ACPL ITEM
DISCARDED

3 1833 01663 3817

332.1

BANKING CRISES

S0-AUG-981

Ba...
Cases and Issues

Banking Crises: Cases and Issues

Edited by V. Sundararajan and
Tomás J.T. Baliño

International Monetary Fund

© 1991 International Monetary Fund

Cover design by IMF Graphics Section

Library of Congress Cataloging-in-Publication Data

Banking crises : cases and issues / edited by V. Sundararajan and Tomás J. T. Baliño.
   p.   cm.
   Includes bibliographical references.
   ISBN 1-55775-187-0 (paper)
   1. Banks and banking. 2. Banks and banking—Case studies. 3. Bank failures.
I. Sundararajan,Vasudevan. II. Baliño, J. T. Tomás.

HG1573.B36 1991   91-37757
332.1—dc20   CIP

Allen County Public Library
Ft. Wayne, Indiana

Price: US$22.50

Address orders to:
International Monetary Fund, Publication Services
700 19th Street, N.W., Washington, D.C. 20431, U.S.A.
Telephone: (202)623-7430
Telefax: (202)623-7201

Foreword

Over the past decade, the macroeconomic consequences of solvency and asset quality problems of banking institutions have attracted growing attention among both policymakers and the academic community. The worldwide trend toward deregulation of financial sectors, and the widespread banking problems of many countries have raised major questions relating to the linkages between deregulation, risks in the banking sector, and a banking crisis. Even if a crisis is avoided, the condition of bank portfolios strongly influences the design and effectiveness of stabilization policies, as was apparent in the recent experiences of many countries. Bank portfolio weaknesses constrain the flexibility in interest rate policy, limit the scope of reforms in the financial sector and in monetary management, distort credit allocation, and can compromise monetary and fiscal stability, particularly if central bank or fiscal assistance is needed to protect the integrity of deposit contracts.

This book considers some of these issues on the basis of the experience of several countries that have faced a banking crisis—defined as widespread insolvencies in the financial sector leading to significant government intervention. The interlinkages between macroeconomic performance and the financial structure of an economy become particularly transparent in times of financial crisis. These crises clearly highlight the importance of appropriate prudential regulations and of the institutional framework to deal with problem banks and problem borrowers in effectively pursuing stabilization goals. This book brings together work of economists in the Central Banking Department of the IMF who have been intimately involved in central banking and financial sector reforms in many developing countries.

It is my hope that the papers will stimulate the interest of policymakers—and their advisors—in attempts to enhance the effectiveness of macro-stabilization policies in the context of structural reforms in the financial sector.

JUSTIN B. ZULU
Director
Central Banking Department

Acknowledgment

The editors wish to thank the contributing authors for their papers, earlier versions of which were issued as IMF Working Papers. The views expressed are those of their respective authors and should not be interpreted as those of the IMF.

The editors are particularly grateful to Justin B. Zulu, Director, Central Banking Department, and Linda M. Koenig, Deputy Director of the same department when this project began, for initiating the project and for providing enthusiastic encouragement and making available the resources needed to complete it.

Also to be thanked are Alfredo Leone, who assisted in the editing of some of the papers, Pierluigi Balduzzi, who contributed to this project while he was a summer intern with the Fund, Dawit Makonnen for his research assistance, and Caroline Cox and Amelita R. Concepcion for their excellent secretarial assistance. Elin Knotter of the External Relations Department provided editorial assistance throughout the production of this book.

Finally, the editors wish to express their gratitude to the many staff members of the IMF Central Banking Department who provided guidance, encouragement, and support for this project.

Contents

The following symbols have been used throughout this paper:

... to indicate that data are not available;

— to indicate that the figure is zero or less than half the final digit shown, or that the item does not exist;

– between years or months (e.g., 1990–91 or January–June) to indicate the years or months covered, including the beginning and ending years or months;

/ between years (e.g., 1990/91) to indicate a crop or fiscal (financial) year.

"Billion" means a thousand million.

Minor discrepancies between constituent figures and totals are due to rounding.

The term "country," as used in this paper, does not in all cases refer to a territorial entity that is a state as understood by international law and practice; the term also covers some territorial entities that are not states, but for which statistical data are maintained and provided internationally on a separate and independent basis.

1

Issues in Recent Banking Crises

V. Sundararajan and Tomás J.T. Baliño

This chapter examines recent experiences with banking crises in seven countries—Argentina, Chile, Malaysia, Philippines, Spain, Thailand, and Uruguay—focusing on the linkages between macroeconomic conditions, financial sector reforms and financial crisis, and the range and effectiveness of measures to deal with financial crises.[1]

The enormous diversity of experiences with crises, owing to cross-country differences in macroeconomic conditions, the regulatory framework, the intensity of the crisis, and the approaches used to deal with it, makes it difficult to generalize and develop stylized descriptions or standardized prescriptions. Nevertheless, certain common features stand out from these experiences; in particular, three key lessons emerge:

- Although macroeconomic instability can weaken the portfolio of financial institutions, weaknesses in the financial sector can have feedback effects on the economy and seriously complicate adjustment and growth policies. Therefore, correcting of the regulatory framework, central bank operating procedures, and portfolio quality in the financial system are important to ensure the effectiveness of adjustment policies.
- Sound prudential policies and their proper enforcement are critical for minimizing major disruptions to growth and stability.
- Measures to recapitalize banks and deal with problem loans and enterprises should be designed to preserve monetary policy independence, promote effective loan recovery and industrial restructuring, and minimize moral hazard. The detailed institutional arrangements that meet these criteria—such as whether to set up a separate agency

[1] Except for Malaysia and Spain, the analysis in this chapter relies heavily on the country studies included in this book.

1

for asset recovery—will vary according to factors specific to the situation. These factors include the legal environment, magnitude of loan losses, and public policy considerations that determine the distribution of losses among various constituencies. However, the chosen arrangement should preserve transparency and avoid shifting the losses to the central bank.

Section I discusses various definitions and models of banking crises, highlighting some key hypotheses with which to interpret the crisis episodes. Section II provides an overview of the case studies by considering the relationship between banking crises and macroeconomic conditions, the propagation of those crises, and the linkages between deregulation and the crisis. The effects of the crises on money demand and credit developments are then examined, and measures used to deal with the crises are analyzed. Section III contains concluding remarks, focusing on lessons for structural reforms and stabilization policies.

I. Definitions and Models of Crisis Situations

This section defines the terms "banking crisis" and "banking distress" and highlights the macroeconomic consequences of such situations. Some models of crises are surveyed to serve as background for the empirical analysis that follows.

Definitions of Financial Crisis

The terms financial crisis and banking crisis are used here interchangeably, an acceptable usage for countries where the banking system dominates financial intermediation.

The definitions of financial crisis in the literature vary with the specific manifestations of the crisis being studied. Samples of definitions are:

- A demand for reserve money so intense that the demand could not be satisfied for all parties simultaneously in the short run (Schwartz (1985); Miron (1986); Wolfson (1986)).
- A liquidation of credits that have been built up in a boom (Veblen (1904); (Mitchell (1941)).
- A condition in which borrowers who in other situations were able to borrow without difficulty become unable to borrow on any terms—a credit crunch or a credit market collapse (Guttentag and Herring (1984); Manikow (1986)).
- A forced sale of assets because liability structures are out of line with market-determined asset values, causing further decline in asset values—the bursting of a price "bubble," for example (Fisher (1933); Flood and Garber (1981); Minsky (1982)).

- A sharp reduction in the value of banks' assets, resulting in the apparent or real insolvency of many banks and accompanied by some bank collapses and possibly some runs (Federal Reserve Bank of San Francisco (1985)).

All of the elements emphasized in these five definitions could be present in a financial crisis and some may be more important than others in a given episode.

For the purposes of this chapter, financial crisis is defined as a situation in which a significant group of financial institutions have liabilities exceeding the market value of their assets, leading to runs and other portfolio shifts, collapse of some financial firms, and government intervention. Thus the term crisis refers to a situation in which an increase in the share of nonperforming loans, an increase in losses (because of foreign exchange exposure, interest rate mismatch, contingent liabilities, etc.), and a decrease in the value of investments cause generalized solvency problems in a financial system and lead to liquidation, mergers, or restructuring. These events usually follow a shock to the economy, and reinforce the subsequent declines in output (or slowing of economic growth) and balance of payments problems.

Banking Distress Versus Banking Crisis: Some Real Consequences

Runs on individual banks—which depend critically on the confidence of their creditors and typically have large gearing ratios—can destabilize banking systems. Destabilization may result either because major macroeconomic or sectoral shocks affect depositors' confidence in a wide range of banks or because the payment difficulties in one bank spread through the system, reflecting the financial interdependence among banks. A bank's failure may jeopardize borrowers' ability to service their loans with other banks, and the lack of adequate information on the relative soundness of various banks may lead bank creditors to lose confidence in the banking system as a whole when an individual bank fails.

The latter contagion effect is a peculiar feature that makes the banking business very different from other businesses. Such contagion is due to (1) the difficulty in knowing the market value of bank loans; (2) the fact that reductions in the value of bank assets do not simultaneously reduce bank liabilities; (3) the fact that depositors are paid back on a first-come-first-served basis; and (4) the relatively low cost (forgone interest) of withdrawing bank deposits compared with the probable cost of losing the capital value of the deposit. Measures to deal with bank runs have addressed one or more of these characteristics (see Section II).

A banking crisis has immediate economic effects. It disturbs normal credit relationships and raises the cost of credit intermediation.[2] It induces a flight to quality by both banks and their creditors; it weakens monetary and budgetary control. For example, the need to support or recapitalize weak banks, and the possible instability in the demand for money—and hence in the price level and economic activity—complicate the task of regulating monetary growth and stabilizing the economy. Propagation of the crisis can be avoided by appropriate lender-of-last-resort intervention and, if the crisis involves only a few banks, by providing information about the true conditions of banks (in order to isolate the unsound from the sound banks).[3] However, the crisis itself generates large and pervasive uncertainty (subjective as it may be), which lowers the perceived return on real assets, and depresses real investment and growth. Some economists have argued that a "crisis" has real effects only insofar as it affects the growth of money stock—either reducing it as in the 1930s, or raising it as in later experiences. However, the weight of evidence seems to suggest that the direct adverse effects of a financial crisis on credit markets, balance of payments, and real economic activity can be substantial, and these are in addition to the impact through changes in interest rates and monetary expansion.[4]

The advent of deposit insurance or implicit guarantees has allowed insolvent financial institutions to stay in business so long as their liquidity position remains manageable (sometimes thanks to central bank assistance). This situation, in which banks are insolvent but not illiquid, is properly called banking distress rather than banking crisis.

A distress situation has effects that resemble those of a crisis, but in a less acute form. Continuing distress perpetuates the resource misallocations that contributed to the distress; prolongs resource allocations that have become inappropriate following a change in the macro-environment; provides incentives for further risk taking, which could aggravate the ongoing losses of financial institutions; and raises the probability of a widespread banking crisis in the event of a major shock—such as a sharp change in relative prices, or a switch in policy regimes as with deregulation. As a result, stabilization and liberalization policies can be effective only if supported by structural reforms that reduce the distress and restore

---

[2] This effect includes, for example, rising interest spreads, collapse of individual credit markets, borrowers forced into nontraditional credit sources at high cost, and untimely recall of loans.

[3] Batcheldor (1985) analyzes the value of providing information to contain a crisis.

[4] For a discussion of the effect of a banking crisis on real economic activity, see Bernanke (1983). Velasco (1987, 1988) discusses the linkages between domestic banking crisis and external debt problems. Misallocation of foreign exchange resources is often reflected in the large foreign exchange exposures and low quality of assets in the banking system. The resulting insolvency and illiquidity of banks weakens monetary control, or induces excessive foreign borrowing, and can precipitate a balance of payments crisis.

and preserve the soundness and stability of financial intermediaries. In the presence of widespread financial distress, however, the design of stabilization-cum-structural reform policies raises complex issues for the speed and sequencing of various structural reforms. These complexities and the cost of adjustment can increase if an actual financial crisis ensues.

Some Models of Financial Crises

In the last few years there has been a great resurgence of academic and popular interest in financial crises. Although a comprehensive review of the literature is beyond the scope of this chapter, it is useful to outline the major analytical approaches that can help in studying the crisis episodes discussed in this chapter. The theories differ regarding (1) the source of financial distress in the nonfinancial sector; (2) the factors affecting the demand and supply of credit; and (3) the specific manifestations of the crisis itself.

The business cycle approach,[5] as modified and extended by present-day writers, holds that the financial environment responds endogenously to the state of the business cycle or to some "displacement" that opens up opportunities for profit. For example, such a displacement could be a liberalization of the financial sector. The key hypothesis is that financial fragility—defined as vulnerability to economic shocks—increases over the course of the business cycle expansion, and in response to some displacement.

An economy's financial fragility stems from factors such as the liquidity of the economy, the proportion of firms that need to borrow in order to honor outstanding debt obligations, debt/equity ratios, and the share of short-term debt in total debt. Financial fragility might also increase because of rising interest rates and overly optimistic expectations that prevail during an investment boom. This does not mean that financial crises occur at the peak of the business cycle as some writers have argued, but rather that crises result from systemic forces that develop near the peak. In particular, interest rates rise partly because of the increase in the interest-inelastic component of the demand for credit. Although velocity of credit rises initially, lenders start to restrict lending as cash flow problems of firms accumulate and nonperforming loans build up. Banks tighten their lending policies, but also attempt to meet loan demands from their prime customers by decreasing the growth of nonloan investments in relation to loans, and, if necessary, reducing excess reserves, and increasing the

[5] This approach is developed in Minsky (1977), Kindleberger (1985), Wojinlower (1980, 1985), Taylor and O'Connell (1985), and Wolfson (1986), by extending and modifying the classical business cycle analysis contained in Veblen (1904) and Mitchell (1941).

recourse to money markets. These developments make the economy more vulnerable to a crisis by reducing the capacity of the financial system to withstand a shock. A surprise event—either a new macro or institutional development or an unexpected bankruptcy (or the threat of one) disturbs these financing patterns, initiating a crisis (defined as a sudden, intense demand for reserve money) which is reflected in investor anxiety, bank runs, and portfolio shifts. Usually the central bank resolves the immediate crisis by acting as a lender-of-last-resort.

Credit market conditions—demand and supply—have received considerable attention among crisis theorists. Some argue that the demand for credit is interest inelastic or that the supply of credit is perversely elastic in certain situations of strong excess demand for credit, such as the peak of the business cycle. Wojinlower (1980) argues that at this peak credit is determined by the availability of funds and credit rationing, since demand is essentially insatiable at any conceivable rate of interest. In such an environment an interruption of the supply of credit triggers a business cycle downturn.

Some economists view credit rationing and credit market collapse as equilibrium phenomena that reflect market failures of various sorts.[6] At certain levels of interest rates, or at certain levels of default risk, a rise in interest rates may not equilibrate the supply and demand for credit. Increases in interest rates will simply reduce the expected profits from lending—assuming additional deposits could be mobilized with higher interest rates—insofar as only higher risk borrowers are willing to borrow ("adverse selection" because of a worsening of the mix of applicants), and borrowers are induced to take on higher risks ("moral hazard").[7] In this framework the default risk is viewed as a positive function of interest rates, debt/equity ratio of borrowers, and the degree of uncertainty in the system. Because raising interest rates beyond a certain point is futile, there will be credit rationing, which could trigger the collapse of some nonfinancial firms. Thus, in the presence of major shocks that raise uncertainty and default risk, a bank has to decide what to do when it feels overexposed to a borrower whose solvency has become questionable. A solution would be to refuse all forms of credit to such a client, including the rollover of existing loans. However, the bank may decide to continue to provide

---

[6] See Stiglitz and Weiss (1981), Guttentag and Herring (1984), and Manikow (1986).

[7] In the context of creditor-borrower relationships, moral hazard usually refers to the risk that "the borrower after obtaining the loan may act in such a way as to increase the probability of default in an effort to raise the probability of very high returns." (Guttentag and Herring (1984), p. 1369.) In the same context, other aspects of moral hazard include the risk that borrowers may not use the cash flow from their projects to service the debt, and the risk that borrowers may pledge their assets to another creditor. The importance of each type of moral hazard will depend on the nature of the loan contract.

finance—increasing its exposure—if it feels that the borrower's situation is likely to improve in the future because of, for instance, anticipated government intervention (e.g., subsidies or a debt bailout).[8] Market failure can also arise if, for many economically sound projects, the demand for and supply of funds do not meet at any interest rate-risk combination because of an exaggerated evaluation of risk on the part of the lenders.

To summarize, the foregoing examples indicate market failures may arise from moral hazard that is costly to monitor privately, adverse effects on the mix of borrowers when interest rates go up, or the inadequacy of lenders' perception of default risk. These market failure theories provide a justification for government intervention in the credit market in the form of tighter banking supervision, loan guarantees, lender-of-last-resort facilities, and direct credit to certain segments of borrowers.[9]

Whereas the above theories focus on the behavior of credit markets, the monetary approach emphasizes the central role of the growth of money stock and its variability in causing crises (Friedman and Schwartz (1963); Brunner and Meltzer (1988)). In this framework, a financial crisis need not occur at any particular stage of the business cycle but could develop whenever the central bank's control of the money supply or reserve money is erratic and results in excessive monetary tightening. Banks are suddenly forced to sell assets in order to obtain needed reserves. This forced sale of assets reduces their price, raises interest rates, threatens bank solvency, and reduces confidence. Banking and debt crises are thus regarded as endogenous events conditioned by economic policy and the banking structure, and not as separate and independent exogenous shocks. In the absence of offsetting action by the central bank, debt and banking crises lead to an excess demand for money, which is an integral part of the monetary policy transmission mechanism.[10] Although bank failures may arise because of exogenous factors such as poor credit decisions, the fall in the money stock propagates and deepens the crisis. Moreover, banking crises are regarded as important mainly because of their effects on money growth.

[8] Borrowers will tend to engage in riskier behavior as their solvency deteriorates because potential losses arising from this behavior are limited to the enterprise's net worth but the gains are not.

[9] The role of banking supervision is to develop procedures for both creditors and supervisors to monitor financial fragility and vulnerability to shocks, identify exposure to moral hazards, and formulate standards (e.g., capital adequacy) for evaluating the appropriateness of particular levels of risk exposure.

[10] The supply of money falls, owing to the rise in the currency/deposit ratio as deposits are reduced in failed banks, and the public want to hold more currency relative to deposits. The demand for money also falls because currency is an imperfect substitute for deposits. The fall in the supply of money will exceed the fall in demand unless the central bank increases base money sufficiently.

II. Crisis and Adjustment—An Overview of Case Studies

The analysis of sample countries considers the following questions that are suggested by the theoretical discussion above. (Appendix I summarizes in tabular form financial reforms and the financial crises in the seven countries.)

1. Did the crises mainly reflect major macroeconomic shocks and macroeconomic instability? Were the banking problems exogenous events that aggravated the effects of macroeconomic shocks?
2. What was the contribution of factors specific to the financial sector (such as financial reform and changes in prudential regulation) in mitigating, aggravating, or causing the financial crises? Did financial reform increase financial fragility?
3. How did the crises alter the behavior of monetary and credit aggregates? What was the contribution of monetary policy in alleviating or aggravating the crises?
4. How did the authorities respond to the crises? What were the key support operations and regulatory adaptations? What principles should govern the design of such support operations?

In most of the sample countries, the banking crisis occurred after a period of economic expansion and was associated with balance of payments problems and substantial changes in relative prices and, in some cases, major political uncertainties. In none of these cases could a monetary contraction have caused the financial crisis, although credit market conditions did play a role in propagating it. Interest rate deregulation and other regulatory reforms took place long before the crisis in some cases and contemporaneously in others. Weakness in bank supervision was a common factor in most cases, even in countries where prudential regulations appeared to be comprehensive. Measures to deal with the crises varied greatly, reflecting a complex set of objectives and institutional constraints.

Banking Crises and Macroeconomic Conditions

Tables 1 and 2 present selected economic indicators for the countries in the sample. In most countries, the banking crisis occurred after a period of rapid economic growth characterized by substantial variations in the relative performance of economic sectors. These variations, in turn, reflected major fluctuations in relative price and general business conditions.[11] The period of the crisis itself was associated with strong reductions

[11] For example, sharp increases in real lending rates as a result of financial liberalization and the introduction and subsequent abandonment of preannounced schedules of devaluation all contributed to major variations in general business conditions in Argentina, Chile, and Uruguay.

Table 1. Macroeconomic Conditions Before and During Banking Crises in Sample Countries

Country[1]	Growth of Real GDP Before[2]	Growth of Real GDP During	Inflation Before[2]	Inflation During	Current Account Deficit/GNP Before[2]	Current Account Deficit/GNP During	Investment Ratio Before[2]	Investment Ratio During	Terms of Trade (1980 = 100) Before[2]	Terms of Trade (1980 = 100) During	Real Effective Exchange Rate[3] (1980 = 100) Before[2]	Real Effective Exchange Rate[3] (1980 = 100) During
				(In percent)								
Argentina (1980–82)	3.1	−3.6	170.3	121.5	1.5	−3.9	12.8	19.0	88.9	99.8	65.0	81.2
Chile (1981–83)	8.1	−3.4	36.2	18.8	−6.6	−9.9	15.0	14.9	97.5	87.4	90.4	103.8
Uruguay (1982–85)	4.8	−4.2	51.6	47.6	−4.7	−2.2	16.0	10.6	102.1	92.7	90.9	81.4
Philippines[4] (1983–86)	4.6	−2.0	14.7	19.7	−6.0	−2.2	25.9	20.5	98.1	86.4	101.3	88.8
Thailand (1984–86)	5.4	4.1	7.2	1.7	−5.8	−4.6	22.7	20.5	87.6	82.8	105.8	95.8
Spain (1978–83)[5]	4.8 (0.6)	1.0 (1.5)	15.2 (15.1)	15.3 (13.3)	−1.8 (−2.6)	−1.3 (−2.1)	26.2 (21.8)	21.8 (20.9)	118.0 (95.0)	99.3 (88.9)	99.2 (97.1)	86.3 (88.2)
Malaysia (1985–86)	7.0	0.1	3.8	0.5	−9.0	−1.2	35.7	26.4	82.9	72.1	113.9	101.5

Source: International Monetary Fund, *International Financial Statistics*, various issues, and IMF staff calculations.

[1] Years in parentheses refer to periods of major bank liquidations, interventions, and restructuring.

[2] Average of the three-year period before the year when the crisis started.

[3] A reduction in the index means a depreciation of the exchange rate of the domestic currency.

[4] There was a bill market crisis in 1981, with repercussions for the banking system.

[5] Although the banking crisis began in 1978, the peak years of the crisis were 1982 and 1983. The figures in parentheses are the values when 1982–83 is considered the crisis period.

in real output in many countries and a sharp deceleration of output growth in others (Table 1). In all cases real investment ratios fell, although to varying degrees. The crisis periods were also marked by major external shocks, balance of payments difficulties, and sharp adjustments in exchange rates and interest rates, although the balance of payments crisis occurred before overt manifestations of the banking crisis in some cases and afterward in others. Owing to the consequences of import compression and other adjustments that typically accompanied the balance of payments problems, it is hard to separate the contribution of the banking sector problems to the severity of the recessions. Nevertheless, evidence from some countries points to the possibility that the credit market disturbances unleashed by the banking crises served to depress output to levels below what might have been expected from the relative price changes and real investment performance.[12]

In most countries external imbalances were fairly severe just before the crisis, which in some cases aggravated them. Misallocation of foreign exchange resources underlay the external debt-servicing difficulties of many countries and was often reflected in large foreign exchange exposures and low quality of assets of the banking system, thereby creating financial fragility and vulnerability to crisis. When the crisis occurred, the growth in central bank credit needed to contain the propagation of the crisis worsened the balance of payments problems. The large devaluations associated with these problems deepened the banking crisis by impairing the debt-service capabilities of debtors with dollar-denominated loans, and by magnifying the losses of banks with large foreign exchange exposures.

Price behavior varied in most crisis episodes. Inflation decelerated—sometimes fairly sharply—particularly at the onset of the crisis (Table 2). In many cases this change was soon reversed, in part because of the expansionary effect of measures to deal with the crisis. Movements in key asset prices were important elements in some crises. A fall in property and share values played a role in the Malaysian crisis, owing to the concentration of the portfolios of many institutions in real estate and shares. A boom and a subsequent fall in land prices were partly responsible for the Uruguayan crisis. In other cases the banking crisis itself and the associated uncertainties seemed to have contributed to a decline in the value of enterprises, making it more difficult to gain access to equity markets just when lenders became more cautious.

---

[12] This point is discussed further below. Bernanke (1983) examines the independent contribution of credit market conditions in causing output declines during the Great Depression.

Table 2. Macroeconomic Indicators in Sample Countries, 1974–86

(In percent)

	1974	1975	1976	1977	1978	1979	1980	1981	1982	1983	1984	1985	1986
Argentina													
Growth rate of real GDP	5.7	−0.4	−0.4	6.3	−3.4	6.6	1.1	−6.5	−5.2	3.3	2.4	−4.5	5.4
Current account/GNP ratio	0.1	−3.3	1.2	2.2	2.9	−0.5	−3.1	−4.0	−4.5	−4.1	...	...	...
Inflation rate (CPI)	23.5	182.3	443.2	176.1	175.5	159.5	100.8	104.5	164.8	343.8	626.7	672.1	90.1
Chile													
Growth rate of real GDP	1.0	−12.9	3.5	9.9	8.2	8.3	7.8	5.5	−14.1	−0.7	6.3	2.4	5.7
Current account/GNP ratio	−2.6	−6.8	−1.5	−4.1	−7.1	−5.7	−7.1	−14.5	−9.5	−5.7	−10.7	−8.3	−6.5
Inflation rate (CPI)	504.7	374.7	211.8	91.9	40.1	33.4	35.1	19.7	9.9	27.3	19.9	30.7	19.5
Malaysia													
Growth rate of real GDP	8.3	0.8	11.6	7.8	6.7	9.3	7.4	6.9	5.9	6.3	7.8	−1.0	1.2
Current account/GNP ratio	−5.7	−5.9	5.4	3.3	0.7	4.6	−1.2	−10.0	−14.0	−12.5	−5.5	−2.1	−0.3
Inflation rate (CPI)	17.4	4.5	2.6	4.8	4.9	3.6	6.7	9.7	5.8	3.7	3.9	0.3	0.7
Philippines													
Growth rate of real GDP	5.0	6.4	8.0	6.1	5.5	6.3	5.2	3.9	2.9	0.9	−6.0	5.3	−7.7
Current account/GNP ratio	−1.4	−5.8	−6.1	−3.6	−4.6	−5.1	−5.4	−5.4	−8.1	−8.1	−4.0	—	3.4
Inflation rate (CPI)	34.2	6.8	9.2	9.9	7.3	17.5	18.2	13.1	10.2	10.0	50.3	23.1	0.8
Spain													
Growth rate of real GDP	5.7	1.1	3.0	3.3	1.8	0.2	1.5	−0.2	1.2	1.8	1.9	2.1	3.6
Current account/GNP ratio	−3.7	−3.4	−4.0	−1.8	1.1	0.6	−2.5	−2.7	−2.4	−1.8	1.3	1.8	...
Inflation rate (CPI)	15.7	17.0	15.0	24.5	19.8	15.7	15.6	14.5	14.4	12.2	11.3	8.8	8.8
Thailand													
Growth rate of real GDP	5.4	7.1	8.7	7.2	10.1	6.1	5.8	6.3	4.1	5.9	5.5	3.2	3.5
Current account/GNP ratio	−0.7	−4.3	−2.7	−5.7	−5.0	−7.8	−6.3	−7.3	−2.8	−7.3	−5.2	−4.2	...
Inflation rate (CPI)	24.3	5.3	4.1	7.6	7.9	9.9	19.7	12.7	5.3	3.7	0.9	2.4	1.8
Uruguay													
Growth rate of real GDP	3.1	5.9	4.0	1.2	5.3	6.2	6.0	1.9	−9.4	−5.9	−1.5	0.3	6.6
Current account/GNP ratio	−3.1	−5.2	−1.9	−4.0	−2.6	−4.9	−7.1	−5.1	−2.6	−1.2	−2.6	−2.2	1.5
Inflation rate (CPI)	77.2	−81.4	50.6	58.2	44.5	66.8	63.5	34.0	19.0	49.2	55.3	72.2	76.4

Source: International Monetary Fund, *International Financial Statistics*, various issues.

Propagation of Financial Crisis: Bank Runs and Contagion

The buildup of depositors' anxiety following the failure of a prominent firm or a financial institution, and the subsequent runs that concentrated in institutions regarded as weak or somehow linked to the initial failure, contributed to the propagation of financial crises, as did the difficulties of weak banks in accessing interbank markets. In some countries the lack of deposit insurance (e.g., the abandonment of full deposit insurance in November 1979 in Argentina) made deposits riskier and helped to propagate the crisis. In the Philippines insufficient resources of the deposit insurance agency and the resulting delays in settling depositors' claims may have contributed to depositors' anxiety and runs.[13] In all cases confidence was restored by the emergency measures taken by the central bank. These measures encompassed lender-of-last-resort facilities, intervention in troubled financial institutions (including some that were initially outside the central bank's jurisdiction), and the re-establishment of deposit insurance (sometimes retroactively).

In some cases the financial crisis spread across country borders. The international propagation of financial crisis could take place either through capital inflows or outflows affecting one country as a result of developments in others or through direct or indirect connections of distressed financial institutions or their customers. A case in point is the demise in March 1981 of the preannounced devaluation scheme for the Argentine peso. This event led to a loss of confidence in Uruguay's similar scheme, causing a massive outflow of capital in that country, and contributing to the Uruguayan crisis. Also, the failure of two banks in Uruguay, Banco Pan de Azúcar and Banco de Italia y Rio de la Plata, was largely the result of the failure of their parent institutions abroad (a Chilean and an Argentine bank, respectively).

Banking Crises and Financial Sector Reform

An often debated issue is whether financial sector reforms helped to trigger or aggravate financial crises. The timing and intensity of the crises and the timing and scope of financial sector reforms—interest rate deregulation and the liberalization of entry and portfolio regulations—varied considerably among the sample countries (Appendix I). In Argentina, Uruguay, and Chile the deregulation of interest rates had been completed and entry and branching restrictions relaxed by the mid-to-late 1970s, but the financial crises were concentrated in the early 1980s. In Spain a gradual deregulation of interest rates was begun in 1974, starting with the

---

[13] In practice, the deposit insurance agency in the Philippines seems to have relied heavily on loans from the Central Bank.

freeing of interest rates on long-term loans and deposits and ending in 1987, when rates on demand deposits and savings deposits of less than six months were freed.[14] By the mid-1970s branching regulations and activity restrictions on various classes of banks had been liberalized. Various portfolio regulations—in the form of mandatory investment coefficients— were reduced beginning in 1974. The banking crisis in Spain was a protracted affair that began in 1977 and intensified during 1982–83 before subsiding. In the Philippines the deregulation of interest rates in 1981 just preceded the first episodes of the financial crisis. In Thailand interest rates remained subject to administrative ceilings, which were adjusted on several occasions. A higher ceiling applied to finance companies, which were the institutions initially affected by the 1983–84 crisis. In Malaysia interest rates were deregulated in 1978, although at various times strong moral suasion was exercised. From October 1985 to February 1987, interest rates on deposits of less than 12 months' maturity were subject to restrictions.[15] This was also a period of recession; authorities faced crises among deposit-taking cooperatives and strengthened a wide range of prudential regulations to contain and manage the risks in the banking system.

These chronologies of financial reforms and crisis episodes should be considered with caution, in part because in many cases the weaknesses of problem banks that surfaced during the crisis had originated well before these weaknesses became obvious. It took some time for the problems to be discovered by supervisory authorities because of the normal tendency of banks in distress to reduce the transparency of their accounts.[16]

To analyze the linkages between financial sector reform and financial crisis in the sample countries, it is useful to identify some ways in which financial sector reforms might increase the fragility of both financial and nonfinancial firms, thereby setting the stage for a crisis.

First, increased freedom of entry into the financial sector and freedom to bid for funds through interest rates and new instruments could lead to excessive risk taking, if such freedom were not tempered with adequate prudential supervision and regulation. For example, implicit guarantees of a government bailout of depositors (and, to some extent, bankers), together with weak prudential legislation and supervision permitting unsound lending patterns, could trigger excessive risk taking following deregulation. Deregulation could also facilitate a too rapid growth of some financial

---

[14] The rates on deposits of one year or more had been free since 1977 and those on time deposits of six months to one year were set free in 1981.

[15] Some restrictions still apply to lending rates. The central bank approves the base lending rate (BLR) of banks and finance companies after analyzing their cost of funds. Actual lending rates can deviate from the BLR only by a margin set by the central bank.

[16] For an elaboration of this point, see de Juan (1987) and Long (1988).

institutions and allow unqualified persons to enter into financial business. Examples of such effects were found in all the sample countries.

Second, the institutional structure of the banking system that emerged from regulatory changes could lead to concentration of power in banking, and interlocking ownership and lending patterns. Such an environment is particularly vulnerable to market failures—because of moral hazard, adverse selection, and oligopolistic pricing, all reinforced by the regulatory environment. This situation could favor excessive risk taking on the part of banks (particularly following deregulation of interest rates), and on the part of nonfinancial firms. This point is illustrated by the large share of credits to related firms in the private banking system of Chile and in the banking groups that failed in Spain. However, loans to directors and insiders, fraud and mismanagement, and loans to political interests have been a perennial source of risk concentration, banking difficulties, and bank failures, and there is no reason why deregulation per se should increase the incidence of such practices.

Third, deregulation could lead to excessive increases in interest rates if euphoric expectations coupled with unsound liability structures of firms cause a sharp increase in credit demand. With high debt/equity ratios, an initial increase in real interest rates, among other things, could lead to distress borrowing and hence fairly inelastic demand for credit (artificial demand for credit), which would perpetuate the high rates. This chain of events seems to have occurred in the Southern Cone countries.[17] High debt/equity ratios of nonfinancial firms developed in the pre-reform period of negative real interest rates and directed credits, leading to distress borrowing when real rates turned strongly positive.[18] Distress borrowing aggravated the financial crises in many of the sample countries (e.g., Chile and the Philippines), but its influence in starting the crises is unclear.

Fourth, following the deregulation of interest rates, the authorities might lack an adequate set of instruments of monetary control to influence interest rates or might follow a hands-off policy in the erroneous belief that domestic interest rates would automatically converge to international rates over time.[19] Or, the authorities might base targets for monetary and credit

---

[17] Sometimes this was coupled with borrowers' stripping their enterprises of most valuable assets, leaving creditors little on which to foreclose.

[18] Distress borrowing typically leads to strong liquidity problems of individual banks. These problems, in turn, are a factor weakening monetary control.

[19] Following deregulation, domestic interest rates would depend upon both domestic monetary conditions and external factors (foreign interest rates plus exchange rate expectations), and the relative importance of the domestic and external factors would be a function of the extent of openness to capital flows. Even in fairly open economies, monetary policy can have a strong effect on interest rates in the short run, and an automatic and immediate convergence to foreign rates cannot be assumed.

aggregates on past behavior, despite massive shifts taking place in income velocity and the money multiplier in response to deregulation and other measures. These factors would cause excessive increases in real interest rates and precipitate a crisis, particularly if the policy error persists.[20] Also, tighter credit policies could widen the interest margin and contribute to excessively high real lending rates, insofar as they are implemented by raising unremunerated reserve requirements, or by forcing banks to hold low-yield government securities. Such outcomes are readily corrected through appropriate refinements of instruments and timely reversals of policy stance (if macroeconomic conditions permit such reversals). There is little evidence that inappropriate monetary policies contributed to the crisis in the sample countries, except insofar as the authorities let interest rates become too high in some cases (e.g., Chile and Uruguay). In all cases monetary policy was complicated by the large portfolio shifts in the banking system (see the following subsection for details).

Fifth, following deregulation, instability in the credit markets could arise not only from an inelastic demand for credit, but also from credit rationing. For example, in times of perceived high risk and uncertainty or merely of tight financial policies, real interest rates could rise sharply. However, lenders will see a rise in interest rates beyond a certain point as counterproductive because of the higher risks associated with that increase, and the markets could resort to credit rationing. This inelastic or even perversely elastic supply of credit could result in instability, characterized by bankruptcies of firms and banks. In some cases this credit rationing behavior would show up in persistently high real interest rates, possibly rising interest margins, and a simultaneous fall in loan/deposit ratios of the banking system. There is evidence of these phenomena in some countries, notably in the Philippines.[21]

Sixth, the supervisory authority might be ill prepared to deal with a financial system that operates with much more freedom than in the past. Both the regulations and the administrative infrastructure might need to be overhauled to focus them on analyzing bank solvency and credit risk rather than on monitoring compliance with control regulations such as interest rate ceilings or selective credit regulations.[22] Although supervision

---

[20] Nominal interest rates could remain high even in times of price stability, owing to temporary uncertainties and stubborn exchange rate expectations. If this is the case even after major corrections to the real exchange rate, nonaccommodating credit policy would soon alter exchange rate expectations and reduce real rates. However, if high real rates persist long enough, they could precipitate a crisis.

[21] Evidence on this topic should be evaluated carefully to distinguish between shifts in the credit supply function and changes in its shape. For instance, a shift in the supply of credit could also lead to most of the phenomena attributed to credit rationing here.

[22] For the case of Argentina, see Banco Central de la República Argentina (1980) and Baliño (1987).

was inadequate in some of the sample countries, in others, despite an adequate supervisory apparatus, the enforcement was weak and indecisive because of political interference. In all the countries in the sample poor risk diversification, inadequate loan evaluation, and plain fraud were the main factors leading to financial institutions' liquidation or intervention. Sometimes these factors were related to the fact that more liberal entry into financial intermediation allowed people with little or no experience in the field to set up or take over a financial institution.

Finally, the deregulation of interest rates could adversely affect financial institutions that have a large exposure to long-term assets funded by short-term liabilities, which carry fixed interest rates. This situation could precipitate a crisis for some segments of the industry, and for the whole system unless appropriate action was taken. However, this factor did not play a significant role in the sample countries.

In sum, the connection, if any, between financial reform and financial crisis derives from an unstable macroeconomic environment, the development of unsound liability structures of nonfinancial firms (before or after the reform), and weaknesses in the institutional structure for banking. Therefore, sound financial policies, vigilant supervision of banks, and well-designed prudential regulations would limit financial crises and help reduce the vulnerability of a financial system to the vagaries of the macro environment.

Banking Crises and Monetary Conditions

Banking crises are often associated with substantial portfolio shifts. The demand for money can rise because crises cause uncertainties and asset liquidations, or fall because savers shift to safer assets such as foreign currency assets, treasury bills, and nonmonetary instruments: the net effect of these two opposing forces is an empirical question. Moreover, different aggregates are likely to be affected differently. Demand will shift in favor of financial liabilities of institutions that are perceived as having no or negligible default risks—such as the central bank and state and foreign banks—and against liabilities of institutions perceived as risky. For instance, sharp—albeit temporary— increases in currency demand occurred in most of the sample countries at the time of bank liquidations. Also, the interest elasticity of the demand for various monetary aggregates might change, often permanently, because of the greater awareness of risks and returns built up in times of crisis. Such portfolio shifts complicate the conduct of monetary policy. The effect of these shifts on monetary aggregates will depend on the policy response. For example, implementation of interest rate controls will diminish the attractiveness of time and savings deposits.

Table 3.   Tests of Shifts in Demand and Interest Elasticities in Five of the Sample Countries

Country	Shift in Intercept		Shift in Interest Elasticities[1]	
	Currency	M2	Currency	M2
Argentina	+0.070	−0.035	Negative	Positive
	(2.4)	(−3.1)		
Chile	Not significant	+0.053	Negative	Positive
		(3.7)		
Philippines	+0.153	+0.032	Negative	Positive
	(5.3)	(3.8)		
Spain	Not significant	Not significant	Not significant	Positive
Uruguay	Not significant	+0.018[2]	Negative	Positive
		(1.26)		

Source: International Monetary Fund, *International Financial Statistics.*
Note: Based on regressions, quarterly changes (1975–87) in the log of currency or M2 on prices, output, and interest rates, using general distributed lags in these variables and lagged values of the dependent variable. Figures in parentheses are at-values.
[1]Direction of change in the absolute value of interest elasticity (sum of all lag coefficients).
[2]Becomes insignificant when shifts in interest elasticities are allowed.

Some portfolio and parameter shifts took place following banking crises in the sample countries. There is evidence of a significant shift into currency or a decline in the interest elasticity of currency demand following the crises in Argentina, Chile, the Philippines, Thailand, and Uruguay (Table 3).[23] Also, in several sample countries the demand for M2 showed an upward shift, and interest elasticities increased following the banking crisis. The shift in money demand in some cases reflected a portfolio switch from nonbank institutions and deposit substitutes into bank deposits. For example, in Thailand deposits switched from finance companies to banks following the crisis among the finance companies. A similar phenomenon was observed in the Philippines following the bill market collapse in 1981.

The behavior of the money multiplier and the stability of the monetary base might also be significantly affected by a banking crisis. The money multiplier would fall because of increased demand for currency and a precautionary rise in banks' excess reserves prompted by greater volatility

[23] Several authors have studied the decline in income velocity of money during the Great Depression in the United States.

in deposits and increased riskiness in lending.[24] Although further work is needed on this topic, preliminary examination of data suggests that multipliers (for M2) showed significant changes during crisis periods (Chart 1). For example, in Spain, despite the progressive reductions in statutory cash reserve ratios, the multiplier declined fairly sharply between 1977 and 1979 before resuming its upward trend. Sharp reductions in multipliers occurred in Uruguay and the Philippines following their crises, and a mild decline and greater volatility were evident in Argentina (where a large drop occurred in 1982). These declines are partly attributable to changes in reserve requirements. However, even after allowing for such changes, a notable fall or a pause in the growth of the multiplier could be detected in many of the sample countries. In the Philippines the sharp increase in currency demand contributed to the decline in the multiplier.

Quarterly growth rates for reserve money showed no significant changes in their level, variability, or seasonality following the crises in most countries, although a brief acceleration in the growth of reserve money or a breakdown of normal seasonal patterns was evident during the crises in some countries (Chart 2).

An important monetary development in most countries, at least for brief periods, was the change in the sources of growth in reserve money. In several cases, central bank credit to banks and other financial institutions rose sharply as the crises unfolded, and its share in reserve money rose (Chart 3). This increase of central bank credit typically served a dual purpose: to assist ailing institutions or borrowers, and to offset the contractionary effect of reductions in the money multiplier. In some cases this growth in central bank credit jeopardized the attainment of monetary and balance of payments targets, forcing the authorities to use other instruments of monetary control to absorb excess reserve money. Although in some countries the initial spurt in central bank credit was reversed within a short period, in others the central bank credit's share in reserve money increased permanently (Table 4).

Banking Crises and Credit Markets

This subsection discusses the relationship between the banking crises and credit markets by focusing on three key questions: (a) What was the role of credit market conditions in initiating or aggravating the crisis? (b) Did the causality run from credit to the real sector or in the opposite direction? (c) What were the effects of financial crises on credit demand?

---

[24] In the case of Argentina, the behavior of excess reserves during the crisis did not seem to deviate significantly from historic patterns.

Chart 1. Banking Crises: Money Multiplier

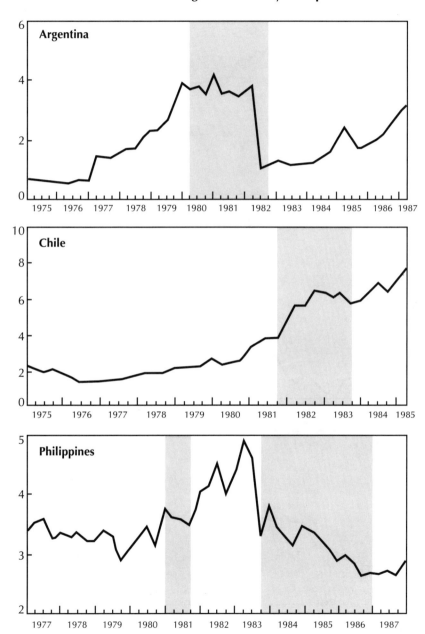

Note: Shaded areas indicate crisis periods.

Chart 1 *(continued).* Banking Crises: Money Multiplier

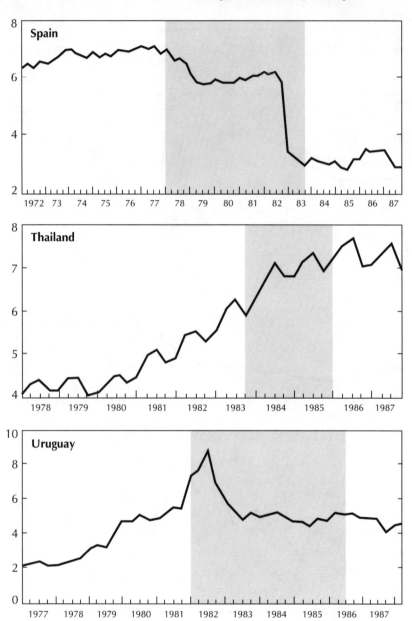

Note: Shaded areas indicate crisis periods.

Chart 2. Banking Crises: Rate of Growth of Reserve Money
(In percent)

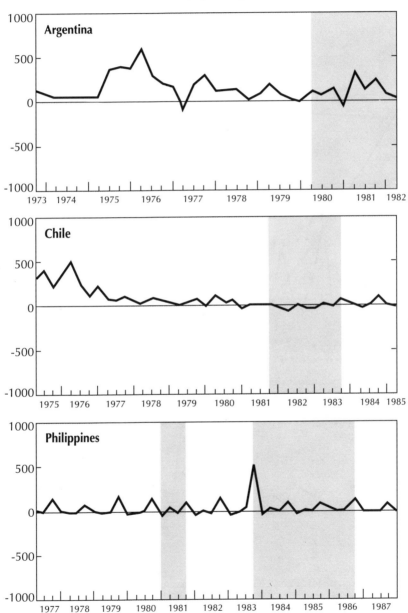

Note: Shaded areas indicate crisis periods.

Chart 2 *(continued)*. Banking Crises: Rate of Growth of Reserve Money
(In percent)

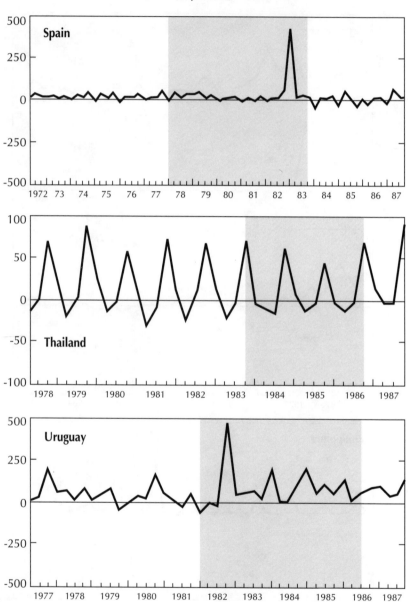

Note: Shaded areas indicate crisis periods.

**Chart 3. Banking Crises: Central Bank Credit to
Nongovernment Agents**
(In real terms)

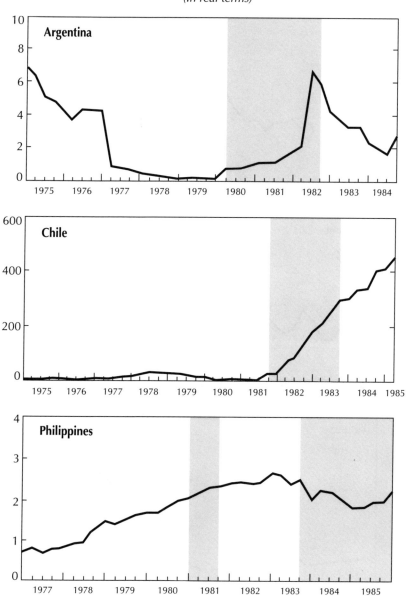

Note: Shaded areas indicate crisis periods.

**Chart 3 *(continued).* Banking Crises: Central Bank Credit to
Nongovernment Agents**
(In real terms)

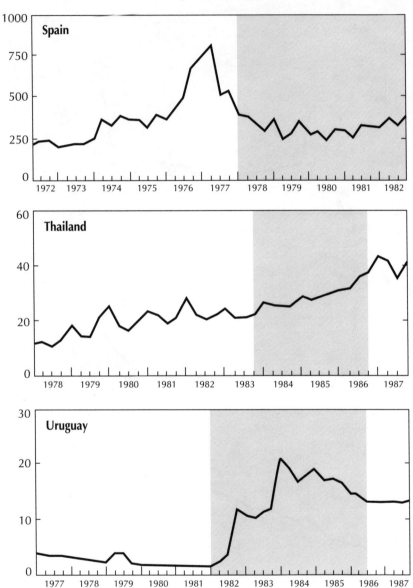

Note: Shaded areas indicate crisis periods.

Table 4. Total Central Bank Credit as a Percentage of Reserve Money in Six of the Sample Countries, 1974–86

Year	Argentina	Chile	Philippines	Spain	Thailand	Uruguay
1974	96.0	398.2	124.7	53.5	69.8	179.8
1975	100.7	552.2	160.9	61.0	73.5	139.6
1976	81.9	327.6	138.6	76.7	78.4	109.1
1977	54.7	328.9	109.3	74.9	90.2	79.5
1978	51.2	280.0	132.5	58.7	105.9	59.7
1979	39.8	245.9	143.0	63.2	126.4	75.1
1980	103.9	171.9	165.6	73.2	142.9	76.5
1981	176.2	156.1	213.4	93.2	157.1	69.8
1982	143.6	452.7	255.2	112.3	166.3	304.3
1983	154.9	907.1	237.8	80.7	170.2	407.5
1984	169.3	1,279.1	238.0	67.1	160.7	648.0
1985	. . .	. . .	219.8	72.9	167.9	473.1
1986	. . .	. . .	153.7	68.9	155.0	541.6

Source: International Monetary Fund, *International Financial Statistics*, various issues.
Note: Although Chart 3 shows central bank credit to nongovernment agents, this table focuses on total central bank credit. In many countries the central bank supported the problem institutions indirectly, with the budget providing the actual support but financing it through central bank credit to the government. This was a particularly significant factor in the Philippines.

The Role of Credit Market Conditions

The role of credit market conditions in crises differed across the sample countries. The extent to which caution on the part of bankers, and the resulting credit rationing, accelerated business bankruptcies in the sample countries is not fully clear, although there is some evidence to this effect. In all cases nonperforming loans rose sharply just prior to and during the crises. The effect of high real lending rates on the financial conditions of already highly leveraged borrowers, and the perpetuation of such high rates because of the resulting distress demand for credit and increased riskiness of lending, was an important factor in Argentina, Chile, the Philippines, and Uruguay. High nominal lending rates in relation to growth of credit—a result of tight monetary policy to attain adjustment—aggravated the crises in both the Philippines and Thailand.[25] The behavior of lending rates had no significant effect on the crisis in Spain, in part reflecting the gradual pace of liberalization there. In the Philippines bank credit to the private sector declined precipitously in nominal terms between 1983 and 1986 (by more than 50 percent in real terms), while nominal bank lending rates averaged 23 percent. Real lending and deposit rates were significantly positive during most of the 1983–86 period, which was marked by asset liquidations and a fall in output. The decline in credit to the private sector in the Philippines could not be attributed to demand factors alone or to simple crowding out by the Government, but also reflected credit rationing by bankers, owing to the increased riskiness in lending.[26]

Comparisons of credit aggregates before and after the crises emerged show that, with the exception of the Philippines and (marginally) Spain, credit continued to grow strongly in real terms after the crises began, despite falls in real output or real growth during the crises (Table 5).[27] In some cases the increase in real domestic credit was accompanied by a sharp fall in the country's total foreign reserves, which suggests that in some countries the central bank ensured the provision of credit to the economy at the cost of losing substantial amounts of reserves.[28] The strong growth in credit in some countries also reflected the rollover of nonperforming

[25] Also, a high or rising nominal loan rate (as a result of inflation) on adjustable-rate loans implies a faster loan repayment, which caused hardship to borrowers in some countries. In addition, uncertainty tends to reduce the maturity of loans, which means that most financing carries a de facto adjustable rate.

[26] See Nascimento (1990) for further details.

[27] This finding does not preclude the possibility of short-term credit disruptions in the early months of the crises. See the next section for further discussions.

[28] As discussed in the next section, central banks provided large sums of credit to ailing institutions and, in some cases, to final borrowers.

Table 5. Change in Real Credit Balances of the Sample Countries
(Percentage change)

Country	Total Domestic Credit	Domestic Credit to Private Sector	International Reserves
Argentina	98.6	73.0	−52.4
Chile	85.0	147.0	24.1
Malaysia	35.3	46.1	37.9
Philippines	−14.2	−29.0	−45.0
Spain	3.6	−2.4	98.7
Thailand	62.8	67.5	57.6
Uruguay	89.5	27.8	−43.1

Source: International Monetary Fund, *International Financial Statistics*, various issues.
Note: For each country the change was calculated using the average levels for the three years immediately before and the three years immediately after the year the crisis began. See Table 1 for the dates of the crises.

loans, interest accrual on them, and new work-out loans to try to rescue ailing borrowers. In addition, the increased demand for M2, noted earlier, might have facilitated a continued strong credit expansion following the crisis.

Causality Between Credit and GDP in the Short Run

Short-run disruptions in credit flows—a common phenomenon during banking crises—can have a serious effect on short-run economic performance. When real credit and real growth fall, the question arises whether the fall in real credit was supply determined (and thus a possible *cause* of the fall in growth) or demand determined (and thus a possible *result* of the fall in growth).

To shed some light on this question, Table 6 shows Granger causality tests to analyze the relationship between real domestic credit and real GDP (quarterly data, seasonally adjusted) for Argentina, Chile, and the Philippines.[29] The data correspond to total domestic credit and domestic credit to the private sector. Four lags for each variable were used in the tests.

The results in this table are generally inconclusive. Only in the case of the Philippines is there evidence of statistically significant causality, which is unidirectional for total credit (running from credit to GDP) and

[29] Data availability allowed the analysis of only these three countries.

Table 6. Granger Causality Tests of the Relationship Between Real Domestic Credit and GDP in Three of the Sample Countries
(In percent)

		F-statistic	
Country	Period	Credit to GDP	GDP to credit
A. For the relationship between total domestic credit and GDP			
Argentina	1975(I)–1987(IV)	F(5,38) 0.88	F(5,38) 1.66
Chile	1975(I)–1985(II)	F(5,28) 1.51	F(5,28) 0.09
Philippines	1981(I)–1988(III)	F(5,17) 3.32*	F(5,17) 0.68
B. For the relationship between private sector credit and GDP			
Argentina	1975(I)–1987(IV)	F(5,38) 1.09	F(5,38) 2.44
Chile	1975(I)–1985(II)	F(5,28) 1.16	F(5,28) 0.42
Philippines	1981(I)–1988(III)	F(5,17) 5.63*	F(5,17) 3.18*

Source: International Monetary Fund, *International Financial Statistics*, various issues.
* Statistically significant at the 5 percent level.

bidirectional for private sector credit. These results are somewhat surprising, given the importance of credit in financing economic growth and the substantial variability in both credit and output in the three countries under consideration. It may be concluded that shocks from other variables overshadowed the importance of credit as a determinant of output—and of output as a determinant of credit—in the countries and the periods considered here. This interpretation appears plausible, because the timing of some of these other shocks (e.g., the collapse of the exchange rate regimes in Argentina and Chile) did not coincide with those of shocks to the supply of credit.[30]

Effects of Financial Crisis on Demand for Credit

Do financial crises affect the demand for credit? As mentioned earlier, some authors have suggested that borrowers become unwilling or unable to pay their loans and are happy to roll over these loans, even at high real rates, because the borrowers expect to be bailed out eventually. A way to test this hypothesis is to estimate a simple model of the demand for credit and see what effect, if any, the crisis had on interest elasticities. Although

[30] A recent study concludes that the data do not support the hypothesis of a simple or unidirectional relationship between bank runs and economic performance for the case of the United States (Dwyer and Gilbert (1989)).

such analysis is not available for all countries, studies with Argentine data suggest that the demand for loans rises in real terms when the real cost of credit goes up, confirming the hypothesis that the demand for credit in Argentina included many loans that were insensitive to interest rates and on which interest was accrued and capitalized but not paid (i.e., effectively nonperforming loans).[31]

Dealing with Banking Crises

The measures to deal with failing and ailing institutions during a banking crisis should aim at arresting the propagation of the crisis, restoring depositors' confidence, and protecting the payments system immediately; and at bringing about an orderly restructuring and recapitalization of problem banks later. Evaluation of any measures should take into account the following factors: monetary and budgetary effects; moral hazard (effects on future risk-taking behavior); distribution of losses among borrowers, depositors, the banking system, and the government; effectiveness of loan recovery; and side effects on solvent borrowers and banks. The measures undertaken in the sample countries varied a good deal, owing to differences in legislative framework and macroeconomic and political constraints. These measures fall into the following categories: (1) emergency measures; (2) measures to deal with failing banks; (3) measures to assist borrowers; and (4) reforms of banking regulations and legislation. Appendix III shows a stylized framework of these measures and the objectives and constraints governing them. Appendix IV outlines the approaches the sample countries used to deal with failing banks and borrowers.

Emergency Measures

In each country emergency measures were aimed at stabilizing the financial system as rapidly as possible. They always included making available lender-of-last-resort facilities, often to replace the loss of deposits of the affected institutions. In many instances normal lender-of-last-resort facilities were not adequate to handle a major crisis, and special credit facilities had to be set up. In some cases the government had to pass emergency legislation to broaden the institutional coverage of the lender of last resort and to put in place other arrangements to on-lend funds through stronger institutions (Philippines) or through special ad hoc funds (Thailand). Central bank intervention in the management of ailing institutions also helped to restore confidence (Argentina, Chile, Malaysia, and Spain). Explicit deposit guarantees, sometimes with retroactive effect, were found useful in Argentina and Chile.

[31] See Appendix II for further details.

In none of the countries studied could the disclosure of information about individual institutions have helped, because insolvency on a wide scale, rather than isolated instances of failure, was a problem.

The traditional prescription that a central bank should lend freely at a penalty rate in times of panic fully applies to situations of illiquidity arising from sudden surges in the demand for reserves. By itself, the willingness to lend freely is often enough to prevent the propagation of a financial crisis. The penalty rate serves to reduce moral hazard, and in open economies helps to induce capital inflows. However, in the crisis episodes considered here, insolvency, rather than illiquidity, was the main problem. Moreover, it was of such a scale that in most countries initial emergency lending at market or penalty rates soon had to be replaced by longer-term lending at concessional rates. Thus, the central bank or the government ended up actively subsidizing many financial institutions. Therefore, to minimize moral hazard, nonpecuniary penalties—such as replacing management, requiring the surrender of shares, or preventing dividend distribution—were often employed.

Measures to Deal with Failing Banks

The fate of failing banks chiefly depended on each country's legislative framework (particularly on the range of enforcement actions available in the legislation), the structure of the banking system, the presence or absence of a deposit insurance agency, and the magnitude of each bank's losses. In Argentina most failed institutions were eventually liquidated, even after the legislation had been amended to allow the Central Bank to arrange for their merger or sale. In Thailand a variety of disposition decisions were employed for finance companies, including liquidations, mergers, restructuring of activities, recapitalization, and support through long-term, soft loans from the central bank. No bank was liquidated, but most troubled banks received subsidies in the form of soft central bank loans, and the government assumed the ownership of one bank.

In Chile, following some initial liquidations of small institutions, troubled banks were recapitalized and assisted through various subsidy schemes. In the Philippines troubled rural and thrift banks, which were numerous and small, were commonly liquidated. For the larger commercial banks, however, the preferred method was takeover by a government-owned financial institution, or acquisition by the government with central bank support and intervention. In Spain, the deposit insurance agency (or a similar agency) typically took control of the problem bank by buying shares at a nominal price, assumed the bad debts, and sold off the clean bank through competitive bidding.[32] As an exception, a large banking

---

[32] This process was similar to the purchase and assumption procedure used in the United States.

group was temporarily nationalized, together with other enterprises belonging to the same conglomerate (RUMASA).

The disposition method and the legal environment affected the distribution of losses among bankers, depositors, borrowers, and the government. Owners experienced their greatest losses when the bank was liquidated or they had to surrender ownership for a nominal price, and their smallest losses when they were allowed to hold on to their shares and the bank received subsidies from the central bank or the government. The loss to depositors was minimal in most countries, except where negative real interest rates were reinstated to reduce the debt burden.[33] Malaysia implemented a scheme to pay off depositors partly with equity in the institutions being recapitalized, and in one case Uruguay followed the same course.[34] In most cases, however, the government or the central bank assumed the bulk of the losses. These losses are difficult to measure, depending inter alia on the chosen method of disposition.[35] In countries with deposit insurance or other arrangements requiring contributions and loans from other banks (e.g., Thailand's Rehabilitation Fund to which all banks contributed), other banks—and indirectly their clients—shared the losses to the extent that the deposit insurance fund or the equivalent agency had insufficient resources to cover the losses.

The methods for recapitalizing banks typically involved various forms of subsidization. Under one approach the central bank (or a separate government agency) purchased bad loans at par, paying with central bank securities (or government bonds) that carried market rates.[36] Such purchases entail recovery risks for the central government or the central bank. To minimize these risks, in Chile the selling bank had to buy back the bad loans from the Central Bank according to a schedule stretching over ten years.[37] Thus, the Central Bank did not assume the commercial risk or management of these loans, but the approach still carried the risk that the continuation of old linkages between the bank and the debtor could weaken loan recovery. In Uruguay the Central Bank assumed the bad

---

[33] In Argentina holders of foreign currency deposits in failing banks lost everything. In Thailand, depositors of failed finance companies were to be paid over a 10-year period, without interest.

[34] For Uruguay, see Cikató (1989).

[35] Baliño (1987) gives partial figures for the Argentine Government's losses.

[36] For some operations the Central Bank of Uruguay issued U.S. dollar claims to purchase bad loans, some of which were denominated in domestic currency.

[37] This condition essentially converted the operation into a rediscount credit against the collateral of bad loans, with the proceeds reinvested in central bank securities. Thus, the objective was to support the profits of the bank for an extended period of time, with a part of the profits being used to repurchase bad loans. This method, based on a prespecified schedule of repurchases, could pose difficulties for bank operations if the profits were not adequate to cover the repurchases. This consideration was not relevant in the case of Chile, however, because the repurchases were stretched out over a long period.

loans, while collection responsibility kept switching between the Central Bank and a state commercial bank, thereby hampering loan recovery. In the Philippines, to facilitate loan recovery, some staff of the commercial banks were seconded to the fiscal agency that assumed the bad loans.

Central banks are ill equipped to assume the administration of bad loans of banks being recapitalized or restructured.[38] Borrowers have little incentive for repaying outstanding loans to an institution that cannot make new loans. Moreover, a central bank usually lacks the expertise in loan administration of a commercial bank or a specialized agency. Also, central bank losses on account of bad loans compromise monetary control, in addition to making the losses less transparent.

The case studies clearly point toward certain significant advantages—and some disadvantages—in shifting the bad assets to a separate agency with explicit funding sources. Such a shift, which took place in the Philippines and Spain, had the advantage of not only making the losses transparent, but also breaking off the linkages between problem banks and problem borrowers, linkages that had contributed to the problems in the first place. The resulting restructuring of banks' balance sheets also facilitated the implementation of monetary policy. Moreover, a separate entity —such as the so-called bad or collecting banks, those found in the United States—could offer greater flexibility and capability to mobilize staff with expertise in loan administration and recovery than a central bank or in some cases even commercial banks.

However, setting up a separate agency also has significant disadvantages. Generally, incentives for repayment by the debtor, and loan recovery efforts by the creditor, are likely to be much higher if the owner of the loan is a functioning commercial bank or a separate specialized agency with its own resources to lend, or if the commercial bank is given incentives to work with the debtor in asset restructuring and recovery. The debtor has greater incentives to restructure and resume normal credit relationships if a lending institution, which offers opportunities for new credits, is involved in loan recovery than if a pure asset recovery agency or a central bank is involved. Moreover, a separate loan recovery agency may lack the depth of knowledge of the debtor's situation and the loan recovery experience that the originating commercial bank is likely to have. In addition, staffing such an agency may deplete the human resources available to commercial banks in countries where loan recovery skills are in short supply.[39]

---

[38] In the case of liquidations, however, it is common for the central bank or the deposit insurance agency to assume the bad loans.

[39] In the Philippines, commercial bank staff with knowledge of debtors were used by the specialized agency, with administrative safeguards to ensure professional independence of such staff from the influence of debtors.

In some cases, rather than purchasing bad loans, the central bank offered a soft loan with which the troubled bank could acquire a government bond or a central bank security at a market-related rate, and thereby start receiving a stream of subsidies. Chile offered cheap government loans to facilitate the purchase of bank stock and tax credits for subscriptions of new issues of bank stock. In Chile and the Philippines, a government agency was charged with underwriting issues of new stock for the intervened banks.

Measures to Assist Borrowers

Measures to assist borrowers included financial support, technical assistance, and debt-equity conversions. Under a typical arrangement, the central bank provided medium-term refinance credit to commercial banks at subsidized rates (or other forms of subsidies) to encourage the banks to consolidate and reschedule their clients' loans.[40] In most cases the rate charged to final borrowers was not concessional. Uruguay enacted special legislation requiring banks to refinance all "insolvent" borrowers, with the terms of refinance depending on the classification of each borrower. A special government commission was to classify each borrower using various solvency and sectoral criteria, and a debt moratorium applied while classification was pending. Loan recovery and administrative costs with this approach have not been satisfactory in Uruguay.

Measures assisting borrowers that had contracted loans denominated in foreign exchange included preferential exchange rates, interest subsidies on foreign exchange swap transactions, and exchange insurance schemes. These measures often resulted in sizable subsidies to borrowers—with corresponding losses to the central bank—because of large devaluations. Malaysia also provided technical assistance to borrowers for restructuring their operations. The Philippines relied extensively on the takeover of ailing nonfinancial companies by government financial institutions (which converted part of the outstanding debt into equity), an action that postponed hard solutions and even led to the insolvency and restructuring of some of the rescuing institutions.

A key issue in formulating an assistance program for borrowers is whether it should be case by case or a blanket program that covers all who request assistance in a given industry or sector. Although care and selectivity can maximize the cost effectiveness of assistance, on occasion practical considerations might require choosing a blanket program. Ideally, debt restructuring should be left to the individual banks and their clients. But in the uncertainty surrounding a major banking crisis, market decisions may

---

[40] In many developing countries, banks are reluctant to provide long-term loans, given the short maturity of deposits and the lack of liquidity facilities.

be influenced by subjective fears and more than the socially optimal amount of caution; such a situation would justify some temporary government action.

The most powerful but probably also the most costly method to help insolvent borrowers and banks is to reimpose interest rate controls and produce negative real interest rates that transfer wealth from depositors to borrowers. This was the solution adopted in Argentina, and for a limited time in Uruguay. But this solution discourages depositors, and therefore over time results in a shrinking of the banking system in real terms.

Regulatory and Legislative Reforms

The emergence of crises highlighted the weaknesses in legislative and regulatory frameworks and triggered substantive regulatory reforms in most of the sample countries. For example, significant changes in regulations occurred in Thailand: central bank supervision was extended to finance companies in addition to banks, the central bank's powers of intervention and enforcement options were broadened, and regulations to limit concentration of ownership and portfolio were strengthened. In Chile comprehensive measures to tighten bank supervision were adopted in late 1981 and 1982; major legislative reforms were accomplished beginning in 1986. These changes provided a more precise definition of the limit on loans to a single borrower, taking into account the interlocking ownership of firms; a formal rating system for financial institutions; public disclosure of information on the nature and quality of the assets of financial institutions; tighter capital requirements; a formal deposit insurance for small savers to replace ad hoc guarantees, and full insurance protection of sight deposits, with the restriction that sight deposits exceeding two and a half times a bank's capital should be invested in central bank and government securities.

In Malaysia formal guidelines on suspension of interest on nonperforming loans and provisions for bad and doubtful debts were more forcefully implemented and industry practices standardized in order to promote consistent and prudent lending policies. Other measures included giving the central bank expanded powers to intervene in all deposit-taking institutions, establishing the Board Audit and Examination Committees to strengthen supervision of bank management,[41] and tightening lending limits per borrower. In the Philippines regulations on bill market practices and dealer supervision were strengthened following the 1981 crisis, and prudential accounting standards and bank liquidation procedures began to be strengthened.

---

[41] Every financial institution was required to establish such a committee, chaired by a non-executive director, to evaluate internal and external audit reports and pursue follow-up action to remedy any inadequacies discovered.

III. Concluding Remarks

A key question in the study of financial crisis is what can be done to prevent it, or at least to minimize its consequences. The answer must address three main problems posed by crisis: how to keep the system liquid, how to restore its solvency, and how to keep it solvent. The structural measures to deal with these problems cannot be fully effective in the presence of major macroeconomic instability and relative price distortions. At the same time, however, eliminating the major portfolio weaknesses in the financial sector can significantly reduce the cost of macroeconomic adjustment measures and make them more effective.

The problem of maintaining liquidity has been resolved through the lender-of-last-resort function of the central bank. However, given the unstable macroeconomic conditions before and during the banking crises in many sample countries, this solution posed difficulties for the design of financial policies—particularly monetary policy. Specifically, central banks had to balance the objective of preserving monetary stability with the fulfillment of their lender-of-last-resort obligations and, at the same time, had to contend with significant shifts in money demand and the money multiplier in times of crisis.

The restoration of solvency of the system in crisis involved a variety of disposition decisions for problem banks, problem loans, and problem borrowers. Because the widespread losses had to be dealt with in some fashion—to protect the depositors and ensure the sound future functioning of the financial intermediaries that would remain—the key issue was how to apportion the losses among depositors, borrowers, the banking system, and the government. In most cases, the government or the central bank assumed the bulk of the losses, because banks could not be expected to outgrow such large losses with only limited initial support. This approach complicated the design of monetary and fiscal policies. However, to ensure monetary policy independence, promote effective loan recovery and industrial restructuring, and minimize moral hazard, there are advantages in solutions that encompass the following elements: make the losses transparent rather than hide them in the books of the central bank or commercial banks; work out institutional arrangements that maximize professionalism in loan recovery, asset liquidations, and asset restructuring; and ensure that original shareholders absorb losses to the maximum extent possible under the law and that the old management is replaced in the problem financial institutions by new management.

After the initial recapitalization and restructuring of weak institutions, complex issues arose in the development of the regulatory and supervisory framework to preserve solvency of the financial system. First, the effectiveness of banking supervision was influenced by the uncertainties in the quality of the loan portfolio of financial institutions. Sharp changes in general business conditions (relative prices, policy regimes, etc.) caused cash-flow problems to businesses and raised loan defaults in some of the crises discussed here (Argentina, Chile, the Philippines, and Uruguay). Even loans that were sound when they were granted became bad loans; thus, major macroeconomic instability and sharp changes in relative prices constrained the effectiveness of vigilant bank supervision and made the identification and treatment of problem loans more complex. Nevertheless, in all the sample countries, factors specific to some institutions (e.g., weak management, fraud, risk concentration) also contributed to the poor quality of the assets of the financial system[42] and highlighted the importance of tighter prudential regulations and enhanced bank supervision.

Second, reforms of bank supervision and regulation raised difficult issues in defining the appropriate roles for the government and the market in maintaining the stability and soundness of the financial system. One area of debate has been the need for and form of deposit insurance. Some authors have argued that stricter supervision entails excessive government intervention in private business; others consider stricter supervision ineffective. These concerns have been reinforced by the moral hazard problem that most deposit insurance schemes pose. Reflecting these concerns, the Chicago plan for monetary reform—which originated in the 1930s and was espoused subsequently by Friedman (1959)—suggested splitting banks into two types of institutions, one allowed to receive demand deposits but subject to a 100 percent reserve requirement, and the other totally free from government regulation that would be able to receive any type of deposit from the public except demand deposits and invest in loans or any other assets. The authors of this plan argued that it would ensure that demand deposits (and hence the narrow money definition they were interested in) would not be subject to the contractions that take place during financial crises. Depositors in the second type of institution would bear the risk of the investments because the government would not bail out these institutions or their depositors.

A similar idea lies behind proposals for financial reform that have been triggered by financial crises in the eighties. For instance, Fernández (1983) advocated changing the nature of banks so that they would no longer undertake to guarantee a certain yield to their depositors. Also, the recent reform of the banking legislation in Chile distinguishes demand deposits from other deposits. The former have a state guarantee, and banks must invest demand deposits in securities issued by the government or the Central Bank. Other deposits have no guarantee and no restriction over

---

[42] The importance of these specific factors is clear from the fact that quite a few financial institutions in all the sample countries emerged from the crises virtually unscathed.

their investment. In the event of insolvency, a bank may enter into agreements with the holders of nonguaranteed deposits to settle claims on the bank; these depositors are treated like any other creditors of the bank. Reforms along these lines aim to preserve the integrity of the payments system by severely restricting the assets in which banks can invest demand deposits, but other types of deposits bear the full market risk.

Some writers have suggested ways to reduce moral hazard problems and minimize losses to deposit insurance schemes without reforming the financial system. For example, banks could be required to value their assets at market prices; large depositors could share in the losses of a liquidation or reorganization mandated by the regulator; banks could be required to partly fund themselves by issuing subordinated debt;[43] deposit insurance premiums could be differentiated on the basis of banks' riskiness; and more information could be provided to the market on the financial condition of individual banks.[44] These proposals reflect the view that with enough information the market will be able to assess, largely on its own, the relative soundness of the financial system.[45] Moreover, market reactions would help the regulator to detect problems in financial institutions and act before their net worth becomes zero, thus avoiding losses to the deposit insurer. Unfortunately, there is little evidence so far regarding the market's ability to judge a bank's soundness.[46]

To summarize, prompt support from the monetary authorities and the government during a financial crisis can prevent problem banks from causing major and lengthy disruptions to the payments system and the economy at large. However, effective restructuring and recapitalization of the problem banks and the banking system may require significant fiscal adjustment, prompt structural reforms of the nonfinancial sector, and

[43] Proponents of this requirement believe that it can reduce moral hazard because holders of subordinated debt would suffer a loss in the event of liquidation (unlike insured depositors) and would not gain from extraordinary profits arising from risky behavior (unlike bank shareholders).

[44] Kuprianov and Mengle (1989) discuss some of these ideas. For detailed proposals on "puttable" subordinated debt, see Wall (1989). Benston and others (1986) present a comprehensive discussion of options to make the banking system more resilient.

[45] Chile's recent legislation mandates the supervisory authority to publish indicators of the financial condition of individual institutions as a way of facilitating the market's assessment.

[46] In a recent article, Randall (1989) casts some doubt on the market's effectiveness in this regard. He suggests that the stock market and bond-rating agencies were too late in identifying the problems in large bank holding companies in the 1980s, and even then underestimated the seriousness of the problems. Moreover, he argues that it would be impractical to give the market the kind of information required for a proper evaluation of the quality of bank assets. In his view many of the market-oriented proposals discussed here would only make the financial system more vulnerable and would fail to protect the deposit insurer.

progress toward macroeconomic stability. Such stabilization and structural policies should be supported by adequate supervision and prudential regulations, which are also necessary to make financial crises less likely and less costly. But regulatory authorities must balance their concerns for the financial system's safety (which requires appropriate regulation and supervision) against the need to maximize its efficiency (which requires that market forces play the main role in shaping the structure and operations of the system). Discussion on ways of attaining this balance is still wide open.

APPENDIX I

Financial Reforms and Financial Crises in the Seven Case Studies: An Overview

Interest Rate and Regulatory Reforms	Openness to Capital Flows	Exchange Rate System	Deposit Insurance	Financial Crisis
ARGENTINA				
Under the financial reform of 1977, interest rate controls were eliminated, branching and entry regulations were eased, and most selective credit controls were abandoned. Interest rate controls were reintroduced during 1982 and 1983. Prudential regulations were comprehensive and somewhat strengthened during the reform. Supervision of asset quality and on-site inspections, which had been inadequate, were strengthened following the crisis.	Foreign borrowing was liberalized during 1976–81, with almost no barriers remaining by 1979. Measures to restrict external debt repayments were adopted in 1982.	Preannounced schedules of devaluation were in effect from December 1978 to March 1981. A dual exchange market was introduced in June 1981, scrapped at the end of the year, and reintroduced in July 1982. The dual system comprised a commercial rate, which was set by the Central Bank, and a financial rate, which was free although the Central Bank intervened in the market as a buyer.	Before 1979 the Central Bank fully insured depositors and bore all costs. Partial coverage was introduced in November 1979. The maximum amount of insured deposits was indexed, and insurance premiums and participation were set. Participation was voluntary. Amounts above the ceiling were insured only up to 90 percent. The maximum amount was adjusted retroactively following the crisis.	The crisis began with the failure of a large private bank in March 1980, leading to runs on three other banks that had to be intervened soon thereafter. Crisis spread rapidly to other banks and nonbank financial institutions; more than 70 institutions were liquidated or subjected to intervention between 1980 and 1982, accounting for 16 percent of the total assets of commercial banks and 35 percent of the total assets of finance companies.

APPENDIX I *(continued)*

Financial Reforms and Financial Crises in the Seven Case Studies: An Overview

Interest Rate and Regulatory Reforms	Openness to Capital Flows	Exchange Rate System	Deposit Insurance	Financial Crisis
CHILE				
The financial reform began in late 1973. Banks were privatized in 1984 and acquired by major conglomerates. Controls on interest rates were lifted in 1975, and selective credit controls were abolished. Entry and branching restrictions were removed. The system moved toward multipurpose banking, as distinctions among commercial, investment, mortgage, and development activities were abolished. Regulations on capital requirements	Capital flows were liberalized gradually. Quantity and term controls were relaxed between 1979 and 1980. Limits on bank borrowing abroad were abolished in 1980. The minimum maturity requirement was abolished in 1982.	Preannounced schedules of exchange rate devaluation were in effect between December 1977 and June 1979, and the nominal exchange rate was unchanged from June 1979 to June 1982. Since the maxi-devaluations in the latter half of 1982, the exchange rate has been adjusted in line with a set of indicators.	Explicit deposit guarantees were granted in January 1983, initially for a limited period. They were extended periodically until a formal deposit insurance scheme was instituted in 1986. There is partial insurance coverage for small depositors, with sight deposits fully protected.	The crisis began with the acceleration of business bankruptcies in 1980; a prominent sugar refining company failed in early 1981. Following bank runs in late 1981, the Government assumed control of three banks, a development bank, and four *financieras*, accounting for more than one third of the loan portfolio of the financial system. Again, in January 1983 seven banks and one *financiera*, accounting for 45 percent of total assets, were put

under government control, and three were liquidated immediately. Central bank inspectors were placed in seven other financial institutions.

were tightened and adjusted in line with inflation. Regulations, legislation, and supervisory apparatus aimed at controlling excessive risk taking and unsound lending patterns—given the interlocking ownership of financial and nonfinancial firms—were weak or nonexistent until 1980. These deficiencies were rectified following the crisis. Also, since 1983 a suggested maximum interest rate on 30-day deposits has been used.

MALAYSIA

All interest rates were formally liberalized in 1978, but effectively so in 1982. Controls on short-term deposit rates were temporarily im-

Capital flows are fairly free in practice. Foreign borrowing by residents and holding of accounts abroad are subject to approval. Banks' foreign proval.

Floating rates with intervention by the central bank using a set of indicators.

No formal deposit insurance system exists.

The crisis began in July 1985 with short-lived runs against some branches of a large domestic bank, stimulated by rumors following the

APPENDIX I (continued)

Financial Reforms and Financial Crises in the Seven Case Studies: An Overview

Interest Rate and Regulatory Reforms	Openness to Capital Flows	Exchange Rate System	Deposit Insurance	Financial Crisis
MALAYSIA (continued)				
posed between October 1985 and February 1987. A ceiling on interest rate margins over the base lending rates was set in late 1987. Prudential regulations and supervision of banks were generally strengthened during reform. Weaknesses in enforcement, coverage of institutions, and intervention options were remedied following the crisis.	exchange operations are subject to open position limits.			collapse of a related bank in Hong Kong. A spell of sporadic runs against weak institutions persisted throughout late 1985 and 1986, culminating in the failure of deposit-taking cooperatives in July and August 1986. This failure led the Bank Negara Malaysia (BNM) to intervene in 24 deposit-taking cooperatives with total deposits of M$1.5 billion. Also, in 1987 the BNM intervened in an apex cooperative with deposits of M$1.5 billion. In addition, in 1985/86 the

BNM had to intervene and inject capital into three ailing commercial banks with total deposits of M$3.9 billion. However, the turnaround in monetary policy in late 1986, economic recovery, regulatory adaptations, and support measures to ailing businesses all helped to restore the health of financial institutions. The BNM has begun to recover its credits to formerly ailing institutions.

PHILIPPINES

Financial reform began in mid-1980. In July 1981 all interest rate ceilings except those on short-term loans were lifted. In 1982 short-term loan rates also were freed. Before the reform (1972–81) interest ceilings were raised and ad-

Capital flows are fairly free in practice, although some controls remain. Capital flows were facilitated during the 1972–80 period by the introduction of foreign currency deposits (1972) and offshore banking units (1976). All foreign

Floating exchange rates, with intervention by the authorities.

A formal deposit insurance scheme has existed since 1970, but the scheme experienced difficulties in settling the growing claims in 1981. It was recapitalized in 1985. As of June 1987, only 52 percent of all claims on insured de-

The first episodes of the crisis were in 1981, when the commercial paper market collapsed owing to the dishonored bills left behind by the textile magnate Dewey Dee, who fled the country. This collapse caused a major confidence

APPENDIX I (continued)

Financial Reforms and Financial Crises in the Seven Case Studies: An Overview

Interest Rate and Regulatory Reforms	Openness to Capital Flows	Exchange Rate System	Deposit Insurance	Financial Crisis

PHILIPPINES
(continued)

justed on several occasions, but fees to circumvent ceilings were common.
Between 1972 and 1980 entry of domestic banks was tightened and mergers were encouraged by higher capital requirements, while foreign bank entry was eased. In 1980 universal banks were authorized and activity restrictions on thrift banks were relaxed.
Prudential regulations and supervisory appa-

borrowing except short-term borrowing by Philippine commercial banks has been subject to prior approval by the Monetary Board. Commercial banks' holdings of foreign assets are subject to limits relating to letters of credit, export bills purchased, and other foreign exchange receipts. Restrictions on external debt repayments introduced in late 1983 and early 1984.

posits had been settled.

crisis, triggered failures and takeovers of non-bank money market institutions, and resulted in a spread of distress among nonfinancial firms. Also between 1981 and 1983, failures among rural and thrift banks (these banks account for only 9 percent of the assets of the financial system) accelerated; government and central bank assistance to troubled financial and nonfinancial firms continued at high rates in 1982 and

1983. Failures of thrift banks accelerated in 1984 and 1985.

Three private banks were liquidated in 1985 and 1986. In all, between 1981 and 1987, 126 rural banks, 32 thrift banks, and 3 commercial banks closed down. These, however, accounted for only 3.5 percent of total financial system assets. In addition, 2 large state-owned banks and 5 private commercial banks accounting for 32 percent of total financial system assets required financial support, subsidies, and restructuring in 1985 and 1986. The 2 government-owned banks were effectively liquidated and bailed out, with their nonperforming loans (about 30 percent of the

ratus were generally comprehensive. Regulations were strengthened in some areas (e.g., capital adequacy) but relaxed in others (e.g., loans to related interests) during the reform period, but the enforcement of powers and regulations was weak.

APPENDIX I (continued)

Financial Reforms and Financial Crises in the Seven Case Studies: An Overview

Interest Rate and Regulatory Reforms	Openness to Capital Flows	Exchange Rate System	Deposit Insurance	Financial Crisis
PHILIPPINES (continued)				banking system's assets) transferred to a separate agency in 1986. The 5 commercial banks are undergoing rehabilitation under the Central Bank's supervision.
SPAIN Financial reform began in 1974. Interest rates were liberalized gradually, starting with the longer maturities. By the beginning of 1981, all interest rates were free, except for some specified priority categories and short-term deposit rates. The latter were freed in 1987.	Capital flows are fairly free.	Floating exchange rates, with intervention by the Bank of Spain.	In November 1977 deposit guarantee funds were established—one for each group of institutions—within the Bank of Spain, offering protection to small depositors based on contributions from financial institutions. Separate Guarantee Funds were organized on March 28, 1980,	A protracted banking crisis began in 1978, when the Bank of Spain had to rescue one of the smaller banks in distress. Between 1978 and 1983, a total of 51 problem banks, accounting for about 19 percent of the total assets of the banking system as of the end of 1977, required in-

Activity regulations were eased and entry regulations were streamlined and liberalized. Bank secrecy laws were drastically modified; commissions and fees were freed.

Prudential regulations were comprehensive and in some cases very detailed, but proved difficult to implement. Supervision was weak.

with the Bank of Spain matching the premiums contributed by banks. The maximum size of an insured deposit was adjusted several times.

tervention and appropriate disposition decisions. The peak of the crisis came in 1982 and 1983, when two large banking groups, owned by large industrial conglomerates, had to be taken over or temporarily nationalized. Two banks were closed; all others were either sold by the Deposit Guarantee Fund or taken over by stronger institutions.

THAILAND

Deposit rates are subject to ceilings. Money market rates, bill rates, and secondary market rates for government debt are relatively free.

The central bank's lack of adequate supervisory and regulatory powers was remedied following the outbreak of the crisis.

Capital inflows are fairly free, with significant scope for foreign borrowing by prime companies. Banks' foreign exchange operations are subject to open-position limits.

Exchange rates are determined on the basis of a basket of currencies.

No formal deposit insurance system exists.

A serious crisis among finance companies—accounting for about 12 percent of the total assets of the financial system—began in the autumn of 1983. Between 1983 and 1985, 19 finance companies were closed. Subsequently, 6 companies were rehabilitated

APPENDIX I (continued)

Financial Reforms and Financial Crises in the Seven Case Studies: An Overview

Interest Rate and Regulatory Reforms	Openness to Capital Flows	Exchange Rate System	Deposit Insurance	Financial Crisis
THAILAND (continued)				with soft loans and 19 others were merged; support has continued for several others. Weaknesses of the banking sector—rising loan losses and declining net profits—began to surface in the early 1980s. Between 1984 and 1987 this problem culminated in regulatory interventions, government and central bank takeovers, soft loans, recapitalization, and other support arrangements involving 5 banks that accounted for about 25 percent of the total assets of the banking system.

URUGUAY

Interest rates began to be liberalized in 1976, and all interest rate ceilings were abolished in 1979. Strong moral suasion was used in 1983 to bring about interest rate reductions. Interest ceilings were reintroduced in 1984 and abolished again in 1985, with the Banco República (state commercial bank) playing a major role in setting market interest rates.

Prudential regulations were relaxed in some areas (e.g., limit on credit to individual borrowers) and strengthened in others (e.g., capital adequacy) between

Capital flows were completely freed in 1974. Open position limits were introduced for all banks in 1984 to limit exposure to exchange rate risk.

In 1974 the peso became fully convertible.

No formal insurance scheme exists. De facto insurance was provided through some bank bailouts before the crisis.

The crisis began in 1982, when many banks were incurring losses and liquidity problems. Three banks were rescued by the Central Bank in that year. Banking distress became more pronounced from 1984 onward. One bank was liquidated in 1984; the two largest private banks were taken over by the Banco República in 1985. The largest private bank became insolvent in 1987 and was recapitalized with the Banco República subscribing the bulk of the equity. Also in 1987, following a bank run, another bank was taken over by a sub-

APPENDIX I *(concluded)*

Financial Reforms and Financial Crises in the Seven Case Studies: An Overview

Interest Rate and Regulatory Reforms	Openness to Capital Flows	Exchange Rate System	Deposit Insurance	Financial Crisis
URUGUAY *(concluded)* 1974 and 1981. Asset quality supervision was inadequate, but was strengthened following the crisis.				sidiary of the Banco República. These interventions, liquidations, and takeovers affected banks that accounted for more than 30 percent of the total deposits of the banking system.

APPENDIX II

Demand for Credit in Argentina

A simple partial adjustment model was postulated for the private sector's demand for credit:

$$(L/P)^*_t = a_o + a_1 y_t + a_2 r_t + a_3 inf_t \tag{1}$$

$$(L/P)_t = v((L/P)^*_t - (L/P)_{t-1}) \tag{2}$$

where L is the outstanding stock of loans; P is the wholesale price index; y is real GNP; r is the bank nominal lending rate; inf is the inflation rate (measured by the wholesale price index); and v is the speed of adjustment. The basic equation estimated was

$$(L/P)_t = b_o + b_1 y_t + b_2 r_t + b_3 inf_t + b_4(L/P)_{t-1} \tag{3}$$

In addition, dummy variables were introduced for the crisis period and for the period in which interest rates were subject to controls. The dummy for the crisis period was statistically insignificant, but the dummy for interest rates controls (D) was significant. The data used corresponded to the period beginning in the third quarter of 1975 and ending in the fourth quarter of 1987. The reduced-form equation was estimated using instrumental variables and yielded the following results (t-values shown in parentheses):

$$(L/P)_t = -4776 \quad + 0.142 y_t \quad + 15.285 r_t \quad - 20.851 inf_t \quad - 430.230D \ +$$
$$(-2.65) \qquad (3.38) \qquad (2.87) \qquad (-4.44) \qquad (-2.56)$$

$$0.916(L/P)_{t-1} \tag{4}$$
$$(36.62)$$

$$DW = 1.89 \qquad R^2 = 0.976$$

The signs for the interest rate and inflation coefficients are the opposite of what would normally be expected; the estimated coefficients indicate that demand for loans rises in real terms when the real cost of credit goes up. This finding is consistent with the hypothesis that a large fraction of the demand for credit in Argentina consisted of loans that were insensitive to interest rates and on which interest was accrued and capitalized but not paid—that is, effectively nonperforming loans. Thus, when nominal interest rates went up, the real stock of credit increased because interest accrued at a faster pace on these loans; when inflation increased, the value of these loans was eroded—which would account for the negative sign for the inflation rate. Estimates also reveal that interest rate controls had a negative effect on the real value of this debt, insofar as real interest rates were negative over the period. Finally, the low speed of adjustment (0.084) suggests that the outstanding stock of debt was determined largely by the previous period's stock—as could be expected when banks make few new loans and simply accrue interest on a large fraction of their portfolios.

APPENDIX III

A Stylized Framework for Dealing with Banking Crises

OBJECTIVES	CONSTRAINTS
• Restore depositors' confidence and protect some or all depositors • Prevent hasty liquidation of assets • Avoid undue monetary fluctuations • Prevent moral hazard • Protect solvent banks and debtors • Protect the payment system • Minimize budgetary costs (or costs to the insurance agency) • Ensure equitable distribution of losses	• Legislation • Limits on budgetary resources • External imbalances and constraints on foreign borrowing • Political considerations in distributing the losses between government, the central bank, bank owners, depositors, and borrowers • Public interest and employment considerations, e.g., effect on competition and banking concentration

Emergency Measures	Long-Term Measures	Measures to Deal with Failing Banks	Measures to Deal with Borrowers
• Financial support and other lender-of-last-resort actions • Guarantees on deposits • Disclosure of information, e.g., to dispell rumors or to revive confidence • Central bank intervention in management of weak banks	• New institution • New legislation • Strengthened supervision	• Liquidation • Merger • Sale • Recapitalization • Restructuring	• Assistance to reschedule domestic debt • Technical assistance • Subsidies and assistance to foreign currency debtors • Negative real interest rates

APPENDIX IV

Measures to Deal with Banks and Borrowers in Distress in the Sample Countries

The authorities took various measures to deal with financial crises in the sample countries. As noted in the text, these measures differed widely from country to country. The following is a list of the measures taken in one or more of the sample countries, classified according to whether they dealt with banks or with bank borrowers.

I. Banks
    Liquidation
    - Bad loans managed by the central bank or supervision agency (acting as receiver and liquidator)
    - Bad loans assumed by the deposit insurance agency
    - Bad loans taken over by a separate government agency
    Merger
    - Provision of tax and regulatory incentives
    - Provision of special lines of subsidized credit from the central bank
    - Information service to facilitate mergers
    Sale
    - Takeover by government
    - Takeover by another bank or government financial institution, sometimes with medium-term credit from the central bank (for acquisition and investment)
    - Sale after bad loans are assumed by the central bank, or deposit insurance agency (purchase and assumption)
    Recapitalization
    - Cash infusion from the government or deposit insurance agency, the central bank, or a special fund created with subscriptions from financial institutions
    - Capital contribution paid with government securities or central bank securities yielding market rates
    - New stock issues underwritten by a government agency (sometimes the central bank) and supported by fiscal and financial incentives
      —cheap loans to buy banks' shares
      —tax credit based on value of shares purchased
    - Purchase of bad loans at par by a government agency with government funds or government securities
    - Unconditional purchase of bad loans by the central bank which pays with central bank securities at market rate (or with central bank obligations in foreign currency)
    - Purchase of bad loans by the central bank, subject to various conditions (on dividend distribution, repurchases of bad loans, provision of foreign currency loans to the central bank)

- Soft loans from the central bank to be invested in government or central bank securities

Restructuring

- Change in management, in internal controls, and in operating procedures
- Authorization of new product or service lines

II. Borrowers

- Central bank credit to banks at low rates to encourage consolidation and stretching out of business firm debt
- Government subsidies to banks, to facilitate rescheduling of business debt
- Credit guarantee schemes
- Preferential exchange rate for foreign currency debtors, interest subsidies on foreign exchange swap operations, exchange insurance programs
- Controls on interest rates, to bring about negative real rates for borrowers and depositors (a reversal of previous deregulation)
- Technical assistance to borrowers
- Conversion of business debt into equity held by the commercial bank
- Legislation on debt refinancing and temporary debt moratorium
- Partial write-off of accrued interest or principal by the central bank (or the government agency) after assuming the problem loan

Bibliography

Altman, Edward I., and Arnold W. Sametz, eds., *Financial Crises: Institutions and Markets in a Fragile Environment* (New York: John Wiley and Sons, 1977).

Argentina, Banco Central de la República Argentina, *Memoria Anual*, 1980.

Baliño, Tomás J.T., "The Argentine Banking Crisis of 1980," IMF Working Paper No. 87/77, International Monetary Fund, November 17, 1987.

Batcheldor, Roy A., "The Avoidance of Catastrophe: Two Nineteenth-Century Banking Crises," in *Financial Crises in the World Banking System*, ed. by Forrest Capie and Geoffrey E. Wood (New York: St. Martin's Press, 1985), pp. 41–73.

Benston, George J., and others, *Perspectives on Safe and Sound Banking—Past, Present, and Future* (Cambridge, Massachusetts: MIT Press, 1986).

Bernanke, Ben, "Nonmonetary Effects of the Financial Crisis in the Propagation of the Great Depression," NBER Working Paper No. 1054:1–54 (Cambridge, Massachusetts: National Bureau of Economic Research, January 1983).

Blinder, Alan, and Joseph Stiglitz, "Money, Credit Constraints and Economic Activity," *American Economic Review*, Papers and Proceedings, Vol. 73 (May 1983), pp. 297–302.

Bordo, Michael D., "Financial Crises, Banking Crises, Stock Market Crashes and the Money Supply: Some International Evidence, 1870–1933," in *Financial Crises in the World Banking System*, ed. by Forrest Capie and Geoffrey E. Wood (New York: St. Martin's Press, 1985), pp. 190–239.

Brunner, Karl, and Allen H. Meltzer, "Money and Credit in the Monetary Transmission Process," *American Economic Review*, Papers and Proceedings, Vol. 78 (May 1988), pp. 446–51.

Capie, Forrest, and Geoffrey E. Wood, eds., *Financial Crises in the World Banking System* (New York: St. Martin's Press, 1985).

Cikató, Manfredo, "La Crisis Bancaria en el Uruguay," in *Saneamiento de Bancos*, ed. by Juan Carlos Casas (Buenos Aires: El Cronista Comercial, 1989).

de Juan, A., "From Good Bankers to Bad Bankers: Ineffective Supervision and Management Deterioration as Major Elements in Banking Crisis" (unpublished; 1987).

Diamond, Douglas W., and Phillip H. Dybvig, "Bank Runs, Deposit Insurance, and Liquidity," *Journal of Political Economy*, Vol. 91, No. 3 (1983), pp. 401–19.

Dwyer, Gerald P., Jr., and R. Alton Gilbert, "Bank Runs and Private Remedies," *Federal Reserve Bank of St. Louis Review* (May/June 1989), pp. 43–61.

Federal Reserve Bank of San Francisco, "The Search for Financial Stability: The Past Fifty Years," proceedings of a conference held June 23–25, 1985.

Fernández, Roque B., "La Crisis Financiera Argentina: 1980–1982," *Desarrollo Económico*, Vol. 23, No. 29 (April–June 1983), p. 55.

Fisher, Irving, "The Debt-Deflation Theory of Great Depressions," *Econometrica*, Vol. 1 (October 1933), pp. 337–57.

Flood, Robert P., and Peter M. Garber, *A Systematic Banking Collapse in a Perfect Foresight World*, NBER Working Paper No. 691: 1–41 (Cambridge, Massachusetts: National Bureau of Economic Research, June 1981).

Friedman, B.M., and F.H. Hahn, eds., *Handbook of Monetary Economics* (Amsterdam: North-Holland, 1990).

Friedman, Milton, *A Program for Monetary Stability* (New York: Fordham University Press, 1959).

————, and Anna J. Schwartz, *A Monetary History of the United States*, 1867–1960 (Princeton, New Jersey: Princeton University Press, 1963).

Guttentag, Jack, and Richard Herring, "Credit Rationing and Financial Disorder," *Journal of Finance*, Vol. 39 (December 1984), pp. 1–37.

————, "Disclosure Policy and International Banking," *Journal of Banking and Finance*, Vol. 10 (1986), pp. 75–97.

Kindleberger, Charles P., *Manias, Panics, and Crashes: A History of Financial Crises* (New York: Basic Books, 1978).

————, "Bank Failures: The 1930s and 1980s," *The Search for Financial Stability: The Past Fifty Years*, proceedings of the conference sponsored by the Federal Reserve Bank of San Francisco, Asilomar, California, June 12–15, 1985.

Kuprianov, Anatoli, and David L. Mengle, "The Future of Deposit Insurance: An Analysis of the Alternatives," Federal Reserve Bank of Richmond, *Economic Review*, Vol. 75 (May/June 1989), pp. 3–15.

Long, Millard, *Crisis in the Financial Sector*, World Bank, EDI Working Papers, 1988.

Manikow, N. Gregory, "The Allocation of Credit and Financial Collapse," NBER Working Paper No. 1786 (Cambridge, Massachusetts: National Bureau of Economic Research, January 1986), pp. 1–19

Massad, Carlos, and Roberto Zahler, "Another View of the Latin American Crisis: Domestic Debt," *CEPAL Review*, No. 32 (August 1987), pp. 11–25.

Minsky, Hyman P., "The Financial-Instability Hypothesis: Capitalist Processes and the Behavior of the Economy," in *Financial Crises*, ed. by Charles P.

Kindleberger and Jean-Pierre Laffarge (Cambridge, England: Cambridge University Press, 1982), pp. 13–39.

———, "A Theory of Systemic Fragility," in *Financial Crisis: Institutions and Markets in a Fragile Environment*, ed. by Edward I. Altman and Arnold W. Sametz (New York: John Wiley and Sons, 1977), pp. 138–52.

Miron, J.A., "Financial Panics, the Seasonality of the Nominal Interest Rate, and the Founding of the Fed," *American Economic Review*, Vol. 76 (March 1986), pp. 125–40.

Mitchell, Wesley Clair, *Business Cycles and Their Causes* (Berkeley, California: University of California Press, 1941).

Nascimento, Jean-Claude, "The Crisis in the Financial Sector and the Authorities' Reaction: The Case of the Philippines," IMF Working Paper No. 90/26, International Monetary Fund, March 1990.

Randall, Richard E., "Can the Market Evaluate Asset Quality Exposure in Banking?" *New England Economic Review*, Federal Reserve Bank of Boston (July/August 1989).

Schwartz, Anna J., "Real and Pseudo Financial Crises," in *Financial Crises in the World Banking System*, ed. by Forrest Capie and Geoffrey E. Wood (New York: St. Martin's Press, 1985), pp. 11–37.

Sheng, Andrew, "Financial Adjustment in a Period of Disinflation: The Case of Malaysia," in *Visiting Specialists' Papers*, 17th SEANZA Central Banking Course, Sydney, Australia, October/November 1988.

Sinai, Allen, "Credit Crunches—An Analysis of the Postwar Experience," in *Parameters, Policies in the U.S. Economy*, ed. by Otto Eckstein (Amsterdam: North-Holland, 1976), pp. 244–74.

Stiglitz, J.E., and Andrew Weiss, "Credit Rationing in Markets with Imperfect Information," *American Economic Review*, Vol. 71 (June 1981), pp. 393–410.

Taylor, Lance, and Stephen O'Connell, "A Minsky Crisis," *Quarterly Journal of Economics* (1985).

Tybout, James, "A Firm-Level Chronicle of Financial Crises in the Southern Cone," *Journal of Development Economics*, Vol. 24 (1986), pp. 371–400.

Veblen, Thorstein, *The Theory of Business Enterprise* (New York: Charles Scribner & Sons, 1904).

Velasco, Andrés, "Financial Crises and Balance of Payments Crises—A Simple Model of Southern Cone Experience," *Journal of Development Economics*, Vol. 17 (1987), pp. 263–83.

———, "Liberalization, Crisis, Intervention: The Chilean Financial System, 1975–1985," IMF Working Paper No. 88/66, International Monetary Fund, July 21, 1988.

Wachtel, Paul, ed., *Crisis in the Economic and Financial Structure* (Lexington, Massachusetts: D.C. Heath and Co., 1982).

Wall, Larry D., "A Plan for Reducing Future Deposit Insurance Losses: Puttable Subordinated Debt," *Economic Review*, Federal Reserve Bank of Atlanta (July/August 1989).

Wojinlower, Albert M., "The Central Role of Credit Crunches in Recent Financial History," *Brookings Papers on Economic Activity*, Vol. 2 (Brookings Institution: Washington, 1980), pp. 277–326.

——— , "Private Credit Demand, Supply and Crunches: How Different Are the 1980s?" *American Economic Review*, Vol. 75 (May 1985), pp. 351–56.

Wolfson, Martin H., *Financial Crises: Understanding the Postwar U.S. Experience* (Armonk, New York: M.E. Shoorpe, Inc., 1986).

2

The Argentine Banking Crisis of 1980

Tomás J.T. Baliño[1]

I. Introduction and Overview of the Literature on Argentina's Financial Crisis

In March 1980, one of the largest private banks in Argentina—Banco de Intercambio Regional (BIR)—failed; within a few days, the Central Bank had to intervene three other major banks, two of which were subsequently liquidated.[2] Thus began a serious crisis of the Argentine financial system, which resulted in the liquidation of 71 financial institutions over the next two years and caused far-reaching changes not only in the financial system but also in economic policies. The restructuring process is still continuing. Most of the authors who have analyzed these developments have concentrated on the broad macroeconomic aspects; a few others have dealt with selected features of the Argentine financial sector in the context of the crisis. This chapter integrates these two sets of analyses and focuses more closely on the financial sector by emphasizing the regulatory aspects that previous studies have largely ignored.

This section provides a brief overview of selected literature on the Argentine financial crisis. The next section presents evidence on the macroeconomic and general business environment, and Section III analyzes the crisis itself. Section IV presents the conclusions. The research strategy followed in the paper reflects the belief that an appropriate analysis of the Argentine banking crisis has to look beyond the financial

[1] I wish to thank Dawit Makonnen for valuable research assistance and José A. Uriarte of the Central Bank of Argentina for his help in obtaining and interpreting some of the data.
[2] Intervention is the power of the central bank to appoint an administrator who displaces the existing administration of a troubled financial institution. (The property of the institution remains with its original owners.) Intervention can be a first step toward liquidation or toward reorganization and sale of the institution.

system, because a main cause of the crisis was the deterioration of the system's loan portfolio—a deterioration that stemmed in part from developments in the general economic environment and their effects on business conditions.

Overview of the Literature

The Argentine financial crisis has been discussed mainly in the context of the economic policies implemented between 1977 and 1981, with only a few studies focusing on the financial system.[3] This section briefly reviews the different approaches that have been followed in the literature. Fernández discusses three causes of financial crises: inadequacies of free market economies, inappropriate monetary policy, and inherent instability of the financial system.[4] For him, the latter best explains Argentina's financial crisis: under a fractional reserve system with state deposit insurance, financial institutions in trouble can delay failure by resorting to "liability administration." Liability administration is described as the policy of an institution that, facing a cash shortfall caused by nonperforming loans, must raise interest rates to attract new deposits to replace those maturing. An explosive situation can result.

According to Fernández, this situation arose during the Argentine financial crisis as firms defaulted on their bank loans. These defaults were due to enterprise failures, which, in turn, were caused by frustrated expectations over macroeconomic policy and over the relationship between interest rates and the rate of change in the price of each enterprise's product. Finally, Fernández finds merit in Simons's proposal for financial reform, under which sight deposits would have a 100 percent reserve requirement to preserve their liquidity while time deposits would be replaced by bank acceptances or shares whose value would be market determined, that is, time deposits would resemble mutual fund shares.

Commenting on Fernández's paper, Feldman (1983) suggests that the financial crisis should not be interpreted in isolation but should be viewed as a reflection of the real sector crisis that resulted from the growing incompatibility between real domestic interest rates and the rates of return of investments in domestic assets. Furthermore, Feldman suggests that high domestic interest rates largely reflected risk premiums owing to devaluation expectations that exceeded the Government's preannounced, and realized, devaluation rates.

Using the framework developed by Minsky (1977), Dreizzen (1984) constructs several indicators to study the financial situation of a sample of

[3] See, for example, Ardito Barletta, Blejer, and Landau (1984).
[4] Fernández (1983a and 1983b). Similar views, in a broader context, appear in Fernández (1985).

industrial firms. He concludes that between 1977 and 1983 the financial structure of firms became increasingly fragile and had to endure strong destabilizing shocks, most of which originated in the financial market. Among the shocks that took place at different times in that period, he cites restrictive monetary policy, bank failures, and devaluations.

Another paper, by Petrei and Tybout (1985), examines firms' indebtedness by analyzing a sample of industrial firms during the period 1976–81. They suggest that these firms originally obtained huge financial subsidies because of "real currency appreciation and unconstrained access to foreign credit, then again in 1981 because of an exchange insurance program." Moreover, the accelerated growth in the debt/capital ratio in 1980, coinciding with lower profit rates for the firms in the sample, contributed to the development of the crisis.

Arnaudo and Conejero (1985) compare the performance of the three banks that failed in 1980 (Banco de Intercambio Regional, Banco de Los Andes, and Banco Internacional) with one another and with the average performance of private domestic banks. They conclude that several indicators warned of the impending failures of these three banks.

Damill and Frenkel (1987) further develop some of the points raised in the earlier literature. They suggest that the negative real rates of 1979 prompted firms to borrow more, thereby increasing their fragility. This fragility was exacerbated by the short maturities of loans, which made firms particularly vulnerable to "exogenous shocks," such as higher interest rates induced by changes in exchange rate expectations. The consequent loss of profitability of some sectors increased the share of nonperforming loans in bank portfolios. Moreover, some banks that went bankrupt in 1980 had spectacular rates of growth, which the authors attribute to "speculative elements."

The literature just reviewed suggests that the economic environment, as well as factors intrinsic to the financial system, led to the crisis in the Argentine financial system.

II. The Economic Environment

The 1976–82 period saw many economic changes in Argentina. The economic team that came to office in March 1976 inherited a high rate of inflation, a serious balance of payments problem, and a substantial fiscal deficit. The new team not only adopted short-term measures to cope with this situation but also carried out some important structural reforms, the most radical of which took place in the financial sector. Many of these measures and reforms were blamed for the serious difficulties that surfaced when the financial crisis erupted. As a result, beginning in March

Table 1. Phases of Reference Cycles, 1961–82

Expansion		Contraction	
Period	Length (months)	Period	Length (months)
July 1963–May 1967	46	Aug. 1961–July 1963	23
Dec. 1967–Dec. 1974	84	May 1967–Dec. 1967	7
Nov. 1975–July 1977	20	Dec. 1974–Nov. 1975	11
Mar. 1978–Feb. 1980	23	July 1977–Mar. 1978	8
		Feb. 1980–Jan. 1981	11
Jan. 1981–July 1981	6	July 1981–Apr. 1982	9
Average length: 35.8 months		Average length: 11.5 months	

Source: Arranz and Elías (1984).

1981, economic policy was significantly modified and most of the reforms begun in 1976 were scrapped.

To facilitate assessment of the contribution of changes in the economic background to the financial crisis, this section presents some evidence on the behavior of the economy between 1976 and 1982: (1) the evolution of GDP and its major components; (2) the evolution of monetary and credit aggregates; (3) the behavior of some important prices (interest rates, the exchange rate, and some asset prices); and (4) the evolution of enterprise debt.

Evolution of GDP and Its Major Components

Consideration of the evolution of GDP and its components is relevant for the analysis of the financial crisis on at least two grounds. First, a significant body of literature produced by Kindleberger, Minsky, and others asserts that financial crises are an integral part of the business cycle, because they are a necessary consequence of the previous boom. Second, a downturn in economic activity can reduce firms' sales and profits in the affected sectors, compromising the liquidity and solvency of these firms and, therefore, their ability to service their debt.

Table 1, which presents the phases of reference cycles for Argentina from 1961 through 1982, shows that the financial crisis followed an economic expansion: the failure of the Banco de Intercambio Regional in March 1980 came immediately after the expansionary period that had lasted from March 1978 to February 1980.[5]

---

[5] The reference cycles have been estimated with the methodology used by the National Bureau of Economic Research for its studies on U.S. business cycles.

The national accounts data confirm that the financial crisis came after a period of economic expansion: although GDP fell by 3.4 percent in 1978, it grew at rates substantially above historical performance in 1977 and 1979; between 1976 and 1979 the growth rate averaged 3 percent. The crisis cannot be dated so easily with reference to investment, however, because investment kept growing at a rate much above historical averages even after the crisis started; only in 1981 did investment begin to fall sharply. Finally, there were sharp differences in the performance of many sectors; in particular, the financial sector grew much faster than total GDP between 1977 and 1980 but shrank sharply between 1981 and 1983. Moreover, in any given year, rates of growth varied substantially across sectors. These sharp fluctuations in performance undoubtedly required various economic sectors to make substantial adjustments, which may have affected their debt-servicing capacity.[6]

Behavior of Monetary and Credit Aggregates

Table 2 presents data on the behavior of monetary and credit aggregates in the 1976–82 period. These data are useful not only to complete the general background but also to analyze whether monetary factors could have caused the financial crisis.

The table presents the data in nominal terms, from which two main conclusions can be drawn: (1) that monetary and credit aggregates grew very fast throughout the period, and (2) that time deposits significantly increased their share in M2, jumping from 36 percent in 1976 to 71 percent in 1981.

The data in Table 2 suggest that the crisis cannot be attributed to monetary causes: money grew in nominal terms at a high rate both before and after the crisis, although the rates of growth of M1 and M2 fell sharply in 1980, once the crisis was under way. The data for domestic credit show a similar pattern.[7]

Further evidence on monetary developments is provided in Table 3, which presents data on the behavior of the ratios of currency/money and of excess reserves/liabilities subject to reserve requirements. According to the monetarist hypothesis, changes in these ratios caused monetary contractions in the United States that resulted in financial crises and recessions.[8] This hypothesis implies that the rise in these ratios depressed the money

[6] See Baliño (1987), pp. 8 and 9.
[7] Domestic credit is the variable that the Government could control throughout most of the period because international reserves were endogenous, with the Government setting the exchange rate.
[8] See, for instance, Friedman and Schwartz (1963) and Cagan (1965).

Table 2. Main Monetary and Credit Aggregates, 1976–82
(In thousands of australes)[1]

End of Year	1976 Amount	1977 Amount	1977 Percentage increase	1978 Amount	1978 Percentage increase	1979 Amount	1979 Percentage increase	1980 Amount	1980 Percentage increase	1981 Amount	1981 Percentage increase	1982 Amount	1982 Percentage increase
In nominal terms													
Monetary aggregates													
Currency	41	107	61.7	333	210.5	787	136.2	1,642	108.6	3,021	84.0	8,736	189.2
Demand deposits	52	101	95.9	230	127.7	596	158.9	1,093	83.4	1,589	45.3	6,128	285.7
M1	93	208	125.1	563	170.4	1,383	145.5	2,735	97.8	4,610	68.5	14,864	222.5
Time and savings deposits	53	292	449.2	868	197.7	2,915	235.8	5,282	81.2	11,368	95.3	23,458	106.4
M2	146	500	243.2	1,431	186.3	4,298	200.2	8,017	86.6	15,978	99.3	38,322	139.9
Deposits of public sector with commercial banks	38	125	229.1	286	127.8	673	135.6	1,413	109.9	2,861	102.5	8,253	188.5
Credit aggregates													
Domestic credit[2]	189	655	246.2	1,829	179.1	5,392	194.8	11,268	109.0	33,457	196.9	104,491	212.3
Credit to private sector[3]	121	433	257.9	1,218	181.0	4,002	228.6	8,345	108.5	22,197	166.0	68,928	210.5
Credit to public sector[2]	68	222	225.4	611	175.3	1,389	127.5	2,923	110.4	11,260	285.2	35,563	215.8

Source: Central Bank of Argentina, *Boletín Estadístico*, various issues.

[1]The austral is the currency unit introduced in Argentina in 1985 to replace the peso (₳1 = $a 10 million).
[2]Includes outstanding balance of "Cuenta de Regulación Monetaria" (Interest Equalization Fund).
[3]Includes loans in foreign currency.

Table 3. Ratios of Currency to Deposits and Excess of Bank Reserves to Reserve Liabilities, 1976–82

Period	Reserve Requirement[1,2]	Currency/ Deposits[3]	Excess Bank Reserves/Reserve Liabilities[1,3]
1976: I	—	0.309	—
II	—	0.252	—
III	—	0.230	—
IV	—	0.260	—
1977: I		0.212	
II	45.0	0.213	4.20
III	45.0	0.190	0.78
IV	44.7	0.207	1.51
1978: I	44.0	0.170	1.07
II	43.0	0.175	1.88
III	40.7	0.164	0.20
IV	31.0	0.229	0.65
1979: I	27.0	0.175	0.52
II	27.0	0.169	0.51
III	25.0	0.149	0.30
IV	20.0	0.183	0.75
1980: I	13.2	0.157	0.66
II	11.3	0.174	0.91
III	12.5	0.162	0.51
IV	10.3	0.204	1.13
1981: I	12.0	0.157	0.16
II	16.0	0.160	0.35
III	18.0	0.133	0.29
IV	15.5	0.183	0.90
1982: I	16.5	0.127	2.21
II	13.5	0.162	13.65
III	100.0	0.160	11.84
IV	100.0	0.205	5.14

Sources: Central Bank of Argentina, *Boletín Estadístico*, various issues; Gaba (1981); and International Monetary Fund, *International Financial Statistics*, various issues.

[1]The series begins with the reintroduction of fractional bank reserves in June 1977.

[2]Period average.

[3]End-of-quarter data.

multiplier, inducing a fall in the money supply or in its rate of growth.

The data do not support this hypothesis for the Argentine financial crisis. As shown in Table 3, the currency/deposit ratio was lower by the end of the first quarter of 1980 (when the Banco de Intercambio Regional was closed) than in the same period of the previous years; although this ratio tended to rise during the rest of 1980, it still remained below the levels of 1976 and 1977. This situation suggests that the crisis undermined the public's confidence in the safety of deposits only briefly. A study of the period from June 1977 to June 1981 finds evidence of a shift in the intercept of the estimated function for the currency/deposit ratio (Demaestri (1982)). This shift was positive for April and May and negative for June 1980. Another study of the period from May 1978 to March 1982 (Dabós and Demaestri (1983)) found that the demand for currency, in real terms, became less sensitive to the deposit interest rate beginning in March 1980 (i.e., before the liquidation of the first major bank but after the liquidation of one of the largest financial companies).

The excess reserve ratio fluctuated widely between the end of the second quarter of 1977 (the start of the financial liberalization) and the end of 1982. Even after the outlier observations for the second quarter of 1977 and for the whole of 1982 are excluded, the ratio remained volatile: for instance, it dropped from 1.88 to 0.20 between the second and third quarters of 1978.[9] Despite this volatility, the data for 1979 are well within the historical range of values, suggesting that bank reserve behavior was not a contractionary influence on the money supply.[10] More important, the fact that the behavior of bank excess reserves in 1980 shows no departure from the historical pattern suggests that the crisis did not reduce the willingness of banks to invest in yield-earning assets.

The Behavior of Interest Rates

Several authors have blamed interest rate behavior during and after the liberalization experience for the business failures that occurred between

---

[9] The 1982 outliers should be disregarded because they reflected the economic and political uncertainties of that year (conflict over the Falkland Islands/Malvinas; change in administration), as well as the reforms introduced to the financial system by midyear. The figure for the second quarter of 1977 should also be disregarded, because it reflects the transitional effect of moving from a 100 percent reserve system to the fractional system rather than the effect of bank decisions.

[10] The Argentine banks' behavior contrasts sharply with the behavior of U.S. banks during the 1930s, when they increased their excess reserves, thus reducing the money supply and deepening the recession, in the view of monetarist writers such as Friedman and Schwartz (1963).

1977 and 1982. The purpose of this section is to present evidence that can help to evaluate the merits of that explanation.[11]

Nominal interest rates jumped dramatically when interest rate controls were lifted at the end of the first half of 1977: both deposit and lending rates more than doubled from the first to the second half of 1977. It is important to gauge the volatility of interest rates before the crisis, because a high volatility could frustrate business planning and undermine the financial health of firms. The monthly variability of interest rates within each year, measured by the coefficient of variation, was lower during 1979 and 1980 than at any other time between 1977 and 1982.[12] This lower variability was probably caused by the policy of preannounced devaluations between December 1978 and March 1981, which encouraged interest rate arbitrage by reducing exchange rate risk.

The data in Table 4 show that annual average lending rates were positive in real terms during the liberalization period. Also, their highest value (4.87 percent a month, using the wholesale price index—WPI) was attained in the last quarter of 1979; moreover, the annual average of lending rates peaked in 1980. Therefore, high lending rates helped to precipitate and aggravate the crisis by making debt servicing more difficult. However, although these rates were positive on average, and sometimes very high, they were negative during many quarters. Thus the effect on each firm depended not only on the sign and size of its net financial position but also on the pattern of this position through time.

The behavior of real lending rates raises several issues. First, did the high loan rates reflect high deposit rates as well as high spreads? Second, why did enterprises not switch to foreign borrowing? Third, why were enterprises prepared to borrow at rates much higher than the marginal rate of return on investment?

Table 4 indicates that, although lending rates fluctuated in line with variations in deposit rates, the large and volatile spreads contributed significantly to the observed high lending rates. In order to explain the high spreads, Gaba (1981) broke them down into the cost of reserve requirements, the cost of excess reserves, and the gross financial yield for the bank (after taking into account the effect of non-interest-bearing deposits). He found that, except for the second half of 1977, when the high reserve requirement accounted for the largest share of the spread, by far the largest component was the gross financial yield required to cover administrative costs and profits.

Some studies have identified high administrative costs as a significant

---

[11] Also, many studies have pointed to high real interest rates as evidence of the failure of the liberalization experience. See, for instance, Díaz-Alejandro (1985).

[12] See Baliño (1987), p. 14.

Table 4. Real Interest Rates, 1974–82
(In percent a month)

Period	Deposit Rate Deflated by[1]		Lending Rate Deflated by[1]	
	CPI	WPI	CPI	WPI
1974	− 1.51	− 1.27	− 1.58	− 0.86
1975	− 10.16	− 10.38	− 8.97	− 9.19
1976	− 8.40	− 9.04	− 7.75	− 8.38
1977 Average	**− 1.86**	**− 1.42**	**− 0.61**	**0.01**
I[2]	− 3.08	− 2.96	− 2.19	− 2.06
III	− 1.68	− 1.22	− 0.83	− 0.38
IV	0.42	1.44	3.51	4.52
1978 Average	**− 1.45**	**− 0.51**	**0.06**	**0.99**
I	− 1.16	0.34	1.57	3.06
II	− 1.84	− 0.71	− 0.50	0.63
III	− 0.31	− 0.13	0.78	0.96
IV	− 2.48	− 1.56	− 1.59	− 0.68
1979 Average	**− 0.93**	**− 0.56**	**− 0.24**	**0.13**
I	− 2.85	− 2.19	− 2.12	− 1.46
II	− 1.35	− 2.13	− 0.73	− 1.51
III	− 1.28	− 2.00	− 0.64	− 1.36
IV	1.76	4.08	2.54	4.87
1980 Average	**− 0.41**	**1.11**	**0.48**	**1.99**
I	− 0.86	1.16	− 0.05	1.97
II	− 1.12	− 0.74	− 0.25	0.12
III	0.93	2.20	1.97	3.23
IV	− 0.60	1.81	0.23	2.65
1981 Average	**0.81**	**− 1.01**	**2.57**	**0.76**
I	1.77	2.64	3.60	4.48
II	0.29	− 4.54	2.32	− 2.49
III	1.38	0.05	3.22	1.90
IV	− 0.19	− 2.19	1.15	− 0.84
1982 Average	**− 3.02**	**− 5.79**	**− 2.02**	**− 4.80**
I	− 0.28	− 1.06	0.85	0.07
II	2.06	− 3.21	3.56	− 1.72
III	− 10.28	− 15.50	− 9.41	− 14.63
IV	− 3.58	− 3.39	− 3.09	− 2.91

Source: Central Bank of Argentina.

[1]The formula used for deflation was: Real rate = (nominal interest rate - rate of inflation)/ (1 + rate of inflation).

[2]Corresponds through the first semester.

Table 5. Administrative Costs of Financial Institutions, 1981–82[1]

	1981 Dec.	1982 June	1982 Dec.	1982 May
Official national banks	6.0	2.8	4.0	5.8
Official state and municipal banks	12.8	9.4	13.3	12.3
Domestically owned private commercial banks	7.7	7.9	9.9	9.8
Foreign-owned private commercial banks	9.2	8.8	9.6	8.9
Investment banks	13.4	8.5	13.0	13.5
Finance companies	9.0	9.5	14.8	15.8
Credit cooperatives	11.9	12.6	21.6	22.7
Savings and loan associations	7.4	10.1	12.9	12.7
Weighted average[2]	8.0	7.0	8.8	8.7

Sources: World Bank (1984), and author's own estimates.
[1]Administrative costs a year as percentage of total loans.
[2]The weights used are the shares in total loans as of end-December 1982.

component of the spreads.[13] Although these costs, shown in Table 5, are sizable, a large residual component of the spread remains to be explained. One explanation of the residual is that banks had some monopoly power, which they exploited by charging rates that included a monopoly rent. On the surface, this explanation is appealing: bank services are differentiated products that offer scope for imperfect competition (e.g., it is costly for borrowers to switch banks). A corollary of this explanation is that more competition should lower spreads. In this regard, the liberalization measures, which not only freed interest rates but also eliminated barriers to entry, should have undermined the monopolistic position of the banking system and thus lowered spreads. But it could be argued that whereas eliminating entry barriers reduced monopolistic rents, dismantling interest rate controls allowed banks to better exploit whatever monopoly power they retained. Thus the net effect of the 1977 reform on the rent component of spreads appears to be ambiguous. Another possible explanation is that high spreads reflected risk premiums on loans, which rose because of uncertainties about the course of economic policy and because banks knew

[13] See, for example, World Bank (1984).

very little about many of their new clients.[14] This explanation helps to explain why borrowers were willing to pay high real rates,[15] but it is inconsistent with the explanation that borrowers were willing to pay high rates because they expected a government bailout—because if bankers shared that expectation they would have viewed their loans as low-risk assets and hence charge a low-risk premium.[16] A detailed analysis of the causes of high spreads is beyond the scope of this paper.[17]

Although the high spreads made domestic loans appear more expensive than foreign loans, firms did not switch to foreign sources of credit, in part because the preannounced devaluation schedule (described in the next subsection) did not eliminate the uncertainty over the course of the exchange rate. In this regard, several authors[18] have suggested that a perceived exchange risk discouraged foreign borrowing. This reasoning is consistent with the fact that the domestic deposit rate exceeded the yield in pesos of dollar deposits abroad until February 1981,[19] thus indicating that borrowers and depositors shared similar expectations over the course of the exchange rate. Another reason is that probably only large enterprises had direct access to foreign credits (Petrei and Tybout (1985)). The evolution of interest rate differentials is depicted in Table 6, where the U.S. prime rate was taken as the representative rate for borrowers and the treasury bill rate as the representative rate for deposits. Analyzing a similar data set, Blejer (1982) concluded that the Argentine financial market was informationally efficient but that an uncorrelated time-varying risk premium was present between June 1977 and August 1981.

Several hypotheses have been offered to explain why firms borrowed at

---

[14] The increase in the real size of the financial market reflected not only the growth of loans to old bank clients but also lending to new borrowers, some of which operated in fields that became more dynamic as a result of the change in relative prices described later in this chapter. Also, personal loans and mortgage loans gained much importance. It is worth noting that, for long periods before the liberalization, banks were not allowed to make personal loans for consumption.

[15] Such borrowers would be investing in risky projects with a high expected rate of return. Therefore, they would be prepared to borrow even at a high rate, because in case of failure they would default on their loan but in case of success they would keep the entire profit.

[16] For the bailout explanation see, for instance, Calvo (1986).

[17] A major problem would be to obtain the required data. For instance, the data on spreads before and after June 1977 cannot be easily compared because lending rates before that date were accompanied by credit rationing, which involved practices like compensating balances which increased the actual cost of borrowing.

[18] See, for instance, Rodríguez (1982) and Feldman (1983).

[19] On February 2, 1981 the Central Bank devalued the peso by 10 percent despite having announced in October 1980 that the monthly devaluation rate for that month and the following months—with no specified time limit—would be 1 percent.

Table 6.   Differentials Between Domestic and
Foreign Interest Rates, 1977–82
(Quarter averages; in percent a month)

		U.S. Rates[1]		Interest Rate Differential	
		Prime rate	Treasury bill rate	With Argentine lending rate	With Argentine deposit rate
1977:	III	6.41	6.29	1.77	1.05
	IV	8.58	8.45	4.58	1.62
1978:	I	7.19	7.06	4.10	1.50
	II	4.45	4.30	3.82	2.63
	III	3.37	3.22	4.35	3.40
	IV	5.62	5.45	1.99	1.27
1979:	I	5.97	5.77	1.26	0.73
	II	5.24	5.05	1.91	1.48
	III	4.84	4.64	3.02	2.58
	IV	4.44	4.19	2.78	2.24
1980:	I	3.90	3.68	2.17	1.58
	II	3.41	2.93	2.24	1.85
	III	2.41	2.23	3.74	2.89
	IV	2.33	2.11	3.29	2.68
1981:	I	6.89	6.52	1.75	0.27
	II	25.91	25.55	−15.32	−17.00
	III	5.29	4.90	6.37	4.92
	IV	9.07	8.68	−0.63	−1.59
1982:	I	15.08	14.80	−6.87	−7.72
	II	12.53	12.20	−3.87	−4.70

Sources: International Monetary Fund, *International Financial Statistics*, various issues; and Central Bank of Argentina.

[1] Adjusted for the actual depreciation of Argentina's currency.

relatively high real interest rates. Besides the high-risk and bailout hypotheses already mentioned, the explanations include distress borrowing by firms in difficulties and speculative borrowing induced by devaluation expectations.[20]

[20] See World Bank (1984), p. 207. A detailed discussion of distress borrowing is presented in Dreizzen (1984) and in Fernández (1985).

Liberalization of Foreign Sector

The policies followed in the external sector, especially exchange rate policies, had important effects on the soundness of the financial system, directly by influencing the capital flows and the value of the foreign debt of firms, and indirectly by dramatically changing many relative prices in the economy—in particular, asset prices.

The lackluster record in the fight against inflation prompted the authorities to use the exchange rate as a stabilization instrument, beginning in December 1978 and ending in March 1981.[21] For this purpose the Central Bank periodically published a schedule of daily devaluations for given periods of time. This strategy was intended to make tradable prices follow international prices (nontradables would follow a similar path, assuming some substitutability between tradables and nontradables). Moreover, the preannouncement of the rate was expected to reduce uncertainty and to help make domestic interest rates move in line with foreign rates.

The first exchange rate schedule covered the period through August 31, 1979. Several others followed, carrying a declining rate of devaluation. On October 1, 1979 the third schedule was issued: it set a 2.8 percent devaluation for January 1980, to be reduced by 0.2 percentage point a month through the end of 1980. In September 1980, however, the authorities revised the schedule and announced that the devaluation rate that had been set for October (1 percent) would be maintained for November and December. This policy led to a substantial real appreciation of the peso, which began to affect the exchange market.[22]

After some failed attempts at restoring confidence in the exchange policy, a new economic team scrapped the policy of preannounced devaluations and sharply devalued the peso (by about 23 percent). In addition, the team stated that, in the future, they would follow a policy of frequent minidevaluations. Despite these statements, further reserve losses prompted a new devaluation of about 23 percent on June 2. Twenty days later, the foreign exchange market was split in two: a commercial market, with the rate to be set by the Central Bank, and a financial market, with the rate to be determined by the market.[23] Transactions to be carried out in the latter market included most new financial transactions, sale of a specified fraction of the proceeds of some exports, and other transactions that were not allowed to be made through the commercial market. In order

[21] Prices had been rising about 7–8 percent a month between the last quarter of 1977 and the last quarter of 1978.

[22] Moreover, the bank failures had begun to erode public confidence in the course of the economy.

[23] In practice, the Central Bank followed a "crawling peg" policy to adjust the commercial rate, while it also intervened to some extent in the financial market.

to reduce the effect of past devaluations on private foreign debt and to encourage renewal of foreign loans, the Government compensated borrowers for the effects of the June devaluation on loans that were rolled over for at least one year. To encourage further rollover of foreign debt, the Government also established an exchange insurance facility; to qualify, new loans or loan renewals had to have a minimum maturity of one and a half years. In the last quarter of 1981, the scope of the exchange insurance facility was broadened and a swap facility was established for six-month operations.

The administration that came to power in December 1981 returned to a more liberal exchange system, unifying the exchange markets, eliminating the exchange insurance and swap facilities, liberalizing sales of foreign currency, and announcing that the peso would be allowed to float. In April 1982, however, drastic exchange controls were imposed to cope with the problems caused by the conflict with Britain over the Falkland Islands/ Malvinas. Subsequently, a new administration, inaugurated in July 1982, reintroduced dual exchange markets, one commercial and the other financial. The Central Bank set the rate in the first market, but in the second it intervened solely as a buyer, at a predetermined rate. Gradually, however, operations initially assigned to the commercial market were transferred to the financial market, and in November both markets were merged.

These policies substantially affected the real effective exchange rate, as depicted in Table 7. These data show a real appreciation of the domestic currency of about 31 percent (export-weighted index) or 35 percent (import-weighted index) between December 1977 and March 1980 (when the financial crisis surfaced). This appreciation continued until the end of 1980 to a cumulative total of 40.5 percent (export-weighted index) or 42.5 percent (import-weighted index); in January 1981, the effective exchange rate began to fall as a result of the faster devaluation of the peso, a process that continued for the rest of the period covered in Table 7.

The uncertainty introduced by shifts in exchange rate policy was compounded by the changes in the degree of openness of the economy to capital and trade flows. Between 1976 and 1982, the openness of the economy to capital flows changed several times. The first period, from April 1976 to March 1981, was characterized by a dismantling of restrictions and a higher degree of integration of the domestic and international financial markets. The problems that surfaced in 1981 and 1982 in the foreign sector increased the risk of foreign borrowing for both borrowers and lenders and reduced that integration; this reduction was aggravated by the increased exchange rate volatility already mentioned, by the dwindling reserves, and by the measures taken in 1982 to restrict debt repayments.

The liberalization of capital flows was coupled with liberalization of trade between 1976 and 1981, but the trade liberalization was never so

Table 7.   Evolution of the Exchange Rate, 1977–82

	Exchange Rate (australes per US$100, period average)		Real Exchange Rate Indices[1]	
			Export weighted (Dec. 1969 = 100)	Import weighted (Dec. 1969 = 100)
1977: IV	0.00599		106.1	109.4
1978: IV	0.01007		91.6	88.4
1979: IV	0.01662		75.3	72.0
1980: I	0.01751		72.8	71.5
II	0.01858		70.3	69.2
III	0.01937		68.7	67.7
IV	0.01996		63.1	62.9
1981: I	0.02339		67.5	66.5
	Commercial	*Financial*[2]		
II	0.04396	0.04974	75.7	77.0
III	0.05578	0.07455	80.9	80.0
IV	0.07679	0.10725	79.7	78.5
1982: I	0.10872		94.3	93.4
II	0.15163		97.3	96.6
III	0.26816		99.9	99.4
IV	0.46021		111.5	111.0

Source: Central Bank of Argentina.

[1]Based on monthly averages of the nominal exchange rate adjusted by price (WPI) and exchange rate movements in Argentina's major trading partners.

[2]From June 22, 1981 to December 24, 1981 and from July 5, 1982 to November 1, 1982 the foreign exchange market was split into a commercial and a financial market. For effective exchange rate calculations, the rate actually applicable to trade transactions (i.e., commercial or mixed rate) was used.

comprehensive as financial liberalization. Two main pieces of trade liberalization were a program of phased tariff reductions to be carried out between 1979 and 1984 and the elimination of import prohibitions. However, the newly inaugurated administration abandoned the tariff reduction program on April 1, 1981.

Wage Policy

The wage policy followed during much of the liberalization period aimed at adjusting salaries more or less in line with inflation, as measured by the consumer price index. This policy, combined with the exchange rate regime just described, dramatically increased real labor costs, particularly in dollar terms: real wages in terms of dollars increased by almost 177 percent between December 1978 and December 1980,[24] while real wages in terms of the CPI and the WPI increased by only 23 and 54 percent, respectively.[25,26] The result was a loss of competitiveness of Argentine tradable goods, which deteriorated the foreign sector position and the economic solvency of producers of those goods.

Changes in Asset Prices

The purpose of this section is to investigate whether a speculative bubble could have played a role in the crisis.[27] A speculative bubble that drove up asset prices could have induced people to borrow in order to purchase those assets. When the bubble burst, the price of assets would suddenly have become lower than the value of the counterpart loans.[28] This situation would have made borrowers unable—and unwilling—to repay their debts, while banks would have found that foreclosing did not allow them to recover their credits in full.

Table 8 presents the prices of some assets deflated by the wholesale price index (WPI) and by the peso/dollar exchange rate. These deflators are particularly useful because of the existence at the time of substantial public holdings of financial assets and liabilities linked to the WPI or the

[24] These dates mark the period when the policy of preannounced devaluations was fully implemented.

[25] Notice the difference in the real wage changes measured with the CPI and WPI. Real wage increases were lower using the CPI probably because services and nontradables have a heavier weight in that price index.

[26] For a detailed evolution of real wages, see Baliño (1987), p. 27.

[27] In the case of Chile, Meller and Solimano (1983) agree that "speculative elements and high real interest rates" were responsible for the crisis of the financial system. Their tests suggest the existence of a speculative bubble in the Chilean stock market.

[28] Falling asset prices have been blamed for some bank crises, such as the "wildcat banking crisis." See Rolnick and Weber (1984).

Table 8. Selected Relative Prices of Assets, 1977–84

		Car Prices Deflated by		Apartment Prices Deflated by		Cattle Prices Deflated by	
		WPI (1)	Exchange rate (2)	WPI (3)	Exchange rate (4)	WPI (5)	Exchange rate (6)
1977:	I	1.052	0.908	0.846	0.730	1.149	0.991
	II	0.917	0.833	1.041	0.946	1.089	0.990
	III	1.032	0.997	1.040	1.004	1.195	1.154
	IV	1.011	0.973	1.024	0.986	1.054	1.015
1978:	I	1.077	1.097	0.866	0.882	0.874	0.890
	II	1.085	1.261	1.137	1.321	0.836	0.971
	III	1.174	1.509	1.055	1.356	1.023	1.315
	IV	1.179	1.659	1.144	1.610	1.270	1.788
1979:	I	1.077	1.686	0.755	1.183	1.217	1.906
	II	0.899	1.586	1.133	1.999	1.319	2.326
	III	0.863	1.769	1.441	2.954	1.648	3.377
	IV	1.073	2.140	1.233	2.460	1.434	2.860
1980:	I	1.081	2.246	1.397	2.901	1.308	2.718
	II	1.065	2.445	1.221	2.805	1.412	3.244
	III	1.088	2.613	1.493	3.586	1.258	3.023
	IV	1.098	2.784	1.520	3.852	1.100	2.789
1981:	I	1.138	2.618	1.490	3.428	1.018	2.342
	II	1.128	1.318	1.210	1.414	1.059	1.237
	III	1.202	1.724	1.078	1.545	0.928	1.330
	IV	1.093	1.491	0.976	1.330	1.277	1.742
1982:	I	1.267	1.908	0.754	1.136	1.113	1.677
	II	1.132	1.060	0.713	0.668	1.226	1.148
	III	1.134	1.009	1.103	0.981	1.496	1.331
	IV	1.212	1.039	0.884	0.758	1.422	1.220
1983:	I	1.189	1.069	0.985	0.886	1.307	1.175
	II	. . .	. . .	0.940	0.925	1.307	1.286
	III	. . .	. . .	0.866	0.619	1.322	0.945
	IV	. . .	. . .	0.773	0.898	1.203	1.397
1984:	I	. . .	. . .	1.082	0.931	1.273	1.096
	II	. . .	. . .	1.007	1.099	1.056	1.153
	III	. . .	. . .	0.884	1.034	1.516	1.773
	IV	. . .	. . .	0.975	1.167	1.018	1.219

Source: Central Bank of Argentina.

U.S. dollar. Thus, the ratios in Table 8 also illustrate the opportunity cost of holding real assets relative to holding such financial assets (or liabilities). The first two columns, which correspond to the price of cars, illustrate the effect of the appreciation of the peso over much of the liberalization period (as well as the restrictions on car imports). Whereas cars appreciated by only 18 percent vis-à-vis the wholesale price index between the second quarter of 1977 and the first quarter of 1980, they appreciated by almost 170 percent vis-à-vis the U.S. dollar over the same period. Furthermore, in this period the rate of appreciation vis-à-vis the WPI was negative in several quarters, whereas the appreciation vis-à-vis the dollar was continuous except for two quarters (last quarter of 1977 and second quarter of 1979). The appreciation vis-à-vis the dollar extended until the end of 1980, just before the policy of preannounced devaluation began to change in February 1981.

Apartments appreciated steadily both with respect to wholesale prices and to the dollar (third and fourth columns of Table 8): between the second quarter of 1977 and the first quarter of 1980 apartments appreciated by 34 percent vis-à-vis wholesale prices and by 207 percent vis-à-vis the dollar; by the end of 1980 these rates of appreciation had reached 46 percent and 307 percent.[29] The last two columns correspond to cattle prices.[30] Again, although cattle appreciated by about 20 percent vis-à-vis wholesale prices between the second quarter of 1977 and the first quarter of 1980, its appreciation vis-à-vis the dollar was much higher—175 percent over the same period.

In summary, Table 8 suggests that no general pattern was evident for asset prices until the second quarter of 1981, when the substantial devaluations of the peso that had taken place during that quarter caused asset prices to plummet in terms of dollars; the dollar prices of assets remained substantially below the 1979–80 values throughout the period under analysis. Apartments depreciated both in terms of dollars and of the wholesale price index: the latter fall began in the first quarter of 1981, and the real price of apartments never returned to the high levels of the period that began in the second quarter of 1979 and ended in the first quarter of 1981.

Table 9 presents series on the index of value of the stock market. This index reflects the value of the outstanding shares of all firms listed in the Buenos Aires Stock Exchange valued at the latest available price. The first

---

[29] This appreciation did not result from higher costs of construction. Although construction costs increased faster than wholesale prices, the ratio of the two indices increased by only 8.5 percent between June 1977 and March 1980 and by 35.6 percent between June 1977 and December 1980.

[30] The price of cattle was included because it was one of the most important asset prices in the Argentine economy for which data were available. However, cattle prices are subject to the livestock cycle, so their level depends to an important extent on the decisions on stocks taken some time before.

Table 9. Stock Market Behavior
(Base: January 1978 = 1)

		Index of Stock Value		
		Nominal value	Deflated by WFI	Deflated by exchange rate
1977:	I	0.853	1.837	1.586
	II	0.712	1.279	1.162
	III	0.528	0.742	0.717
	IV	0.565	0.622	0.599
1978:	I	1.786	1.555	1.584
	II	1.667	1.165	1.354
	III	3.195	1.837	2.360
	IV	3.177	1.439	2.026
1979:	I	6.416	2.265	3.547
	II	13.493	3.715	6.554
	III	11.320	2.402	4.923
	IV	12.139	2.403	4.795
1980:	I	21.488	3.772	7.836
	II	14.578	2.179	5.003
	III	15.382	2.109	5.066
	IV	12.477	1.569	3.976
1981:	I	15.198	1.692	3.892
	II	13.035	1.007	1.177
	III	14.578	0.853	1.222
	IV	22.918	1.028	1.403
1982:	I	19.809	0.706	1.064
	II	34.384	0.917	0.858
	III	57.926	0.872	0.776
	IV	61.150	0.667	0.572
1983:	I	98.127	0.744	0.669
	II	181.043	1.018	1.002
	III	287.462	0.988	0.706
	IV	468.200	1.001	1.162
1984:	I	1,184.650	1.658	1.427
	II	1,323.600	1.117	1.220
	III	1,487.820	0.715	0.836
	IV	2,345.670	0.691	0.827

Sources: FIEL, *Indicadores de Coyuntura,* various issues; and Bolsa de Comercio de Buenos Aires, *Boletín,* various issues.

column shows the average value of the index over each month; the other two columns present the deflated values using the wholesale price index (second column) and the exchange rate index (third column). The series displays a high degree of variability;[31] nevertheless, the index appreciated, both in terms of the wholesale price index and of the dollar, between the last quarter of 1977[32] and the first quarter of 1980—which is the peak period of the two series. The behavior of the stock value index differs sharply from the behavior of the relative price of the other assets just discussed. Stock prices dropped in both nominal and relative terms (compared with wholesale prices and the U.S. dollar) immediately after the start of the financial crisis (March 1980); in contrast, the dollar price of the assets included in Table 8 continued to increase while their price relative to wholesale prices showed no significant change in the next few quarters after that date.

The evidence in Tables 8 and 9 does not support the hypothesis that a bursting speculative bubble caused the first episodes of the crisis (i.e., the bank failure and interventions of March–April 1980). However, the value of enterprises declined dramatically after the crisis began, partly as a result of the uncertainty induced by the crisis. This decline deepened the financial crisis by reducing the value of collateral and making it more difficult for enterprises to substitute capital market financing for banking loans.

The Combined Effect of Changes in Interest Rates and Relative Prices

The variability of interest rates and relative prices, including the prices of assets, complicates the analysis of the effects of lending interest rates on various sectors during the liberalization period. Gauging these effects helps in evaluating the merit of some demands for debt relief, which were based on the assertion that extended periods of high interest rates had driven many borrowers into insolvency. A way to analyze this issue is to compute the cumulative effect of real lending rates on a loan, using different price indices. This is done in Table 10 for selected prices. Figures in that table correspond to the ratio between the value of a loan[33,34] and the price index indicated at the top of each column. Therefore, if a ratio rises between two dates, the debt burden of the borrower rises, measured as the

[31] For instance, the coefficient of variation for the data in the second column equaled 0.524 for monthly data between January 1977 and December 1984.

[32] The monthly series allow for a more precise dating of the trough in October 1977.

[33] It is assumed that interest on the loan, at the average lending rate, is compounded monthly and that there are no payments of interest or principal until the loan matures. Because loans in Argentina were made at an adjustable rate, both new and old loans paid the same rates.

[34] The value of the loan is set equal to one in January 1978.

units of the price index that would be needed to repay the loan. Alternatively, in the case of an asset, the rise in the ratio indicates what yield of the asset, compounded and net of depreciation, would have allowed borrowers to keep their wealth unchanged between the chosen dates.

The data in Table 10 show substantial volatility in most of the series: in particular, this is so when wages and cattle prices are chosen as denominators (first and sixth columns). The data also indicate that the debt burden, measured by the wholesale price index or by the stock price index, had begun to increase about two quarters before the first episodes of the crisis and continued to do so until the end of the first quarter of 1982. The next quarter the debt burden began to fall because of a rise in stock prices and a fall in real interest rates (the latter resulted from the establishment of interest rate ceilings in July 1982). For the same reasons, the debt burden measured in dollars also went down dramatically after the first quarter of 1982, using the exchange rate as the denominator (column 3).[35]

Enterprise Debt

The previous discussion suggests that economic agents had to face important shocks during the financial liberalization, which included significant changes in key relative prices—including assets—and, during some periods, high borrowing costs. The vulnerability of firms to such shocks depends, inter alia, on the ratio of debt to total assets ("gearing ratio"); a high ratio not only magnifies the effect of interest rates on firm profits but also indicates that the firm has a low capital base to absorb losses.

Petrei and Tybout (1984) have analyzed the evolution of the gearing ratio and similar indicators between 1976 and 1981. Their analysis is based on financial statements of 155 publicly traded industrial corporations, classified into three major categories: exportable goods producers, importable goods producers, and nontradable goods producers. Their work suggests that, except for exportables, the gearing ratio increased over the liberalization period, whereas liquidity fell and foreign debt increased as a proportion of total assets. They conclude:

> During the late 1970s, firms appear to have substituted dollar debt for peso debt, keeping their overall leverage stable. But beginning in 1980, when earning rates fell sharply, firms steadily increased their reliance on debt finance. So this year and thereafter, some of the increase in firms' financial riskiness may have been

---

[35] The devaluation of the domestic currency helped to restore the competitiveness of many firms but also increased the debt burden of those that had borrowed in foreign currency. The latter obtained debt relief later.

Table 10. Real Interest Rates for Selected Price Indices, 1977–84
(*Base: January 1978 = 1*)

		Wages (1)	WPI (2)	Exchange rate (3)	Deflator Index[1] Cars (4)	Secondhand apartments (5)	Cattle (6)	Stock prices (7)
1977:	I	0.631	0.895	0.772	0.851	1.058	0.779	0.487
	II	0.730	0.864	0.785	0.942	0.829	0.793	0.675
	III	0.797	0.856	0.827	0.829	0.823	0.717	1.154
	IV	1.122	0.972	0.936	0.962	0.950	0.922	1.562
1978:	I	1.215	1.058	1.078	0.982	1.221	1.211	0.680
	II	1.185	1.078	1.252	0.993	0.948	1.290	0.925
	III	1.481	1.108	1.424	0.944	1.050	1.083	0.603
	IV	1.082	1.088	1.532	0.923	0.951	0.856	0.756
1979:	I	1.188	1.045	1.636	0.970	1.383	0.859	0.461
	II	1.053	1.003	1.769	1.116	0.885	0.760	0.270
	III	1.108	0.970	1.988	1.124	0.673	0.589	0.404
	IV	1.214	1.115	2.225	1.040	0.904	0.778	0.464
1980:	I	1.150	1.180	2.451	1.091	0.845	0.902	0.313
	II	1.205	1.185	2.720	1.113	0.970	0.839	0.544
	III	0.867	1.300	3.122	1.195	0.871	1.033	0.616
	IV	0.908	1.404	3.559	1.278	0.924	1.276	0.895

1981:	I	1.081	1.594	3.666	1.400	1.069	1.565	0.942
	II	1.031	1.496	1.747	1.326	1.236	1.413	1.485
	III	1.183	1.576	2.259	1.310	1.462	1.698	1.848
	IV	1.093	1.541	2.102	1.410	1.580	1.207	1.499
1982:	I	1.384	1.552	2.338	1.225	2.059	1.394	2.197
	II	1.776	1.488	1.393	1.314	2.087	1.214	1.623
	III	0.881	1.018	0.906	0.898	0.923	0.681	1.167
	IV	0.722	0.941	0.808	0.777	1.065	0.662	1.411
1983:	I	0.717	0.893	0.803	0.752	0.907	0.684	1.200
	II	0.546	0.897	0.883	…	0.955	0.686	0.881
	III	0.548	0.774	0.553	…	0.893	0.585	0.783
	IV	0.502	0.741	0.860	…	0.958	0.616	0.740
1984:	I	0.437	0.673	0.579	…	0.621	0.528	0.406
	II	0.384	0.601	0.656	…	0.597	0.569	0.538
	III	0.298	0.548	0.640	…	0.620	0.361	0.766
	IV	0.354	0.566	0.678	…	0.581	0.556	0.819

Sources: Raw data provided by the Central Bank of Argentina and author's own estimates.

[1]Value of loan deflated by different price indices. The loan takes a nominal value of one in January 1978 and its quarter-to-quarter variations are due to accumulated interest (at the average market lending rate). Nominal values of the loan are deflated by the price indices indicated in the table.

due to distress borrowing. The beginning of the upward leverage trend corresponds to the emergence of banking sector crises, and may well have been a causal factor. (p. 50)

Using the same data base, Dreizzen (1984) constructed an indicator of financial fragility f, based on Minsky's theories. This indicator is defined as the ratio of debt-service payments to self-generated funds where debt service is defined as debt amortization plus interest payments, and self-generated funds are defined as profits plus asset depreciation and interest, minus taxes. Dreizzen's sample included 143 "normal" enterprises and 23 that had to renegotiate their debts under judicial surveillance. Therefore it is possible to compare the behavior of these two categories of enterprises. His data suggest that the firms that eventually fell under judicial surveillance had a much higher increase in the index of fragility than normal firms. However, it is unclear whether this index provides an explanation of why some firms had difficulties or whether it just states those difficulties—that is, being unable to service debts with their own resources.

Business Failures

The economic developments just summarized caused business failures, which in turn contributed to the failure of banks and other financial institutions. Table 11 presents some data on the liabilities of failed business firms for the Buenos Aires court district. The table shows quarterly total liabilities in nominal terms (first column), deflated by the wholesale price index (second column), and as a ratio to bank credit to the private sector (third column). Inflation makes it difficult to interpret the first column. However, the last two columns give the same broad picture: business failures increased in real terms every year until 1982, peaking in the first quarter of that year, while the ratio of business failures to total private credit shows the same pattern, except for 1980 when the ratio fell.[36] Moreover, the highest real rate of increase of business failures (76 percent) was in 1980 (i.e., when the financial crisis started), although this development is masked in column 3 by the expansive credit policy followed vis-à-vis the private sector. Industry was the sector most seriously hit in the early stages of the crisis: its share in total liabilities of bankrupt firms jumped from 53.7 percent in 1979 to 83.9 percent in 1980.[37]

---

[36] The data in column 2 are easier to interpret than those in column 3, which require two special—though plausible—assumptions: that financial liabilities in failed firms can be proxied by total liabilities and that business failures in the entire country can be proxied by business failures in Buenos Aires.

[37] Baliño (1987), p. 35.

Table 11. Total Liabilities of Bankrupt Firms

		Liabilities of Firms Declared Bankrupt over the Quarter[1]		
		In nominal terms (1)	Deflated by WPI (2)	Deflated by bank credit to private sector (3)
		(*In australes*)		
1977:		*3,404*	*3,985*	*4,693*
	I	7	16	48
	II	66	121	76
	III	248	380	913
	IV	3,083	3,468	3,656
1978:		*17,499*	*10,099*	*16,057*
	I	2,293	2,143	7,615
	II	2,151	1,639	3,302
	III	1,768	1,094	2,155
	IV	11,287	5,223	2,985
1979:		*73,693*	*16,452*	*28,788*
	I	2,854	1,033	8,123
	II	3,387	1,055	2,975
	III	25,201	5,720	9,469
	IV	42,251	8,644	8,221
1980:		*209,485*	*29,024*	*22,517*
	I	23,563	4,249	7,969
	II	22,195	3,509	4,072
	III	39,969	5,639	4,870
	IV	123,758	15,627	5,606
1981:		*440,127*	*35,799*	*41,854*
	I	102,124	11,768	19,118
	II	171,123	15,059	11,556
	III	58,260	3,776	8,013
	IV	108,020	5,196	3,167
1982:		*1,382,678*	*39,151*	*43,733*
	I	758,210	28,021	27,960
	II	170,760	5,105	9,013
	III	112,261	2,062	4,522
	IV	341,447	3,963	2,238
1983:		*2,049,399*	*7,781*	*12,695*
	I	187,910	1,553	4,955
	II	168,024	1,078	1,533
	III	688,781	2,851	3,464
	IV	1,004,684	2,299	2,743
1984:		*15,317,202*	*10,741*	*18,956*
	I	1,810,683	2,879	5,841
	II	2,238,114	2,145	3,026
	III	5,527,367	3,874	8,671
	IV	5,741,038	1,843	1,418

Sources: FIEL, *Indicadores de Coyuntura*, various issues; and International Monetary Fund, *International Financial Statistics*, various issues.

[1]Comprises data for firms filing for bankruptcy or for judicial surveillance in Buenos Aires courts in each quarter.

III. The Financial Crisis

The Financial System Before the Crisis

Argentina's financial crisis was the result of the economic developments discussed in the previous section and of developments within the financial sector itself. A key aspect of the latter was the financial liberalization that was implemented in 1977, which drastically changed the functioning of the financial system. The delay in fully adapting the supervisory apparatus to these changes played a major role in deepening the crisis. Once the crisis started, the Central Bank acted swiftly to prevent the collapse of the financial system. However, the measures adopted over time to deal with the crisis had a long-term influence on the structure of the financial system and on the economy as a whole.

The Argentine financial system underwent radical changes in the 1970s. Before 1977, it was heavily regulated. This regulation had been reinforced by the law of nationalization of deposits enacted in 1973 and by the ensuing complementary measures adopted by the Central Bank. The nationalization law had established that commercial banks would receive deposits only for the account and on behalf of the Central Bank; the banks had to keep these deposits in the form of cash-in-vault or deposits with the Central Bank. In other words, banks had a reserve requirement of 100 percent.[38,39] Banks could only lend out their own capital and reserves and the funds received via rediscount. The aim of that law was to empower the Central Bank to allocate credit selectively to different sectors and regions. The Bank also set the interest rates on loans and deposits.[40] However, the system of nationalized deposits and regulated interest rates soon proved to be too rigid, particularly when the inflation rate, which had been repressed by price controls in 1973, went up significantly in 1974 and jumped dramatically in 1975. In addition, the lack of an explicit link between deposits and loans reduced bank incentives to attract deposits. Therefore the system had to be made more flexible. In 1975, interest rates on certificates of deposit were freed, and automatic rediscount facilities, linked to the growth of specified deposits, were introduced; interest rates on time deposits were also raised significantly. Despite these measures, the yield on nonindexed financial assets was negative in real terms. As a result, over the nationalization period (1973–77), M2 fell by 50 percent in real terms, time deposits by 56 percent, and M1 by 46 percent. This

[38] A similar system had existed between 1946 and 1957 (see Baliño (1982)).

[39] The Central Bank paid a commission to commercial banks as compensation for the administrative cost of deposits.

[40] The Central Bank also set maximum fees and commissions on other bank operations.

shrinkage of the financial system was made easier by the existence of indexed government bonds, which not only provided a hedge against inflation but also were very liquid.[41]

Entry into the financial system also was heavily regulated. The Central Bank had to approve the establishment of new banks and the opening and closing of branches of existing banks.[42,43] The approval process included an evaluation of the need for new banking services and the prospective bank's capital adequacy.

The administration that came to power in March 1976 immediately decided that a profound reform of the financial system was needed. The economic program announced on April 2, 1976 stated the need "to give back to the financial and banking system its flexibility and efficiency [by] eliminating the system of deposit nationalization that is inoperative from the point of view of official credit control and that also conspires against the development and agility of financial activity."[44] The reform legislation was enacted in early 1977; its two main pieces were Law 21495, which authorized the Central Bank to convert the financial system back to a system of fractional reserve requirements, and Law 21526, which provided a new legal framework for financial institutions.[45]

These laws provided the legal basis that allowed the Central Bank to deregulate the Argentine financial system to an unprecedented degree. The Central Bank freed interest rates, which had been totally or partially regulated since 1935. At the same time, in order to facilitate competition by improving market transparency, the Central Bank enjoined banks from charging commissions and special fees on loans, practices that had been widely used to raise the cost of credit when rates were regulated. The Central Bank also abandoned most selective credit practices, returning the responsibility for credit allocation to the commercial banking system; however, the Bank established a special refinance line to facilitate export financing at preferential rates.

Prudential Regulations and Bank Supervision Before the Crisis

Adapting prudential regulations and bank supervision to the new, more liberal, system created by the financial reform was difficult because the

---

[41] Indexed bonds issued by the Treasury coexisted with nonindexed assets: the former became very popular as a hedge against an increasing and volatile rate of inflation.

[42] State banks, however, were free to open new branches within their jurisdiction, subject only to a communication to the Central Bank.

[43] Argentine legislation has traditionally vested the powers of chartering, bank regulation, and supervision in the Central Bank.

[44] Central Bank of Argentina (1977, p. 25).

[45] The conversion to the fractional reserve scheme became effective as of June 1, 1977.

many years of heavy regulation provided no guidance on how the Argentine financial system would function in a more liberal environment.

The Central Bank of Argentina has traditionally enjoyed wide powers over the regulation and supervision of banks and other financial institutions. Such powers were preserved by the financial reform, thus allowing the Central Bank to revise existing regulations. The revised regulations covered four areas: capital requirements, asset immobilization, liabilities/capital ratios, and ratios between the amount of the loan and capital (of the lender and of the borrower).

Minimum capital requirements varied according to the type and location of financial institutions. These requirements were adjusted annually by the wholesale price index.

The regulations on asset immobilization required that immobilized assets could not exceed 100 percent of the capital and reserves of financial institutions.[46] For this purpose, immobilized assets were defined as physical assets, prepaid expenses, all kinds of noncurrent and value-impaired loans, and some other assets of lesser importance. In addition, noncurrent and value-impaired loans could not exceed 5 percent of the capital and reserves of financial institutions.

For all financial institutions, the maximum ratio of financial liabilities to net capital and reserves was set at 25. Limits were also set on the maximum financing, including both loans and bank guarantees, that a given client could obtain. These limits were set at 50 percent of the borrower's capital and reserves for borrowing from any individual financial institution and at 80 percent for total borrowing from the financial system. Financial institutions could exceed these limits when clients offered real assets as collateral; moreover, loans to promote exports, some loans to state suppliers, and seasonal loans were not included in these ceilings. In addition, total financing to an individual client could not exceed 40 percent of the lender's equity, and a sublimit of 30 percent was set for actual financing of any kind (i.e., excluding guarantees). There were some exceptions for these limits in the case of foreign trade operations.

At the same time, branching regulations were eased. The new law eliminated the requirement that the Central Bank had to approve branch openings of domestic banks. Thereafter, domestic financial institutions simply had to comply with some specific requirements and advise the Central Bank in advance of their intention to open a new branch. But, the Central Bank specified that institutions located outside the major centers

[46] For new institutions, the limit was set at 50 percent initially and increased 10 points annually until it reached 100 percent.

would temporarily receive preference for opening branches.[47] Local branches of foreign banks remained subject to prior authorization. Moreover, the establishment of new institutions and the transformation of existing ones were facilitated; many formerly nonbank institutions became banks, and thus could broaden the scope of their activities.

These regulations were revised over the years of the reform. Most of the revisions in 1978 and 1979 aimed at increasing the freedom of financial institutions. For instance, in 1978 the Central Bank eliminated the limit on maximum bank lending defined as a proportion of the borrower's capital, but the limit defined as a proportion of the lender's capital remained in force.[48] In 1979 however, the Central Bank increased the minimum capital requirement for financial institutions, measured in real terms.[49]

An important change in deposit insurance took place in 1979. Until then, the Central Bank had fully insured depositors and had borne the full cost of the insurance scheme. The scheme that became effective in November 1979 provided limited coverage, and financial institutions were free to join or not. Those that decided to join had to pay a monthly fee equal to 3/10,000 of their average liabilities subject to reserve requirements. The scheme was not a funded insurance system, however, because the coverage provided was independent of the insurance fees collected. Domestic currency deposits of up to 1 million pesos[50] were fully insured, whereas those above that amount would be insured only up to 90 percent; the amount that received full insurance would be adjusted monthly with the WPI. Deposits in foreign currencies were not insured.

These measures dramatically changed the perceived riskiness of financial assets, although the perception of risk became widespread only when failures of large institutions began. The public believed that one particular

---

[47] It is interesting to note that the three banks that failed in March/April 1980, which included the largest private bank, as well as the largest nonbank financial institution in the country, which had failed in the previous year, all had their head offices in the interior and had used this preference to extend their branch network dramatically.

[48] The new regulations established that maximum lending to an individual client would fall gradually, to reach 5 percent of the bank's capital as of January 1, 1980. The purpose of these changes, according to the Central Bank, was to allow financial institutions "to amply recover their rights to consider and determine, for each operation, the amounts of assistance technically appropriate to the activity and size of the borrower" (Central Bank of Argentina (1978, p. 15)).

[49] There was some hesitation in the Bank's regulatory action. For instance, as of March 1, 1979 the Bank established that at least 50 percent of a financial institution's portfolio had to be covered by domestic collateral or by guarantees from foreign banks. This requirement was dropped in late 1979 with the argument that financial "institutions [themselves should] determine the . . . collateral requirements to be provided by their borrower" (Central Bank of Argentina (1979, p. 17)).

[50] Equivalent to about US$640.

group of institutions provided de facto full insurance, despite the fact that most of them chose not to participate in the Central Bank insurance scheme. This group comprised state banks, usually guaranteed by the corresponding government (national, provincial, or municipal), and branches of foreign banks, which people thought would receive help from their parent banks in case of need. The riskiness of the rest of the system remained to be evaluated by the public, usually on the basis of scant information.

All in all, the prudential regulations in place at the time were fairly comprehensive. Moreover, lack of observance of central bank regulations carried penalties ranging from fines to withdrawal of the charter. However, the Central Bank lacked the supervisory structure to cope with a financial system that was growing fast and was experiencing a dramatic increase in its freedom of action. In addition, the liberalization of the system generated many mergers, transformations of one type of financial institution into another, and an expansion in the number of branches. Many new participants entered the financial system. Moreover, the Central Bank's supervisory mechanism was biased toward monitoring compliance with regulations rather than analyzing the quality of bank assets—and poor quality assets would become an important cause of failures.

The Central Bank recognized these difficulties and started to study ways to improve its supervision of banks and nonbank financial institutions.[51] However, a new comprehensive system of bank supervision became operative only as of January 1, 1981, well after the crisis had begun.[52] In the meantime, the Central Bank supervised financial institutions through an analysis of the reports that those institutions had to submit periodically and through on-site inspections. It is hard to evaluate the quality and scope of this supervision, but the annual reports of the Central Bank usually provide some data on the number of inspections carried out over the year. Although the data are fragmentary, they suggest a drop in the percentage of institutions inspected between 1977 and 1981, which began to be reversed only in 1982.

The foregoing discussion suggests that the main supervisory problems were the lack of an appropriate supervisory mechanism and the scant use of the one available, rather than the lack of regulations or supervisory power, which were quite comprehensive. The Central Bank began to work on the first problem soon after the start of the reform, but it began to

---

[51] See Central Bank of Argentina (1979 and 1980).

[52] The new system involved substantial changes in bank accounting and reporting, standardization of auditing procedures, and reorganization of the bank supervision area at the Central Bank.

revamp the supervisory mechanism only in 1981, well after the crisis had begun.

Early Warning Indicators

The question arises as to whether the Central Bank, using available information, could have detected that a crisis was imminent. A way to answer this question is to construct some indicators and test their power in predicting the crisis; this was done in two papers on the Argentine crisis. The first, by Dueñas and Feldman (1980), presents a set of six indicators based on the financial statements (balance sheet and profit and loss statement) that banks have to file with the Central Bank of Argentina: (1) liquid assets/deposits; (2) capital, reserves, and nondistributed profits/risk-bearing assets; (3) problem loans/total loans; (4) risk-bearing assets/income-earning assets; (5) total operating costs/ total operating income; and (6) net income from exchange operations/total net income. The data sample runs from June 1977 to June 1979 and comprises 17 banks, 2 of which were later liquidated by the Central Bank. The study shows that those indicators would have provided early warning about the problems of those 2 banks. Only in January 1981, however, did the Central Bank begin to compute and use such indicators systematically—even though the necessary data had been available for a long time.

The second paper, by Arnaudo and Conejero (1985), also concludes that individual bank failures could have been predicted. Relying only on published sources, the authors considered several indicators to analyze the behavior of the four major banks that collapsed in March–April 1980. Their approach was to compare these banks with one another and with the average behavior of private domestic banks. Several indicators are discussed, including the "unit defensive position,"[53] growth of deposits in relation to interest rate premium paid, cost per unit of deposits, share of foreign exchange operations, and branch expansion. Of these, the first three were effective in warning of the impending collapse. These two studies suggest that some indicators could have predicted the onset of the crisis. Other information regularly received by the Central Bank—such as bank reserve positions—could have provided additional warning of individual problem banks.

The studies just described suggest methods for detecting when individual banks depart from the system's norm for some performance ratios. Although the Argentine crisis initially affected only a few banks, it

---

[53] The authors define the "unit defensive position" as loans/deposits (1 − legal reserve requirement) and interpret it mainly as an indicator of bank capitalization. They are assuming implicitly that changes in other assets and liabilities (such as excess reserves or foreign exchange operations) do not distort the values of this indicator.

**Table 12.   Share of Problem Bank Loans
by Economic Sector, 1974–80**

(In percent)

Economic Sector	Share of Problem Loans at End of Period[1]						
	1974	1975	1976	1977	1978	1979	1980
Primary sector	1.71	1.70	0.35	2.15	2.73	3.52	11.71
Manufacturing	1.80	3.00	0.70	1.07	1.95	3.43	12.83
Electricity, gas, and water	0.02	1.08	0.47	0.02	0.37	0.17	0.33
Construction	4.93	2.44	1.43	1.85	1.74	2.32	6.28
Commerce	4.93	1.26	0.60	3.70	3.72	3.28	10.61
Services	0.51	0.27	0.19	0.85	1.23	0.71	3.45
Total[2]	1.95	1.79	0.53	1.52	2.22	2.62	9.13

Source: Central Bank of Argentina, *Boletín Estadístico*, various issues.
[1]Includes all loans currently overdue for more than 10 days, and those that were overdue for more than 10 days in the past and for which special agreements were reached to regularize payments.
[2]Excludes personal loans and loans to unclassified activities.

became evident fairly soon that most of the system had substantial portfolio problems. Therefore, it is useful to analyze whether there were some leading indicators of the condition of the whole banking system.

Table 12 presents data on problem loans, as reported by banks to the Central Bank between 1974 and 1980. In the case of loans to the primary sector and manufacturing, the share of problem loans increased continuously beginning in 1976; the heavy weight of those two sectors in total loans then caused a similar increase in the overall ratio. But the other sectors do not show such a clear pattern until 1980, when every sectoral ratio increased dramatically and the overall ratio jumped by almost 250 percent. These data suggest that until the end of 1979 the deterioration of the portfolio of the banking system as a whole was not particularly alarming, especially given the structural changes that were taking place in the economy. But in 1980 that deterioration became alarming because the economy decelerated (Table 1 suggests that a recession began in February of that year). Moreover, indicators of the firms' situation, such as earnings, liquidity, and profits, worsened.[54] This worsening is also reflected in the jump in enterprise bankruptcies in 1980 (Table 11).

[54] See Petrei and Tybout (1984).

The Crisis

Although many of the problems that led to the financial crisis had been discussed for some time, until 1980 the evolution of the financial system had suffered no major setbacks. The first overt signs of a financial crisis were the failure of one bank, the Banco Intercambio Regional, on March 28, 1980; the intervention of three others by the Central Bank almost immediately afterward;[55] and a significant reshuffling of deposits within the financial system. The failed bank had, in a few years, become one of the largest private banks in the country, with a network that had increased from 46 branches in 1977 to 96 in 1979. Its failure caused important losses to its depositors: those that had dollar deposits lost everything[56] and those that had peso deposits lost the fraction uncovered by deposit insurance (at least 10 percent) plus the cost of having the insured fraction immobilized until the Central Bank actually paid off insured deposits.[57] This failure made the public acutely aware of the fact that bank deposits had some risk, which varied widely from one institution to another. People withdrew funds from institutions whose solvency they questioned and deposited the funds with institutions the depositor considered solvent. In addition, operators in the interbank money market became more cautious because participants would have little chance of recovering loans made to a failed financial institution. Among the institutions whose solvency was questionable were those that had expanded enormously in a short time, largely because they paid high interest rates on deposits—in other words, institutions whose performance resembled that of the Banco de Intercambio Regional. The institutions that were considered solvent were those backed by the Government at any level (national, state, or municipal) or by a foreign parent institution, or, to a lesser extent, those domestic private banks that had a well-established reputation. Deposits could be reshuffled rapidly owing to their short maturities—time deposits were concentrated in maturities no longer than 30 days. This reshuffling and the drying up of interbank funds helped to propagate the crisis: The

---

[55] Some of the interventions that took place in 1980 were challenged in court—unsuccessfully—because, at the time, the law did not grant explicit intervention powers to the Central Bank.

[56] Their only hope was that the failed bank would have some funds to repay dollar depositors, at least partially, once the liquidation proceedings were finished. But bank liquidations are usually lengthy proceedings, and in this case there was little chance that any funds would remain to pay back dollar deposits.

[57] This period was longer than usual in the case of the Banco de Intercambio Regional owing to its extensive network and chaotic administration. The law only required the Central Bank to pay back insured deposits of a financial institution within 30 days of each deposit's maturity. The depositor earned no interest over this period.

Central Bank had to intervene three banks within a month of the Banco de Intercambio Regional's failure. Although the economic situation of these banks might have required some central bank action, the run on their deposits made urgent intervention the only policy option open to the Bank.

The Authorities' Reaction to the Crisis

The authorities had to act on several fronts to cope with the crisis. First, they had to take emergency measures to avoid a bank panic; second, they had to search for longer-term solutions to the private debt problem and its effects on financial institutions; and third, they had to find ways to restructure the financial system.

Emergency Measures. When the Banco de Intercambio Regional was closed, the Central Bank had to address the solvency problem of those institutions that faced massive deposit withdrawals. Its first measure was to create a new credit facility to aid financial institutions whose deposits were falling. This step was taken on April 3, 1980, when it became evident that existing lender-of-last-resort facilities were inadequate to cope with the size of the withdrawals. The second measure was to increase by a multiple of 100 the maximum size of fully insured deposits retroactively to November 18, 1979, which was the date when the reduction in deposit insurance had come into effect.[58] The third measure was the authorities' intervention, on April 28, 1980, of the three banks that had suffered the biggest drain in deposits (Banco Internacional, Banco Oddone, and Banco de los Andes).

These measures gradually succeeded in stabilizing the situation. Aggregate deposits fell in real terms immediately after the start of the crisis, but by August they had already exceeded the March levels. However, the distribution of deposits among financial institutions changed in favor of state and foreign institutions, a pattern that persisted over time (Table 13).

Solutions to the Private Debt Problem. Once the immediate danger of a panic had been averted, the authorities turned their attention to the problem of private debt.[59] The first actions attempted to provide relief by encouraging the lengthening of loan maturities, most of which had been very short (i.e., below one year). In November 1980, the Central Bank announced that it would be prepared to make advances to financial institutions at a much longer term (one year) than prevailing deposit

---

[58] The maximum size was increased from 1 million to 100 million pesos (10 australes), which at the time represented an increase from US$600 to US$60,000.

[59] Some estimates suggest that total private debt (gross debt, i.e., without subtracting private holdings of financial assets) had increased from about 18 percent of GDP in 1976 (year-end) to about 32 percent in 1980 and reached a peak of 39 percent in 1981. These figures are from Arriazu, Leone, and López-Murphy (1985).

Table 13.   Distribution of Deposits Among Groups of Institutions at Selected Dates, 1980–84

(In percent)

End of Period	State Banks	Foreign Banks	All Other Financial Institutions
March 1980	35.7	8.6	55.7
April 1980	40.9	10.2	48.9
May 1980	43.6	10.6	45.8
June 1980	42.7	10.4	46.9
September 1981	38.9	12.2	48.9
June 1982	40.0	12.7	47.3
June 1983	48.0	12.0	40.0
March 1984	44.7	15.1	40.2

Source: Central Bank of Argentina, *Boletín Estadístico*, various issues.

maturities. By reducing the maturity risk of financial institutions, these loans would encourage those institutions to extend the maturities of their own loans. However, this measure was in operation only in November and December 1980. A second effort was made in April 1981 when a new scheme of central bank advances to financial institutions was announced. Financial institutions were allocated funds, first by auction and later by direct allocation, up to 12 percent of their deposits, at market-related rates. These funds had to be used to refinance existing business debt—mainly debts of the agricultural, manufacturing, and construction sectors. This scheme was abandoned in November 1981, when a special law established a more ambitious refinance program with the following characteristics:

(a) Banks and other financial intermediaries should refinance 50 percent of the liabilities of the manufacturing sector and 40 percent of the debt of other industrial sectors (excluding personal and mortgage debts) outstanding at the end of August 1981. The refinanced portion of the debt would be payable over seven years, with a three-year grace period. Borrowers would pay a yearly interest of 3 percent, and the principal would be fully indexed to the Financial Adjustment Index (*Indice de Ajuste Financiero—IAF*), which was computed by annualizing the interest rate paid by a sample of banks on 30-day deposits (*tasa testigo*).

(b) Banks and other financial intermediaries were authorized to rediscount with the Central Bank the full amount of the refinanced debt. This rediscount carried a zero rate of interest and was fully indexed to the IAF.

(c) Along with the rediscount, the banks had to lodge with the Central Bank a government bond for an amount equivalent to the rediscount. This bond had a maturity of seven years with a three-year grace period, was not transferable or negotiable (except between banks), and paid a yearly interest rate of 6 percent (tax free), with full indexation of the principal to the IAF.

(d) Private financial institutions were free to participate or not in the scheme. Participating institutions had to provide refinancing to all client firms requesting debt consolidation. Participation was compulsory for all official banks.

(e) Participating private institutions had the option to contribute 1.5 percent of the amount refinanced to a guarantee fund administered by the Central Bank. The guarantee fund applied to 75 percent of the refinanced debt, and provided banks with protection against bankruptcy or default by firms receiving refinance. If a firm defaulted, the guaranteed portion of the principal would be frozen, interest free (although it would continue to be indexed to the IAF), for the remainder of the seven-year period, at the end of which the guarantee would be made effective. The rediscount of that transaction and the equivalent bond amount would be canceled.

(f) Firms benefiting from the debt consolidation would have to increase their capital by 10 percent of the refinanced amount (IAF-adjusted) over a two-year period. Any distribution of dividends, moreover, would have to be matched by an equivalent cancellation of the (indexed) refinanced debt at the moment the distribution took effect. By March 1, 1982, this refinancing program had provided funds for 4,709 billion pesos—equivalent to about 2 percent of total loans to the private sector.

The mechanisms just outlined were, in essence, refinancing schemes with an element of subsidy, but they still preserved the principle of free rates. Near the end of 1981 the authorities diluted this principle by setting a so-called reference rate and establishing that any interest differential over that rate had to be deposited with the Central Bank. This measure did not have much effect because the reference rate was rapidly phased out when the administration changed soon thereafter. This administration—in office between December 1981 and July 1982—restored free interest rates and tried to follow a free-market approach to economic management. However, the conflict over the Falklands/ Malvinas caused the authorities to intervene more actively in the economy—though not in the financial market—and eventually led to the downfall of the administration.

The administration that came to power in July 1982 believed that "there is a manifest disproportion between the magnitude of enterprise and household liabilities, both in pesos and dollars, and also the liabilities of the public sector itself, in relation to the value of real assets, especially productive assets (farm land, urban industrial, and commercial real estate, machinery, etc.)."[60] To solve this problem, the authorities decided to

---

[60] Interview with Domingo Cavallo, President of the Central Bank of Argentina in July 1982 (de Pablo (1986)).

introduce a drastic reform in the financial sector, the major aim of which was to generate negative real interest rates for a limited time in order to erode the value of existing bank loans and deposits.[61] At the same time, new financial assets were created in order to give the public some protection against future inflation, and thus encourage the financial savings needed for new lending. In broad terms, the strategy called for a transitional period during which the financial system would have three main segments: a regulated segment, whose relative importance would fall over time as negative real rates shrank the value of its assets and liabilities until the segment disappeared altogether, and two other segments, one with free rates and the other indexed, whose combined relative importance would grow over time.

Although the financial system that emerged from these reforms was supposed to evolve back to a free system, later adjustments moved it in the opposite direction: the regulated segment grew in size while the free segment languished. Finally, in August 1983 the Central Bank prohibited the acceptance of any new deposits for the free segment, which was phased out as outstanding deposits matured.

The effects of the reform on the real value of the outstanding debt and on the size of the financial system were dramatic: negative real regulated rates eroded the outstanding real value of bank loans and reduced the demand for financial assets. Table 10 shows that the real value of debt deflated by the WPI had fallen by almost 37 percent between the second and fourth quarters of 1982 and by 62 percent by the end of 1984; all the other deflators in that table give a similar picture. Moreover, the size of the banking system shrank significantly below its prereform size, as measured by the real value of loans and deposits (Table 14). Table 14 shows that the real claims of the system on the private sector outstanding by the end of 1982 represented only 85 percent of those outstanding in June 1982, a proportion that fell to 70 percent by the end of 1983 and to 63 percent by the end of 1984. For total claims (i.e., including claims on the Central Government) the corresponding figures are 65 percent for the end of 1983 and 60 percent for the end of 1984. Moreover, the proportion of total claims financed by private sector peso deposits declined from 39 percent in June 1982 to 26 percent three months later, and then began to increase—but without reaching the levels that existed during most of the financial liberalization experience.

Table 15 presents quarterly data on deseasonalized monetary aggregates

---

[61] Other measures taken simultaneously sought to encourage the refinancing of private foreign debt and to reduce further the attractiveness of public sector securities through the advance repayment of outstanding public debt denominated in pesos. Also, the peso was sharply devalued and the exchange market was split in two—one market for commercial transactions and another for financial transactions.

Table 14. Evolution of the Banking System
(In thousands of australes)

End of Period		Real Claims of the Banking System[1]		Share Funded by Domestic Currency Deposits	
		On private sector	Total	Of claims on private sector	Of total claims
1977:	I	329	407	0.497	0.403
	II	410	508	0.609	0.491
	III	465	560	0.635	0.528
	IV	478	584	0.672	0.550
1978:	I	471	642	0.742	0.544
	II	485	677	0.789	0.565
	III	518	684	0.825	0.624
	IV	552	703	0.713	0.559
1979:	I	542	716	0.784	0.593
	II	581	744	0.782	0.611
	III	604	753	0.791	0.635
	IV	792	989	0.728	0.584
1980:	I	873	1,086	0.716	0.575
	II	910	1,122	0.634	0.514
	III	989	1,215	0.662	0.539
	IV	1,049	1,261	0.633	0.527
1981:	I	1,148	1,396	0.611	0.502
	II	1,099	1,333	0.520	0.429
	III	1,021	1,317	0.578	0.448
	IV	996	1,285	0.534	0.414
1982:	I	936	1,259	0.592	0.440
	II	881	1,216	0.535	0.388
	III	798	1,109	0.366	0.264
	IV	752	999	0.383	0.288
1983:	I	694	929	0.466	0.348
	II	692	918	0.467	0.352
	III	600	785	0.473	0.362
	IV	621	785	0.505	0.400
1984:	I	597	757	0.548	0.432
	II	550	701	0.557	0.437
	III	501	650	0.562	0.433
	IV	556	731	0.543	0.413

Source: International Monetary Fund, *International Financial Statistics.*
[1]Deflated by the WPI.

Table 15. Monetary Aggregates in Real Terms, Deflated by the CPI, 1977–84
(In thousands of australes)

Period[1]		M1[2]	Quasi-Money[3]	M2[4]
1977:	I	23,480	17,831	41,354
	II	25,023	24,293	49,510
	III	23,339	28,644	51,767
	IV	19,699	30,468	50,303
1978:	I	19,214	33,158	52,317
	II	19,254	34,758	53,856
	III	19,839	37,710	57,660
	IV	19,215	36,809	56,142
1979:	I	19,068	37,188	56,288
	II	18,930	40,332	58,909
	III	18,542	41,867	60,680
	IV	19,897	49,629	69,539
1980:	I	21,147	51,642	72,928
	II	21,020	48,607	69,132
	III	21,633	51,435	73,441
	IV	21,360	50,127	71,446
1981:	I	18,539	46,499	65,266
	II	15,259	42,855	57,663
	III	14,670	44,589	59,697
	IV	14,870	45,686	60,308
1982:	I	14,033	44,305	58,581
	II	17,329	44,652	61,587
	III	16,155	33,801	50,172
	IV	15,216	30,005	45,232
1983:	I	13,784	29,072	42,967
	II	13,487	28,811	42,050
	III	12,794	27,144	40,123
	IV	12,822	27,354	40,128
1984:	I	13,740	27,902	41,732
	II	12,986	26,085	38,850
	III	11,344	23,488	34,996
	IV	10,464	23,045	33,440

Source: Central Bank of Argentina, *Boletín Estadístico*, various issues.

[1]Quarterly average of end-of-month balances.

[2]M1 = Currency in circulation plus demand deposits of the private sector.

[3]Quasi-money: Savings and time deposits and "other deposits" of the private sector (accrued interest is a major component of "other deposits").

[4]M2 = M1 plus quasi-money.

in real terms, for the period beginning in the first quarter of 1977 through the fourth quarter of 1984. Two major conclusions can be drawn from that table. First, although the crisis caused monetary aggregates to fall in the second quarter of 1980, there was a recovery in the third quarter, when M2 reached its peak for the whole period included in Table 15. Also, the fall in the demand for monetary aggregates became increasingly pronounced between the fourth quarter of 1980 and the second quarter of 1981. These two facts suggest that uncertainty about economic policies (related to an impending change in administration) was more important than the earlier bank failures in undermining people's willingness to hold peso-denominated assets. Second, only after the reintroduction of interest rate controls in the third quarter of 1982 did quasi-money and M2 fall below the levels they had reached immediately before the liberalization.

As the system shrank, banks had to rely less on the public for their funding and more on the central bank rediscount, which became a major source of funding.[62] Also, as the importance of bank lending fell, the market sought alternative financial sources. Some, like bank acceptances, went through official channels; others, like inter-enterprise loans, did not. Lack of information on these alternative sources prevents us from analyzing them in this paper. As a general proposition, however, a financial market with regulated and unregulated segments entails a loss of economic welfare and macroeconomic control, compared with a free, integrated market. In particular, financial savings will tend to be lower and the cost of capital higher, on average, because of the market imperfections created by the segmentation.

Besides relieving the burden of domestic currency debts, successive administrations also took measures to relieve the burden of foreign currency debts. One of the first measures was to compensate some borrowers for the increase in the domestic currency value of their debts that resulted from the devaluation of June 1981. This compensation covered debts incurred or renewed between January 1 and May 29, 1981 that matured until the end of that year, provided that the debts were rolled over for at least one year. In addition, the Central Bank established an exchange insurance scheme that subsidized borrowers insofar as the premium charged was below the actual rate of devaluation.[63] Over time, the scheme

---

[62] This increase in central bank funding began in 1981, when debt relief mechanisms were put in place.

[63] The criteria to calculate the premium varied over time, but two were used quite often: the wholesale price index and the domestic deposit interest rate. The subsidy in the insurance scheme resulted from the significant real depreciation of the peso over the period and from the fact that the domestic deposit rate did not fully reflect the peso depreciation. Moreover, in many cases borrowers could choose the criteria for the adjustment of their exchange

was enlarged and made even more attractive as Argentina's reserve position deteriorated and the authorities tried to induce borrowers to renew their foreign credits.

Measures to Restructure the Financial System. The Central Bank acted to facilitate the restructuring of the financial system not only by liquidating failed financial institutions but also by encouraging mergers and sales and by increasing the Bank's own flexibility to deal with problem institutions.

In October 1980 the Central Bank established a special line of credit to finance a fraction of the cost of mergers and purchases of financial institutions. The financed fraction could vary in each case and the interest rate on this line of credit was below market rates.[64] Later, the Central Bank created a formal service to help financial institutions meet partners for mergers or purchases.

In 1982, a new law broadened the powers of the Central Bank to deal with problem financial institutions. The purpose of this law was to give more flexibility to the Central Bank, which, under the old law, had very few options besides liquidating insolvent financial institutions. Liquidation has always been the last-resort remedy provided by the Argentine banking legislation to deal with institutions in serious difficulties; in addition, liquidation has been the most severe penalty that could be inflicted on a financial institution. When the Central Bank approves the liquidation of a financial institution, a liquidator—usually from the Central Bank staff—is appointed to replace the chief executive officer and the board of directors of the institution. The liquidator's first task is to pay the insured part of maturing deposits with funds advanced by the Central Bank.[65] The liquidator does not make new loans but is responsible for collecting those outstanding as they mature. The liquidator also has broad powers in administering the institution on a day-to-day basis, subject to the approval of senior central bank management. The liquidator's task is completed once court approval has been obtained for the final disposition of the institution's assets and liabilities.

The liquidation process is quite costly. First, announcement of the

---

insurance premium between at least two indices. The cost of the subsidies implicit in the insurance scheme was borne by the Central Bank, which also bore the losses caused by swaps.

[64] In 1981, 227.1 billion pesos were granted under this facility. To have an idea of its relative importance, in September 1981 the average capital and reserves of a private bank in the Province of Buenos Aires approached 36 billion pesos; the corresponding figure was lower for most other areas.

[65] The Central Bank usually recovers only a fraction, in real terms, of the funds so advanced. Such recovery takes place only as the credits made by the failed bank are repaid and other assets are sold.

liquidation of a large financial institution can create a confidence crisis. Second, both depositors and borrowers have to transfer their business to another institution. Third, funds advanced by the Central Bank for the liquidation are a source of monetary expansion that may be difficult to sterilize. Fourth, the physical and human resources that were employed by the liquidated institution may lay idle for a relatively long time. Fifth, borrowers tend to give relatively low priority to repaying loans made by a liquidated bank, because they prefer to honor their commitments to operating banks, which can provide new credits; this attitude introduces a rigidity in credit distribution in favor of the clients of the liquidated institution. Sixth, the cost escalates if the liquidated institution has acquired assets from bankrupt borrowers that must be administered by the liquidator. Few liquidators have expertise in administering assets that belonged to the bankrupt borrower (e.g., a steel mill), but many liquidators have had to deal with such a situation.

Because liquidation proved to be a rather costly solution to the problems of financial institutions, the new law was intended to reduce the need for liquidation by allowing different solutions to be applied at the discretion of the Central Bank.[66] For instance, the Central Bank could authorize one sound financial institution to administer a troubled institution for a given period of time, at the end of which the first institution had the option of purchasing the second.[67] In addition, the Central Bank was granted explicit powers to intervene troubled financial institutions; the Bank had exercised such powers since the crisis started but their legality had been challenged. The new law also expanded the Central Bank's choices in liquidation cases: for example, the Bank could decide to liquidate an institution without revoking the institution's charter.

The financial crisis and the actions of the Central Bank added impetus to the restructuring of the financial system that was already under way when the crisis began. The number of nonbank financial institutions fell sharply beginning in 1979, largely as a result of mergers, transformation into banks, or absorption by banks; also, 97 institutions were liquidated between May 1977 and December 1983. The number of banks increased almost continuously until 1981, but this increase was more than offset by the decrease in the number of nonbank financial institutions. Despite the reduction in the total number of financial institutions, however, the number of branches increased steadily throughout the period.

---

[66] The Central Bank's decisions can be appealed to the Ministry of Finance or to the courts.

[67] This solution was tried on one of the largest and oldest private banks, the Banco Español del Rio de la Plata, but the administering institution decided not to exercise its purchase option. The Banco Español was finally auctioned, and the buyer received central bank assistance for the purchase.

Steps to Streamline the Liquidation Process

The Central Bank tried several mechanisms to shorten the length and reduce the cost of the liquidation process. The law approved in 1982 had authorized the Bank to sell the assets of failed institutions under the terms and conditions that it deemed most appropriate. It also specifically allowed the Bank to delegate to other financial institutions the task of collecting the loans made by failed institutions. Thus, by 1985, the Central Bank had arranged for some government-owned commercial banks to manage 39 portfolios of failed institutions, but the results were disappointing. Therefore, following the recommendations of an ad hoc advisory commission, the Central Bank began to allow private banks to purchase the portfolios of some failed institutions or to administer them on behalf of the Central Bank. When portfolios were sold, however, the selling price reflected a discount as high as 80 percent of the face value of the loans.[68] Also, in order to speed up the sale of the real estate held by the Central Bank (which had probably become the largest landlord in the country), the Bank provided preferential financing to buyers. These advantages, together with a more aggressive sales attitude, resulted in the sale of more than 1,500 real estate units between 1985 and 1987—a pace that accelerated later. Before 1985, only 500 units had been sold out of a total of about 5,200 that had been received by the Central Bank.[69]

Beginning in December 1987, the Central Bank also began to sell branches of banks under liquidation. These branches were sold as operating units, and their staff transferred to the purchasing bank. This practice allowed the purchasing banks to expand at a time when it was very difficult to obtain central bank approval for new branches.

Effects of the Crisis on Monetary and Credit Policy

The measures that the Central Bank took to cope with the crisis had important implications for monetary and credit policy. The immediate effect was a significant change in the sources of reserve money: as Table 16 shows, central bank loans to the financial system were equivalent to less than 2 percent of reserve money just before the crisis began (February 29, 1980). But that share increased dramatically once the Central Bank started to aid troubled financial institutions: by the end of April 1980 it had jumped to almost 31 percent, and at the end of the year it exceeded 50 percent. During 1981 and 1982 it kept increasing. The need to accommodate financial institutions—and, at a second stage, borrowers—put a

---

[68] Casas (1989).
[69] Ibid., pp. 112–13.

**Table 16.   Changes in Sources of Base Money
Creation, Selected Months, 1980–83**

(In percent)

Date	Ratio of Central Bank Loans to Financial Institutions to Reserve Money
February 29, 1980	1.87
March 31, 1980	2.76
April 30, 1980	30.82
June 30, 1980	32.24
December 30, 1980	50.12
December 30, 1981	81.61
December 30, 1982	110.11
December 30, 1983	69.03

Source: Central Bank of Argentina, *Boletín Estadístico* and *Memoria Anual,* various issues.

heavy burden on the Central Bank. The rapid growth in credit to financial institutions, coupled with faster growth in credit to the Government, resulted in a jump in central bank domestic credit (Table 17). Moreover, net international reserves of the Central Bank fell by US$2.9 billion in 1980, US$3.5 billion in 1981, and US$5.5 billion (including accumulated arrears) in 1982.

Part of this loss of reserves—and the contemporaneous acceleration in inflation—can be attributed to the faster expansion in net domestic credit of the financial system that started in 1981. Another cause of the loss was the fall in demand for peso-denominated assets that resulted from a loss of confidence in the value of the peso. The financial crisis and the measures taken to cope with it were major factors in this loss of confidence. First, the public realized that a bank failure could entail losses to depositors.[70] Second, it also realized that much of the financial system was unsound, and that any measures taken to solve the problems were likely to entail losses to holders of financial assets in pesos. These losses would occur because (a) the Central Bank would be forced to provide assistance to distressed financial institutions (or final borrowers), and this assistance could lead to excessive monetary expansion, immediately if financed by

[70] Even though most of these fears were allayed when practically full insurance for peso deposits was restored retroactively, dollar depositors in the Banco de Intercambio Regional have not yet recovered their deposits.

Table 17.   Sources of Expansion of Central Bank Liabilities, 1977–84

(In percent)

	End-of-Year Data							
	1977	1978	1979	1980	1981	1982	1983	1984
In reserve money								
Net foreign assets	48.33	87.08	129.74	65.71	61.39	36.91	14.59	30.65
Net claims on the Government	37.22	41.85	31.94	53.62	94.06	26.49	79.76	78.93
Claims on financial institutions	17.22	8.85	7.44	50.11	81.61	110.42	70.53	89.78
In total central bank liabilities								
Net foreign assets	47.28	63.27	76.72	38.78	25.89	21.24	8.85	15.38
Net claims on the Government	36.41	30.41	18.89	31.65	39.67	15.24	48.38	39.60
Claims on financial institutions	16.85	6.43	4.40	29.57	34.42	63.52	42.78	45.04

Source: International Monetary Fund, *International Financial Statistics Yearbook,* 1985.

expanding the money supply, or later if financed by issuing interest-bearing debt; or (b) interest rate regulation could be used to erode the real value of the assets and liabilities of financial institutions by generating negative real interest rates.

Costs and Distribution Effects of the Crisis

It is easy to list the types of costs generated by the financial crisis: welfare losses of lower money balances, temporary disruptions of the credit and payments system, deterioration and unemployment of the physical assets of failed financial institutions and bankrupt borrowers, unemployment of labor, misallocation of credit, untimely capital out-flows, and the like. The list would be even longer if wealth and income redistribution effects were also considered, but complete quantification of these costs and distribution effects is practically impossible: not only is it hard to identify many of these categories, but also data often are unavailable. Nevertheless, this section presents some estimates to illustrate typical costs and effects.

Costs to the Central Bank of Liquidating a Financial Institution.   When the Central Bank liquidates an institution, it advances the funds needed to pay back all insured deposits and it bears the cost of administering the institution until the liquidation process is finished. Because this process ends only when all assets, including loans, have been sold or recovered, it usually takes several years. Only when the process is completed can the Central Bank get reimbursement for its advances and other expenses, but only to the extent that the liquidated institution had valuable assets.[71] Typically, the Bank cannot recover the full value, at constant prices, of its advances and expenses. Few figures are published on the losses incurred by the Central Bank in this regard. Moreover, the process of liquidation is still unfinished for most of the financial institutions that have been closed since the financial crisis began. However, each year the Central Bank sets aside reserves to cover the estimated cost of various contingencies. By the end of 1982, the reserves earmarked to cover losses from the liquidation of financial institutions totaled the equivalent of US$364 million. This figure underestimates the true expected losses because the Bank can also use non-earmarked reserves to cover such losses.

Wealth Redistribution Effects. Some of the data just discussed suggest that significant wealth redistribution effects took place during the period under analysis, even before the crisis came into the open. For instance, the movements in relative prices, particularly those of assets and liabilities, undoubtedly entailed redistribution of wealth among the owners of real and financial assets. Moreover, the crisis also had wealth effects, for example, on holders of foreign currency deposits, which were uninsured. Finally, many of the measures taken to cope with the crisis gave rise to a further wealth redistribution. For example, exchange rate insurance transferred the cost of devaluation from those enterprises that had borrowed abroad to the Central Bank. Given the complexity of wealth redistribution effects and the difficulty in obtaining relevant data, only one particular measure—the introduction of interest rate controls in July 1982—will be discussed here. These controls caused significant redistribution of wealth because they resulted in negative real rates, which eroded the value of existing loans and deposits in the financial system.[72]

Table 18 presents data for 1982 and 1983, which illustrate the size of these effects. The first two columns show the implicit subsidy for borrowers, measured as the difference between the flow of interest accrued at the regulated rate and the flow that would have accrued in the absence of interest rate regulation. There are two columns because the latter flow is defined according to two alternative assumptions about the nominal interest rate: (a) equal to the rate of inflation (wholesale prices); and (b) equal to

---

[71] Under the law, the Central Bank's claims on failed financial institutions take precedence over other claims.

[72] As explained earlier, the maturity of outstanding debts also was extended.

Table 18.   Initial Wealth Redistribution Effects of 1982 Interest Rate Regulation of Commercial and Savings Banks, 1982–83

| | Borrower Subsidy with Respect to | | Depositor Cost | | |
| | | | Time and savings deposits[1] | | |
Quarter	Inflation WPI (1)	Real lending rate, 1977–82 (2)	WPI (3)	Real deposit rate, 1977–82 (4)	Checking deposits WPI (5)
	(As percent of GDP)				
1982: III	6.80	7.34	4.87	4.76	1.13
IV	1.13	1.56	0.84	0.76	0.48
Total	7.93	8.90	5.71	5.52	1.61
1983: I	0.70	1.12	0.77	0.68	0.63
II	−0.04	0.38	0.25	0.15	0.55
III	1.68	2.07	1.51	1.41	0.85
IV	0.58	0.94	0.65	0.57	0.72
Total	2.92	4.51	3.18	2.81	2.75
Total for 1982/83	10.85	13.41	8.89	8.33	4.36

Sources: Central Bank of Argentina, *Boletín Estadístico*, various issues; data furnished by the Central Bank of Argentina; and author's own estimates.

[1]In columns (3) and (4) savings accounts are assumed to earn the same rate of interest as time deposits.

the nominal rate that would reflect the average real lending rate that prevailed in the liberalization period (June 1977–June 1982). A similar procedure is used in the third, fourth, and fifth columns to estimate the cost to depositors; for checking deposits, only the rate of inflation alternative is used. The estimates in the table indicate that in the one and a half years under consideration borrowers benefited from an income transfer that ranged between 10.8 and 13.4 percent of GDP, while holders of time and savings deposits lost between 8.3 and 8.9 percent, and holders of checking deposits lost about 4.4 percent of GDP. These substantial redistributions have extended beyond the period covered in Table 18, although the size of the yearly redistribution has probably been falling as the size of the financial system shrank in real terms. As noted at the time by the authorities, however, this redistribution of wealth between holders of financial assets and liabilities through the measures adopted in July 1982 could be regarded as an acknowledgment of the reality that many borrowers could not repay the full value of their debts, necessitating a corresponding reduction in the value of deposits.

IV. Summary and Conclusions

Because this study has covered a broad range of issues, it is useful to summarize its main points before drawing more general conclusions:

- The financial crisis occurred after a period of economic expansion, which was uneven by sector and during which substantial changes in relative prices took place.
- There is no evidence of a monetary contraction that could have caused the financial crisis, as some authors have claimed was the case during the U.S. crisis of the 1930s. On the contrary, monetary aggregates were growing rapidly before the crisis began and continued to do so thereafter.
- When interest rate ceilings were lifted in 1977, nominal interest rates more than doubled and remained significantly higher and more variable than controlled rates had been. This variability was lower during the period of preannounced devaluations.
- High real lending rates helped to precipitate and aggravate the crisis, but because negative real rates prevailed in many periods, the effects of real rates on borrowers varied according to the timing of their borrowing.
- Although lending rates fluctuated with deposit rates, large and volatile spreads had a major influence on them. These spreads largely reflected the gross margin that served to cover administrative costs and profits. Risk premiums and monopolistic behavior are hypotheses that could explain these margins, but they are not tested in this chapter.
- Imperfect access to foreign loans and uncertainty over exchange rate policies can explain why borrowers continued borrowing domestically.
- Financing of high-yield and high-risk projects, expectations of a bailout, and speculative borrowing are the main hypotheses that have been advanced to explain borrowing at high real rates, as observed in Argentina.
- The policy of preannounced exchange rates—and to a lesser extent, trade policies—substantially increased the price of nontradable goods relative to tradable goods beginning in early 1979 and lasting until the exchange rate policy was changed in 1981. The policy changes forced

enterprises to adapt to a dramatically changed economic environment; this adaptation was made more difficult by growing uncertainty about the sustainability of exchange and trade policies.

- Stock prices, which had been increasing significantly before the financial crisis started, dropped immediately thereafter, both vis-à-vis the wholesale price index and the dollar. This drop made access to finance more difficult for enterprises just when lenders became more cautious and lending rates were high in real terms.
- The debt burden, measured as the ratio of a hypothetical debt to selected prices, shows substantial variability over the liberalization period. Nevertheless, the burden continuously increased, in terms of foreign currency, between the first quarter of 1977 and the first quarter of 1981, when the situation reversed itself as a result of the devaluation. Thus, whether a firm was better off by borrowing in domestic currency or in dollars hinged on the period over which the debt was outstanding. Also, between the first quarter of 1980 and the second quarter of 1982, the debt burden for homeowners more than doubled; this burden became a major argument in favor of debt relief at the time.
- Distress borrowing aggravated the crisis, but its influence in starting the crisis is unclear. Some evidence suggests that when enterprise profitability fell, beginning in 1980, gearing ratios increased.
- Business failures increased during the liberalization period and jumped when the crisis broke out in 1980; industry was the most affected sector.
- The financial reform of 1977 not only freed interest rates but fostered competition by liberalizing entry into the financial market and the opening of branches.
- The abandonment of full deposit insurance in November 1979 made deposits riskier and helped to propagate the crisis, until mid-April 1980, when full insurance for most deposits was re-established. Reluctance of the interbank market to lend to troubled institutions contributed to propagating the crisis.
- The prudential regulations and penalties for noncompliance that were in effect during the liberalization period were fairly comprehensive, but the emphasis in supervision was on monitoring compliance with regulation more than on analyzing the quality of the portfolio of financial institutions. Indicators that might have given advance warning on troubled institutions were not available until 1981. Moreover, the percentage of institutions inspected on site fell between 1977 and 1981.
- Bank reports indicated a steady deterioration in bank portfolios, starting in 1976 but accelerating dramatically in 1980.

- The emergency measures taken by the Central Bank succeeded in stopping the run on deposits that started with the Banco de Intercambio Regional's liquidation.
- Some evidence suggests that currency holdings became less elastic to the deposit interest rate after the start of the crisis. Also, uncertainty over the course of economic policy late in 1980 and early in 1981 appears to have been more important than bank failures in reducing the demand for monetary aggregates.
- The Central Bank adopted various measures over time to provide debt relief to the private sector. In 1980 and 1981 the Bank implemented schemes to encourage banks to refinance outstanding loans. In July 1982 it took a more drastic approach, the main elements of which were interest rate ceilings on most financial assets and debt refinancing. Also, the Bank provided inducement, such as exchange rate insurance, to encourage the rescheduling of foreign debts.
- The reintroduction of interest rate controls in 1982 was coupled with a rise in the inflation rate. The resulting negative real interest rates caused a dramatic fall in the value of the outstanding stock of debt and a fall in the demand for monetary assets. At the same time, central bank credit became a major source of funding for the financial system and of growth of reserve money. This situation contributed to the loss of reserves and the rise in inflation experienced after the crisis started.
- The Central Bank established new facilities, including credit lines, to facilitate absorptions and mergers. The costs implicit in liquidating financial institutions, which was the remedy mandated by law in some situations, induced the Government to give more flexibility to the Central Bank in dealing with troubled institutions, and the Bank to devise means to speed up the liquidation process.
- Figures for the cost of bank liquidations are hard to obtain. By the end of 1982, the Central Bank had earmarked provisions equivalent to about US$364 million, which probably underestimates the cost. Moreover, the costs of keeping resources idle or using them suboptimally are impossible to estimate. These resources include not only typical bank assets such as bank buildings and computers but also property acquired by banks through foreclosure that the Central Bank has to manage in the case of failed banks.
- The financial crisis and the measures taken to cope with it entailed significant redistribution of wealth. Depositors in foreign exchange in failed institutions lost their deposits. A further redistribution resulted from the negative real rates that prevailed after interest rate controls were reintroduced. The latter redistribution transferred the equivalent of at least 11 percent of GDP to borrowers over one and a half years.

A broad conclusion that can be drawn from the analysis is that, although elements endogenous to the financial system, such as the high level of interest rates following the liberalization and loans of dubious quality, contributed to the crisis, elements exogenous to the system played a major role in determining the extent of the crisis. Macroeconomic policies, particularly with regard to the exchange rate, forced enterprises to adjust to substantial changes in economic conditions. Uncertainty about policy continuity exacerbated the costs of adjustment. These elements contributed to a recession and to the collapse of many firms, which, in turn, caused the quality of the loan portfolio of the financial system to deteriorate.

Inadequate supervision of the financial system also contributed to the crisis. Financial institutions that were liquidated in the early stages of the crisis had particular problems that early warning indicators and closer monitoring could have detected more promptly. Earlier detection not only would have given more time to find solutions but also could have reduced the size of the problem by limiting the growth of those institutions. But even with better supervision, some deterioration of the quality of bank portfolios could not have been avoided in light of the instability of economic conditions that made forecasting and planning very uncertain. Be that as it may, there is little doubt that improved supervision would have enabled the financial system to withstand such deterioration better.

The Central Bank was able to contain the propagation of the crisis by granting emergency credits to troubled institutions and by eventually reversing its previous policy of gradually reducing the scope of deposit insurance. The crisis gave impetus to improvements in bank supervision and prompted the introduction of more flexible ways to deal with troubled institutions in order to reduce the need for the inherently costly liquidations. Measures to speed up the liquidation process had mixed success; the most promising of such measures appear to have been the sales of branches as operating units, sales of real estate, and sales of failed institutions' portfolios.

The reintroduction of interest rate controls brought relief to borrowers but it also shrank the size of the financial system, as depositors became reluctant to hold financial assets carrying a negative real yield. This situation, together with other measures taken to help borrowers and financial institutions, such as increased central bank funding of the financial system, undoubtedly made monetary management more difficult and contributed to the higher inflation and loss of international reserves that had started with the crisis. The huge debt relief granted in 1982 also raises difficult questions about the fairness of the substantial redistribution of wealth that it entailed and about the extent to which more selective relief could have improved bank portfolios and helped problem borrowers at less cost.

References

Ardito Barletta, Nicolas, Mario Blejer, and Luis Landau, eds., *Economic Liberalization and Stabilization Policies in Argentina, Chile, and Uruguay. Applications of the Monetary Approach to the Balance of Payments* (Washington: The World Bank, 1984).

Arnaudo, Aldo A., and Rafael Conejero, "Anatomía de las Quiebras Bancarias de 1980," *Desarrollo Económico*, Vol. 24, No. 96 (January–March 1985).

Arranz, Juan M., and Lidia R. Elías, "Ciclos de Referencia para la Economía Argentina," *Serie de Estudios Técnicos*, Centro de Estudios Monetarios y Bancarios, Banco Central de la República Argentina, No. 60 (July 1984).

Arriazu, Ricardo H., Alfredo M. Leone, and Ricardo H. López-Murphy, "Políticas Macroeconómicas y Endeudamiento Empresario" (unpublished; Buenos Aires, 1985).

Baliño, Tomás J.T., *La Reforma Monetaria y Bancaria Argentina de 1946–57 un caso de encaje bancario total?* (Mexico City: CEMLA, 1982).

————, "The Argentine Banking Crisis of 1980," IMF Working Paper No.87/77, International Monetary Fund, November 17, 1987.

Blejer, Mario I., "Interest Rate Differentials and Exchange Risk: Recent Argentine Experience," *Staff Papers*, International Monetary Fund, Vol. 29 (June 1982), pp. 270–79.

Bolsa Comercio de Buenos Aires, *Boletín de la Bolsa de Comercio de Buenos Aires*, various issues.

Cagan, Philip, *Determinants and Effects of Changes in the U.S. Money Stock, 1875–1960* (New York: National Bureau of Economic Research, 1965).

Calvo, Guillermo A., "Fractured Liberalism: Argentina under Martínez de Hoz," *Economic Development and Cultural Change*, Vol. 34 (April 1986).

Casas, Juan Carlos, "El Saneamiento de Bancos en la Argentina" in *Saneamiento de Bancos*, ed. by Juan Carlos Casas (Buenos Aires: El Cronista Comercial, 1989).

Central Bank of Argentina, *Boletín Estadístico* (Buenos Aires), various issues.

————, *Memoria Anual* (1978).

————, *Memoria Anual* (1979).

————, *Memoria Anual* (1980).

Dabós, Marcelo P., and Edgardo C. Demaestri, "La Demanda de Billetes y Monedas en la Argentina. Un Análisis Empírico," *Serie de Estudios Técnicos*, Centro de Estudios Monetarios y Bancarios, Banco Central de la República Argentina, No. 59 (October 1983).

Damill, Mario, and Roberto Frenkel, "De la Apertura a la Crisis Financiera. Un Análisis de la Experiencia Argentina de 1977–82," *Ensayos Económicos*, No. 37 (March 1987).

Demaestri, Edgardo C., "Estimación de una Función para el Coeficiente de Circulante en los Recursos Monetarios," *Serie de Estudios Técnicos*, Centro de Estudios Monetarios y Bancarios, Banco Central de la República Argentina, No. 46 (January 1982).

de Pablo, Juan Carlos, "La economía que yo hice," *Ediciones El Cronista Comercial*, Vol. 2 (Buenos Aires, 1986).

Díaz-Alejandro, Carlos, "Good-Bye Financial Repression, Hello Financial Crash," *Journal of Development Economics*, Vol. 18 (1985), pp. 1–24.

Dreizzen, Julio, "El Concepto de Fragilidad Financiera en un Contexto Inflacionario" (unpublished M.A. dissertation, Pontificia Universidade Catolica do Rio de Janeiro, 1984).

Dueñas, Daniel E., and Ernesto V. Feldman, "Indicadores Financieros de Alerta Anticipada del Desempeño de las Firmas Bancarias," paper presented to the Jornadas de Economía Monetaria y Sector Externo, Banco Central de la República Argentina, Buenos Aires, October 1980.

Feldman, Ernesto V., "La Crisis Financiera Argentina: 1980–1982: Algunos Comentarios," *Desarrollo Económico*, Vol. 23, No. 91 (October–December 1983).

Fernández, Roque B. (1983a), "La Crisis Financiera Argentina: 1980–1982," *Desarrollo Económico*, Vol. 23, No. 29 (April–June 1983).

———— (1983b), "La Crisis Financiera Argentina: 1980–1982, Réplica," *Desarrollo Económico*, Vol. 23, No. 91 (October–December 1983).

————, "The Expectations Management Approach to Stabilization in Argentina During 1976–82," *World Development*, Vol. 13, No. 8 (August 1985), pp. 871–92.

FIEL, *Indicadores de Coyuntura* (Buenos Aires), several issues.

Flood, R.P., Jr., and Paul M. Garber, "A Systematic Banking Collapse in a Perfect Foresight World," NBER Working Paper No. 691 (Cambridge, Massachusetts: National Bureau of Economic Research, 1981).

Friedman, Milton, and Anna J. Schwartz, "Money and Business Cycles," *Review of Economics and Statistics*, Vol. 45, No. 1, Part 2, Supplement (1963).

Gaba, Ernesto, "La Reforma Financiera Argentina—Lecciones de Una Experiencia," *Ensayos Económicos*, No. 19 (September 1981).

International Monetary Fund, *International Financial Statistics Yearbook*, 1985 (Washington: International Monetary Fund).

Kindleberger, Charles P., *Manias, Panics, and Crashes: A History of Financial Crises* (New York: Basic Books, 1978).

Meller, Patricio, and Andrés Salimano, "Inestabilidad Financiera, Burbujas Especulativas y Tasa de Interés: La Economía Chilena de 1975–83," paper presented to the "Encuentro Nacional de Economistas 1983," Instituto de Economía, Pontificia Universidad Católica de Chile, Punta de Tralca, Chile, December 1983.

Minsky, Hyman P., "A Theory of Systemic Fragility," in *Financial Crises, Institutions and Markets in a Fragile Environment*, ed. by Edward I. Altman and Arnold W. Sametz (New York: John Wiley & Sons, 1977).

Petrei, A. Humberto, and James R. Tybout, "How the Financial Statements of Argentine Firms Reflected the Stabilization and Reform Attempts During 1976–81," World Bank Staff Working Papers, No. 706 (1984).

————, "Argentina 1976–81: La Importancia de Variar los Niveles de Subsidios Financieros," *Cuadernos de Economía*, No. 65 (April 1985).

Rodríguez, Carlos A., "La tasa real de interés," in Roque B. Fernández and Carlos A. Rodríguez, eds., *Inflación y Estabilidad*, Ediciones Macchí (Buenos Aires, 1982).

Rolnick, Arthur J., and Warren E. Weber, "The Causes of Free Bank Failures," *Journal of Monetary Economics*, Vol. 14 (1984), pp. 267–91.

The World Bank, *Economic Memorandum on Argentina* (Washington: World Bank, 1984).

3

Liberalization, Crisis, Intervention: The Chilean Financial System, 1975–85

Andrés Velasco

In the mid-1970s, the Government of Chile undertook a comprehensive program of economic liberalization. A central component of this program, particularly after 1977, was a drastic overhaul and deregulation of the country's financial system. This reform was carried out in the spirit of the well-known McKinnon-Shaw prescription that abolishing "financial repression" is essential for sustained economic development (McKinnon, 1973; Shaw, 1973): banks were privatized, regulations were relaxed, interest rate ceilings were abolished, and integration with world capital markets was increased. The financial reform was accompanied by stabilization policies aimed at reducing the persistent macroeconomic disequilibrium, which was reflected particularly in hyperinflation during the early 1970s.

During the stabilization cum reform program, both the financial and the real sectors of the economy appeared to be making progress for several years before a major financial crisis developed. Between 1977 and 1981, inflation fell (albeit slowly), and output boomed while domestic capital markets vigorously expanded (Table 1). But, by late 1981 the financial system was indisputably submerged in a major crisis. By the end of 1981, the nonperforming assets of banks had reached an estimated 22 percent of capital and reserves and were to rise to 47 percent at the end of 1982 and 113 percent in May of 1983 (Arellano, 1983a). Two successive waves of government "interventions" (one in November 1981 and one in January 1983) were necessary to rescue or liquidate the troubled financial intermediaries. By early 1983, 11 commercial banks (including the nation's 2 largest private banks) and 5 financial companies (*financieras*) were under government intervention or had been liquidated. Many other financial institutions survived only because of a generous infusion of government

113

Table 1. Main Macroeconomic Indicators, 1975–86

	1975	1976	1977	1978	1979	1980	1981	1982	1983	1984	1985	1986
Inflation[1,2]	340.7	174.3	63.5	30.3	38.9	31.2	9.5	20.7	23.1	23.0	26.4	17.4
	(343.3)	(197.7)	(84.2)	(37.2)								
Devaluation vis-à-vis U.S. dollar[3]	354.5	104.9	60.5	21.4	14.9	0.0	0.0	88.3	19.2	46.5	43.4	11.4
Real exchange rate[4]	97.9	79.9	90.0	100.0	92.4	79.8	70.5	99.4	93.4	106.1	135.7	146.8
M1 growth[3]	254.8	195.3	108.2	66.9	64.5	56.8	-6.0	9.4	26.6	13.1	11.3	41.3
Real wages[5]	-3.2	2.9	10.4	6.4	8.3	8.4	9.0	0.5	-10.9	—	—	—
Unemployment[6]	16.7	16.8	13.2	14.0	13.6	11.8	11.1	22.1	22.2	—	—	—
Fiscal deficit[7]	-1.7	3.7	1.7	2.1	4.8	5.5	0.8	-3.4	-2.8	-4.4	-2.6	-1.9
Current account deficit[7]	-4.5	0.9	-3.7	-5.3	-5.5	-7.8	-14.3	-9.5	-5.4	-10.7	-8.2	-6.3
Real GDP growth[8]	-12.9	3.5	9.8	8.2	8.3	7.8	5.7	-14.3	-0.7	6.3	2.4	5.7
Stock price index[9]	4.2	13.7	46.3	100.0	202.7	381.5	284.2	254.1	213.3	258.1	330.3	—
International reserves[10]	55.9	405.1	426.5	1,090.1	1,938.3	3,123.2	3,213.3	1,815.0	2,036.3	2,302.9	2,449.9	2,351.3

[1]December to December percentage change; Central Bank of Chile. CPI base:1978 = 100.
[2]Figures in parentheses are from Cortázar and Marshall (1980) CPI.
[3]December to December percentage changes, International Monetary Fund, *International Financial Statistics*.
[4]Measured in December of each year. Nominal exchange rate adjusted by a trade-weighted index of the exchange rates and CPIs of Chile's 16 major trading partners. Base: December 1978 = 100.
[5]Cortázar (1983). Uses Cortázar-Marshall price index as deflator.
[6]United Nations (1983). Arithmetic average of quarterly survey results. Does not include Minimum Employment Plan.
[7]Overall deficit of the nonfinancial public sector, as a percent of GDP.
[8]*IFS*, 1980 prices.
[9]Central Bank of Chile, *Boletín Mensual*, December Indice General de Acciones. Base: December 1978 = 100.
[10]*IFS*, in millions of U.S. dollars.

subsidies. The severity of the crisis contributed to a substantial weakening of macroeconomic performance and major readjustments in policies. The fixed exchange rate regime, maintained for almost three years, collapsed in June 1982. During 1982 and 1983, inflation rebounded somewhat, and real output fell by more than 14 percent in 1982 alone.

This chapter focuses on the possible causes of the crisis in the Chilean financial system and analyzes the measures adopted to deal with the crisis and their effects. The Chilean process resembles the "classical" boom-and-bust cycle of financial crises, as described by Minsky (1977) and Kindleberger (1978).[1] The study therefore examines the upswing in financial intermediation that occurred in the late 1970s and analyzes the weaknesses that eventually led to systemic difficulties. The analysis focuses on the interaction among financial and macro variables and policies.

The macroeconomic policies and outcomes up to the 1982 crisis are well known and have attracted ample academic attention (Corbo (1985); Dornbusch (1984); Edwards (1985); Foxley (1983); Harberger (1985); Sjaastad (1983); Zahler (1983)).[2] It suffices here to outline some of the main changes in the macroeconomic environment that accompanied the financial reform. A major aim of the stabilization policy during this period was to lower the rate of inflation, which had approached hyperinflationary levels in 1973. To a large extent, the inflation reflected the need to finance huge fiscal deficits, which in 1973 had reached 22 percent of GDP.

A tighter fiscal policy was an important component of the policy package. Although the growth of fiscal expenditures was reduced, the Government took mainly strong measures to increase revenue, including tax reform, price increases for goods and services produced by the public sector, and the sale of many enterprises that the previous administration had nationalized. As a result, the public sector achieved a significant overall surplus by 1979.

Monetary and exchange rate policies also were modified. The Government followed a policy of moderate expansion in domestic credit combined with exchange rate adjustments that followed a crawling peg. The strategy was to lower the rate of inflation gradually while improving the reserve position of the Central Bank and preserving the competitiveness of Chilean exports.

The exchange rate policy was changed in December 1977, when the Government introduced a daily schedule for the exchange rate for the ensuing 2 months. In February 1978, this schedule was extended for 11

---

[1] This point has been stressed by Barandiarán (1983).

[2] The microeconomic aspects of policy changes and their effects have also been described in some detail by Arellano (1983a); Barandiarán (1983); Díaz-Alejandro (1985); Zahler (1985); and Luders (1986).

months, and at the end of that year, it was extended through December 1979. These schedules implied a declining rate of devaluation, with the aim of driving inflation closer to international levels. In addition, it was hoped that preannouncement of the devaluation rates would help remove uncertainty and align domestic interest rates with those abroad. In June 1979, the exchange rate was pegged at Ch$39 per U.S. dollar—the level that, according to the schedule, would have been reached only in December. Moreover, the Government announced that there would be no further devaluations.

Perhaps the most dramatic policy changes occurred in the foreign sector. The authorities moved rapidly to eliminate trade restrictions and sharply reduced both the dispersion and the levels of tariffs, but they moved more slowly in freeing capital movements. Most capital outflows remained restricted through the 1970s, and all new foreign borrowing or refinancing of existing credits by commercial banks, except for short-term lines of credit, remained subject to prior approval of the Central Bank.

These policies succeeded in lowering inflation to less than 10 percent per year by 1981, while achieving a rate of growth in GDP of 7 percent per year over the 1976–81 period. But in 1982, and 1983, the country plunged into a major recession; GDP fell 14 percent in 1982, and unemployment increased from a low of 11 percent in 1981 to more than 22 percent in 1982. This recession had both foreign and domestic causes. The most important foreign causes were the collapse in the prices of Chile's main export commodities (especially copper), the appreciation of the U.S. dollar, and higher interest rates abroad. The main domestic cause was a deterioration of competitiveness, caused by the combination of a fixed exchange rate and backward-looking wage indexation. The cumulative effect of high domestic interest rates since 1975, following the liberalization of the financial sector, weakened the financial health of enterprises and served to deepen the recession. Furthermore, the Chilean Government addressed the declining competitiveness and deteriorating external balance by restraining domestic demand and lowering nominal wages. When those measures proved insufficient, the Government abandoned the fixed exchange rate of the peso; on June 15, 1982, the peso was devalued by 15 percent. Following further sharp depreciation, the peso declined to Ch$66 per U.S. dollar by September 1982, when it was announced that exchange rate adjustments would follow a crawling peg.

Although inflation accelerated from 10 percent in 1982 to 23 percent in 1983, the economy then began to recover. In 1984, real GDP grew by almost 6.3 percent, while inflation continued at about 23 percent. Recovery continued in 1985, when GDP grew by about 2.4 percent, although inflation accelerated to about 26.5 percent. The rate of unemployment fell sharply to about 12 percent by 1985; real average wages declined steadily between 1982 and 1985.

Against this background, this chapter systematically analyzes the connection between macro and purely financial developments and separates the micro from the macro causes of the financial crisis. It is usually taken for granted that undesirable macro outcomes such as high real interest rates and overvalued exchange rates adversely affect the position of borrowing firms, and thus the financial system as a whole. However, the more subtle question of how the financial sector disequilibrium affects the health of the macroeconomy is seldom asked. This chapter discusses the possibility that the troubles in the financial sector may have contributed substantially to the creation of instability elsewhere in the Chilean economy. In turn, the macro disturbances that those troubles helped create would come back to haunt the banks, via a weakened pool of borrowers and large quantities of nonperforming assets.

This chapter also examines the interrelationships among several widely accepted hypotheses concerning Chile's financial crisis. The financial reform was quite controversial when implemented, but ex post there is remarkable agreement as to "what went wrong." Many such explanations, however, are partial equilibrium analyses that focus only on a particular feature of the financial problem (high interest rates, for instance). This paper juxtaposes these explanations and explores their mutual compatibility. Finally, this paper benefits from recently published work (Gálvez and Tybout (1985); Corbo and Sánchez (1985); Arriagada (1985)) on the microeconomic performance of Chilean firms during the relevant period. This information permits a better discussion of some common assumptions about the link between firm bankruptcies and bank problems.

Distributional and welfare issues are dealt with only superficially. The process of financial reform and the measures to deal with the financial crisis have probably had major distributional and welfare consequences, but their measurement and evaluation should be the subject of a separate study.

I. Financial Reform

The process of financial reform began shortly after a new administration came to power in 1973. Broadly speaking, the reform included institutional, regulatory, and international aspects, which will be considered in this section. By 1980, the process of liberalization was essentially completed. From 1981 onward, the changes would be mostly in response to the growing imbalances.

Institutional Changes

The financial system was almost entirely under state control in late 1973. After a long period of mixed ownership, virtually all financial institutions had been nationalized during the period of 1970 through 1973. In addition, a number of entities linked to ministries and state agencies directly supplied credit to sundry activities.

In 1974, Chile had 20 domestic nationalized commercial banks. The following year all but the Banco del Estado were sold to the private sector. The system thus became a predominantly private one, although the Banco del Estado has maintained a large and active presence.

The process and terms by which the banks were transferred to private groups have been criticized. Differential access to credit and weak (and eventually abolished) legislation against concentration of ownership meant that the bulk of commercial banks ended up in the hands of a few large conglomerates, some of which had also recently acquired scores of reprivatized manufacturing and service enterprises (Arellano (1983b)).[3] Interlocking ownership and management patterns were eventually blamed for some of the mistakes made by these institutions.

Even before the commercial banks were privatized in May 1974, short-term transactions at free interest rates had been allowed. As a result, a new kind of financial entity arose, the *financieras*, which initially enjoyed great flexibility and a competitive advantage (interest rates on commercial bank deposits were not freed until a year later). In December 1976, problems in some of the *financieras* prompted an increase in their supervision.[4]

The development of *financieras* was only one manifestation of a general increase in new financial intermediaries during the 1970s. The authorities' efforts to lower barriers to entry brought in foreign banks. The evolution of the system is described in Table 2, which shows that by 1981, Chile had 23 domestically owned banks (1 of which was state owned), 18 foreign banks, and 13 finance companies (*financieras*).

During this process, the *Sistema Nacional de Ahorros y Préstamos* (SINAP) (National Savings and Loan System) faced serious difficulties. Founded in 1960 to provide housing credit, it captured a large portion of domestic financial savings during the 1960s. The SINAP had made long-term commitments (housing loans) financed with short-term indexed deposits, which were inexpensive as long as interest rate ceilings existed. When the

---

[3] It is also sometimes argued that the banks were privatized at unusually generous terms, but it is hard to reconcile this argument with the accompanying critiques of ownership concentration. If the banks were sold cheaply, then not only large *grupos* (financial and manufacturing conglomerates) would have had access to them, unless the Government had intentionally discriminated against other potential buyers.

[4] Both "formal" and "informal" *financieras* were in operation until December 1976, when the informal ones were eliminated by the institution of a formal approval procedure for institutions or individuals desiring to receive deposits from the public. Accounting standards were tightened and capital requirements increased to a level equivalent to 75 percent of the capital required from commercial banks.

Table 2. Structure of Financial System, 1974–84

	1974	1975	1976	1977	1978	1979	1980	1981	1982	1983	1984
Total number of banks and finance companies	21	21	20	39	47	54	56	54	49	45	45
Domestic banks[1]	20	20	18	18	22	24	25	23	21	19	19
Foreign banks	1	1	2	3	4	12	13	18	19	19	19
Finance companies	—	—	—	18	21	18	18	13	9	7	7

Source: Larrain (1985).
[1] Only one domestic bank has been state owned since 1975.

ceilings were abolished in 1975, the SINAP was caught in a squeeze. It effectively went bankrupt in 1976, and the state guaranteed its deposits.

Regulatory Reform

Chilean bank regulations changed often during the reform period, so space limitations permit only a general description here. The general aim of these changes was twofold: to promote the rapid growth of the financial system and to increase competition.

As has been noted already, controls on interest rates were lifted in 1975. During the period of so-called financial repression (1930–75), the combination of interest rate ceilings and high inflation had consistently yielded negative real rates, but this situation changed after liberalization. It was hoped that positive real yields on domestic financial assets would reduce preferences for foreign or nonproductive assets. Indexed savings instruments and domestic dollar assets were to help in this task. The attractiveness of domestic financial investments was also to be enhanced by changes in tax legislation, which took account of inflation and ensured that thereafter only real interest earned counted as taxable income.

Another much-criticized feature of the previous system—an array of quantitative controls on credit—also was eliminated. Selective credit controls had been a widely used tool of economic policy until 1975, but after that date, it was expected that the market mechanism alone would allocate credit and improve the allocation of resources.

To reduce the cost to banks of holding required reserves, which could become quite substantial under inflationary conditions, the Central Bank began paying competitive interest on such reserves in May 1976. Subsequently, reserve requirements were gradually lowered, to 10 percent for sight deposits and 4 percent for time deposits, and interest payments on reserves were phased out.

At the same time, the system moved toward multipurpose banking. To increase competition and lower costs, distinctions among commercial, investment, mortgage, and development activities were abolished. In addition, foreign banks were also allowed to open branches in Chile and to purchase Chilean banks. The result was rapid financial widening. According to Luders (1986):

> Savings operations (before a monopoly of the Banco del Estado) were permitted for all banks, and housing mortgage transactions (previously a virtual monopoly of the SINAP) were also expanded to all banks. The volume and diversification of government and Central Bank papers in the market increased noticeably; the range and number of mutual funds increased manifold; businesses began to issue significant amounts of commercial paper which were intermediated by depository institutions, stock exchanges and mutual funds; the insurance business

expanded its list of products; consumer credit offered by financial institutions expanded noticeably, etc.

New regulations also increased the powers of the bank supervisory agency (Superintendency of Banks) and changed various aspects of financial activity, such as capital requirements and credit limits. Those that are most relevant for the purpose of this paper are as follows:

- The jurisdiction of the Superintendency of Banks was broadened to include all financial institutions and its name was changed to Superintendency of Banks and Financial Institutions.
- The Superintendency was authorized to provide general information about the quality of the assets and liabilities of financial institutions in order to increase market transparency.
- In November 1974, the capital requirements for banks were increased to take account of past inflation; thereafter, these requirements were automatically adjusted once a year in accordance with the Consumer Price Index (CPI). The maximum debt/capital ratio was maintained at 20, but noncompliance was penalized more strictly, at the rate of 2 percent daily on the excess debt.
- In 1974, the law limited the maximum individual holdings of bank shares to 1.5 percent (for individuals) and to 3 percent (for firms and organizations). However, these limits were abolished in 1978 because they had proved very difficult to enforce.
- In 1980, the treatment of bank borrowers was made more uniform, with regard to their credit limits in relation to bank capital and reserves. Previously, the legislation favored corporations over other organizations and individuals. The new regulation set a uniform limit at 5 percent for unsecured credits and at 25 percent for secured credits. These limits were halved in the case of borrowers linked to the bank.
- In 1980, to facilitate underwriting operations, the limit on bank investment in a given enterprise's shares was raised from 10 percent to 20 percent of the bank's paid capital and reserves, but the limit of 10 percent of the firm's capital was maintained.
- Limits on bank borrowing abroad were modified several times, and finally abolished in 1980.

These changes gave more freedom to the financial markets and placed more emphasis on rules than on the authorities' discretion in supervising the system. As the financial crisis unfolded in late 1981, some of these regulatory provisions were modified, as discussed in Sections IV and VII.

Capital Flows

The liberalization of international capital flows has been one of the most widely discussed features of the Chilean experience. The process is discussed in detail in Arellano and Ffrench-Davis (1981), Ffrench-Davis (1983), Mathieson (1979), McKinnon (1982), and Edwards (1984).

After many years of controls, the capital account was liberalized gradually. Starting in August 1976, capital inflows were subjected to a minimum maturity requirement of two years (between 1974 and 1976 the minimum requirement was only six months), and to a varying but small deposit requirement (non-interest-bearing) with the Central Bank.[5] This minimum maturity remained in force until the crisis in 1982, when it was abolished.

Banks were allowed to borrow abroad in dollars but not to assume the exchange risk. The principal of the counterpart domestic loans had to be indexed to the exchange rate (i.e., de facto denominated in foreign currency). There were also some limits (relaxed over time) on banks' foreign indebtedness as a percentage of capital and reserves.

The chief purpose of such restrictions was to ensure some control over domestic monetary policy. It was feared that, given very high domestic interest rates, total liberalization would induce huge and destabilizing capital inflows.[6] Despite the restrictions on capital inflows, the inflows proved massive, as seen from Table 3, reflecting in part the policy of preannouncing the exchange rate until mid-1979, which made investing in Chile very appealing.[7] Particularly massive inflows of capital occurred after the change in the exchange rate regime to fixed rates. The monetization of the ensuing reserve buildup was blamed for the slow progress in reducing inflation (Harberger (1985); Corbo (1985)).

As Table 4 suggests, this process led to the rapid accumulation of external debt. In contrast to the situation in Brazil, Mexico, and other Latin American countries, the bulk of the borrowing in Chile was done by the private sector: by 1982, 73.2 percent of net foreign debt had been incurred by the private sector. Most important for the discussion here, financial institutions accounted for the lion's share of private external borrowing (72.9 percent of total inflows, private and public, in 1981).

A drastic and thoroughgoing trade liberalization also was carried out. Quantitative controls were abolished and tariffs swiftly rationalized and

---

[5] These required deposits not only varied over time, but also depended on the maturity of the transaction. For instance, in 1980 they were 15 percent for loans with maturities of less than four years, 10 percent for those between four years and 66 months, and zero for any above 66 months.

[6] See Minister de la Cuadra, quoted in Ffrench-Davis (1983).

[7] To the extent that they were credible, the preannouncements reduced the exchange rate risk, while domestic interest rates remained high. Although formally correct, this argument does not necessarily explain fully the extraordinary size of the capital inflows. It has been argued (see Edwards (1986)) that these inflows were not particularly sensitive to interest rate differentials.

Table 3. Net Capital Inflows, 1977–82
(In millions of U.S. dollars)

Year	Semester	
	First	Second
1977	96.4	471.7
1978	793.6	1,152.5
1979	1,103.4	1,144.7
1980	1,239.1	1,921.0
1981	2,044.2	2,425.1
1982	889.2	415.1

Source: Le Fort (1985).

lowered; by June 1979 a uniform tariff of 10 percent (excepting automobile imports) was in place. The fact that liberalization of the capital account lagged substantially behind that of the current account in Chile has been much discussed. Both ex post and ex ante it has been argued that this sequence maximized the chances for adequate macroeconomic control (McKinnon (1982); Edwards (1984); and Calvo (1986)). Indeed, McKinnon (1982) has gone as far as to say that "Chile is to be treated as a norm or standard of reference" in this regard. But experts disagree on whether the speed and magnitude of the liberalization process were adequate.

II. Effects of the Financial Reform: Some Macroaggregates

A central objective of financial reform is the improvement of the economy's savings and investment performance. This section reviews some of the available evidence on the course of domestic savings and real investment. The discussion, which is far from exhaustive, is intended only as background for subsequent sections.

Domestic Savings

The impact of financial liberalization on the economy's overall rate of savings is difficult to determine a priori. First, liberalization affects only the institutionalized part of the financial market: little can be said about its effects on noninstitutionalized sources of finance, which tend to be important in repressed financial systems. Second, microeconomic theory provides no unambiguous propositions on the effect of higher interest rates in the institutionalized market—a typical first-round effect of financial liberalization—because the income and substitution effects point in opposite

Table 4. Outstanding External Debt, 1975–83

	1975	1976	1977	1978	1979	1980	1981	1982	1983
					(In millions of U.S. dollars)				
Medium- and long-term public debt[1]	3,504	3,488	3,513	4,336	4,810	4,720	4,504	5,157	8,588
Other external liabilities[2]	1,042	1,028	1,349	2,071	3,391	6,026	9,979	11,796	8,827
					(In percent of GDP[3])				
Medium- and long-term public debt[1]	41.8	31.0	26.2	28.2	23.2	17.2	13.7	21.4	43.6
Other external liabilities[2]	12.1	9.2	10.1	13.5	16.4	21.9	30.3	48.9	44.8
Total external debt[4]	53.9	40.2	36.3	41.7	39.6	39.1	44.0	70.3	88.4

Source: Central Bank of Chile.

[1]Outstanding medium- and long-term public and publicly guaranteed debt repayable in foreign currency.

[2]Includes suppliers' credits to private sector; lines of credit for imports of capital goods to commercial banks, Banco del Estado, and development banks; credits to private sector under Articles 14, 15, and 16 of International Exchange Law and DL 600; and short-term lines of credit to commercial banks, Banco del Estado, and Central Bank of Chile.

[3]GDP in current Chilean pesos converted to U.S. dollars at the following exchange rates: 1975, 4.911; 1976, 13.054; 1977, 21.529; 1978, 31.656; 1979, 36.80; 1980, 39.0; 1981, 39.0; 1982, 50.91; and 1983, 78.60.

[4]Sum of medium- and long-term public debt and other external liabilities.

directions. Moreover, higher interest rates may affect the distribution of income among sectors whose propensity to save may be different (e.g., enterprises and households). Empirically, the matter is also far from being settled.[8] In his recent empirical paper Giovannini (1985) concludes that in developing countries, the interest elasticity of savings is likely to be small. The experience of Chile also seems to point in this direction.

Table 5 presents some evidence on the evolution of savings in Chile. The data show significant year-to-year variation in the ratio of gross national savings to GDP, with a peak of almost 20 percent in 1974 and a trough of about 2 percent in 1982. Moreover, the average saving ratio for the liberalization period (1974–83) did not differ significantly from previous periods: for that period the saving ratio averaged 10.7 percent, compared with about 12 percent between 1966 and 1973; however, excluding the recession years of 1982 and 1983, the ratio increases to just 12.6 percent (only 11.6 percent, if the 1974 peak is excluded). The paucity of data makes it even harder to draw conclusions about the distribution of savings between the private and the public sector. Nevertheless, available evidence suggests that the private sector was almost always in deficit and the public sector in surplus, and that the sectoral saving ratios also show substantial variation during the period. The privatization of the social security system completed in 1981 may have had a negative impact on total savings, insofar as part of the contributions previously paid into the state social security were spent instead of saved.

Investment

The data in Table 6 indicate a significant increase (as a percentage of GDP) in private investment over the 1975–81 period followed by a sharp decline between 1982 and 1985, reflecting the effects of the recession and the financial crisis. The sharp increase until 1981 is particularly significant in light of the high real interest rates on loans charged during this period. To a large extent, this increase in private investment was offset by a decline in public investment, which was part of the program to reduce the fiscal deficit and the size of the Government. As a consequence, average gross fixed investment as a percentage of GDP was only marginally higher between 1975 and 1982 than it had been between 1966 and 1974.

Therefore, the effect on GDP growth of the shift in the composition of investment would depend on whether the marginal productivity of the projects undertaken by the private sector was higher or lower than the marginal productivity of alternative public sector projects. A definite

[8] For discussion and estimation, see not only McKinnon (1973) and Shaw (1973), but also Fry (1978), van Wijnbergen (1983), Giovannini (1985), and Molho (1986).

Table 5. National and Domestic Savings, 1960–85
(As percentage of GDP)

	Net National Savings (1)	Capital Consumption (2)	Gross National Savings (3) = (1) + (2)	Net Factor Payments Abroad (4)	Gross Domestic Savings (5) = (3) + (4)
1960–65	1	10	11	. . .	. . .
1966–70	7	8	15	. . .	. . .
1971–73	−1	10	9	1	10
1974	9 (9)	11	20	2	22
1975	−7 (4)	15	8	4	12
1976	1 (8)	13	14	3	17
1977	−1 (8)	12	11	3	14
1978	1 (5)	11	12	3	15
1979	2 (7)	10	12	3	15
1980	4 (9)	10	14	3	17
1981	1	9	10	4	14
1982	−9	11	2	8	10
1983	−7	11	4	9	13
1984	−9	11	2	10	12
1985	−6	11	5	12	17

Sources: United Nations, *National Accounts Statistics: Analysis of Main Aggregates, 1983/84*, New York (1987); and Central Bank of Chile.

Note: Figures in parentheses relate to net savings of the public sector.

Table 6. Gross Domestic Capital Formation, 1960–85

(In percentage of GDP)

	Gross Fixed Capital Formation	Change in Stocks	Gross Domestic Capital Formation		
			Private	Public	Total
1960–65	15.1	−0.9	3.8	10.5	14.3
1966–70	14.5	1.6	4.7	11.3	16.0
1971–73	13.4	−1.9	−0.9	12.4	11.5
1974	17.4 (0.5)	3.8	8.4	12.8	21.2
1975	15.4 (2.6)	−2.3	4.6	8.5	13.1
1976	12.7 (3.0)	0.1	7.4	5.4	12.8
1977	13.3 (6.4)	1.1	7.7	6.7	14.4
1978	14.5 (8.0)	3.3	11.6	6.2	17.8
1979	15.6 (9.8)	2.2	12.6	5.2	17.8
1980	17.6 (11.1)	3.4	15.6	5.4	21.0
1981	19.5 (13.4)	1.2	15.6	5.1	20.7
1982	15.0 (10.0)	−3.7	. . .	. . .	11.3
1983	12.0 (7.3)	−2.2	. . .	. . .	9.8
1984	12.3 (6.4)	1.3	. . .	. . .	13.6
1985	14.2 (7.2)	−0.5	. . .	. . .	13.7

Source: Central Bank of Chile, Dirección de Política Financiera, *Cuentas Nacionales de Chile.*

Note: Figures in parentheses relate to private sector fixed investment.

answer to this question would require further study, which is beyond the scope of this paper.

III. Effects of Financial Reform: Growth of Financial Assets

One of the most remarkable features of the Chilean experience after 1975 is the tremendous expansion of financial intermediation. As Table 7 shows, total financial assets rose from 19.7 percent of GNP in 1975 to 48.1 percent in 1982. The share of the organized financial system in overall financial intermediation rose as well: papers issued by commercial and development banks and *financieras* rose from 16.2 percent to 70.7 percent of

Table 7.   Financial Assets[1]

Year	Total Financial Assets Year-End Balance		Monetary Assets[2]	Nonmonetary Assets in Financial System[3]
	In billions of current pesos	In percentage of GNP	In percentage of total assets	
1973	0.47	14.9	53.0	14.3
1974	2.99	20.0	27.7	14.0
1975	11.36	19.7	26.1	16.2
1976	33.75	19.0	25.4	25.0
1977	75.80	21.0	24.1	38.6
1978	123.10	23.0	24.6	48.6
1979	237.80	29.6	21.1	50.1
1980	395.70	34.9	19.8	59.8
1981	510.80	39.0	14.7	69.8
1982	578.40	48.1	14.0	70.7

Source: Central Bank of Chile, *Boletín Mensual.*
Note: Definition of total financial assets excludes equity and time and demand deposits held by the public sector.
[1]These are financial assets held by the public (i.e., liabilities of the financial system).
[2]Includes currency and demand deposits and time deposits held by the private sector.
[3]Paper issued by commercial banks, development banks, and *financieras.*

total financial assets in the same period. Between 1976 and 1981, value added from financial services expanded at a real annual average of 18.4 percent, more than two and a half times the rate of expansion of the economy as a whole.[9]

At the same time, there were significant shifts in the composition of financial assets. A crucial shift was the move away from money and toward short-term, highly liquid, interest-bearing assets. Quasi-money accounted for 8.16 percent of GDP in 1975 and 22.32 percent in 1986.[10] This tendency follows naturally the upward trend of short-term interest rates paid on quasi-money after liberalization and the richer menu of financial assets available to the public.

The boom in financial intermediation, however, did not substantially lengthen the average maturity of financial instruments. As shown in Table 8, much of the expansion in financial instruments came from the shift from money to interest-earning assets with maturities of less than 90 days. Longer-term assets (with maturities over 90 days) languished. They accounted for 54 percent of total assets in 1975, and for only 44.4 and 37.2 percent in 1980 and 1981, respectively.[11]

These figures do not include equity markets, which experienced a boom of their own. The (real) stock price index rose by 2,685 percent between 1976 and the peak year of 1980 (Table 1). Prices of real estate, land, and other comparable stores of value rose dramatically as well.

This boom in financial intermediation seems inconsistent with the poor performance of domestic savings. An influential view, formulated for the general Southern Cone case, offers an explanation that may be worth quoting at some length:

> In a financially repressed economy with a history of persistent inflation, wealth is held as money, land and capital . . . . Money is held because of its property as a means of payment; capital, because of its expected yield in use; and land, as a shelter against inflation. Expected land yields may be low, but they are strongly correlated with inflation rates . . . . In this context, financial reform-mongers typically propose introducing an indexed government bond as an instrument of financial liberalization.[12] In the presence of such an attractive asset with a strong back-up market, saving propensities should increase and a higher proportion of wealth should be held as productive capital . . . . (However), indexed bonds tend to replace capital (and money) rather than land in private portfolio holdings. True-market-oriented financial reforms are accompanied by a general liberaliza-

---

[9] Central Bank of Chile, *Boletín Mensual*.

[10] See International Monetary Fund, *International Financial Statistics*.

[11] There was a healthy shift, however, from assets with maturities of 90 days to one year to those extending beyond one year (see Table 8).

[12] For the purposes of this study, the introduction of any asset that pays a consistently positive rate of return will play this role.

tion of interest rates, in the context of a demand-contractionary package of policies. . . . An excess supply of money may also obtain, in spite of contractionary policies, if the demand for money is sufficiently lowered by the introduction of the indexed bond (Díaz-Alejandro and Bacha (1982)).

This critical view of the consequences of financial liberalization captures some of the tendencies described so far: the extent to which the growth in

Table 8. Maturities of Financial Assets, 1973–82
(In percentage of total)

Year	Monetary Assets (1)	Less than 90 Days (2)	90 Days to 1 Year (3)	More than 1 Year (4)
1973	53.0	3.1	40.5	3.4
1974	27.7	18.3	47.2	6.8
1975	26.1	19.9	39.0	15.0
1976	25.4	27.2	28.8	18.6
1977	24.1	38.0	25.4	12.5
1978	24.6	44.7	19.5	11.2
1979	21.1	37.6	20.6	20.7
1980	19.8	35.8	22.7	21.7
1981	14.7	48.1	13.3	23.9
1982	14.0	44.0	16.7	25.3

Source: Arellano (1983b).

Monetary assets   = Private money holdings: Currency + demand deposits.

Less than 90 days = Pagarés Descontables Banco Central (PDBC), Depósitos y Captaciones Bancos y Financieras, Ventas PDBC con pacto retrocompra, Ahorro a la vista, Emisión Pagarés Descontables de Tesorería (PDT), PDBC Reserva Técnica, CEPAC, Venta Cartera Bancos, Operaciones con Cuentas de Ahorro Sistemático (CAS).

90 days to 1 year = Cuotas Ahorro Corvi, Depósitos y Captaciones Bancos y Financieras, Ahorro a Plazo, Depósitos de Ahorro e Inversión (DAI), Cuentas de Ahorro SINAP, Valores Hipotecarios Reajustables (VHR), Ahorro Sistemático Cooperativo, Depósitos Plazo Banco Estado.

More than 1 year = Cuentas Ahorro Reajustables (CAR), Pagarés Reajustables de Tesorería (PRT), Bonos y Letras Hipotecarias, Bonos Hipotecarios SINAP, Debentures, Pagarés Banco Central Sistemático Previsión, Bonos de Reconstrucción, Pagarés Reajustables Caja Central.

Note: Until 1975 all time deposits in banking system are classified in column (2).

some financial assets was the consequence of substitution away from money; the boom in interest-bearing financial assets; and the sluggishness in the demand for real capital. But, it fails to account for the boom in overall financial intermediation, not just in close money substitutes. It also neglects the upward dash of the price of the existing capital stock, which took place even as the demand for investment goods remained low. An explanation of these phenomena requires a closer look at the details of the Chilean situation.

A commonly mentioned cause for the spectacular growth of financial assets is the increase in private wealth. It is conjectured that increases in expected permanent income or in the yield of assets held by the public created an upward wealth effect, some of which spilled into higher demand for financial assets. As Barandiarán (1983) puts it:

> The change in expectations toward higher wealth was the decisive factor in the extraordinary expansion of private demand for goods and services. . . . The financial system grew alongside private sector wealth: capital gains realized by the owners of real assets turned in part toward the financial system, producing a monetization of real private assets (in the sense that highly liquid paper was issued on the basis of these assets).

How solid a foundation this process constituted for the growth in bank and *financiera* liabilities is hard to assess. Whether increases in expected permanent income were effective or only perceived must be a moot question, but some of the optimism displayed at the time seems justified in the wake of a massive removal of distortions, a change that had the potential for increasing real income. High interest rates produced attractive short-term yields on financial assets, which also created a perception of increased wealth. Finally, booming stock, land, and real estate prices certainly increased wealth and hence the accumulation of financial assets. However, it seems very likely that such exploding asset prices were unrelated to market fundamentals (like the conceivable real yield on capital and land) and hence unsustainable. In fact, econometric evidence (Meller and Solimano (1983)) suggests that indeed there was a speculative bubble in stock prices, of the sort described by Blanchard and Watson (1982).

Another key element in the expansion of financial assets was the reorientation of savings toward the financial system.[13] During the period of "financial repression," the Government served as a channel for an important portion of national savings. These were in turn directly invested by the Government or lent to state enterprises and the public. As these uses of funds declined after 1973, more and more of the resources obtained by the Government were channeled through the financial system (the liabilities of

---

[13] This point has been stressed by Arellano (1983b).

the consolidated financial system vis-à-vis the Government rose). Another important change was privatization of the social security system, beginning in May 1981. The bulk of social security contributions were thereafter deposited in the financial system. By year-end 1982 such funds accounted for 7.7 percent of total deposits.

Finally, the single largest source of the expansion of domestic bank liabilities was foreign borrowing. Particularly between 1978 and 1981, capital inflows exceeded current account deficits, leading to a buildup of international reserves (Table 1). Whether the borrowers were domestic banks or firms, such funds would eventually find their way into higher deposits in the financial system.[14] At the end of 1981, reserves amounted to almost 10 percent of GDP and to 35 percent of all paper issued domestically by the financial system.

Of course, capital inflows are not an exogenous variable. In Chile, the bulk of foreign borrowing was contracted by domestic banks, which actively sought foreign loans. The same can be said of domestic deposits: banks and *financieras* have ample means at their disposal to regulate their acquisition of deposit liabilities and are willing to attract funds only insofar as they expect to lend them out again, at a profit. The expansion in bank liabilities described must have had a counterpart in a corresponding increase in bank loans. Indeed, it is likely that vigorous growth in the demand for bank credit may have acted as a "pull" factor, prompting banks to attract additional resources to meet this demand. To explore such a conjecture we must examine the course and nature of bank lending, a subject to which we now turn.

IV. Effects of Financial Reform: Expansion of Domestic Debt

Between 1974 and 1982, the accumulated stock of debt of the nongovernment sector went from 5.0 percent of GDP to 61.7 percent (Table 9). The inability of private economic agents to pay interest and principal on such a staggering stock of debt was eventually to become the key weakness of the Chilean experiment.

Much of the debt was denominated in dollars, a factor that increased the service burden after the 1982 maxi-devaluation. Table 10 offers a breakdown of total loans of the financial system by currency and maturity. In 1981, peso loans accounted for almost 62 percent of the total, and dollar loans for the rest. Moreover, such debt was predominantly short term: 67 percent of loans denominated in pesos in 1981 had maturities of less than

---

[14] Unlike many other countries in the hemisphere, in Chile the Central Bank borrowed little in this period.

**Table 9. Loans of Financial System
to Nongovernment Sector, 1969–82**

| End of Year | Total | | Banking System[1] | Central Bank |
	In billions of pesos, 1977	In percentage of GDP	In percentage of GDP	In percentage of GDP
1969	51.5	18.6	8.3	10.3
1970	53.4	18.9	8.4	10.5
1973	82.4	28.7	4.4	24.2
1974	87.7	30.2	5.0	25.2
1975	92.7	39.0	6.4	32.6
1976	87.2	33.3	8.9	24.4
1977	110.7	38.5	14.8	23.7
1978	130.4	41.9	20.3	21.6
1979	150.0	44.5	28.2	16.3
1980	183.8	50.7	40.2	10.5
1981	234.8	61.5	54.9	6.6
1982[2]	251.9	76.3	61.7	14.6

Sources: 1969–78, Central Bank of Chile, *Series Monetarias*; 1979–82, Central Bank of Chile, *Boletín Mensual*; and 1979–82 (total loans only), Superintendency of Banks and Financial Institutions, *Información Financiera*.
[1] Starting in 1979 includes development banks and *financieras*.
[2] November.

one year. Dollar loans were somewhat longer term, given the two-year minimum maturity required of capital inflows, but cheaper dollar credit tended to be rationed and was inaccessible to many.[15] The short-term nature of credit available to firms was a cause of concern throughout the period. As early as 1976 Corbo warned, "Domestic currency debt is made up almost entirely of 30-day loans. These credits are renewable according to different mechanisms, but firms are subjected to a rate of interest they

[15] Regulation on foreign borrowing (see Section I) had the effect of excluding smaller borrowers from the external market. Collateral and creditworthiness considerations may have also played a role. Domestically, then, banks that did borrow abroad had some market power over dollar credit allocation. See Section V for further discussion of this issue.

Table 10. Currency and Maturity Structure of Loans, 1978–82
(In billions of pesos)

End of Year	Below 1 year	Above 1 year	Total
	Domestic Currency Loans		
1978	65.5	19.2	84.7
1979	120.7	41.0	161.7
1980	238.9	90.9	329.8
1981	328.6	164.6	493.2
1982	283.3	236.6	519.9
	Foreign Currency Loans		
1978	45.1	31.8	76.9
1979	71.6	55.1	126.7
1980	116.1	l07.1	223.2
1981	143.3	163.3	306.6
1982	147.1	306.3	453.4

Source: Arellano (1983b).
Note: Overdue loans are excluded.

cannot predict beyond thirty days and are faced with the problem of renegotiating each month the total of their credits."

The first factor to explain the growth in debt ratios (Table 9) is the financial euphoria that seems to have overtaken Chilean economic agents starting sometime in 1977 and peaking in 1980 and 1981.[16] Barandiarán (1983) has maintained that "the generalization of optimistic expectations about the prospects for the national economy was the main cause of the increased indebtedness of firms and households in 1980 and 1981." But as Barandiarán himself emphasizes, such euphoric expectations are hard to justify, even after taking into account hopes about increased national permanent income: these hopes cannot explain a tenfold increase in real domestic indebtedness.

A substantial amount of bank credit directly or indirectly financed an

---

[16] The Chilean economy grew rapidly between 1977 and 1980 despite the modest improvement in investment performance (Tables 1 and 6). Such growth was probably associated with increased capacity utilization or with efficiency gains in the use of capital.

increased demand for consumer durables. As already mentioned, years of import restrictions had created pent-up demand for imported consumer durables, whose low relative price during the period of peso overvaluation made them even more attractive. At the same time, expectations of a real devaluation or of a return to higher tariffs or both made overstocking a rational course of action (see Calvo (1986)). As a result, there was a flood of consumer imports, many of which were purchased with bank credit at variable interest rates. This last feature made repayments particularly difficult in 1981 and 1982, as real peso rates rose. Similarly, dollar credit was contracted for cheaply, but it became almost prohibitively expensive after the devaluation. Repossession of items purchased on credit became common in 1982.

Other practices added a great deal to this boom in credit demand. An important share of credit was extended to *grupos* (financial and manufacturing conglomerates) seeking to purchase firms or other existing assets. An unusual sort of competition took place among these conglomerates, in which market share or sheer size seems to have mattered more than profitability or efficiency. In a few years, these groups had acquired practically all the nation's largest manufacturing and banking firms, and in the process had sent stock prices soaring. Whether these groups acted speculatively (expecting to sell later at a higher price) or whether they thought the exorbitant purchase prices were justified by high present value of expected real return is irrelevant. The point is that asset prices behaved "as if" a speculative bubble were taking place (Meller and Solimano (1983)), and the process probably absorbed a significant share of the nation's available credit.

Stock prices also were inflated by the practice of *grupo* firms of trading stock among themselves, thus boosting the price of their shares above market value. These stocks were then used as collateral for bank credit. This was but one of many practices intended to facilitate the use of bank credit by *grupo* firms.[17] Often such credit was used to purchase banks themselves, in an operation that Luders (1986), following the terminology of the time, terms a "bicycle": "The bank would grant a loan to a corporation controlled by the new owners of the same bank; and the corporation would use the proceeds of the loan to pay for the shares it was acquiring."

The consequences were twofold. First, a good portion of bank credit went to finance the consolidation or expansion of *grupos*. Second, loans to firms belonging to the same conglomerate as the lending bank came to account for a substantial portion of the banks' portfolios; this problem

[17] *Grupos* purchased both firms that were being "reprivatized" and firms that had always been in the private sector.

became known as the problem of the *cartera relacionada*. By June 1982, the *cartera relacionada* accounted for 21.1 percent of the loans of the five largest private banks. In the case of the Banco de Santiago, the nation's largest private bank, this figure was 45.8 percent (Arellano (1983b)).

Finally, perhaps the single most important factor behind the growth of domestic indebtedness was the rolling over of credits and the capitalization of interest. As Arnold Harberger (1985) has put it, in Chile there existed "substantial 'false demand.' The false demand for credit consists of the rolling over of what are essentially bad loans." By 1981, many borrowers were in a tenuous situation. As Gálvez and Tybout (1985) have documented, real peso overvaluation and sustained high real interest rates were major sources of difficulties for manufacturing firms, particularly those competing in the export and import sectors. Tables 11 and 12 show estimates of firm bankruptcies and of loans in default, respectively. By 1981, the figures for loan defaults amounted to 2.3 percent of the portfolio of the total financial system. This share rose to 8.2 percent in 1982 and 18.5 percent in 1983 (see Table 12). The implicit dangers, however, were greater than these figures would suggest. Chilean banks as a whole were undercapitalized with respect to their historical averages (Behrens (1985)), so that the ratio of nonperforming assets to total capital and reserves was extremely high: Arellano (1983a) estimates the ratio at 11 percent in 1980,

Table 11.   Number of Total Bankruptcies, 1974–82

Year	Corporate Enterprises	General Establishments
1974	. . .	75
1975	. . .	81
1976	. . .	131
1977	. . .	224
1978	2	312
1979	4	344
1980	15	415
1981	29	431
1982	75	810

Source: Fiscalía Nacional de Quiebras, taken from Luders (1986).

Table 12. Loan Defaults, 1974–83
(As percentage of total loan portfolio)

Year	Commercial Banks	Finance Companies	Financial System
1974	1.4	. . .	. . .
1975	2.8	. . .	. . .
1976	1.7	. . .	. . .
1977	1.4	. . .	. . .
1978	1.2	. . .	. . .
1979	1.1	. . .	. . .
1980	0.9	. . .	. . .
1981[1]	2.4	2.1	2.3
1982[1]	8.2	8.1	8.2
1983[1]	18.7	5.9	18.5

Source: Behrens (1985) , taken from Luders (1986).
[1]Including "risky portfolio" loans sold to Central Bank.

22 percent in 1981, 47 percent in 1982, and 113 percent in 1983.

Furthermore, the line between a performing and a nonperforming asset becomes fuzzy when rollovers and capitalization of interest are widely used to keep many problem loans on the books. There is substantial consensus (Arellano (1983b); Zahler (1985); Harberger (1985); and Luders (1986)) that such practices accounted for a large share of the expansion in bank credit. Under the extremely high interest rates, interest accumulated on domestic currency loans between 1977 and 1982 would add up to 72 percent of outstanding peso loans by year-end 1982.

Real interest rates (corrected by the CPI) on loans averaged 77 percent per year between 1975 and 1982 (see Table 13). Why would firms and households continue to borrow in pesos at rates so far above any conceivable return on real investment? One possibility is that, locked into short-term credits, firms continued to borrow with the expectation that "interest rates would soon decline." Another possibility is that the real rates we can compute are ex post, while ex ante expected rates were much lower. In 1981 and 1982, for instance, real rates rose largely because of a swift decline in inflation associated with the appreciation of the dollar in inter-

Table 13. Alternative Real Loan Rates, 1975–83
(In percent)

Year	Corrected by CPI[1]	Corrected by Capital Goods Prices[2]	Corrected by Stock Market Index[3]
1975	164.9	38.9	−1,494.4
1976	176.4	150.7	124.5
1977	92.9	60.3	−81.5
1978	55.0	26.3	34.1
1979	23.1	24.3	−40.7
1980	15.7	19.5	−35.3
1981	42.4	38.6	77.4
1982	42.4	47.0	73.7
1983	15.9	21.8	58.8
1975–82[4]	76.6	50.7	—

Sources: Central Bank of Chile, *Boletín Mensual*, Cuentas Nacionales, 1960–83.
[1]Nominal loan rate in pesos corrected by CPI.
[2]Nominal loan rate in pesos corrected by the implicit deflator of fixed capital formation statistics. See *Cuentas Nacionales*.
[3]Nominal loan rate in pesos corrected by IGPA (Indice General Precios de Acciones).
[4]Arithmetic average.

national markets.[18] Such mistakes in expectations can perhaps explain a one-time increase in indebtedness, but not a sustained increase such as that witnessed by Chile. In the latter part of the period it is likely that many firms were willing to borrow at any ex ante rate simply to stave off bankruptcy. On the basis of data obtained by Gálvez and Tybout (1985), net earnings dropped sharply after 1980, especially for firms producing tradables, and the gearing ratio of firms began to rise. This situation is consistent with the hypothesis that capitalization of interest and other related lending can be considered "distress borrowing" for a significant number of firms.

It has been argued that firms acted this way because continued post-

[18] See Corbo (1985). Because the peso was pegged to the dollar, dollar appreciation was tantamount to a revaluation of the peso vis-à-vis other major currencies. Hence, the reduction in Chilean inflation in 1981 may well have been unexpected.

ponement of bankruptcy made a government bailout more likely. According to Arellano (1983b),

> As borrowers become aware that this is a generalized phenomenon that has no micro but only macroeconomic solutions, they become indifferent to the interest rates they are charged. Debts become mere entries in the books—banks cannot collect them. This must have been the perception of large debtors—certainly the conglomerates—during much of the period, and has certainly been the perception of the immense majority of debtors since 1982.

What borrowers expected ex ante we may never know; but ex post those who expected that mounting debts would bring some kind of official help turned out to be correct.

Although many institutional features of the post-reform Chilean financial system facilitated excessive risk taking and unsound lending patterns, the legislation aimed at curtailing such patterns was weak or nonexistent until 1980, and the Superintendency of Banks allowed those practices insofar as they did not violate the letter of the law. In 1980, the Superintendency began to set up a system for the classification of loans according to risk—irrespective of whether they were overdue—and the corresponding rules were established for "individual" provisions for nonperforming loans to supplement the "overall" provisions.[19] In late 1981, the authorities adopted measures that limited the amount of bank exposure to a single enterprise and to a bank's own subsidiaries. But it was not until 1982 that a set of comprehensive measures that tightened bank supervision were approved. The regulations included a more precise definition of the limit on loans to a single enterprise, which took into account the interlocking ownership of firms.[20] In the case of banks classified as unstable or poorly managed, the Superintendency was empowered to regulate the bank's new lending, rolling over of existing credit, and collateral requirements. The Superintendency also began to develop a formal system of rating financial institutions based on "CAMEL" (capital, asset quality, management, earnings, and liquidity) indicators, and commercial banks were prohibited from investing in equity capital, agricultural land, merchandise, or livestock and from accepting stock as loan collateral (so as to limit the use of inflated stocks as collateral).

Minimum capital asset ratios in force in Chile at the time also made it expensive for banks to write off loans. When a loan is declared to be bad,

---

[19] Loans were ranked in five categories according to their soundness, and specific provisioning requirements were applied against all loans ranked in the third category or below.

[20] Although the limit of 5 percent (of a bank's capital and reserves) for unsecured loans—and any excess up to the limit of 10 percent to be secured—was retained, the limit covered not only the loans made directly to an enterprise but also a share of loans made to other institutions which hold stocks of the enterprise.

capital and surplus must be reduced by the amount of bad debt, but the loan portfolio must be reduced by an even greater amount because of regulations on the minimum capital asset ratio. Banks were quite unwilling to do this at a time of high loan rates and booming credit demand.

Furthermore, banks were able to engage in this sort of risky lending because they were not subject to the discipline of depositor or state supervision. There were no explicit peso deposit guarantees in Chile until January 1983, but apparently there was a widespread perception that the Government would rescue depositors in the event of a bank crunch. This perception was reinforced at the time of the collapse of Banco Osorno in 1976, when the Government granted a 100 percent bailout of depositors and other creditors.

The issue of implicit guarantees in Chile has been widely discussed. That peso deposits were perceived to be guaranteed seems clear: there were no major bank runs even as practically all the nation's major banks teetered on the verge of collapse, and this fact was amply discussed in policy circles and even in the press.[21] Whether bank owners or managers perceived their investments or reputations to be guaranteed is clearly a different matter.[22] If this was the case, it has been argued, bankers had incentives to undertake excessively risky investment. Again, ex ante expectations are unclear, but some ex post observations can be made. Starting in late 1981 many bank managers lost their jobs, and some even went to jail. When the Government intervened in a bank, the owners temporarily lost control over the bank, and eventually saw their ownership diluted by the issuance of new stock. Many banks, whether subjected to intervention or not, received generous subsidies.[23] The alternative outcome for comparison is not the entirely unrealistic one in which bank owners or managers lose nothing, but the one in which banks are immediately liquidated, asset prices plummet, and bankers are left with little or nothing in their hands. Compared with the alternative outcome, Chilean bankers appear to have enjoyed a substantial government "guarantee" ex post.

At any rate, if an implicit *deposit* guarantee had not existed, the logic of the market would have necessarily disciplined bankers. Realizing that many banks were in difficulties, depositors would have transferred their funds toward the more solid institutions. If accounting were pristine and

[21] An explicit deposit guarantee was granted in January 1983, initially for the period up to December 31, 1983, but it was extended periodically, until a formal deposit insurance scheme was instituted in 1986 (see Section VII).

[22] The distinction is difficult to make, because often major *grupo* shareholders were directly involved in bank management.

[23] See subsequent sections for a further treatment of this issue.

information flows efficient, the collapse of unsound banks would not have affected the rest. If, conversely, a panic had been generated, the system might have failed anyway, but much earlier.[24,25]

The issue of guarantees to foreign creditors warrants special mention. As Díaz-Alejandro (1985) has emphasized, the Chilean foreign borrowing was largely private and was contracted under explicit government assurances that it would remain so, but the story turned out to be very different. In the words of Arnold Harberger (1985),

> The major international banks seem to have acted in concert, leaving the Chilean government no serious alternative but to assume the position of a reluctant guarantor. There can be little doubt that if each foreign creditor bank and each Chilean debtor bank had been left to work out its financial affairs under the applicable laws, a fair share of the foreign debt of the (failed or failing) Chilean banks would have been written off, and Chile's current debt service problems would consequently have been less.

V. Effects of Financial Reform: Interest Rates

One of the most puzzling features of the Chilean experience is the behavior of interest rates. Accordingly, it is one of the most thoroughly studied (Arellano (1983a and 1983b); Sjaastad (1983); Cortés (1983); Ffrench-Davis (1983); Meller and Solimano (1983); Corbo and Matte (1984); Rosende and Tosso (1984); Zahler (1985); Harberger (1985); Edwards (1986)) with a variety of methods. Zahler (1985) examined events chronologically and attempted to ascertain the changing weight of different factors in interest rate determination. But it is also possible to put forth a few hypotheses that, with some caveats, could apply to the period as a whole. We have taken the latter approach here, drawing generously from the published work on the subject.

Three main features characterize the behavior of Chilean interest rates in this period:

- High nominal peso rates, not easily explainable by international interest parity considerations;
- Extraordinarily high real interest rates on peso loans, exceeding an annual average of 76 percent between 1975 and 1982; and
- A high spread between loan and deposit rates denominated in pesos.

The subsections that follow discuss these features in some detail.

---

[24] Presumably because depositors could not distinguish between sound and unsound banks.

[25] Perhaps also at less cost to the economy at large, but the cost would depend on the magnitude and timing of the bank run.

Table 14. Dollar Interest Rates, 1975–83
(Annual percentages)

Year	Loan Rate[1] (1)	Deposit Rate[1] (2)	LIBOR[2] (3)	Spread[3] (4) = (1) − (3)	Spread[3] (5) = (2) − (3)
1975	86.7	3.1	7.7	79.0	−4.6
1976	118.3	44.3	6.1	112.2	38.2
1977	58.2	19.6	6.4	51.8	13.2
1978	51.1	32.7	9.4	41.7	23.3
1979	40.5	25.9	12.0	28.5	13.9
1980	46.9	37.4	14.1	32.8	23.3
1981	51.9	40.8	16.5	35.4	24.3
1982	−12.1	−20.4	13.2	−25.4	−33.6
1983	18.6	6.4	9.8	8.5	−3.4
1975–82[4]	55.2	22.9	10.7	44.5	12.2

Source: Zahler (1985).
[1]Nominal peso rates on short-term operations (30–90 days) minus actual exchange rate devaluation.
[2]Annual average of monthly data on six-month dollar rates.
[3]Loan rate minus LIBOR.
[4]Simple arithmetic average.

Nominal Interest Rates

As Table 14 reveals, nominal peso deposit rates (corrected for ex post devaluation) exceeded LIBOR for much of the period, except for the quarters after the maxi-devaluation of June 1982. A similar phenomenon emerges for peso loan rates. The differential is also substantial in this latter case, and highly positive for all years except for 1982. Only a small fraction of this differential can be attributed to the premium over LIBOR charged by international lenders to Chile. The average premium charged on loans to Chile was 1.55 percent in 1978, 0.99 percent in 1979 and 1980, 0.89 percent in 1981, and 0.97 percent in 1982 (Edwards (1986)). In short, nominal interest rates were "abnormally" high, given that accepted theory would predict a tendency toward interest rate equalization.

Of course, such a prediction assumes substantial capital mobility. It is useful to recall, however, that there were restrictions on capital inflows (albeit in declining magnitude) throughout the reform period.[26] These might explain a small portion of the remaining differential, but as these restrictions were relaxed over time, the spread fell only slightly.

Restrictions were applied not only on the length and type of capital inflows but also on the uses to which they could be put by domestic banks. As already mentioned, domestic banks were not permitted to take positions in foreign currency, and hence to arbitrage directly.[27] Sjaastad (1983) has argued that these restrictions, by requiring several transactions, made arbitrage very costly and therefore may be held responsible for the stubborn spread. Under such circumstances, "a Chilean banker may be indifferent between paying 3 percent per month for domestic funds as opposed to 1.5 percent for dollars." But as Cortés (1983) has pointed out, Chilean banks at no time seemed bent on arbitraging, and they did not oppose the restrictions. The two principal uses of foreign credit were for *grupo* loans and foreign trade financing. Hence, Cortés concludes that the Sjaastad hypothesis, although theoretically correct, is probably quantitatively unimportant.

Another commonly held explanation of deviation from interest parity (Arellano (1983b), and Zahler (1985)) alludes to market segmentation: borrowers who were privileged by their contacts or collateral (presumably the *grupos*) could borrow cheaply abroad; other borrowers had to resort to expensive credit in pesos. The idea is appealing in its simplicity and informal observation suggests that it probably has some validity, but it is difficult to test rigorously. Further doubts are cast by the Gálvez-Tybout observation (1985) that *grupo* firms do not seem to have enjoyed abnormally low borrowing costs.

Other authors (Corbo and Matte (1984)) have emphasized that Chilean and foreign assets were imperfect substitutes, and hence there was little reason to expect a convergence to interest parity. They have provided evidence to this effect by estimating a simple monetary model with three assets: money, domestic interest-earning assets, and foreign assets. In this model, under perfect substitutability and no sterilization, a decrease in domestic credit by the Central Bank should be matched by an *equal* capital inflow (reflected in higher reserves), which would leave the monetary base constant. For Chile, the estimated offset coefficient was -0.34, suggesting that asset substitutability was less than perfect (Corbo and Matte (1984)). The logic of this argument is indisputable, but once again its applicability to the specifics of the Chilean interest rate situation is unclear. Whatever the reason (and despite this apparent limitation in asset

[26] See Section I of this paper.
[27] Banks had to lend in dollars domestically, and another nonbank Chilean institution would subsequently carry out the lending in pesos.

substitutability), capital inflows to Chile were massive and unprecedented. That they had only a second-order impact on interest rates is still puzzling, even in the context of imperfect asset equivalence.

What about devaluation expectations? Even in a partially open economy, expectations of devaluation must have had some effect on peso interest rates. The problem, of course, is how to compute such expectations. Ex post devaluation was zero in 1980 and 1981 and very large in 1982, but fears of an abandonment of parity may have already been alive in 1981. Using Bayesian methods, in fact, Le Fort (1985) has estimated that the expected rate of devaluation rose from 2 percent in July 1979 (a month after the nominal rate was fixed) to more than 26 percent in May 1982, just prior to the maxi-devaluation. Assuming away such expectational problems, Edwards (1985) estimated an equation for the *nominal* interest rate as a function of ex post realized devaluation and other variables. The coefficient on the devaluation variable was significant and had the right sign, which suggests that devaluation expectations did indeed play a role.

Real balances (lagged one period) also were included in the Edwards equation, and also proved to be significant. This result fits the framework postulated by Edwards and Khan (1985): in an economy that is only partially integrated with world capital markets, domestic monetary policy will normally play a role in determining interest rates.

Real Interest Rates

Real interest rates in pesos (for both loans and deposits) were extraordinarily high between 1975 and 1983 (Table 15). In the words of Meller and Solimano (1983), "This sole fact inevitably had to lead to an economic and financial collapse." Certain features of the evolution of real rates over time can be explained with ease: After the capital account was partially liberalized in 1979, rates tended to fall; in 1981 and 1982, when inflation was lower than expected,[28] rates surged upward. Rosende and Tosso (1984) have suggested such a sequence. Using a simple Fisher-type consumption-savings model, they argue as follows: In the early years of the period, increases (real or perceived) in permanent wealth tended to reduce savings and to push up the real interest rate. This pressure was relieved somewhat by the entry of large amounts of foreign savings after 1979. As the crisis approached, capital inflows dried up. In the midst of a recession, domestic savings dried up as well, and the real interest rate shot up once again. The dynamics of such a process are highly plausible. However, even at their lowest in 1979 and 1980, real interest rates on peso loans averaged 19.4

---

[28] See discussion in Section IV of this paper.

Table 15. Real Interest Rates, 1975–83

Year	Real Peso Loan Rate	Real Peso Deposit Rate
1975	164.9	68.7
1976	176.4	125.1
1977	92.9	58.9
1978	55.0	38.6
1979	23.1	10.9
1980	15.7	8.5
1981	42.4	32.2
1982	42.4	29.7
1983	15.9	3.9
1975–82[1]	76.6	46.3

Sources: Central Bank of Chile; monthly rates taken from *Boletín Mensual* (several issues) annualized and corrected by official CPI. Rates correspond to short-term (30–90 days) bank transactions.
[1]Arithmetic average.

percent (LIBOR in those two years averaged 13.05 percent). Additional explanations still seem to be warranted.

As Edwards and Khan (1985) have emphasized, in a semi-open economy both "external" and domestic factors should help determine interest rates. The obvious external factors in this case are the international real interest rate and the expected real devaluation. Edwards (1985) reports that both factors seem to have been significant.[29] By contrast, Meller and Solimano (1983) attempted to assess the impact of the expected *nominal* devaluation (estimated with parallel exchange market data on ex post devaluation) on the real interest rate. Estimation of a reduced form of the Dornbusch (1980) model yielded a coefficient with a "wrong" sign for expected devaluation, suggesting no effect. Hence, the evidence is mixed concerning the effect of devaluation expectations on the real rate of interest. Casual empiricism, however, suggests that in 1979 and 1980 (at least) both the policymakers' commitment to the fixed exchange rate and the level of international reserves were high. At that time, expectations of devaluation

[29] Edwards (1985) apparently used the *realized* real devaluation as a proxy for expected changes.

Table 16. Nominal Interest Rates, 1975–83

Year	Nominal Peso Loan Rate	Nominal Peso Deposit Rate	Spread
1975	505.6	409.4	96.2
1976	350.7	299.4	51.3
1977	156.4	122.4	34.0
1978	85.3	68.9	16.4
1979	62.0	49.8	12.2
1980	46.9	39.7	7.2
1981	51.9	41.7	10.2
1982	63.1	50.4	12.7
1983	42.7	30.7	12.0
1975–82[1]	175.9	135.3	30.0

Sources: Central Bank of Chile; monthly rates taken from *Boletín Mensual* (several issues) and annualized. Rates correspond to short-term (30–90 days) bank transactions.
[1]Arithmetic average.

must have been very low, yet nominal deposit interest rates were still in the 40 to 50 percent range (Table 16). As far as demand factors are concerned, demand for real liquidity was fueled, as already mentioned, by the "bad loan problem" faced by banks. Harberger (1985) identifies this "artificial demand for credit" as one of the two key reasons why real interest rates in Chile were so high (the other being the "decapitalized" state of Chilean firms).

On the supply side, various authors have singled out a "credit crunch" as a cause of high real rates. Edwards (1985) expresses the view that the absence of sufficient real liquidity stands out as a significant factor. Meller and Solimano (1983) conclude that "monetary policy plays an important role in the determination of the real interest rate."

Care must be exercised, however, in ascertaining the source of this alleged credit crunch. Domestic credit grew 47.2, 30.4, and 97.1 percent in 1980, 1981, and 1982, respectively. (The corresponding inflation rates were 31.2, 9.5, and 20.7 percent.) Hence, booming demand, not tight supply, seems to have been at the root of this excess demand for credit, as Harberger hypothesized.

Spread Between Loan and Deposit Rates

Table 16 also suggests that there was a substantial spread between lending and deposit rates over the period, which accounts for part of the high absolute level of real loan rates. Although real interest paid on deposits was high (particularly in 1981 and 1982), it cannot fully explain the high rates charged for loans. Meller and Solimano (1983) maintain, as a result of their econometric work, that the spread is totally independent of the variables that determine the real interest rate. Hence, microeconomic factors must have been at work in maintaining the wedge between loan and deposit rates.

Early in the financial reform period the combination of high reserve requirements and substantial inflation was blamed for the spread. But as has been discussed in Section I, interest began to be paid on bank reserves in May 1976, and required reserve ratios were gradually brought down to very low levels. Hence, the effect of reserve requirements on bank costs was minimized over time. Another cost-based argument is that made by Sjaastad, and mentioned earlier, about the existence of arbitrage restrictions, but this argument is probably unimportant. Finally, it is commonly conjectured that Chilean banks' unit operating costs were much higher than those for comparable institutions in more developed countries. This feature has been variously attributed to inefficiency, inexperience, setup costs, and economies of scale, among other things, but assessment of its importance must await a detailed microanalysis of the banks' books. It is also possible that bank managers attempted to offset the high risk of their portfolios with a higher spread, or that bad loan reserve provisions forced the spread upward—such provisions constitute an "operating cost," after all.

Frequent mention is also made in the literature (Arellano (1983b); Meller and Solimano (1983); Zahler (1985)) of the oligopolistic characteristics of the Chilean banking system, but the dynamics of the process remain unclear.[30] Barriers to entry were reduced, and monopoly rents should have fallen over time. Vigorous competition seems to have existed among banks and *financieras*, but for some reason it focused on quantity and product differentiation and seems to have had little effect on financial prices.

A plausible though imperfect hypothesis to explain this puzzle goes like this: for a given market-determined deposit rate, the spread will depend on the cost of holding reserves, on operational costs, and on dividends paid to stockholders. Other things being equal, the higher the dividends paid, the larger is the spread. In Chile, banks found themselves with a large portion of nonperforming loans, so that their effective cash inflow was small

---

[30] Monopolistic competition actually seems a better label.

despite the high loan rates charged. Had nonperforming loans been of manageable size, banks could have lowered dividends or management salaries or other flexible costs to cushion the blow. Given the magnitude of accumulating bad debt, however, a crisis was inevitable.[31] Bankers then faced a dilemma: the higher the bank earnings and dividends are, the worse the cash flow of the firm and the sooner the crash would come. At one end, if dividends were infinity, the crisis would have occurred immediately; at the other extreme, if dividends were zero, the crisis would be postponed but the sum of dividends paid over the period also would be zero. Somewhere in between there had to be a rate of earnings/dividends —and hence the spread—that maximized the present value of bank owners' earnings. This was presumably the stable state the Chilean bankers chose.

VI. Four Theories of the Financial Crisis: Separating Micro from Macro Causes

The macroeconomic environment began to deteriorate dramatically in 1981. According to the indices computed by Corbo (1985), the real exchange rate appreciated about 45 percent between the second quarter of 1979 (when the nominal parity was fixed) and the end of 1981.[32] The trade balance worsened accordingly, and, for 1981, the current account deficit reached a staggering 14.3 percent of GDP (Table 1). Between October 1981 and June 1982, the Central Bank of Chile lost US$555 million in international reserves. The need for a real devaluation was by then beyond doubt. Policymakers considered a mandatory cut in money wages as a possible alternative to nominal devaluation, but the idea was soon dropped. The devaluation (18 percent in nominal terms) came in June, and it was accompanied by a relaxation of the indexation of minimum wages, which had put a floor to private sector wage adjustments, to ensure that a real devaluation would take place as well.[33] The public deemed the devaluation insufficient and speculation continued. An additional US$890 million in reserves was lost in the rest of the year, as floats and crawls were tried to stabilize the exchange market. An almost 90 percent nominal devaluation was to occur before the exchange market was stabilized. To cushion the impact, the authorities swiftly set up preferential exchange rates for dollar debtors.

[31] Losses per unit of time could not be fully offset by lowering costs and dividends.

[32] The actual figures are 46.8 percent for the ratio of nontradables' prices to export prices, and 38.3 percent for the ratio of nontradables' prices to import prices.

[33] Minimum wages had been readjusted at fixed intervals. Each such government-decreed rise matched the CPI inflation accumulated since the previous readjustments.

The Chilean financial crisis had begun to unfold in late 1981. By then the difficult macroeconomic conditions were taking their toll on the profit statements of firms, and business bankruptcies surged—most prominently, CRAV, a large sugar refining company, failed in May 1981. During the year, real interest rates, which had fallen in 1980, began climbing again, placing further strains on a weakened financial structure characterized by high debt/equity ratios among enterprises and a significant amount of nonperforming assets in the portfolios of banks.

The first public shock came in November 1981, when the Government decreed the "intervention" of three banks, a development bank, and four *financieras* that together accounted for more than one third of the loan portfolio of the financial system. Two of the banks were among the six largest private commercial banks in the country (Banco Español de Chile and Banco de Talca); the other was a small regional bank. The banks that were subjected to intervention began losing deposits in September 1981; the decline in deposits from August to December amounted to Ch$24 billion, of which almost Ch$16 billion took place in November. Throughout 1982, Chile was plagued by rumors and by evidence of further firm and bank problems, made more urgent by the rapidly worsening macroeconomic situation.[34] Fears were confirmed in January 1983, when the Government placed seven banks and one *financiera* under temporary government management.[35] These institutions held 45 percent of the outstanding loans and 41 percent of the total deposits in Chile. They included the nation's two largest private commercial banks (Banco de Chile and Banco de Santiago), which served as standard-bearers for the two most powerful *grupos*. Thereafter, a wide array of programs would be put into effect to stabilize the remaining institutions and to restructure and restore to health the ones in which the Government had intervened.[36]

What triggered a crisis of this magnitude? The financial system had long been engaged in a rather unstable process of credit expansion, but until sometime in 1981 international reserves and the real economy seemed to be booming anyway. There were two immediate activators of the collapse: First, capital inflows declined sharply (Table 3). In the first half of 1982, net capital inflow totaled US$889.2 million—only 36 percent of the inflow in the previous semester. Of course, much of this reduction had exogenous causes—the conflict between Britain and Argentina over the Falkland/

[34] The Government had to intervene two banks and one *financiera*, all quite small, accounting for 1.5 percent of total loans, during 1982.

[35] Three were immediately liquidated. In contrast with previous intervention, the Government guaranteed only 70 percent of deposits this time, but it became necessary to compensate 100 percent of the foreign creditors' claims.

[36] These measures are described in the next section of this paper.

Malvinas Islands, the Mexican problems of August 1982, and the generalization of the Latin American debt crisis. Second, asset prices dropped as a result of bankruptcies and the reversal of previously optimistic expectations. This drop had an unusually large effect on the financial health of firms, because a good portion of profits until then had consisted of (unrealized) capital gains.[37] After the fall in asset prices, many firms that had apparently suffered only from short-term liquidity problems were revealed to face long-term insolvency.

The hypotheses about the deeper or structural causes of the financial sector problem can be classified into four groups:

- External shock explanations: The negative impact from abroad (higher interest rates, deterioration of the terms of trade, credit rationing) was so large that no domestic financial system could have withstood it.
- Macro-shock explanations: The macroeconomic environment was sufficiently hostile, and variables (like the real interest rate and exchange rate) sufficiently out of line, to ensure the collapse of the financial system.
- Inherent market instability explanations: Unregulated markets can be destabilized by random events. This is especially true of financial markets, where elements such as expectations and trust play a key role. What happened in Chile was nothing but the unfortunate disequilibration of an otherwise sound market.
- Inadequate financial reform explanations: Reforms in Chile were carried out with little or no regard for possible market imperfections. Competition and the free flow of information were not sufficiently encouraged. The outcome was a predictable combination of several market failures (oligopoly pricing, moral hazard, adverse selection, etc.).

Of course, these four views are but caricatures that require appropriate qualifications. They serve, however, as focal points to structure our discussion.

From the point of view of the interaction of a troubled financial system with the economy at large, the first two explanations above are equivalent: both maintain that the problems came from outside the financial system. Two counterexamples are available to evaluate such an argument. First, consider what happened to the Chilean financial system the last time it suffered an external shock of this magnitude—in the 1930s. Despite all the caveats that such a comparison requires, it can be noted that during the Great Depression no Chilean bank went bankrupt; nor did any bank from the "major countries" in Latin America: Argentina, Brazil, and Mexico (Díaz-Alejandro (1983)). A second counterexample is the recent fate of Latin American countries that did not liberalize their financial systems but suffered great external stress as Chile did. Brazil, Peru, Colombia, and

[37] See Barandiarán (1983).

Venezuela experienced many macro and micro problems over the past decade, but not financial problems of the magnitude experienced by Chile. Of course, maintaining financial repression probably entails substantial costs, and so does keeping banks alive through more or less open subsidization (as some Latin American governments seem to have done in the 1930s). Such counterexamples, however, do suggest that governments have tools at their disposal that can, to some extent at least, reduce the vulnerability of a financial system to the vagaries of the macro environment. It seems undeniable that the Chilean Government did not use such tools in time during the crisis of the early 1980s.

It is also important to note that not all banks in Chile experienced the same difficulties in the recent period. The conservatively managed Banco del Estado (the nation's second largest) emerged from the crisis practically unscathed. So did the various foreign banks operating in Chile. Of course, all banks, private and state-owned, domestic and foreign, were subjected to the same macroeconomic storms. The key to their different fates seems to be in the differences in micro management, to which we now turn.

In contrast to the first two hypotheses, the last two hypotheses focus on the financial system itself in searching for the causes of the crisis. The third hypothesis stresses that such a crisis could have happened to any market system, given the inherent instability of financial markets and the severity of exogenous shocks during the period; the last hypothesis is that a crisis was bound to happen to *this* particular market system because of the nature of the institutions with which it had been endowed at the time of the financial reform. Obviously, severe shocks can disequilibrate even the soundest of markets. But whereas a sound market tends to cushion the effects of perturbations, an unsound one tends to magnify them. Unfortunately, the Chilean market seems to belong in the latter category. Regardless of the role played by other factors, it is difficult to escape the conclusion that the Chilean financial problem had perverse *micro* dynamics of its own, which in turn was made possible only by the peculiar pattern of ownership and regulation with which the system emerged from the process of reform. Ex post at least, the market failures visible in the Chilean financial markets belong to the textbook variety (moral hazard, adverse selection, oligopolistic pricing), which were fostered by certain government policies (implicit guarantees, lack of portfolio supervision, allowance of interlocking ownership, and lending patterns).

Furthermore, a strong case can be made that financial sector imbalances contributed to create the macro disequilibrium, and not just the other way around. Theorists of stabilization increasingly recognize the crucial role that credibility plays in disinflation-cum-reform programs.[38] Announced

---

[38] For a general treatment, see Sargent and Wallace (1986). For a treatment focused on the Southern Cone case, see Calvo (1986).

exchange rate policy clearly enjoyed substantial credibility until sometime in 1981, and such confidence was buttressed by healthy international reserves. But the stabilization program coexisted with a mounting private financial deficit that was clearly unsustainable in the long run and that, under the (apparently justified) assumption of implicit guarantee, would eventually become the responsibility of the Government. What measures (domestic credit creation, inflation, etc.) the Government would choose to deal with this problem could not be anticipated, but they were unlikely to be compatible with the maintenance of a fixed exchange rate, a cautious monetary policy, and careful management of expectations as the backbone of the anti-inflation policy.[39]

The point can be put slightly differently. It is often argued, as in the Argentine case, that the combination of a slow crawl of the exchange rate with a large fiscal deficit would make the policy package inconsistent and hence unworkable. What, then, was the inconsistency in the Chilean program, in which fiscal deficits had been contained? What variable played the role that the budget deficit played in Argentina? One possibility is the system of backward full wage indexation (Edwards (1985) and Corbo (1985)); combining it with a fixed exchange rate was tantamount, it is argued, to imposing two numeraires on the economy. Eventually, one had to give. The financial deficit can be suggested as an additional source of "incredibility" in the Chilean case. Díaz-Alejandro (1985) has hinted at this possibility:

> The massive use of Central Bank credit to "bail out" private agents raises doubts about the validity of pre-1982 analyses of the fiscal position and debt of the Chilean public sector. . . . Ex post, it turned out that the public sector, including the Central Bank, had been accumulating an explosive amount of contingent liabilities to both foreign and domestic agents, who held deposits in, or made loans to, the rickety financial system.

In other words, it is conceivable that the financial sector deficit played the role usually reserved for the fiscal deficit. As is the case with any deficit, it can be financed with bonds or with money creation. The Chilean deficit was financed at first with "bonds": banks borrowed abroad and central bank reserves swelled but domestic credit creation was cautious. Eventually, as the limit on foreign borrowing was reached and domestic bankruptcies increased, many banks were revealed to be significantly overextended. The Central Bank had to intervene or heavily subsidize them; in addition, it had to assume responsibility for servicing the foreign debt contracted by banks. The prudent fiscal and monetary stance had to be abandoned (at least temporarily), and the end of the exchange

---

[39] Aimed, of course, at maintaining the fixed parity.

rate regime could not be far away.[40] In the last quarter of 1981, the Central Bank extended almost US$1 billion of credit to the financial sector and lost about US$230 million in net foreign reserves; in the first six months of 1982 the Central Bank extended a further US$535 million of credit to the financial system, and lost an additional US$325 million of foreign reserves. There can be little doubt that the financial crisis contributed significantly to the loss of reserves and eventually to the collapse of the stabilization plan. First, the intervention of financial institutions led to a rapid expansion in net domestic credit of the Central Bank to support those institutions. Second, those interventions undermined confidence in the financial system, which contributed to the decline in the demand for domestic financial assets observed in 1982 and 1983. These two factors played a major role in generating expectations of higher inflation and of a depreciation of the peso, as international reserves were drawn down.

This is of course a highly stylized account, but it captures one crucial feature of the Chilean problem. The stabilization plan relied heavily on the moderation of inflationary expectations. This aim was initially achieved, but public confidence could not be sustained as long as a good share of the nation's banks and firms were perceived to be insolvent. After a period of confidence the public eventually adopted precautionary measures (such as beginning to accumulate foreign exchange) to protect itself from future policy changes. As a result, the Government's stabilization policy became even more difficult and costly to apply.

VII. Reacting to the Crisis

The Government's reaction to the macroeconomic troubles that became evident in 1981 appeared at first to be guided by the expectation that an "automatic adjustment" would occur in response to such disequilibrium. In particular, high real interest rates would reduce the pressure of domestic demand. The problem of an overvalued exchange rate also would correct itself: in the event of a balance of payments deficit, reserves would flow out and the resulting lower money base would push down the price of nontradables. But because such adjustments appeared to take too long, the Government decided to take a more activist policy stance beginning in May 1982. The Government aimed at easing the adjustment in relative prices by devaluing the peso. Moreover, it began to use monetary policy

---

[40] The amounts of central bank credit extended to the financial system appear in Table 18. This drastic increase was not matched immediately by a comparable increase in monetary aggregates for two reasons: (1) international reserves and hence the monetary base declined and (2) a massive amount of illiquid central bank paper was issued as part of the bank rescue package.

actively to moderate increases in interest rates, especially as external financing increasingly dried out. These efforts to reduce domestic rates were later helped by the decline in international interest rates; in this regard, beginning in 1984, the Central Bank strove to keep domestic rates competitive with international rates. In 1985, repayment of domestic debt of the nonfinancial public sector and increased reliance on foreign borrowing eased the need for public sector domestic borrowing. The Central Bank provided large credit flows at predetermined rates to financial institutions and "suggested" deposit rates to banks.

At the micro level, the Government's reasoning before the devaluation was similar: If any firms were near bankruptcy, they would voluntarily declare themselves so. The judicial system would carry out the necessary settlements and liquidations. If asset prices fell as a result, that would only reflect equilibrium conditions in the corresponding markets. The main exception to this hands-off position was a tightening of bank supervision by the Superintendency of Banks. As mentioned, in 1982, the Government attempted to encourage *grupos* to reduce their debt to the public and particularly to their own banks. The problem of the *cartera relacionada* was on its way to becoming a public issue.

Barandiarán (1983) conjectures that in mid-1981 firms' problems were still of a manageable magnitude so that a wave of liquidations would have been feasible both economically (asset prices would not have plummeted) and logistically (the judicial system could have handled the resulting workload). By mid-1982, a drastic solution of this sort was no longer feasible. A macro relief package was necessary, and it had to come from the Government.

The first round of intervention of financial institutions involving eight of them, came in November 1981. At this time, substantial amounts of credit began to flow from the Central Bank to the banking system. The June 1982 devaluation put further strains on the ability of banks and firms to service dollar debts, and more vigorous palliative policies began to be adopted. Further rescue measures would be put into effect as part of the early 1983 bank interventions and until early 1985.

Measures to Aid Domestic Borrowers

Reprogramming of Loans to Firms

In 1983 and 1984, the Central Bank established schemes to enable banks to reschedule a portion of their loans to firms. Lenders granted firms lower interest rates and longer maturities. Because these measures would worsen banks' liquidity and reduce their profits, the Central Bank introduced a scheme of subsidization that is described in the next subsection.

Under the 1983 program, rescheduled debts of firms in pesos carried a real interest rate of 7 percent. The terms for dollar loans were identical except that the 7 percent interest applied to each payment in U.S. dollars (equivalent) on the basis of the current exchange rate. All borrowers were to repay the rescheduled credits in ten years, with a grace period of five years for principal and one year for interest. The second debt rescheduling, implemented in 1984, expanded the amounts eligible for rescheduling, lowered interest rates (5 percent real for the first two years, rising in steps to 7 percent from the sixth year), lengthened the maturities to up to 15 years, and granted more favorable treatment for smaller debtors.

From the point of view of debtors, these were not easy terms. In the first round (1983) 51 percent of the financial system's loans were reprogrammed at subsidized interest rates (7 percent in real terms). The remainder was left at market rates (15 percent, real). The resulting average effective real rate—more than 11 percent—was still quite onerous, especially given the recessive economy.

This program was substantial: by the end of 1984 rescheduled loans accounted for 21.4 percent of domestic credit.[41] There were some restrictions on eligibility: foreign trade credit and loans to legally bankrupt firms, to other financial institutions, and to holding companies could not be reprogrammed. Nevertheless, this "blanket" program made no effort to separate viable borrowers from those that were not. Whereas, under the 1983 program, the Central Bank sought to reschedule a mandatory minimum 30 percent of the debts of all eligible debtors, the 1984 program varied the rescheduled percentage according to the size of loans. Since late 1985 the possibility of a "case by case" rescheduling exercise had been discussed, but only a program for small debtors was implemented—in 1986—and without any subsidy or credit from the Central Bank. This program included supervisory incentives and penalties aimed at encouraging banks to regularize the situation of small borrowers.

Reprogramming of Housing Loans (Mortgages)

A similar program was established for mortgage debts. Amounts to be rescheduled included installments unpaid since 1981 and a decreasing percentage of installments payable between 1983 and 1987. The rescheduled amounts became loans denominated in UFs (for *Unidad de Fomento*, a unit of account indexed to the CPI) and carrying 8 percent annual interest. The Central Bank purchased part of the rescheduled loans from the financial institutions with a note in UFs also at 8 percent, and refinanced the remainder of the rescheduled payments with a central bank line of credit carrying 7 percent real annual interest.

Under this scheme, more than 36,000 loans were reprogrammed. Re-

---

[41] This figure was to drop to 16.4 percent in the course of 1985.

scheduled amounts were not very large—about US$120 million outstanding as of August 1985.

Sectoral Lines of Credit

As part of efforts to cushion the effects of the crisis on some sectors and to revive other sectors, the Central Bank established some special lines of credit. Some of these have been targeted to working capital needs, payroll financing, labor hiring incentives, construction and public works, and reforestation. They all provide credit to firms at below-market rates. They also carry an implicit subsidy for the financial intermediary involved, because the cost of central bank credit for these lines of credit is lower than banks are allowed to charge the user.

Measures to Aid Financial Intermediaries

Emergency Loans to Banks

At the start of the crisis, emergency loans were granted to banks in which the Central Bank had intervened and others. When more comprehensive aid packages were put in place, loans were repaid and converted to equity.

Subsidies to Facilitate Reprogramming of Loans

As noted earlier, the loan reprogramming was facilitated by the provision of subsidies to the banks and *financieras* involved: The Central Bank extended to financial institutions lines of credit to be repaid within ten years at a real interest rate of 5 percent, with a grace period of five years for principal and one year for interest; in turn, financial institutions were to use the funds to buy six-year central bank notes on which payments were made quarterly at an annual rate of 12 percent.[42,43] In short (and abstracting from the different maturities), banks exchanged their own paper yielding 5 percent for central bank paper yielding 12 percent, thereby receiving a 7 percent spread (with no risk) as subsidy.

Purchase of Risky Loans by Central Bank

Beginning in 1982, the Central Bank decided to facilitate the recapitalization of the banking system. The first scheme, announced in July 1982, involved a central bank purchase of the substandard loan portfolio of banks

---

[42] Credits are denominated in UFs.

[43] The rates on dollar-denominated notes carried a yield of LIBOR plus 2.125 percent or the prime rate plus 2 percent, at the financial institution's option. These notes (both domestic and dollar denominated) were transferable only among financial institutions.

up to 100 percent of the capital and reserves of each bank. The Central Bank would pay for this purchase by issuing non-interest-bearing central bank bonds. Banks would have to repurchase 5 percent of these loans every six months for ten years. Both the loans and the bonds would be adjusted for inflation. This scheme improved the balance sheet position of the banks involved by temporarily removing substandard assets from their portfolios and by effectively giving them the possibility of writing off bad loans over a ten-year period.

A more comprehensive recapitalization scheme was introduced in February 1984.[44] In essence, the new scheme provided for the Central Bank to purchase with cash substandard loans at par for up to 150 percent of capital and reserves of each bank. To reduce the monetary effect of this cash purchase, the selling bank had to use the proceeds to repay any outstanding emergency loans from the Central Bank, and had to use any remaining balances to purchase central bank *pagarés* (IOUs). Once again, the implicit subsidy was substantial: the central bank *pagarés* carried a real rate of return of 7 percent (UF plus 7 percent) and a four-year maturity. Banks could also exchange an additional amount of substandard loans (up to 100 percent of their capital and reserves) for a non-interest-bearing, nontransferable central bank note. Loans exchanged for central bank notes had to be repurchased over ten years at their initial real value. Loans sold for cash had to be repurchased at their initial value plus a 5 percent real interest rate over ten years. Bank shareholders were required, at the time of sale, to devote all dividends on their shareholdings to this repurchase until the repurchase was completed. New capital contributions also faced a partial limitation on dividends—only up to 30 percent of earnings could be distributed as dividends—until the loan repurchase was completed. By the end of August 1985, the amount of bad loans sold by the commercial banks had reached US$2.36 billion (domestic banks accounted for 96 percent; and "intervened" banks for 75 percent). Although initially only banks that had not been subjected to intervention were allowed to sell substandard loans to the Central Bank, from 1985 the intervened banks also were allowed to participate. As a result, the purchases of substandard loans continued through 1987.[45]

In addition, the Government decided to recapitalize intervened banks directly. A law passed in February 1985 allowed the Superintendency of Banks to require intervened institutions to increase their equity to make

[44] Loans repurchased in 1982 had to be converted to the 1984 scheme. The new scheme also aimed to increase the liquidity of banks.

[45] To facilitate this process, new regulations approved in May 1986 allowed for the purchase by the Central Bank as substandard portfolio up to 350 percent of new capital contributions. As of March 1987, total purchases of substandard loan portfolios by the Central Bank amounted to about Ch$676 billion.

them financially viable.[46] The new stock would be offered first to existing stockholders and then to third parties. Any portion of the required capital stock that was not subscribed would be purchased by CORFO, Chile's state development agency. CORFO would pay for these shares by assuming the emergency credits that intervened banks had earlier received from the Central Bank. In other words, the Central Bank emergency credits were converted to equity. CORFO would have to sell its bank shares within five years, at a rate of 20 percent per year as a minimum. Any unsold stock would be automatically transferred free of cost to the shareholders that had already contributed to the equity increase. Moreover, the law established that at no point could CORFO shares of a bank exceed 49 percent of the bank's capital. Any losses under this program would accrue to the Central Bank, although the law provides for reimbursement from the Treasury up to a certain amount.

To attract interest in the shares of effectively bankrupt institutions, CORFO made the terms very attractive. Only a small down payment was necessary; the balance was payable in 10 years at 5 percent real interest.[47] With some limits, individuals with no tax arrears enjoyed even more favorable conditions: 15 years and no real interest. Buyers of such stock also enjoyed substantial fiscal advantages: not only tax-exempt dividends but also a tax credit equivalent to 20 percent of the value of shares purchased.

Through these mechanisms, the five intervened banks were returned to the private sector during 1986. Four were fully capitalized and sold, including the largest two in the nation, Banco de Santiago and Banco de Chile. The shares of these two banks were sold to more than 57,000 shareholders by December 1986, and their management was subsequently fully privatized. The fifth bank, Colocadora Nacional de Valores, was merged with the Banco de Santiago.

Other Relief Measures

Preferential Exchange Rate

In mid-1982, the Central Bank established a preferential exchange rate for debt-service payments on certain dollar-denominated loans.[48] Since December 1982, the resulting subsidy has been paid with negotiable

---

[46] Recapitalization was a prerequisite for selling substandard loans to the Central Bank.

[47] UF adjustment plus 5 percent.

[48] In effect, the program provided debtors with access to foreign exchange at a below-market price. The implicit subsidy can be calculated as $S = D(E_o - E_p)$, where S = subsidy (in pesos), D = dollar amount purchased by domestic resident to service dollar debt, E_o = official exchange rate, and E_p = preferential exchange rate.

central bank notes that have a maturity of six years.[49] In 1984, the Central Bank introduced some restrictions on access to this program. In 1985, further restrictions were enacted, and it was decreed that the program would be gradually phased out.[50] As a result, although the devaluation of the peso in February and June of 1985 increased the total cost of the program for that year, the cost subsequently dropped.[51]

Interest Subsidies on Swap Operations

Since 1983, swap operations have provided a hedge to domestic agents possessing dollar liabilities. Outstanding swaps of dollars derived from the repayment of certain foreign currency loans by domestic residents to local banks were converted into dollar-denominated accounts at the Central Bank, carrying a yield of six-month LIBOR plus a spread.[52] Banks can only draw funds from these accounts in order to purchase foreign exchange to service their external debt. Against the remaining balance the Central Bank issues peso-denominated lines of credit to banks at a predetermined real interest rate. In the course of 1985, measures were taken to moderate the effect of the subsidy. The premium over LIBOR that the Central Bank paid on these deposits was gradually reduced, and eliminated by February 1987, and the Government made efforts to decrease the immediate monetary effect of the program. The Central Bank also established a schedule for the elimination of the subsidy on swaps; for new operations, this subsidy was eliminated by the end of April 1987.

The most important result of all these relief programs is that they kept the banking system functioning, however tenuously. The importance of this development for an economy trying to climb out of a deep recession cannot be overstated. As the overall economy recovered somewhat (real GDP grew by 6.3 percent in 1984 and 2.4 percent in 1985), the business bankruptcy problem was less dramatic than it was in 1982, and banks' fortunes rose accordingly. In 1985, the banking system as a whole showed after-tax profits amounting to 6.2 percent of capital, the first such profits

---

[49] Before that it was paid in cash, with the consequent expansionary impact.

[50] In February 1984, most public enterprises were excluded from the subsidy, and the access of firms engaged in export activities was limited. In 1985, when the Government decided to phase out the system, the subsidy was maintained for debts of US$50,000 or less outstanding.

[51] Until mid-1985 the preferential rate was indexed to inflation. Hence, real devaluations increased the spread between the preferential and market rates, and the size of the subsidy.

[52] Notice that devaluation of the peso increases the domestic currency value of these deposits and creates a loss for the Central Bank. Devaluation adjustments are accrued but not paid in cash, thus postponing the monetary effect. Only the interest on these accounts is paid in cash, and then only in pesos.

since 1981. In 1986, the system registered profits of about 4 percent of capital.[53]

The bank rescue operation, together with the decline in international interest rates, may also have facilitated a moderation of domestic interest rates (Table 17). This overall encouraging trend obscures some short-term cyclical fluctuations. In the course of 1985, for instance, as banks tried to shield themselves from the losses from certain problem loans, real loan rates rose slightly (even as deposit rates edged down). But real rates declined again in 1986, presumably aided by the fall in international rates.

The counterpart to the improved asset position of many banks (fewer problem loans, less *cartera relacionada*) has been a dramatic increase in central bank financing of commercial banks. For instance, this financing became more important than deposits as a source of funding (Table 18). Moreover, as of June 1985, outstanding borrowing in pesos from the Central Bank amounted to four times the capital and reserves of the banking system and was equivalent to almost 50 percent of the sum of loans and foreign assets of the system. A similar point can be made for the income figures, dependent as they are on central bank support. As a result of the support extended to the rest of the financial system and of the preferential exchange rate subsidy, central bank credit (in terms of liabilities to the private sector) rose by 94 percent in 1982 and by a further 433 percent in 1983 (Table 19). The bulk of central bank credit in 1983 consisted of credit to financial intermediaries and transfers to banks and the corporate sector as part of the preferential exchange rate and other programs involving subsidies. During 1984, the credit expansion of the Central Bank slowed down to 174 percent, even though the Central Bank continued to be the principal channel of foreign loans to Chile.

During 1985, central bank credit increased by about 200 percent, largely reflecting the losses arising from the preferential exchange rate and swap subsidies discussed earlier, which are registered as "other assets" in Table 19. Credit expansion was financed to a much larger extent from domestic sources in 1985 than in 1984: liabilities to the private sector increased by about 90 percent, especially reflecting the issuance of medium-term notes to finance the preferential exchange rate subsidy. The issuance of central bank paper limited the immediate liquidity effect of the subsidies, which nevertheless has had to be offset as this paper matured and its interest was paid.[54]

---

[53] The decrease reflected the reduction in central bank subsidies summarized earlier.

[54] The spectacular growth of central bank credit to the financial system is in evidence in Table 19. The effect of such credit on monetary aggregates, however, has been moderated by the massive issue of central bank paper (Table 20). Such bond financing of government spending is subject to the limits discussed by Sargent and Wallace (1986).

Table 17. Interest Rates on 30–89–Day Operations of Commercial Banks, 1981–86

(In percent per month)[1]

	Nominal		Real[2]	
	Loans	Deposits	Loans	Deposits
Annual average				
1981	52.0	40.8	38.7	28.6
1982	63.1	47.8	35.1	22.4
1983	42.7	27.9	15.9	3.9
1984	37.2	26.1	11.4	2.3
1985	40.4	31.6	11.4	4.1
1983				
March	3.1	2.2	1.2	0.3
June	3.0	2.1	1.4	0.4
September	2.8	1.9	0.5	− 0.4
December	2.6	1.8	2.0	1.2
1984				
March	1.7	0.9	− 0.8	− 1.5
June	2.1	1.4	0.8	0.1
September	2.1	1.2	− 0.8	− 1.7
December	4.2	2.9	2.7	1.5
1985				
January	3.0	1.9	− 0.1	− 1.2
February	3.5	2.6	1.5	0.6
March	3.3	2.7	0.5	− 0.1
April	3.9	3.4	1.6	1.1
May	3.4	2.9	1.4	0.9
June	3.1	2.6	− 0.6	− 1.0
July	3.6	3.1	2.3	1.8
August	2.3	1.8	1.4	0.9
September	1.9	1.4	0.7	0.2
October	2.1	1.7	0.6	0.2
November	2.1	1.7	0.5	0.1
December	2.3	1.9	1.0	0.6
1986				
January	2.2	1.7	− 0.5	− 0.9
February	2.7	2.0	1.8	1.1
March	1.9	1.3	0.4	− 0.2
April	2.1	1.6	0.7	0.2
May	2.0	1.5	1.3	0.8
June	1.6	1.0	0.3	− 0.3
July	1.8	1.4	0.8	0.4
August	1.7	1.2	1.1	0.6
September	1.5	0.9	—	0.6
October	1.9	1.6	0.4	0.1
November	2.0	1.6	0.6	0.2
December	2.0	1.6	0.5	0.1

Source: Central Bank of Chile, *Síntesis Monetaria y Financiera.*
[1]Weighted average of the rates on all operations during the month.
[2]The nominal rate less variation in the CPI during the month.

**Table 18. Central Bank Financing
of Commercial Banks, 1981 and 1985**
(In percent)

Credit from Central Bank Relative to	June 1981	June 1985
Commercial bank deposits in domestic and foreign currency	6.9	117.2
Domestic loans and foreign assets of commercial banks	3.4	49.8
Commercial banks' capital accounts	26.9	400.1

Source: International Monetary Fund, *International Financial Statistics.*

Similarly, despite the progress on the interest rate front, some problems proved to be more difficult. Despite the fall in deposit and lending rates, spreads continued to be substantial, as banks attempted to offset losses from bad loans not sold to the Central Bank (Table 17). The reduction in interest rates owed a great deal as well to government aid. Without these transfers from the Central Bank, interest rates charged to new borrowers would probably have been much higher.

A reasonable case can be made that the measures taken since 1982 served to postpone and dilute over time the effects of the crisis. Progress was made in many areas, but key issues remained to be settled.

One such issue was the determination of conditions that would enable individuals and enterprises to service their rescheduled debts without incurring further unpayable obligations. As mentioned earlier, the conditions faced by borrowers (unlike those for lenders) were quite stringent from the start, creating great pressures for further reprogrammings and concessions. According to Arellano (1984),

> The granting of very strict reprogramming conditions—which are not sustained later on—has been typical since 1982. . . . In the end, experience has demonstrated that unrealistic conditions such as the ones that prevailed both before and after the reprogrammings cannot be applied to debtors, and in the long run they end up raising costs and further eroding credibility.

Even after loans had been reprogrammed, the bad debt problem persisted: in 1985, overdue loans as a percentage of all loans started to rise

Table 19. Central Bank Operations, 1982–85
*(Percentage change with respect to liabilities
to private sector at beginning of period)*

	1982	1983	1984	1985
Net international reserves	−94.5	−93.2	−13.0	−1.6
Net domestic credit	94.4	433.4	174.3	199.6
Net credit to nonfinancial public sector[1]	−36.9	−9.8	69.8	−50.1
SINAP	15.2	26.5	18.0	21.0
Credit to private sector	−0.4	21.2	−0.9	0.4
Net credit to financial intermediaries	167.0	375.8	−30.4	18.6
Capital and reserves[2]	−77.2	−56.1	55.0	−29.9
Other assets	26.7	75.9	62.8	239.6
Net medium- and long-term foreign liabilities[3]	6.4	235.0	133.6	108.2
Liabilities to private sector	−6.4	105.2	27.5	89.7
Currency	−1.6	18.0	10.6	10.9
Other[4]	−4.9	87.2	17.0	78.8
Memorandum items:				
Total net foreign liabilities (in billions of pesos)	101.1	328.2	146.7	109.9
Inflation rate (CPI)	20.7	23.1	23.0	26.4

Source: Central Bank of Chile.

[1]Excludes holdings of treasury notes on account of the 1983–85 capitalization of the Central Bank. These notes are included in other assets.

[2]A negative sign implies an increase in capital and reserves.

[3]Includes foreign liabilities on account of deposits placed by the corporate sector in the Central Bank in the context of the 1983–85 rescheduling agreements with foreign commercial banks.

[4]Includes medium-term notes issued by the Central Bank to finance the preferential exchange rate subsidy.

Table 20. Holdings of Financial Assets by Private Sector, 1982–85

(Rate of growth, in percent)

	1982	1983	1984	1985 I	1985 II	1985 III	1985 IV	Year
Changes in nominal stocks[1]	*13.6*	*21.4*	*30.0*	*13.8*	*9.5*	*11.3*	*9.0*	*51.2*
Money	7.3	27.7	12.0	5.8	1.6	-1.9	5.6	11.3
Other assets	14.9	20.2	33.8	15.2	10.8	13.3	9.4	58.2
Quasi-money[2]	11.1	1.3	36.4	11.4	11.4	11.5	7.5	48.9
Central bank notes	38.5	424.0	32.5	44.1	15.2	26.5	16.5	144.5
Treasury notes	—	263.8	-0.4	11.0	-5.7	2.6	14.2	22.7
Changes in real stocks[1,3]	*-5.9*	*-1.4*	*5.7*	*5.2*	*1.2*	*7.6*	*4.3*	*19.6*
Money	-11.1	3.8	-9.1	-2.2	-6.1	-5.2	1.1	-11.9
Other assets	-4.8	-2.3	8.8	6.5	2.4	9.5	4.8	25.1
Quasi-money[2]	-8.0	-17.8	10.9	3.0	3.0	7.8	3.0	17.8
Central bank notes	14.7	325.6	7.7	33.2	6.5	22.3	11.6	93.5
Treasury notes	—	195.6	-9.5	2.6	-12.9	-0.8	9.3	-2.9
Memorandum items:								
Changes in real stocks[3]	-5.9	-1.4	5.7	5.2	1.2	7.6	4.3	19.6
Held by private social security funds	213.1	78.0	32.1	8.6	7.2	10.5	8.0	38.9
Held by rest of private sector	-12.1	-10.2	0.5	4.3	-0.4	6.8	3.3	14.6

Source: Central Bank of Chile.

[1] Foreign currency deposits are valued at the end-of-period exchange rate.

[2] Includes time and savings deposits, mortgage bonds, and foreign currency deposits.

[3] Nominal changes deflated by changes in CPI.

again. Improved economic conditions beginning in 1986 have gradually diminished the importance of this problem.[55]

Reform of Bank Regulations and Legislation

As part of the response to the financial crisis, the prudential regulations were strengthened (as discussed in Section IV) and a new legislative framework was developed to govern the restructured financial system. But, in the immediate aftermath of the crisis, it was necessary to allow sufficient flexibility in the application of various legal and accounting regulations to permit time for adjustment. In the period following the 1981 and 1983 interventions, this flexibility encompassed the time allowed for an overdue loan to be transferred to the nonperforming portfolio, the term for constituting individual provisions, the rules governing disposal of physical assets acquired by banks from debtors, the accruals of interest, and the definition of capital and reserves for the purpose of capital adequacy regulations. Only in late 1984, new regulations were issued to return to more orthodox accounting practices. Also, since January 1983, the general deposit guarantee had been extended from time to time, and in June 1986, deposit insurance was granted only to domestic Chilean banks that met specified minimum capital requirements and only upon application by each bank.[56]

In November 1986, a new banking law was enacted that modified several key aspects of existing legislation in order to give formal status to existing supervisory practices, to further strengthen prudential regulations, and to streamline the deposit guarantee scheme. The main aim of the reform was to minimize the need for state intervention in the financial system by facilitating market self-regulation.[57] The law also tried to

[55] The indicators prepared by the Superintendency of Banks and Financial Institutions show that overdue loans that had represented 3.5 percent of banks' loan portfolios as of December 1985 and 3.8 percent as of December 1986 had fallen to 2.9 percent as of August 1987. However, for the same dates, the ratio of loans sold to the Central Bank over all loans (i.e., loans in banks' loan portfolios plus loans sold to the Central Bank) equaled 20.9, 23.8, and 23.0 percent. Thus, part of the improvement in the quality of banks' portfolios might have been attributable to further sales of bad loans to the Central Bank.

[56] Financial institutions that receive a state guarantee pay a commission of 0.0625 percent on the average amount of guaranteed deposits.

[57] In explaining the measures, the Superintendency of Banks and Financial Institutions pointed to the need "to emphasize the private nature of the financial system, not only as regards its operation and ownership but, especially, its mechanisms to distribute risks and absorb losses . . . agents participating in the market—bankers, debtors and depositors—have a central responsibility to oversee the good use of the funds entrusted to financial institutions." *Información Financiera*, Superintendencia de Bancos e Institutiones Financieras, December 1986, p. IX.

eliminate some of the practices that had led to problems in the past, such as lending to related groups.

To increase information to the public, the new law directed the Superintendency to publish detailed information on the type and quality of the assets of each of the financial institutions it supervises, at least three times a year. The law also sets different levels of confidentiality. Strict confidentiality applies only to deposits and other sources of funds to the financial system. Banks are allowed to release other information to firms specializing in the analysis of financial institutions and, more generally, to anyone with a legitimate interest—provided such disclosure cannot be seen to harm a bank customer.

The law also strengthened bank supervision by converting previous superintendency regulations into law and making some superintendency powers more explicit. It also defined more precisely the concept of bank client, in order to take into account interrelated ownership.

The foregoing measures were intended to give depositors better information about the soundness of financial institutions. As a consequence, the authorities thought that state deposit insurance should be reserved only for small savers, for whom 90 percent coverage of their time deposits with a maximum of 120 UFs remained. The elimination of the state insurance on other deposits has been taking place gradually, and was to have been completed in 1989. Sight deposits, however, will still be fully protected. Banks have to maintain in liquid central bank or treasury assets the equivalent of sight deposit balances exceeding two and a half times the bank's capital. Moreover, should a bank be unable to meet its sight deposit obligations by selling off those liquid assets, the Central Bank would advance the necessary funds. In other words, sight deposits remain fully protected, but banks' freedom to invest such deposits has been circumscribed. A bank with insolvency problems can, subject to approval by the Superintendency of Banks and Financial Institutions, enter into agreements with its creditors proposing ways to meet its obligations. All bank creditors are eligible for these agreements, except holders of sight deposits and time deposits—to the extent that the latter are covered by the state deposit insurance. These agreements may include partial or total capitalization of eligible bank liabilities, extension of the maturity of the liability, and partial write-off. Lack of agreement of an insolvent bank with its creditors is one of the grounds for the Superintendency to liquidate the bank.

The new law has tightened capital requirements. A bank has to increase its capital not only when it no longer meets the minimum capital requirement, as previous law mandated, but also when it does not comply with the required ratio between its capital and reserves, and deposits and other liabilities. The law establishes the period within which recapitalization must take place; in case of noncompliance, the bank is forbidden from increasing its loans or any other investments, except central bank instruments. The law also facilitates the rescue of one troubled bank by another bank. The rescuing bank can lend up to the equivalent of 25 percent of its capital to the troubled bank for two years. The loan can only be repaid if the latter bank has been sufficiently recapitalized, without including the loan for this computation. If the loan is not repaid within two years, it can be used as a capital contribution, in case of merger of the two institutions, or to capitalize the borrowing bank, but with the shares remaining in the hands of the borrowing bank.

Although it is too soon to assess the effects of the new legal framework on the functioning of the banking system, the foregoing reforms constitute an interesting attempt to balance the desire to minimize the state's interference with private banks against the state's perceived responsibilities in monetary policy. The law appears to assign a much greater degree of responsibility to the state to ensure the smooth functioning of the payments system than to protect the private sector's time deposits and other liabilities.[58]

VIII. Avoiding and Managing Financial Crises: Some Lessons from the Chilean Experience

This section presents nine lessons about managing (and avoiding) financial crisis from the Chilean experience:

- Financial liberalization is likely to be characterized by rapid growth in quasi-money and the creation of new forms of financial intermediation. But conventional indicators of financial "deepening" or "widening" may be misleading in two senses.

First, ratios like M2/GDP may rise precipitously as a result of substitution away from other assets or sudden inflows of foreign savings. The growth of short-term financial assets does not imply (or require) a better national savings performance; nor does it necessarily entail an efficiency gain, as, for instance, in the channeling of resources away from stores of value with low marginal product toward more productive assets.

Second, financial "deepening" and "widening" are not necessarily tantamount to the emergence of well-developed financial markets, if "well-developed financial markets" means a situation in which key markets exist and relative prices are reasonably close to any conceivable range of social optima. Markets for long-term transactions, in particular, develop only

---

[58] This differential treatment of sight and time deposits resembles the ideas included in the "Chicago plan for monetary reform" advanced in the 1930s, which are discussed in Friedman (1959), Chap. 3.

slowly, even in the context of cautious fiscal and monetary policies and declining inflation. Real interest rates can remain extremely high and erratic, far from the course of variables like the marginal product of real capital. For these and other reasons, investment can stagnate even as financial intermediation booms.

- Conceptually, two internally consistent ways of organizing a financial system can be distinguished: (1) laissez-faire, without supervision but also without government insurance and a binding and credible pre-commitment ruling out future bailouts; and (2) government-provided deposit insurance, which is then sold to banks at actuarially fair prices (to reduce the adverse selection and moral hazard problems typical of insurance schemes, the Government exercises stringent supervision of bank activities).

The choice between the two systems (or combinations of them) should ultimately be guided by empirical considerations, but one warning should be kept in mind: Laissez-faire will work in financial markets only if information flows are efficient and inexpensive, so that customers can easily assess the soundness of a bank's operations; and if the behavior of depositors and creditors is rational, so that problems in one bank will not lead to runs at other otherwise sound institutions. If these two rather demanding conditions are not met, then government-provided deposit insurance ought to be the choice of the cautious policymaker.

- The Chilean experience suggests that effective bank supervision should not be limited to the enforcement of certain key required minimum ratios. Interlocking ownership patterns cause such huge problems that they breathe new life into the old-fashioned principle that cautions against banks' ownership of firms, or vice versa. It is highly doubtful that Chilean banks would have extended so many unsound loans if many of them had not gone to banks' own related enterprises. Without this sizable *cartera relacionada*, a financial crisis of Chile's proportions could never have occurred.

- When financial liberalization is carried out in a high-inflation setting, a special problem arises. Highly negative (controlled) real interest rates usually are a serious problem under financial repression, and reformers clamor for their elimination. The Chilean experience from 1975 to 1985 suggests that sustained highly positive real rates can constitute at least as serious a problem. When real rates stubbornly remain above any conceivable rate of return on investment, problems among businesses will become widespread. A business's borrowing decision is then distorted: rather than borrow to invest or to finance working capital, many businesses will borrow to pay interest or simply to stave off bankruptcy. Under institutional arrangements such as Chile's, the problem can quickly snowball and will inevitably lead to a systemwide crisis.

It is also important to notice that even in an economy as open as Chile's, policy can have an important effect on domestic interest rates, both nominal and real. A central conclusion of this paper is that *domestic* supply and demand factors were the most important causes of high interest rates. This suggests, among other things, that it may have been a mistake to assume, without further verification, that only fully open economy models were to be used in designing and evaluating policies in Chile.

- An "artificial demand" for credit, arising from continuous bank lending to troubled enterprises, seems to have been a major force behind high domestic interest rates. The rolling over of scheduled principal payments and the capitalization of interest tended to increase the demand for credit. In turn, banks tended to raise deposit rates in order to attract domestic resources to finance these practices. Loan rates went up correspondingly, bringing further difficulties to the immense majority of firms whose peso borrowing was short term.

  It is noteworthy that the upward pressure on interest rates remained even at times when monetary policy was somewhat expansionary. This suggests that, when setting monetary targets, architects of stabilization programs should closely monitor institutional developments in credit markets and the composition of credit recipients. What may seem like a generous rate of credit expansion to the private sector may turn out to be unduly restrictive if the lion's share is taken up by the needs of troubled firms.[59]

- Although macroeconomic shocks can aggravate economywide financial problems, the ways in which financial crises can aggravate macroeconomic disequilibrium are less well understood. As already mentioned, business problems, credit demand, and interest rates will probably be connected. In the presence of high real interest rates, private investment will predictably suffer. But most important, the accumulation of "excess" domestic debt can introduce serious distortions into the formulation and effects of macroeconomic policies. If the perception exists that depositors, borrowers, or financial intermediaries are under the Government's protective umbrella, agents in the economy can come to expect that future bailouts will require the abandonment of fiscal and monetary prudence. Even if explicit or implicit insurance does not exist, a wave of bankruptcies may induce policymakers to adopt expansionary policies. Alternatively, the authorities may choose to create inflation in order to wipe off part of the debt and shift some of the adjustment burden from debtors to creditors. In short, the presence of a serious financial imbalance calls into question the credibility of any stabilization program that

---

[59] Possible inflationary consequences of increased credit expansion remain, of course.

may be put into practice. Moreover, this loss of credibility can become a self-fulfilling expectation.

- Voluntarily declared bankruptcies (of firms or banks) will not act as a brake to the unstable financial dynamics that this paper has described. Managers face great incentives to postpone bankruptcy almost at all costs, realizing that the bigger the problem, the more likely it is that some sort of relief will be forthcoming. In the early stages of the problem, the authorities would be well advised to use all measures within their power to counter this logic. Practices like distress borrowing should be monitored and discouraged. The price of financial stability may well be eternal vigilance. This maxim holds even for governments with a preference for laissez-faire: when the bad debt problem becomes sufficiently large, prior commitments against bailouts become unenforceable and hence less credible.

- If the problem becomes so widespread that government intervention is inevitable, a central aim of policy should be to uproot the problem as decisively as possible. Decisive action begins with taking stock of the situation at once and avoiding the temptation publicly to minimize the importance of the problem—or worse, implying that with a bit of patience it will go away. It is important to make a realistic estimate of the present value of the transfers necessary to restore troubled banks and firms to health. If subsidies are to be granted, debts rescheduled, and so on, the terms should be sufficiently generous—given a cautious assessment of the market prospects of the enterprises involved—to make them definitive. Otherwise, firms will soon come to realize that another round of government assistance is necessary. But uncertain of the terms, managers are likely to postpone important investment decisions. The propagation of a wait-and-see attitude among business groups unnecessarily delays macroeconomic recovery.

- In designing aid packages, policymakers face a trade-off between the across-the-board and the case-by-case approaches. The former fails to distinguish between firms suffering different degrees of difficulties and may turn out to be unnecessarily expensive; the latter system not only is cumbersome and administratively costlier, but also can run into sticky political complications. In most cases, some combination of these two approaches is likely to be optimal. Whatever the combination, at some point, the decision has to be made to stop subsidizing nonviable enterprises, to the extent that they can be identified. Moreover, any case-by-case reschedulings should be unanticipated (not announced in advance) and definitive: unanticipated, so that moral hazard problems will be avoided (managers who expect that troubled firms will get better deals in the future may have an incentive to slacken or to manipulate the company books); definitive, so that the expectation of additional case-by-case reschedulings will not create moral hazard problems in the future.[60]

References

Arellano, José Pablo (1983a), "El Financiamiento del Desarrollo," in *Reconstrucción Económica para la Democracia* (Santiago: Editorial Aconcagua, 1983).

———— (1983b), "De la Liberalización a la Intervención: El Mercado de Capitales en Chile 1974–1983," *Colección Estudios CIEPLAN*, No. 11 (December 1983).

————, "La Difícil Salida al Problema del Endeudamiento Interno," *Colección Estudios CIEPLAN*, No. 13 (June 1984).

————, and R. Ffrench-Davis, "Apertura Financiera Externa: La Experiencia Chilena en 1973–80" (unpublished; *CIEPLAN*, 1981).

Arriagada, Pedro, "Adjustments by Agricultural Exporters in Chile during 1974–82," in *Scrambling for Survival*, ed. by V. Corbo and J. de Melo, Staff Working Paper No. 764 (Washington: World Bank, 1985).

Barandiarán, Edgardo, "La Crisis Financiera Chilena," *Documento de Trabajo*, Centro de Estudios Públicos, No. 6 (October 1983).

Behrens, R., "Los Bancos e Instituciones Financieras en la Historia Economíca de Chile" (unpublished thesis, Catholic University of Chile, 1985).

Blanchard, O., and J. Watson, "Bubbles, Rational Expectations and Financial Markets," in *Crises in the Economic and Financial Structure*, ed. by Paul Wachtel (Lexington, Massachusetts: Lexington Books, 1982).

Calvo, Guillermo, "Incredible Reforms," paper prepared for the Conference on Debt, Stabilization, and Development, Helsinki, August 1986.

Central Bank of Chile, *Boletín Mensual*.

————, *Síntesis Monetaria y Financiera*.

————, Dirección de Política Financiera, *Cuentas Nacionales de Chile*.

————, *Series Monetarias*.

Corbo, Vittorio, "Necesidades Financieras de las Empresas: La Función de las Instituciones Financieras," *Estudios Monetarios V*, Banco Central de Chile (1976).

————, "Reforms and Macroeconomic Adjustment in Chile During 1974–84," *World Development*, Vol. 13, No. 8 (August 1985).

————, and Ricardo Matte, "Capital Flows and the Role of Monetary Policy: The Case of Chile," *Documento de Trabajo*, Economics Institute, Catholic University of Chile, No. 92 (1984).

————, and José Miguel Sánchez, "Adjustments by Industrial Firms in Chile during 1974–82," in *Scrambling for Survival*, ed. by V. Corbo and J. de Melo, Staff Working Paper, No. 764 (Washington: World Bank, 1985).

Cortázar, Rene, "Wages in the Short-Run: Chile, 1964–1981," Corporación de

---

[60] This problem is related to the distinction between anticipated or unanticipated shocks in the rational expectations literature. For example, an unexpected devaluation may serve certain purposes, but an expected one can only cause a loss of reserves.

Investigaciones Económicas para Latinoamerica, *Notas Tecnicas*, No. 56 (April 1983).

————, and Marshall Jorge, "Indice de Precios del Consumidor en Chile: 1970–1978," *Colección Estudios, CIEPLAN*, No. 4.

Cortés, Hernán, "Políticas de Estabilización en Chile: Inflación, Desempleo y Depresión 1975–1982," *Cuadernos de Economía*, No. 60, Catholic University of Chile (1983).

Díaz-Alejandro, Carlos F., "Good-bye Financial Repression, Hello Financial Crash," *Journal of Development Economics*, Vol. 18 (September/October 1985).

————, "Stories of the 30's for the 1980's," in *Financial Policies and World Capital Markets: The Problems of Latin American Countries*, ed. by R. Dornbusch, M. Obstfeld, and P. Aspe-Arnella (Chicago: University of Chicago Press, 1983).

————, and Edmar Bacha, "Tropical Reflections on the History and Theory of International Financial Markets," in *For Good or Evil: Economic Theory and North-South Negotiations*, ed. by Gerald K. Helleiner (Toronto: University of Toronto Press, 1982).

Dornbusch, Rudiger, "External Debt, Budget Deficits and Disequilibrium Exchange Rates," NBER Working Paper, No. 1336 (April 1984).

————, "Inflation Stabilization and Capital Mobility," NBER Working Paper, No. 555 (1980).

Edwards, Sebastian, "The Order of Liberalization of the External Sector in Developing Countries," Princeton Essays in International Finance, No. 156 (December 1984).

————, "Stabilization with Liberalization: An Evaluation of Ten Years of Chile's Experiment with Free-Market Policies," *Economic Development and Cultural Change*, Vol. 32 (January 1985).

————, "Monetarism in Chile 1973–1983: Some Economic Puzzles," *Economic Development and Cultural Change*, Vol. 33 (June 1986).

————, and Mohsin Khan, "Interest Rate Determination in Developing Countries:A Conceptual Framework," *Staff Papers*, International Monetary Fund, Vol. 32 (September 1985).

Fernández, Roque, "La Crisis Financiera Argentina: 1980–1982," *Desarrollo Económico*, Vol. 23, No. 89 (April–June 1983).

Ffrench-Davis, Ricardo, "El Problema de la Deuda Externa y la Apertura Financiera en Chile," *Colección Estudios CIEPLAN*, No. 11 (December 1983).

Foxley, Alejandro, *Latin American Experiments in Neoconservative Economics* (Berkeley, California: University of California Press, 1983).

Friedman, Milton, *A Program for Monetary Stability* (New York: Fordham University Press, 1959).

Fry, Maxwell J., "Money and Capital or Financial Deepening in Economic Development?" *Journal of Money, Credit and Banking* (November 1978).

Gálvez, Julio, and James Tybout, "Microeconomic Adjustments in Chile During 1977–81: The Importance of Being a Grupo," *World Development*, Vol. 13 (August 1985).

Giovannini, Alberto, "Saving and the Real Interest Rate in LDCs," *Journal of Development Economics*, Vol. 18 (August 1985).

Harberger, Arnold, "Observations on the Chilean Economy, 1973–1983," *Economic Development and Cultural Change* (April 1985).

International Monetary Fund, *International Financial Statistics*.

Kindleberger, Charles P., *Manias, Panics and Crashes: A History of Financial Crises* (New York: Basic Books, 1978).

Larrain Garces, Mauricio, "Treatment of Banks in Difficulties: The Case of Chile (unpublished paper; International Monetary Fund, Seminar on Central Banking, July 1–12, 1985).

Le Fort, Guillermo, "The Real Exchange Rate and International Capital Flows: The Case of the Southern Cone Countries" (doctoral dissertation, Los Angeles: UCLA, 1985).

Luders, Rolf, "Lessons from the Financial Liberalization of Chile: 1974–1982" (unpublished; World Bank, Washington, June 1986).

Mathieson, Donald J., "Financial Reform and Capital Flows in a Developing Economy," *Staff Papers*, International Monetary Fund, Vol. 26 (September 1979).

McKinnon, Ronald I., *Money and Capital in Economic Development* (Washington: The Brookings Institution, 1973).

————, "The Order of Economic Liberalization: Lessons from Chile and Argentina," in *Economic Policy in a World of Change*, Carnegie-Rochester Conference Series on Public Policy, ed. by Karl Brunner and Allan Meltzer, Vol. 17 (1982).

Meller, P., and A. Solimano, "Inestabilidad Financiera, Burbujas Especulativas y Tasa de Interés: La Economía Chilena en 1975–83"(unpublished; Santiago, Chile, 1983).

Minsky, Hyman, "A Theory of Systemic Fragility," in *Financial Crises, Institutions and Markets in a Fragile Environment*, ed. by E. I. Altman and A. W. Sametz (New York: John Wiley & Sons, 1977).

Molho, Lazaros, "Interest Rates, Saving and Investment in Developing Countries," *Staff Papers*, International Monetary Fund, Vol. 33 (March 1986).

Rosende, F., and R. Tosso, "Una Explicación para la Tasa de Interés Real en Chile en el Período 1975–1983," *Cuadernos de Economía*, No. 62 (April 1984).

Sargent, Thomas, and Neil Wallace, "Some Unpleasant Monetarist Arithmetic," in *Rational Expectations and Inflation*, ed. by Thomas Sargent (New York: Harper and Row, 1986).

Shaw, Edward S., *Financial Deepening in Economic Development* (New York: Oxford University Press, 1973).

Sjaastad, Larry A., "Failure of Economic Liberalism in the Cone of Latin America," *World Economy*, Vol. 6 (March 1983).

Solimano, Andrés, "Liberalización Financiera y Crisis: Aspectos Teóricos y Consideraciones de Política Económica" (unpublished; Santiago, Chile, 1985).

Superintendency of Banks and Financial Institutions (Chile), *Información Financiera*.

United Nations, *National Accounts Statistics: Analysis of Main Aggregates* 1983/89 (New York, 1987).

————, Economic Commission for Latin America (CEPAL) and United Nations Environment Programme, "Estilos de Desarrollo, Energía y Medio Ambiente: Un Estudio de Caso Exploratorio" (Santiago de Chile: Naciones Unidas, 1983).

van Wijnbergen, S., "Interest Rate Management in LDC's: Theory and Some Simulation Results for South Korea," *Journal of Monetary Economics*, Vol. 12 (September 1983).

Velasco, Andrés, "Financial Crises and External Balance," *Journal of Development Economics*, Vol. 27 (October 1987).

Zahler, Roberto, "Recent Southern Cone Liberalization, Reforms and Stabilization Policies: The Chilean Case 1974–1982," *Journal of Interamerican Studies and World Affairs* (November 1983).

————, "Las Tasas de Interés en Chile: 1975–82" (unpublished; CEPAL, Santiago, January 1985).

4

Crisis in the Financial Sector and the Authorities' Reaction: The Philippines

Jean-Claude Nascimento

Between 1981 and the middle of 1987, the Philippine economy faced a major crisis in the financial sector. Three commercial banks, 128 rural banks, and 32 thrift institutions failed, and 2 other private banks were under intervention. In addition, the biggest commercial bank, the Philippines National Bank, and the Development Bank of the Philippines, both government owned, became de facto insolvent and, in 1986, were bailed out by a transfer of their nonperforming assets (about ₱ 108 billion, equivalent to 80 percent of their combined assets) to the Asset Privatization Trust (APT), specially constituted to administer problem assets. The crisis began on a limited scale during 1980 and 1981 and intensified thereafter, culminating by the end of September 1986 in a significant contraction of the financial system (excluding the Central Bank of the Philippines—CBP). For the purpose of analysis, three distinct phases of the crisis have been identified.

The first phase, which spanned all of 1981, featured a crisis of confidence triggered by fraud in the commercial paper market.[1] Although the crisis initially affected only a small part of the system outside the commer-

---

[1] This event was known as the Dewey Dee Affair. In January 1981, Dewey Dee, an industrial magnate who had borrowed heavily in the commercial paper market, fled the country, leaving behind an estimated ₱ 500–800 million of debt. The news sent a wave of panic through money market investors and small depositors. The former did not renew their funding, causing commercial paper borrowers to default on a large scale. The small depositors shifted their deposits to large commercial banks, perceived as sounder financial institutions.

cial and development banks, whose combined assets accounted for 16.5 percent of total assets of the financial system in 1980, the crisis had a lasting impact on confidence. The commercial paper market collapsed and many nonbank money market institutions went out of business. The two largest investment houses belonging to two major holding companies went bankrupt, provoking the failure of the holding companies themselves and leading to the bankruptcy or takeover of their numerous corporate subsidiaries. Wealth holders shifted funds to the highest-quality paper and to more stable and conservative banks.

The loss of confidence spread to the thrift banking system. Also, failures of rural banks, which had sharply increased in 1980, continued to rise in 1981. However, the assets of failed rural and thrift banks accounted for only 1.6 percent of the total assets of the banking system in 1981, and the failures among them did not pose a threat to stability but served to weaken confidence further.

In the second phase, which spanned 1982(I)–1983(III), the Government intensified its assistance to nonfinancial and financial institutions, which served to alleviate the growing distress among nonfinancial corporations but widened the budget deficit. The Government increased its emergency lending and equity contributions to public corporations, arranged for the takeover of troubled private banks by government financial institutions[2] in order to facilitate their restructuring and eventual disposition, and supported the takeover by the government financial institutions of numerous nonfinancial firms in distress. The Government was attempting to prevent widespread private corporate failures and banking problems, while stepping up public investment to offset the slump in private sector investment. During this phase, political uncertainty became widespread and foreign exchange difficulties grew, although the problem was initially masked by swap and forward cover operations by the CBP as well as by irregular banking operations.[3]

When the third phase, which spanned 1983(IV)–1986(IV), began, there was widespread uncertainty in the economy, stemming from the unstable political environment of the first half of 1983 and the balance of payments crisis of October 1983. The effects spilled over to the banking system. Indeed, in October 1983, the authorities' announcement of a moratorium on external debt payments to foreign commercial banks provoked financial panic; a series of runs on the banks ensued, and this time commercial banks

---

[2] Government financial institutions include the Development Bank of the Philippines (DBP), the Philippines National Bank (PNB), the Land Bank of the Philippines (LBP), the Government Service Insurance System (GSIS), and the Social Security System (SSS).

[3] Some of these deficiencies are discussed in Central Bank of the Philippines (1988, p. 6; and 1989, p. 15).

were included. Large-scale flight to currency and outflows of capital occurred. The capital outflows that were recorded during this period may have occurred even earlier and been obscured by the banking irregularities. The disclosure or sudden loss of reserves in mid-October undermined confidence and exacerbated the crisis.

By the end of this phase the hardest hit financial institutions were the two largest government-owned banks—the DBP and the PNB. The depth of the crisis during this phase is illustrated by three events:

- A staggering decline in commercial bank credit to the private sector, which fell by 53 percent in real terms between the end of September 1983 and the end of September 1986.
- A massive restructuring of the DBP and the PNB, which led in November 1986 to a transfer of ₽ 108 billion of nonperforming assets (representing nearly 30 percent of total bank assets) to a government agency—the APT.[4] Included in the transfer were ₽ 23.4 billion of nonperforming assets from the PNB, which contributed to a decline of 20.5 percent, in real terms, in commercial bank credit to the private sector during the last quarter of 1986.
- Continued government intervention in weak private banks and the closing of three private commercial banks.[5]

Against this background, this chapter examines the causes and manifestations of the crisis in the Philippine financial sector and the reaction of the authorities to that crisis. Attention here is on the behavior of the financial system before and during the crisis; the aim is to clarify the linkages among financial reform, financial crisis, and macroeconomic performance.

The main conclusion of the chapter is that factors within the financial system caused and exacerbated the crisis. Although the political and economic climate of the late 1970s and early 1980s increased the fragility of the financial sector, weaknesses of the regulatory framework and loose banking practices triggered and exacerbated the crisis. In the end, the interventions by the authorities prevented the banking sector from collapsing, but at a high financial cost to taxpayers.

Section I discusses the background to the crisis and the role of the macroeconomic and regulatory environment. Section II discusses the manifestations of the crisis, with emphasis on money and credit developments. Section III describes the measures taken to deal with the crisis. Section IV highlights the main findings.

---

[4] This agency was set up in December 1986 to take over the nonperforming assets of state banks and to resell them to private investors. In 1986, the value of these assets was estimated at ₽ 20 billion (i.e., 19 percent of their book value).

[5] The fate of one insolvent commercial bank remained undecided as of the end of 1987 because of litigation contesting the liquidation.

I. Setting of the Crisis

Three factors within and outside the financial system are examined here in order to differentiate their effects on the crisis: (1) the macroeconomic setting and political climate before and during the crisis; (2) the structure of the financial sector and its liberalization initiated in 1972 and completed in 1981; and (3) prudential regulation and supervision of financial institutions and related institutional practices.

Macroeconomic Setting

During the 1970s the economy experienced strong growth in real GNP, despite the low productivity of investment (see Table 1 and Chart 1). The unprecedented, demand-driven economic boom reflected the authorities' development strategy based on intensive investment growth.[6] The financing of the investment boom resulted in a widening of external imbalances and a sharp rise in foreign savings (in percent of nominal GNP) (Table 1). Also, the growth of domestic bank credit accelerated, particularly to the private sector (see Table 2). PNB and DBP accounted for a substantial portion of credit to the private sector, which often was granted on the basis of political, rather than economic, considerations.

During the late 1970s and early 1980s, a deterioration in world economic conditions further weakened the external position, while the limited crisis of confidence in 1981 seemed to dampen investors' expectations regarding growth projections; these developments affected private investments adversely in the 1980s.[7] By the second half of 1983, the effects of rapid expansion in earlier years, the growing uncertainty in the political climate, and unfavorable external conditions combined to cause a balance of payments crisis, which led to the announcement of a temporary moratorium on external debt repayments in October. This event triggered a run on banks, a cut-off of external financing, and some capital flight, all of which had significant feedback effects on the macroeconomy, particularly the balance of payments. In late 1983, CBP reacted by injecting reserve money to meet the increase in currency demand (see Table 2). The sharp increase in reserve money during 1983 also reflected large losses on swap

---

[6] In line with this strategy, the authorities carried out inward-looking and expansionary macroeconomic policies during the 1970s, namely, protectionist trade policies, widespread tax incentives, and preferential lending by government financial institutions to priority sectors (i.e., construction, manufacturing, and energy).

[7] The sharp decline of private investment (in percent of GNP) in 1980/81 is overstated because the investment data during the 1970–80 period are unreliable. However, the magnitude of the decline and the downturn in economic growth point to more sluggish investment in the 1980s than in the 1970s.

Chart 1. Selected Macroeconomic Indicators, 1970–86
(In percent)

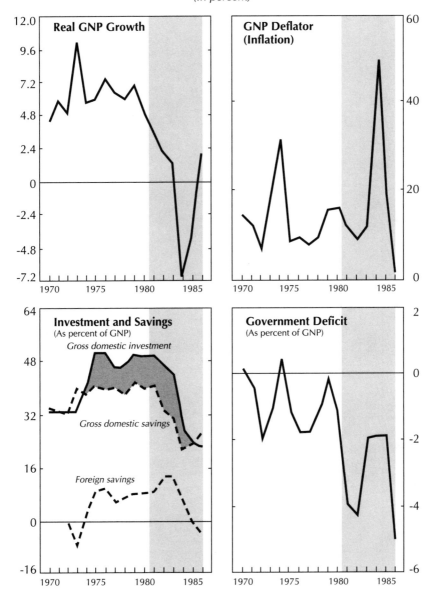

Note: Shaded areas indicate crisis periods.

Sources: International Monetary Fund, *International Financial Statistics, 1988*; and Table 1.

Table 1. Selected Macroeconomic Indicators, Selected Years, 1970–86

(In percent)

Indicator	1970	1975	1980	1981	1982	1983	1984	1985	1986
Growth rate of real GNP (at 1980 prices)	4.3	5.8	5.0	3.4	1.9	1.1	−7.1	−4.1	2.0
Implicit GNP deflator (at 1980 prices)	14.5	8.3	15.6	11.0	8.3	11.6	50.0	18.2	1.6
Gross domestic investment (in percent of GNP)	21.5	29.6	30.7	30.7	28.8	27.1	17.4	14.3	13.8
Of which: Private investment[1]	(19.1)	(27.0)	(27.4)	(16.2)	(16.1)	(17.6)	(14.5)	(11.4)	(10.0)
Gross national savings	20.6	25.2	24.8	25.3	20.7	19.0	13.4	14.3	16.5
Of which: Private savings	(18.6)	(21.8)	(19.4)	(21.1)	(16.5)	(14.5)	(11.9)	(13.2)	(17.8)
Foreign savings (in percent of GNP)	—	5.8	5.4	5.4	8.1	8.1	4.0	0.1	−3.3
National government balance[2] (deficit −) (as percent of GNP)	—	−1.1	−1.3	−4.0	−4.3	−2.0	−1.8	−1.8	−5.1
Net foreign assets (in billions of pesos)	−0.6	2.8	−21.1	−30.1	−50.5	−95.3	−125.0	−94.0	−28.5
Inflation rate[3]	14.0	8.2	18.2	13.1	10.2	10.0	50.3	23.1	0.7
Real GNP per capita (in thousands of pesos)	3.9	4.64	5.47	5.52	5.50	5.43	5.03	4.7	4.6

External debt/GNP	...	31.3	48.9	54.4	62.8	72.7	80.6	81.7	92.9
Of which:									
Total short-term/GNP	(...)	(12.4)	(21.2)	(24.9)	(22.4)	(37.9)	(37.3)	(32.7)	(19.0)
From commercial banks	(...)	(6.3)	(19.5)	(11.5)	(12.4)	(10.9)	(11.0)	(7.7)	(2.7)
Debt service ratio[4]									
Exports of goods and services	29.2	18.1	20.9	25.2	38.1	38.9	44.6	48.3[5]	46.9[5]
Of which: Share of interest payment	(29.8)	(38.6)	(58.5)	(63.3)	(65.2)	(62.7)	(65.2)	(57.7)	(50.6)
Exchange rate (peso/U.S. dollar at end of period)	6.4	7.5	7.6	8.2	9.17	14.0	19.8	19.0	20.5
Terms of trade (growth rate)	17.0	−46.0	−15.9	−12.0	−2.8	4.4	−2.3	−6.6	7.5
Memorandum item:									
Consolidated public sector balance (deficit −) (in percent of GNP)	—	—	−3.9	−5.8	−5.3	−9.0	−8.2	−5.9	−5.4

Sources: International Monetary Fund, *International Financial Statistics*, 1986, and IMF staff estimates.

[1]Figures for 1970–80 are official data from the National Economic and Development Authority (NEDA); because these data are overstated, they are not comparable with the 1981–86 series, which represent IMF staff estimates.

[2]Includes losses of government financial institutions (PNB, DBP, and CBP).

[3]As measured by the consumer price index in Manila.

[4]Before rescheduling.

[5]Preliminary.

Table 2. Monetary Conditions, Selected Years, 1970–86

	Reserve Money	Of which		Liquidity[2]	Of which		Bank Credit[1]	Of which	Interest Rates (in percent)		
	Total	Currency with the public	Excess reserves[3]	Total	M1	M3	Total	To private sector	12-month treasury bill	Lending rate (one year and less)	Deposit rate (one year and less)
	(In billions of pesos)								*(In nominal terms)*		
1970	3.2	2.4	−0.5	9.1	4.3	9.1	10.6	8.1	13.7	12.0	6.5
1975	7.1	4.8	. . .	34.9	10.3	34.9	32.8	26.9	10.9	12.0	9.0
1980	17.0	10.2	0.6	79.2	22.5	79.2	94.6	79.7	12.8	14.0	14.0
1981	18.7	11.6	−0.4	87.2	23.5	82.1	114.3	97.0	13.1	16.0	15.3
1982	19.7	12.7	0.1	99.7	23.5	95.3	133.1	110.1	15.0	16.8	14.1
1983	29.1	19.6	−3.4	118.6	32.5	113.0	173.6	139.9	14.9	18.8	13.7
1984	34.9	21.8	−1.8	139.5	33.6	120.4	183.3	139.4	41.5	26.7	23.2
1985	39.9	24.1	−3.1	178.7	35.8	132.8	171.5	115.3	35.1	28.8	21.8
1986	52.3	29.3	−0.2[4]	205.9	42.6	141.4	118.9	89.2[5]	13.2	17.1	12.3
	(In billions of pesos at 1980 prices)								*(In real terms)[6]*		
1970	12.7	9.5	−2.0	36.9	16.9	36.9	42.5	31.6	−1.6	−3.3	−8.5
1975	12.7	8.5	. . .	51.7	18.4	51.7	59.8	48.3	4.1	5.2	−1.5
1980	17.0	10.2	0.6	79.2	22.5	79.2	89.9	75.8	−5.4	−4.2	−4.2
1981	16.5	10.3	−0.4	74.7	20.1	70.3	97.8	83.0	0.1	2.9	2.2
1982	15.8	10.2	0.1	78.1	18.4	74.6	104.3	86.2	4.8	6.6	3.9
1983	21.2	14.3	−2.5	78.9	17.1	73.1	115.5	93.1	−4.9	8.8	3.7
1984	16.9	10.6	−0.9	58.7	14.2	50.7	77.1	58.6	8.8	−23.6	−27.1
1985	15.7	9.5	−1.2	69.8	14.0	51.9	67.0	45.6	12.0	5.2	−1.3
1986	20.4	11.5	−0.1	80.7	16.7	51.3	46.5	35.0	14.4	16.3	11.5

Sources: International Monetary Fund, *International Financial Statistics*, 1987; and data provided by the authorities.

[1] Starting in 1977, the authorities adopted a new classification system.

[2] Starting in 1981, the figures include treasury bills and central bank certificates of indebtedness (CBCIs) held outside the banking sytem. Thus, between 1970 and 1980, liquidity is equal to M3, which includes demand, savings, and time deposits collected by the banking system.

[3] Between 1970 and 1980, excess reserves were calculated by multiplying the required reserve ratio by the deposit base and subtracting the result from bank reserves. Afterward, data are from IMF country reports.

[4] End of November.

[5] After transfer of ₱ 23 billion of nonperforming loans from the PNB to the Government.

[6] Calculated by subtracting the inflation rate as measured by the consumer price index in Manila.

operations.[8] As a result, inflation and depreciation of the peso accelerated during 1983/84.

The subsequent tightening of monetary policy, the soaring interest rates during 1984/85, and the continued devaluations of the peso all contributed to the spread of distress among financial and nonfinancial corporations. Indeed, the high real interest rate and the peso devaluation aggravated the debt-servicing problems of firms with foreign currency debt.[9]

With very high interest rates, growing uncertainty, and weakening of confidence, aggregate demand dropped, leading to a deep recession. Bank credit, especially to the private sector, fell sharply in real terms.

Structure of Financial Sector and Its Liberalization

To finance the development strategy based on intensive investment growth, CBP introduced numerous reforms between 1972 and 1981. Institutional reforms included the liberalization of controls on foreign capital. Regulatory reforms included the progressive liberalization of interest rates and the introduction of "universal banks."[10] Prudential reforms included the elimination of restrictions on the entry of foreign banks and on their equity participation in domestic banks, and higher barriers to entry for domestic banks (e.g., higher minimum capital requirements).

Liberalization of Controls on Foreign Capital

Evidence shows that the liberalization of controls on foreign capital, together with lending practices largely influenced by political considerations, increased the financial fragility of nongovernment entities. In the subsections that follow, the specific policy measures are presented and their impact on the external debt burden and the financial structure of nongovernment entities is discussed.

Measures. During the 1970s, CBP introduced the foreign currency deposit (FCD) system, created offshore banking units, and eased controls on direct foreign investment. These measures were aimed at attracting foreign capital and permitting wider portfolio selection for domestic investors.

Under the foreign currency deposit system, resident and nonresident

---

[8] These losses amounted to about ₱ 5 billion in the last quarter representing half of the yearly increase in reserve money from end-1982 to end-1983.

[9] The share of foreign currency debt in the total debt of the nongovernment sector rose from an average of 44 percent between 1980 and 1982 to 60 percent between 1983 and 1985.

[10] Commercial banks with a capital of ₱ 500 million or more can apply to become a universal bank or "unibank" and, upon approval, are authorized to expand their activities to include investment banking services, securities transactions, credit guarantees, leasing, and equity investments in allied and nonallied undertakings.

nationals could hold foreign currency deposits with eligible banks.[11] In turn, CBP allowed foreign currency deposit banks to make foreign currency loans to domestic residents subject to prior CBP approval, or peso loans after these banks had converted their foreign currency into pesos under a swap arrangement with CBP.[12] Secrecy laws protected investors' deposits. Depositors were also free to withdraw their funds or transfer them abroad. Interest rates on these foreign currency deposits were unregulated. Beginning in 1978, these banks' foreign exchange operations were subject to open position limits.[13]

Under the offshore banking unit system, both domestic banks and nonresidents were allowed to hold foreign currency deposits with offshore banking units. Banks' lending operations required prior CBP approval. In addition, banks were not allowed to make loans with a maturity exceeding 360 days.[14]

The relaxation of foreign capital controls included the following measures:

(1) Foreign direct cash investment made after 1973 became freely repatriable;

(2) Foreign-owned companies were granted authorization to raise loans in domestic currency;

(3) Foreign banks were allowed to take equity participation, with minority or majority ownership, in domestic banks. Although significant capital controls remained, the removal or relaxation of restrictions stimulated capital inflows.

Overindebtedness and Unsound Debt Structure.   As a result of these developments and of the foreign financing of the investment boom, the external debt burden rose sharply while the maturity of this debt shortened (see Table 1). These developments disputed the contention that liberalization of capital controls would reduce foreign borrowing.[15] Rather, these devel-

[11] Eligibility criteria included competence in the conduct of foreign exchange operations as well as the minimum unimpaired capital requirement. Liability restrictions consisted of holding a minimum foreign currency reserve ratio with CBP. Furthermore, foreign exchange receipts from exports and most invisible transactions could not be deposited in these FCD accounts.

[12] Banks were prohibited from converting foreign currency into pesos, except under swap arrangements with CBP.

[13] Under Circular No. 547, issued in 1978, banks were required to cover at least 70 percent of the foreign currency liabilities with eligible assets in the same currency. This foreign currency cover included deposits with the CBP and other Philippine-based commercial banks, deposits with foreign banks and offshore banking units, foreign currency loans or securities, foreign currency notes and coins, and foreign currency swapped with the CBP.

[14] This restriction applied also to domestic banks operating under the FCD system.

[15] According to McKinnon (1973), freer capital flows would deter capital flight and boost the national saving rate, thereby reducing external borrowing.

opments suggested that liberalization of the foreign capital flow contributed to excessive external borrowing, which permitted domestic investment to accelerate before the crisis.[16]

Incomplete financial reforms, combined with the political climate, encouraged such borrowing. Indeed, the authorities eased capital controls while maintaining controls in other areas, such as credit allocation and trade transactions.[17] Excessive foreign borrowing and domestic protection contributed to weakening the financial position of nongovernment entities.

As large foreign capital inflows exerted strong inflationary pressures during the second half of the decade, real lending rates became negative by 1980 (see Table 2). Along with high trade barriers, these negative rates created widespread misallocation of resources and encouraged debt finance. Indeed, during the 1970s enterprises and banks had relied heavily on debt finance, especially foreign, to expand their activities.[18] Consequently, the total outstanding debt of the nongovernment sector (both in real terms and in percent of national income) doubled between 1972 and 1980; the share of this debt denominated in foreign currency quadrupled to 40 percent in 1980 (see Table 3). For enterprises, the changes in the level and structure of indebtedness were even more dramatic. As a result of these changes, the quality of banks' portfolios (especially of the DBP and PNB) and the soundness of their liability structure had deteriorated by 1980.

Until 1983, the rise in the debt burden and the weakening of the liability structure of nongovernment entities accelerated, reflecting the end of the economic boom and deterioration in the political and economic climate during that period. Thereafter, a massive liquidation of debt took place, as domestic and foreign creditors curtailed sharply the supply of funds (see Tables 1 and 3).

Interest Rate Liberalization

The statistical analysis in the subsections that follow suggests that despite a fairly open capital account, domestic monetary conditions played a significant role in explaining the behavior of interest rates after the

[16] As Fry (1988) notes: "Foreign capital flow liberalization can stimulate investment more than domestic savings, causing excess indebtedness" (p. 345).

[17] For instance, banks were required to allocate 15 percent of their total deposit base for credit to the rural sector. This was known as the agri/agra requirement. Other portfolio restrictions included banks' minimum holdings of government securities. Furthermore, selective credit policies designed to allocate credit to priority sectors (e.g., exports of traditional products) were maintained. DBP was a main conduit for channeling these funds to the priority sectors.

[18] Individuals also resorted to domestic debt to finance their rapidly rising consumption.

Table 3. Indicators of Indebtedness of Nongovernment Sectors

	1972	1980	1981	1982	1983	1984	1985
Debt, by borrowers				*(In billions of pesos at 1980 prices; end of period)*			
Total nongovernment[1]	104.5	246.7	255.8	281.3	320.6	245.3	185.9
Enterprises[2]	(30.2)	(117.4)	(123.7)	(134.2)	(169.1)	(133.4)	(95.3)
Commercial banks	(62.5)	(113.7)	(116.6)	(131.5)	(136.0)	(101.3)	(84.5)
Individuals	(11.8)	(15.6)	(15.5)	(15.6)	(15.5)	(10.6)	(6.1)
Denomination of debt				*(In percent of total)*			
Nongovernment							
Total	100.0	100.0	100.0	100.0	100.0	100.0	100.0
In pesos	90.0	60.9	52.4	55.1	45.0	38.7	37.0
In U.S. dollars	10.0	39.1	47.6	44.9	55.5	61.3	63.0
Enterprises							
Total	100.0	100.0	100.0	100.0	100.0	100.0	100.0
In pesos[3]	100.0	42.4	37.7	34.1	24.9	15.8	12.2
In U.S. dollars	—	57.6	62.3	65.9	75.1	84.2	87.8
Commercial banks							
Total	100.0	100.0	100.0	100.0	100.0	100.0	100.0
In pesos	83.0	74.7	74.9	71.2	64.8	62.4	67.7
In U.S. dollars	17.0	25.3	25.1	28.8	35.2	37.6	32.3
Debt burden ratio				*(In percent of nominal income of each sector)*			
Nongovernment	65.7	116.9	120.5	131.9	155.9	141.6	115.3
Enterprises	20.0	55.6	58.3	63.0	82.2	77.0	59.1

Memorandum items:

Enterprises' foreign debt (in billions of U.S. dollars)	—	8.9	10.8	12.4	13.4	14.0	12.8
Of which: Short-term	(—)	(2.5)	(3.7)	(4.0)	(4.0)	(4.2)	(3.0)
CPI (1980=100)	28.8	100.0	114.6	126.8	147.1	246.1	290.8
National income[4] (at current prices)	45.8	211.0	243.2	270.4	302.4	426.2	468.8

Sources: Central Bank of the Philippines, *Statistical Bulletin,* 1982 and 1983; and *Philippines Financial Statistics, 1982–1985;* and International Monetary Fund.

[1]Domestic and foreign debt (converted into pesos at the peso/U.S. dollar rate at end of period) of the nongovernment sector composed of enterprises, commercial banks, and individuals.

[2]Composed of private and public corporations, single proprietorships, partnerships and associations, and cooperatives. The overwhelming share of the debt belonged to corporations.

[3]Excludes the peso loans that were re-lent by the Central Bank of the Philippines or a commercial bank. As the ultimate borrowers (i.e., enterprises) assumed the exchange rate risk, this debt was included in foreign debt contracted in U.S. dollars. These data also exclude: overdue loans, items in litigation, domestic and foreign bills, "clean."

[4]Calculated by netting out indirect taxes (net of subsidies) and income *plus* profit taxes from nominal GNP.

liberalization. Between 1984 and 1986 these conditions, reflected in indicators of excess demand for real money (M3),[19] were influenced largely by the uncertain environment and by CBP policy efforts to bring down inflation. The main reforms are presented first and the behavior of interest rates following the reforms is discussed.

Reforms. During the 1970s CBP administered the level and structure of interest rates. It tried to maintain positive rates in real terms and to keep nominal interest rates aligned with foreign interest rates. In 1976 the usury law was abolished, and CBP introduced ceilings on money market rates applied to deposit substitutes.[20]

In 1981, CBP deregulated all bank rates except short-term lending rates. Ceilings on all deposit rates were lifted in July; those on medium- and long-term lending were lifted in October. The ceiling on short-term lending rates was eliminated at the end of 1982. Meanwhile, in March 1982, to enhance transparency in the credit and deposit markets, both a Prime Rate and a Manila Reference Rate (MRR) began to be compiled and announced.[21]

Determinants of Interest Rate Levels. Following the liberalization, nominal interest rates first rose gradually, then shot up between 1984 and 1985, before declining in 1986 (see Chart 2). Despite a fairly open capital account, foreign factors (e.g., foreign interest rates and expected exchange rate changes) were not the only determinants of nominal interest rates after the liberalization.

Indeed, the uncovered interest arbitrage relation explained only part of the interest rate fluctuation from 1981(I) to 1986(IV). Empirical equations for domestic interest rates (nominal) indicated that the estimated short- and long-run coefficients of the foreign interest rate (adjusted for ex post devaluations) were 0.1 and 0.5, respectively (see Table 4).[22] The estimated

---

[19] M3 consists of M2 (currency, demand deposits, time and savings deposits) *plus* deposit substitutes (interest-bearing securities issued by banks to their customers).

[20] This measure was aimed at curbing the flow of financial savings from bank deposits into deposit substitutes whose yield was unregulated. The ceiling on short-term deposit substitutes was set at 17 percent in 1976 and then lowered to 16 percent in 1978. Both ceilings were higher than the rates on savings and short-term time deposits.

[21] Under the Prime Rate system, a sample of ten commercial banks regularly publicized the rate that they charged to their best customers on a 90-day loan. Under the MRR system, CBP compiled an average cost of bank funds—of 30-day, 60-day, and 90-day maturities—from a sample of ten commercial banks. These costs of funds were market determined and known as the Manila Reference Rates or MRRs.

[22] A simple equation for uncovered interest arbitrage was estimated for the 1981(II) to 1986(IV) period. Because the financial market was assumed to adjust with a lag, a lagged dependent variable was introduced in the tested equation. A dummy variable (1 from 1981(II) to 1983(III) and 0 for the remaining quarters) was added to detect the presence of a structural

coefficient of the dummy variable was statistically insignificant—a fact that points to a stable interest arbitrage relationship before and after the announcement of the moratorium. To test the significance of domestic factors affecting nominal interest rates, a more general relationship was estimated by including a variable measuring monetary disequilibrium.[23] The statistical significance of this variable (defined as the difference between actual M3 and the estimated value of the demand for money, both in real terms) was evidence of the strong presence of the "liquidity" effect on nominal interest rates (see Table 4).

This liquidity effect was governed by both the CBP's policy stance and the banks' behavior. In 1982 and 1983 expansionary policies created an excess supply of real balances, which, in turn, put downward pressure on interest rates (see Chart 2). Although the expansionary stance was maintained in the first half of 1984, a shortage of real balances subsequently emerged because of the sharp decline in the money multiplier, which put strong upward pressure on interest rates; the fall in the money multiplier resulted from banks' cautious lending policies in the presence of widespread economic uncertainty. The upward pressure on interest rates persisted in 1985 and 1986, as the monetary policy stance became tight (see Section II below).

Determinants of Interest Rate Structure. The gross margin between lending and deposit rate fluctuated by an average of about 4 percentage points annually between 1980 and 1984, and rose sharply between 1985 and 1986 (see Table 5).[24] But quarterly data show that this margin was often larger and that it fluctuated sharply, particularly for short-term rates (see Chart 3). The larger margin for short-term rates was caused by the inverted term structure of bank lending rates which reflected the increase of inflationary

---

shift in the equation after the announcement of the debt moratorium. The Orcutt-Cochrane estimation procedure was used. The results reported in Table 4 were quite satisfactory. The coefficients for the foreign interest rate (adjusted for ex post devaluation) and the lagged dependent variable were significant at a 5 percent significance level.

[23] The empirical specification builds on Edwards and Khan (1985). Domestic interest rate is related to a weighted average of the foreign interest rate adjusted for expected exchange rate changes and of domestic factors, namely, monetary disequilibrium, expected inflation, and the long-term equilibrium rate of interest in real terms—a constant. Equations were estimated by the Orcutt-Cochrane procedure and two types of tests were performed. First, the interest rate equation was estimated in both an unrestricted form and a restricted form that posited that the liquidity effect was absent (i.e., monetary disequilibrium has no short-term effect on the real interest rate); a Chow test was applied to test the statistical significance of this restriction. Second, a dummy variable was used to test the stability of the slope coefficients during the two periods 1981(I) to 1983(III) and 1983(IV) to 1986(IV).

[24] Using a weighted average interest rate on secured loans (lending rate) and MRRs (banks' costs of funds) for a sample of ten commercial banks.

Chart 2. Movements of Nominal Rates, 1982(I)–1986(IV)
(In percent per annum; period average)

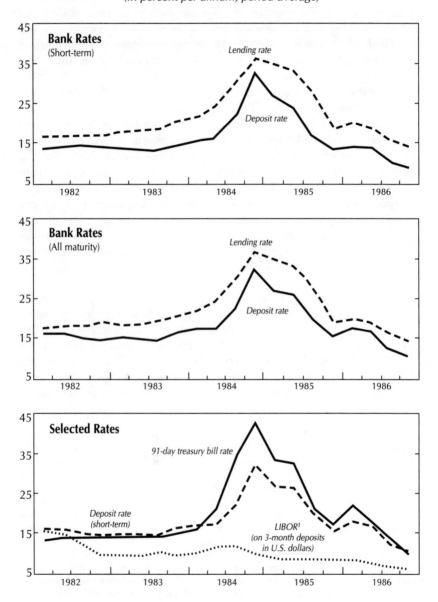

Sources: Central Bank of the Philippines, *CB Review,* Vols. 38 and 39, 1986.
[1] London interbank offered rate.

Table 4. Estimates of Selected Financial Relationships, 1981(II)–1986(IV)[1]

(Annual percentages)

Estimated Equations[1] Dependent Variable	Estimated Coefficients							Adjusted	
	Constant	Dummy variable	Real GNP	Actual inflation	M_t/P_{t-1}	Rho	Rss	R^2	DW
1. *Demand for money[2]* Real M3	-4.695 (-24.031)	0.076 (10.646)	0.082 (1.769)	-0.001 (-10.515)	0.783 (41.968)	-0.009	-0.002	0.998	1.989
2. *Uncovered interest arbitrage[3]* Deposit rate (i_t)	1.165 (0.860)	$(i^* + e)_t$ 0.097 (3.889)	i_{t-1} 0.726 (7.704)			-0.018	135.1	0.824	-0.103
3. *Generalized version of interest rate equation[4]* Deposit rate (i_t)	0.267 (0.226)	$(i^* + e)_t$ 0.092 (4.368)	EMS_t -0.511 (-1.861)	i_{t-1} 0.799 (9.495)		0.017	118.7	0.877	0.094

Source: IMF staff calculations.

Notes: Table shows quarterly average data. Note also that: (i) Figures in parentheses represent the *t*-statistic whose critical value at 95 percent significance level is t_c = 1.708 for 25 observations; and (ii) DW is the Durbin-Watson statistic.

[1]Their specification posits a slow market-clearing process. Thus, the estimates reported are short-term coefficients with the coefficients of (M_t/P_{t-1}) and i_{t-1}, representing the adjustment lag coefficient in equations (1), (2), and (3), respectively.

[2]The demand for real money (defined as M3) was assumed to depend positively on real GNP, and negatively on inflation (used as the opportunity cost variable capturing the substitution effect between money and goods). The adjustment process in the market for real money assumed that prices adjust to monetary imbalance with a time lag; this process is described by the following equation:

$$\ln P_t - \ln P_{t-1} = [\ln M_t - (\ln m_t^e / P_{t-1})].$$

The estimated equation was specified in semilog linear form. The reduced-form equation of this demand for money was tested, using an Orcutt-Cochrane procedure. The dummy variable taking a value of one before the announcement of the moratorium and zero thereafter was included to test the presence of a structural shift between these two periods.

[3]A constant was added to this regulation to assess the presence of persistent deviation between domestic and foreign rates. Following a liberalization of foreign capital flows, the constant is expected not to be significant, while the long-run coefficient of ($i^* + e$) would be close to one. Because of an adjustment lag, the short-term coefficient could be much lower than one within the period.

[4]In essence, this equation tests the presence of a "liquidity" effect in the uncovered interest arbitrage relationship. In the short run, an excess supply of real money (demand) would cause the real interest rate to fall (rise); through the Fisher equation, this would cause the nominal interest rate to fall (rise). The monetary disequilibrium variable (i.e., actual real money minus the predicted value of the estimated demand for real money—equation (1)) is negatively correlated with the interest rate.

Chart 3. Banks' Gross Interest Margins, 1982(I)–1986(IV)
(In percent per annum; period average)

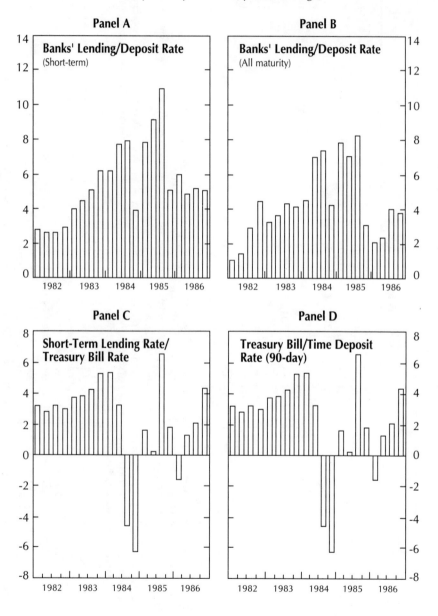

Sources: Central Bank of the Philippines, *CB Review,* Vols. 38 and 39.

Table 5. Banks' Interest Margins, Selected Years, 1970–86

(In percent; period average)

	Gross Margins			Net unitary income (i_n) per peso lent				Net Margins
	$i_L - i_d$	r	i_r	i_L^n	$i_r.r$	$i.a(1-r)$	i_n	$(i_n - i_d)$
	(1)	(2)	(3)	(4)	(5)	(6)	(7)	(8)
1970	6.8	20.0	3.0	8.88	0.60	0.00	9.48	5.18
1975	7.4	20.0	3.0	7.94	0.60	1.31	9.85	4.95
1980	4.5	20.0	3.0	8.72	0.60	1.54	10.86	1.86
1981	3.6	20.0	3.0	9.82	0.60	1.58	12.00	0.40
1982	3.0	18.0	3.0	12.05	0.54	1.85	14.44	−0.76
1983	4.3	23.0	1.0	12.00	0.23	1.72	13.95	−1.05
1984	4.5	24.0	4.0	16.38	0.96	4.73	22.07	−0.13
1985	7.1	24.0	4.0	17.31	0.96	4.00	22.27	1.17
1986	6.4	22.0	4.0	11.40	0.88	1.54	13.82	2.12

Sources: Buhat (1987); and IMF staff calculations.

Definitions:

$i_L - i_d$ = difference between lending (i_L) and deposit rate (i_d), as defined in footnote 21, page 188.

r = Required reserve ratio.

i_r = Interest rate on required reserves deposited at the CBP.

i_L^n = Net interest income per peso lent.

$$i_L^n = i(1 - t)(1 - a)(1 - r)$$

t = Gross tax receipts on lending operations; t = 5 percent on each unit income from lending.

a = Agri/agra required ratio; a = 15 percent of banks' loan portfolio.

i_a = Interest rate on treasury bill that banks can hold to meet other agri/agra required ratio. Thus, the net income per peso lent is derived by adding interest earnings on treasury bills held to meet the agri/agra requirement and on required reserves:

$$i_n = i_L^n + i_r.r + i_a.a(1 - r).$$

expectations.[25] Indeed, bankers took a cautious stance, incorporating a risk premium for inflation in their lending rates (see Buhat (1986)).[26] Also, the gross margin between the short-term lending rate and the short-term deposit rate measured by the 90-day MRR rose steadily until 1983(III);

[25] Growing macroeconomic imbalance and large devaluations contributed to increased inflationary expectations.

[26] The gross interest margins (for short-term rates) was regressed on inflation, the ratio of overdue to total loans outstanding, and the Herfindahl-Hirschman index (a measure of concentration in the banking industry) to identify the determinants of banks' gross spread after the liberalization. Only inflation and overdue loan ratios were found to be statistically significant; the other coefficient had the right sign (see Appendix Table 1).

this rise reflected a decline in the MRR soon after its introduction (see Chart 3, Panel (A). Fry (1988) suggests that the initial decline in the MRR pointed to oligopolistic pricing, whereas Buhat (1987) interprets this decline as a move by banks to offset the increase in other elements of their costs of funds (e.g., the cost of the promotional campaign for deposits). Evidence supports the latter interpretation, especially in view of the low concentration ratio in the banking industry (described later) and of the evolution of the net interest margin.

The net interest margin—after allowing for the cost of reserve requirements and other regulatory factors[27]—fell sharply between 1980 and 1983, but rose between 1984 and 1986 (see Table 5). The regulatory factors contributed about 5 percentage points to the average intermediation cost between 1984 and 1986; their impact on the marginal intermediation cost was even higher (around 8 percent) particularly in times of inflation and high interest rates. Thus, the reserve requirements and other regulatory factors served to aggravate the crisis by disproportionately raising the borrowing costs of firms. As noted earlier, the increase in overdue loans also contributed to widening the margins (to reflect risk premiums) and further raised borrowing costs. Particularly during 1984 and 1985, the increase in loan losses and the resulting caution in lending policies by banks served to raise lending rates and both gross and net margins.

Monetary Control Reforms

The reforms of monetary policy instruments facilitated greater flexibility in interest rates and rapid adjustments to major shocks, but the financial crisis itself strongly influenced the evolution of the instruments.

First, during the 1970s, CBP set a uniform legal reserve ratio of 20 percent across both institutions and instruments. In 1980, CBP announced a plan to lower gradually the legal reserve ratio to 16 percent, beginning in January 1982. The plan was to reduce the ratio by 1 percentage point every six months. During 1982, the plan went into effect and the legal reserve ratio declined from 20 percent to 18 percent at the end of 1982. As the crisis worsened in 1983, the plan was frozen; in 1984, CBP raised the legal reserve ratio to 24 percent in order to contain liquidity pressures.

Second, until 1983, CBP actively pursued selective credit policies. Special rediscount facilities were opened as an incentive to banks, especially development banks, to extend credit to priority sectors and activities (e.g., foodgrain production, land irrigation, promotion of small busi-

---

[27] The authorities applied a lower reserve ratio of 5 percent on long-term deposits, compared with the ratio on shorter time deposits in column (2) of Table 5. Other regulatory factors include gross receipts, tax, agri/agra requirements, and the 3 percent (now 4 percent) interest paid on required reserves.

nesses). Following the crisis of confidence in 1981, CBP also opened a special rediscount window for medium- and long-term loans and equity investment to help government financial institutions finance the takeover and acquisition of troubled entities hit by the crisis. In November 1983, CBP also opened a liquidity window to counter the increasing pressures on the banking system. During 1984 and 1985, however, CBP drastically modified the rediscounting policy. It set access limits on the refinance facilities, raised the rediscount rates to market-related levels, unified the terms of access of these facilities, and, in November 1985, reduced the number of regular rediscount windows from five to one.

Third, beginning in the mid-1970s, CBP relied increasingly on open market operations, based on its own securities, to regulate the domestic liquidity of the banking system. Indeed, until 1981, CBP used central bank certificates of indebtedness (CBCIs) with maturities longer than 180 days.[28] In 1983, however, CBP stopped issuing CBCIs by auction and sold them on tap at a fixed yield.[29] In 1984, CBP introduced central bank bills with maturities of less than 180 days; during 1985 and 1986, auctions of central bank bills would become the main instrument for the dramatic tightening of monetary policy.

Finally, CBP introduced swap operations in 1982. This instrument, which became more important as the 1980s progressed, aimed at improving CBP's foreign exchange position and providing liquidity to deposit money banks so as to smooth out short-term interest rates. Because of the fall in the value of the peso, CBP incurred huge foreign exchange losses on these swap operations.

On the whole, these reforms had positive effects, because they allowed CBP to react promptly to the numerous monetary shocks (e.g., bank runs, portfolio shifts, increased domestic financing of budgetary deficits) that buffeted the economy between 1983 and 1986, and to transmit its policy actions to the banking system swiftly via interest rates. Through high interest rates, CBP was able to meet its reserve money targets and to bring down inflation by 48 percentage points within two years; in 1986, inflation stood at 1.8 percent.[30] The adaptations of discount window policies served to prevent a collapse of the banking system.

The timing and sequencing of some measures, however, seemed to

[28] Owing to their unattractive features and low budgetary pressures, treasury bills played no role in the conduct of open market operations. After an unsuccessful attempt to restore the primacy of treasury bill issues in 1981, CBP pursued the conduct of open market operations using primarily its own securities until 1986.

[29] Treasury bill issues were also being sold on tap at that time.

[30] The management and impact of monetary policy at the height of the crisis (i.e., between 1984 and 1986) are discussed in greater detail in Section II.

exacerbate instability. In view of expectation of further devaluation of the peso against the U.S. dollar as a result of the persistent weakening of the external position and accelerating rate of devaluation of the peso between 1979 and 1982, the introduction of swap operations with foreign exchange guarantees seemed ill-timed; CBP was able to finance unsustainable balance of payments deficits, but it risked large exchange losses if the trend in the peso depreciation continued.[31] Furthermore, the opening of numerous special rediscount facilities, in addition to the emergency facility, between 1981 and 1983 was inconsistent with interest rate deregulation, insofar as access to these facilities by financial institutions weakened the effectiveness of open market operations. (Banks could obtain refinancing from CBP at below-market rates and at their own initiative.) As expected, these measures had inflationary effects between 1981 and 1983. The appropriate sequencing of the regulatory reforms should have been to modify the rediscount mechanism while interest rates were deregulated, not after.

Banking Structure

Measures. Between 1971 and 1981 CBP attempted to consolidate the domestic banking system while promoting greater competition by allowing foreign banks to enter. In 1972, CBP substantially raised the minimum capital requirement for all banks (see Table 6). After 1975, banks that could not comply with this requirement were permitted to merge with other domestic and foreign banks. However, CBP also actively encouraged banks to open branches, particularly in rural areas.

In 1980, CBP enacted legislation permitting the establishment of "universal" banks.[32] They also raised the minimum capital requirement again. The previous functional classification of thrift banks into savings banks, private development banks, and savings and loan associations was eliminated. Thrift banks were allowed to carry on all operations performed by commercial banks except foreign exchange operations. The fact that they were also subject to lower reserve requirements gave them a cost advantage. Entry requirements for rural banks, which lend to farmers and rural entrepreneurs, were very liberal; capital requirements were low and limited management experience was accepted.[33]

Impact of the Crisis. The crisis significantly altered the banking structure. First, in terms of the volume of assets, by 1980 banks had increased

[31] Actually, in 1983, CBP had abandoned its earlier stance and indicated that the outstanding amount of swap operations at end-1982 would not be increased.

[32] Nine commercial banks converted to unibanks, one of which (Manila Bank) was recently liquidated and another (Philippine National Bank) was subject to major restructuring. Unibanks did not actively pursue the opportunities in near-banking activities permitted to them because of the unstable environment and the preoccupation with survival.

[33] The banking experience of management often consisted of only a few weeks of training.

Table 6. Selected Prudential Ratios of Central Bank, 1972 and 1980

	1972	1980
	(*In millions of pesos*)	
Minimum capital requirement[1]		
Extended commercial banks (unibanks)	. . .	500.0
Commercial banks[2]	900.0	300.0
Thrift banks (in Manila)[3]	—	20.0
Rural banks	—	0.5
Investment houses		20.0
	(*In percent*)	
Limits on equity investments		
by commercial banks		
including unibanks in:		
Allied undertakings		
Financial		
Commercial banks	49.0	30.0
Others	49.0	100.0
Nonfinancial	100.0	100.0
Nonallied undertakings[4]	0.0	35.0
Total equity investments		
(in percent of net worth)		
For commercial banks	35.0	25.0
For unibanks		50.0
Single-equity investments	15.0	15.0
Capital risk assets ratio	15.0	10.0
Borrowings by directors, officers,		
stockholders, and their		
related interest (DOSRI)	$\leq K$[5]	$\leq K$[5]

Source: Central Bank of the Philippines.
[1]Applies to newly established institutions.
[2]For existing ones, it remains at ₱ 100 million.
[3]In other places, it is ₱ 10 million for new institutions and ₱ 5 million for existing ones.
[4]By unibanks; for commercial banks, it remains at zero percent.
[5]CB Circular No. 357 dated January 22, 1973. K = the aggregate ceiling on capital accounts net of recommended valuation reserves. (This refers to net value of capital accounts.)

their dominant position among financial institutions (see Table 7), but tiers had developed in the banking sector. The first tier consisted of a few commercial banks and development banks whose size had increased sharply during the 1970s. The second tier consisted of a large and growing

Table 7. Assets of Financial Institutions, Selected Years, 1970–85

	Amount				Distribution			
	1970	1975	1980	1985	1970	1975	1980	1985
	(In billions of pesos; end of period)				(In percent of total)			
Central Bank	6.0	26.0	65.4	251.6	17.6	21.2	20.9	33.7
Banks	19.1	69.9	188.8	395.2	56.0	57.0	60.3	52.4
Commercial	14.1	53.2	138.4	283.3	41.3	43.3	41.6	37.6
Of which:								
Government	(. . .)	(18.1)	(34.6)	(70.3)	(. . .)	(14.8)	(11.1)	(9.3)
Foreign	(—)	(—)	(18.7)	(45.0)	(—)	(—)	(6.0)	(6.0)
Thrift	1.0	2.11	0.6	15.1	2.9	1.7	3.4	2.0
Rural	0.7	2.8	5.6	8.8	2.1	2.3	1.8	1.2
Specialized	3.3	11.8	34.2	88.0	9.7	9.6	10.9	11.7
Of which:								
DBP	(. . .)	(9.6)	(28.0)	(74.4)	(. . .)	(7.8)	(8.9)	(9.9)
Nonbanks	9.0	26.8	58.7	107.2	26.4	21.8	18.7	14.2
Total	34.1	122.7	313.1	754.0	100.0	100.0	100.0	100.0

Source: Central Bank of the Philippines.

number of rural and thrift banks, mostly small ones (see Table 8). A disproportionate number of institutions in this segment of the banking system were hit hard by the crisis, partly as a result of the weaknesses in entry regulations and the limited subsequent supervision. At the end of 1986, a total of 30 commercial banks in the Philippines (9 unibanks, 17 domestic commercial banks, and 4 foreign banks) accounted for 41 percent of the gross assets of the financial system (60 percent in 1980). In addition, there were 3 specialized government banks (16 percent),[34] 114 thrift banks (2.7 percent), and 877 rural banks (1 percent). Between 1981 and 1986, the relative position of banks was eroded somewhat by the growing role of the CBP in financing government budget deficits and in supporting troubled financial institutions because of the crisis itself.[35]

Second, government-owned banks played a central role within the banking system, and the concentration of risks in some of them was a critical factor in the crisis.[36] Their share of total bank assets, which averaged about 33 percent between 1970 and 1980, rose to 36 percent by the end of 1985. DBP alone accounted for 29 percent of total bank assets. Their troubles threatened the stability of the banking system and culminated in the major restructuring and rehabilitation of two of the largest state-owned institutions that became insolvent.

Third, significant parts of the banking system were characterized by a bank-holding-company structure. Twelve holding companies had interrelated ownership and interests in private banks and nonfinancial corporations. They controlled commercial or savings banks, investment houses, and insurance companies. Such was the case with the Herdis Group,[37] which, between 1979 and 1980, controlled Summa Savings and Mortgage Banks, the Summa Insurance Corporation, the Equipment Credit Corporation, and Interbank and Commercial Bank of Manila.[38] Furthermore,

[34] The specialized government banks are DBP, LBP, and the Amanah Bank.

[35] As the crisis worsened after 1981, CBP granted massive indirect financial assistance to public corporations through some government financial institutions. This aid allowed these financial institutions to finance their acquisition of troubled nonfinancial entities between 1982 and 1985. Furthermore, CBP accumulated huge losses on foreign exchange swap operations linked to successive and massive devaluations during the first half of the 1980s.

[36] Government-owned banks included the DBP, LBP, PNB, the Amanah Bank, and the Philippines Veterans' Bank.

[37] This group effectively went out of business after the 1981 crisis, and many of its companies and subsidiaries were bought out by the Government.

[38] Similar cases included the Ayala Group, which controlled 37.0 percent of the paid-up capital of the Bank of Philippine Islands (the second-largest commercial bank after PNB), the Bancom Group, the Cojuango Group (United Coconut Planters Bank, the seventh-largest commercial bank in 1981); the First Philippine Holding Group (Philippine Commercial and International Bank, the fifth-largest bank in 1981).

Table 8. Number of Banking Institutions, Selected Years, 1975–86

	Total Offices				Head Offices			
	1975	1980	1981	1986	1975	1980	1981	1986
Total Banks	2,156	3,364	3,652	3,774	892	1,171	1,222	1,025
Commercial	996	1,503	1,732	1,716	33	32	33	30
Domestic	996	1,499	1,728	1,716	33	28	29	20
Of which:								
Government	. . .	. . .	. . .	. . .	(2)	(2)	(10)	(10)
Foreign[1]	. . .	4	4	4	. . .	4	4	4
Thrifts[1]	259	673	631	665	88	144	140	116
Rural	834	1,096	1,167	1,293	768	985	1,040	877
Specialized government[2]	67	92	122	100	3	3	3	2
Concentration ratio of commercial banking industry (in percent)[3]	. . .	9.99	10.03	10.00				

Sources: Central Bank of the Philippines, Private Development Banks, *Annual Report, 1981*.
Note: For 1975, data reproduced from World Bank (1979).
[1]Includes private development banks, savings banks, and stock savings and loan associations.
[2]Includes DBP, Land Bank, and, starting in 1980, the Philippine Amanah Bank, which operates under Islamic principles.
[3]As measured by the Herfindahl-Hirschman index.

most groups had many interlocking directorships within the corporate business sector (see Doherty (1983)).

The number and size distribution of banks—the Herfindahl-Hirschman index showed a ratio of only 0.10 as of December 31, 1986—suggest that the degree of concentration was not a problem.[39] The previously noted fall in net interest margins between 1980 and 1983 following the deregulation of interest rates also suggests a competitive banking system. The rise in net interest margins between 1984 and 1986 was attributable to tighter monetary policies, high reserve requirements, and an increase in loan losses. Thus, oligopolistic pricing does not seem to have been a factor in interest rate developments. However, the bank-holding-company structure, together with the supervisory weaknesses discussed in the next section, permitted excessive risk taking following deregulation, and this risk taking seems to have helped cause and aggravate the crisis.

Prudential Regulation and Supervision and Related Institutional Practices

Supervisory weaknesses were conducive to loose banking practices, which later led to numerous bank failures. Also, the existence of a deposit insurance scheme did little to prevent or contain the crisis. In the following subsections, the supervisory system that regulates and oversees the conduct of banks' operations is described, and the role of this system in ensuring the soundness and stability of the financial sector is discussed.

Supervisory Authority

Although CBP exercises supervisory authority over the banking institutions, the ultimate supervisory authority is the Monetary Board (MB), the policymaking body of CBP.[40]

The Department of Bank Supervision and Examination is the operational arm of CBP for supervision. Supervisory procedures in the Philippines, which include reporting requirements and examination, are regular, comprehensive, and thorough.[41] Officers of the Department of Bank

---

[39] The number of banking institutions, including branches, is shown in Table 8.

[40] The MB is composed of the Governor acting as chief executive, the Minister of Finance, the Director General of the National Economic Development Authority, the Chairman of the Board of Investments, the Minister of the Budget, and two part-time members of the private sector.

[41] For instance, the reporting system covers every item of banks' balance sheets, and information such as credit to directors, officers, and shareholders and their related interest (DOSRI credit) is even reported daily. On-site examinations and inspections, patterned after the U.S. system, focus on the quality of banks' assets, which are classified accordingly. A rating system, CAMEL (Capital Asset, Management, Earning, and Liquidity), is used to assess quantitatively a bank's soundness, along with a questionnaire for a qualitative assessment.

Supervision and Examination are responsible for bank examination to assess the soundness of operations and the solvency and liquidity of the bank. Reports of these bank examinations are then transmitted to the MB, which decides what action to take when a bank is found to be in trouble.

When a bank faces protracted liquidity or solvency problems, the MB may appoint a conservator to take charge of the assets, liabilities, and management of the bank in order to protect depositors and other creditors. If the conservator is unable to restore the viability of the bank, the bank is declared insolvent.[42] The MB then appoints a receiver to take charge of all assets and liabilities of the bank, and forbids the bank from doing business. Within 60 days, the MB decides whether to liquidate the bank or to reorganize it to permit the resumption of business. In the former case, CBP appoints a liquidator to carry out the decision, provided no court challenges the decision.

The ultimate enforcement resides with the MB, and the closing of a troubled bank is subject to due process, which may take a long time, especially when litigation is brought by owners.

Supervisory Rules

Between 1972 and 1982, CBP also modified the main prudential regulations on commercial banks. Capital requirements, defined as a ratio of net worth to risk assets, were lowered from 15 percent in 1972 to 10 percent in 1973 (see Table 6). After 1980, ratios as low as 6 percent became permissible with the prior approval of the MB. The authorities sought to provide banks with greater leverage to expand their asset portfolios.

CBP relaxed its rules regarding credit accommodation to directors, officers, stockholders, and related interests (DOSRI). In 1973, DOSRI credit had an upper limit equal to a bank's total capital account, net of valuation reserves.[43] By 1980, this limit had become less restrictive for commercial banks, because the authorities had somewhat relaxed the provisions designed to limit conflicts of interest between a bank and another financial or nonfinancial institution that were linked by interlocking directorate.[44] In addition, regulations governing relations between a bank and its subsidiaries were eliminated.

To restrict banks' risk exposure, the authorities established a single-

[42] Insolvency is defined in the law as the inability of a bank to pay its liabilities as they fall due in the usual and ordinary course of business. One important limitation of this definition is that it does not apply to insolvency stemming from extraordinary deposit withdrawals caused by a financial panic.

[43] See CB Circular No. 357 dated January 22, 1973.

[44] See CB Circular No. 596 dated March 1, 1978, whereby the Central Bank amended CB Circular No. 357 to exclude from the maximum credit accommodation to DOSRI, among

borrower limit of 15 percent (including loans and equity investment) of the bank's net worth; the rule had been in force during the 1970s and is still valid, although exceptions have been made. For example, in 1983, the Government's takeover of the Construction and Development Corporation of the Philippines (CDCP) through the PNB violated this limit. After the takeover, PNB's total exposure (in equity alone) in CDCP went to 60 percent of its net worth.

In contrast to the trend toward relaxation of prudential regulations, CBP expanded the institutional coverage of bank supervision after 1972 in order to include the nonbank quasi-banks (NBQB). CBP also monitored the nonbank quasi-banks' issues of commercial paper "with recourse" and regulated its terms, conditions of rollover, physical delivery, and the like.

Loose Lending Practices

As a result of the political climate both before and during the crisis, CBP failed to enforce supervisory rules regarding DOSRI credit, supervision of nonbank quasi-bank activities, and, most important, the treatment of past due loans and their provisioning.

DOSRI Credit. Failure by the MB to enforce the rules reportedly led to substantial bank lending to DOSRI, to the detriment of other legitimate borrowers.[45] Inappropriate loans to DOSRI are cited as a major contributor to bank failures over the past decade. In reaction to the 1981 crisis, CBP tightened the regulations on DOSRI credit.[46] Bank credit to firms with interlocking directorship/officership was tightened again (reversing the earlier stance), but the restrictions regarding institutional relationships between holding companies and subsidiaries were loosened.

Supervision of Money Market Operations.[47] Prior to 1980, regulations governing the functioning of the money market were differentiated by type of participant and type of operation, each type falling under the purview of a different supervisory authority. CBP supervised only banks and nonbank quasi-banks and monitored only transactions on a "with

---

others, "the credit accommodations to a corporation in whose board of directors, a director or officer or stockholder of the lending bank seats as a representative of the bank. However, the bank representative's equity interest in the borrower corporation shall only be the minimum shares required by law, rules and regulations, or the by-laws of the corporations to qualify a person as director to the corporation." (Sycip and others (1978), p. 15.)

[45] Central Bank of the Philippines (1980).

[46] The CBP adopted new ceilings on unsecured DOSRI credit of 30 percent of total credit accommodations for each DOSRI. Total DOSRI credit was subsequently limited to 15 percent of a bank's loan portfolio or its entire capital account, whichever was lower. Also, new accounting and reporting standards for DOSRI loans have been adopted.

[47] The money market in the Philippines is characterized by a variety of participants, including all financial institutions; the Treasury and nonfinancial corporations; and a wide

recourse" basis. The Securities and Exchange Commission supervised other participants, while monitoring transactions on a "without recourse" basis. Subsequently, CBP imposed regulations on nonbank quasi-banks. These regulations included the requirement that nonbank quasi-banks hold 20 percent of their liabilities—deposit substitutes—in the form of deposits with the CBP; a ceiling on interest rates of these institutions (the maximum rate paid for borrowing was 17 percent; the rate charged for lending was 18 percent); and a minimum trading lot. Because nonbank financial institutions were not subject to such regulations by the Securities and Exchange Commission, nonbank quasi-banks lost their competitiveness. In response, nonbank quasi-banks started to deal in paper on a "without recourse" basis; this paper was issued mostly by subsidiaries or affiliates of "groups" to which the nonbank quasi-banks belonged. This practice allowed nonbank quasi-banks not only to circumvent CBP regulations and monitoring of their money market activities, but also to help businesses of their "group" to mobilize short-term funds by issuing less-than-prime commercial paper. These unsound lending practices contributed to the collapse of the commercial paper market in 1981.[48]

Accounting Rules. The 1980 reforms did not cover CBP rules governing the treatment of overdue loans, the provisioning for bad debt, and scrutiny of deposit transactions by CBP examiners. The inadequacies of these rules, which remained unchanged until 1986, played a significant role in the worsening of the financial crisis.

CBP used the following rules for its own assessment of bank conditions: demand loans were considered past due if payment was not received within six months of a written demand. For loans payable in installments, the determining factor was the number of payments in arrears, a number that varied with the repayment schedule of the loan (monthly, quarterly, semiannually, or annually). The threshold for monthly installment loans was ten missed installments. For other loans, the period varied between one and two years. Whenever 20 percent of the outstanding balance of a

---

range of instruments such as promissory notes issued by banks and nonbank quasi-banks, government securities, central bank bills, certificates of participation/assignments, and commercial paper issued by corporations. Commercial paper can be issued "with or without recourse." Deposit substitutes issued by nonbank quasi-banks are also referred to as commercial paper issued by these institutions. See Lontoc (1981), p.8.

[48] In reaction, the authorities modified the regulations governing money market operations. Among other things, the new regulations limited the issuance of commercial paper to prime companies; required that issuers have at their disposal a bank credit line covering 35 percent of their money market issues; and required that all commercial papers be registered with the Securities and Exchange Commission and be printed serially on security paper, by the Central Bank Printing Plant.

loan was in arrears, the entire loan was to be considered overdue; once a loan was classified as overdue, interest could no longer be accrued. In practice, however, banks differed considerably in their treatment of overdue loans. Conservatively managed banks generally placed loans on a nonaccrual status more promptly than did the schedule used by CBP, in order to avoid the tax on gross revenues; other banks followed loose practices, especially as they began facing financial distress.

Regarding provisions for bad debt, CBP is empowered by law to establish rules, either generally or in individual cases. CBP has not enforced the rules, however, leaving reserve or provisioning policies to bank managements.[49] In the supervisory process, the CBP does compare the reserves established by a bank with those it believes are required on the basis of its own assessment of asset quality. Under the law, banks are allowed to write off bad loans up to ₱ 100,000, but they must have CBP approval before writing off loans above that amount. Requests for writeoff approval concerning DOSRI loans are passed on to the MB; other requests are handled by CBP staff.

Examiners are not allowed to investigate deposit transactions that are protected by strict secrecy rules, unless they are duly authorized by the MB. The MB may permit scrutiny of deposit transactions only if it is satisfied that a bank fraud or serious irregularity has been committed and that it is necessary to look at deposit transactions to determine the facts.

Negligible Role of Philippines Deposit Insurance Company (PDIC). Because of its severe staffing constraints and low capital base, PDIC played no significant role in improving depositors' confidence in the banking system during the crisis period of the 1980s.[50] Despite the capital increase from ₱ 20 million to ₱ 2 billion in 1985, PDIC's resources, human and financial, were insufficient.[51] As a result, PDIC faced major difficulties in settling the growing claims of insured depositors of failed banks (see Table 9).[52] Thus, CBP was compelled to tie up most of its supervisory staff in helping PDIC settle these claims.

Summary

The absence of significant reforms in prudential supervision aggravated the banking crisis. First, the existing rules were not enforced in practice,

---

[49] The policy was formalized in 1987, when the MB passed a resolution requiring all banks to set up a system for reviewing loans and other assets for the purpose of establishing appropriate and adequate reserves.

[50] Deposit insurance limit was ₱ 10,000.

[51] Annual premium contribution by financial institutions amounted to ₱ 100 million.

[52] However, in the case of the largest failed bank, PDIC quickly settled the claims of insured deposits.

Table 9. PDIC Payments to Insured Depositors of Failed Banks as of June 1987

	Deposit Liabilities (1)	Estimated Insured Deposits (2)	Total Payments (3)	Ratio (3)/(2)	Ratio (2)/(1)
Commercial banks	4,447.3	1,463.1	226.5	15.5	32.9
1970–80	338.7	45.2	45.2	100.0	13.3
1981–87	4,108.6	1,417.9	181.3	12.8	34.5
Savings and mortgage banks	1,015.9	815.8	771.7	94.6	80.3
1970–80	16.4	11.5	11.5	100.0	70.1
1981–85	999.5	804.3	760.2	94.5	80.5
Private development banks[1]	294.6	183.4	124.2	67.7	62.2
Savings and Loan Associations[1]	1,310.3	1,083.8	740.7	68.3	82.7
Total	7,068.1	3,546.1	1,863.1	52.5	50.2
1970–80	355.1	56.7	56.7	100.0	16.0
1981–87	6,713.0	3,489.5	1,806.4	51.8	52.0

Source: Philippine Deposit Insurance Corporation.
[1]Covers the 1981–87 period; figures for the 1970–80 period amount to zero.

although the MB was informed promptly of the problem-bank cases. Second, some of the accounting rules themselves were not codified to ensure consistency and transparency. This situation encouraged troubled banks to book accrued interest on nonperforming loans and to distribute the book profits. The main problem with provisioning rules arose after the crisis of 1981. The MB had to decide between forcing banks to provision for bad debt so as to maintain confidence in banking institutions or remaining tolerant on this issue to give troubled banks time to overcome their financial difficulties. The MB took the second option, which accelerated the deterioration of bank finances.

II. Manifestations of the Crisis and Its Monetary Effects

The manifestations of the crisis—loss of public trust in the banking system and the spread of financial distress and bank failures— and the monetary effects of the crisis, which complicated the conduct of CBP monetary policy and caused a severe credit crunch, are described in this section.

Loss of Public Trust

During the crisis, financial wealth holders lost trust in the banking system, causing both runs on banks and "flight to quality."[53] The spread of banking distress weakened the public's confidence in financial institutions, adding fears about the safety of banks' deposits.

Surge in Demand for Reserve Money

As noted earlier, the Dewey Dee affair triggered a crisis of confidence that provoked bank runs and capital flight in 1981.[54] The bank runs caused an increase in the ratio of currency to narrow money in 1981, which was a sharp reversal of the declining trend in the ratio during the 1970s. Evidence pointed also to capital flight (see Table 10).

The currency ratios continued to increase in 1982 and jumped in 1983; these increased ratios reflected a major erosion of confidence in the banking system. The largest increase occurred in the last quarter of 1983 after the authorities announced, in late September 1983, the suspension of repayments on external debt. Capital flight intensified in 1983 (see Table 10), because the announcement of the moratorium raised concern among foreign creditors and led to the cutoff of suppliers' credit.

"Flight to Quality"

The 1981 panic also caused a redeployment of funds, mostly to institutions perceived as sound, namely, the commercial banks. As already noted, investors in the commercial paper market switched to bank deposits. Indeed, as shown in Table 11, banks' deposit accounts increased as a whole by ₱ 1.6 million (from ₱ 21 million in 1980 to ₱ 22.6 million in 1981), but there was also a switch of deposits away from thrift banks. Whereas total bank deposits increased by 11 percent between 1980 and 1981, deposits of thrift banks fell by 9 percent, triggering failures among these institutions.[55] In addition, commercial banks gained 3.2 million

[53] A "flight to quality" refers to financial wealth holders' shift from deposits to safer assets such as treasury bills, or from weak banks to banks perceived to be more sound.

[54] Capital flight is defined here as "the *acquisition* or *retention* of a claim on nonresident that is motivated by the owner's concern that the value of his asset would be subject to discrete losses if his claims continued to be held domestically." See International Monetary Fund (1988).

[55] The collapse of the commercial paper market had also triggered a panic in the thrift banking sector.

Table 10.   Selected Financial Ratios and Years, 1970–86

Year	"Financial Deepening" Ratios			Ratios Measuring Stability of Banking Sector			
	$\dfrac{M1}{GNP}$	$\dfrac{L}{GNP}$	$\dfrac{M3}{GNP}$	$\dfrac{C^P}{M1}$	$\dfrac{C^P}{L}$	$\dfrac{K1^1}{\Delta D}$	$\dfrac{\Delta C^P}{\Delta D}$
	(In percent at end of period)						
1970	10.3	21.8	21.8	55.8	26.4	20.0	30.0
1975	9.0	30.5	30.5	46.6	13.8	43.9	11.4
1980	8.5	29.9	29.9	45.3	12.9	31.3	10.1
1981	7.7	28.7	27.0	49.4	13.3	−51.6	7.5
1982	7.0	29.7	28.4	54.0	12.7	−17.6	8.8
1983	8.5	31.3	29.8	60.3	16.5	−46.0	36.5
1984	6.4	26.5	22.8	64.9	15.6	6.2	10.5
1985	6.0	30.0	22.3	67.3	13.5	−33.9	5.9
1986	6.9	33.5	23.0	68.8	14.2	−52.9	19.1

Sources: International Monetary Fund, *International Financial Statistics*, 1987; Table 2; and IMF staff estimates.

[1]Short-term capital (net), including errors and omissions (these flows represent nonmonetary capital flows); this ratio is used as a rough measure of capital flight (minus sign), including the trade credit squeeze.

deposit accounts in 1981—a 32 percent increase over 1980, while thrift and savings banks lost 2.1 million accounts—a decline of about 30 percent over the same period.

After 1983, financial investors again redeployed their funds, this time toward safe securities with high yields. Specifically, the public shifted out of deposits and into treasury and central bank bills. The ratio of M3 to total liquidity fell sharply after 1983 (Table 2), owing in part to the sharp increases in interest rates on treasury and central bank bills beginning in 1984. Banks as a group lost a large number of deposit accounts.

Banking Distress

Between 1981 and 1985, financial difficulties of corporate businesses steadily worsened, increasing the distress among banking institutions.[56] The limited data on the financial performance of the top 1,000 corpora-

---

[56] Official figures on business failures do not exist. In this section, partial data from nongovernment sources are relied on to provide an idea of businesses' financial distress.

tions from 1980 to 1984 showed a sharp increase in debt/equity ratios in 1982, declining profitability from 1981 to 1983 with negative net incomes in 1982 and 1983, and a sizable weakening of the liquidity positions of firms (as measured by the ratio of current assets to current liabilities) between 1980 and 1984 (Appendix Table 2). The sharp increase in the debt/equity ratio and in the indebtedness of the nongovernment sector (Table 3) in 1982 and 1983 when real lending rates were at a peak seems to suggest that distress borrowing was a significant factor. These developments were reflected in the evolution of overdue loans in the banking system. Overdue loans rose from ₱ 12.5 billion (11.5 percent of total loans) in 1980 to ₱ 16.6 billion (13.2 percent) in 1981. The situation deteriorated sharply after 1983, and overdue loans rose to a record high of 19.3 percent in 1986.

Until 1983, the ratio of nonperforming loans to banks' loan portfolio remained below the critical ratio of 15 percent that is perceived by bankers and the public as a threshold for individual banks' solvency.[57] Between 1981 and 1984, banks' ratio of capital to outstanding loans remained above banks' ratio of overdue to outstanding loans. Hence until 1983, banks as a whole appear to have been sufficiently capitalized to provision for bad debt and absorb eventual losses from bad loans. Beginning in 1985, the ratio of capital to outstanding bank loans fell below the ratio of overdue loans, indicating major solvency problems in the banking system. The size of overdue loans was contained in part by the authorities' rescue of (at least) 123 failing businesses and by the troubled banks' practice of keeping bad loans current by renegotiating them at maturity.[58] In addition, the Government alleviated the banking distress by acquiring six troubled commercial banks between 1981 and 1983.

The authorities' rescue of distressed banks significantly helped to limit the number of liquidations among commercial banks. By the end of 1986, only three sizable commercial banks had failed. The liquidations occurred mostly among the many small rural and thrift banks.

Between 1981 and 1983, 138 thrift and rural banks failed; this number amounts to 12 percent of all banks existing in 1980 (Table 10). Although these failures did not threaten the stability of the banking system, they tied down CBP supervisory staff. In addition, the Philippines Deposit Insurance Corporation, with its low capital base and inadequate contributions, found it increasingly difficult to settle the growing claims of depositors of the failed banks.

---

[57] See *Business Day* (1982), p. 139.

[58] Renegotiated loans doubled between 1984 and 1985 while loans past due for more than one year rose steadily from ₱ 6 billion in 1984 to ₱ 8 billion in 1986.

Table 11. Indicators of the Financial Crisis, Selected Years, 1970–87

(In percent)[1]

	1970	1975	1980	1981	1982	1983	1984	1985	1986	June 1987
Number of bank failures[2]	6	7	24	30	8	7	26	44	26	22
Of which:										
Commercial banks	(3)	(1)	(0)	(0)	(0)	(0)	(0)	(2)	(0)	(1)
Thrift	(. . .)	(. . .)	(0)	(4)	(2)	(1)	(16)	(6)	(0)	(3)
Ratio of failed bank assets to total assets[2]										
Commercial banks	1.9	1.0	0.0	0.0	0.0	0.0	0.0	1.2	0.0	4.0[3]
Thrift banks	5.2	0.0	0.0	0.4	0.3	1.3	10.8	35.4	0.0	5.0[4]
Rural banks	0.3	0.3	1.1	1.2	0.2	0.2	0.4	1.9	1.4	1.0
Ratio of overdue loans to total outstanding loans	16.7	19.2	11.5	13.2	13.0	8.9	12.7	16.7	19.3	. . .
Of which:										
Commercial banks	(. . .)	(. . .)	(11.9)	(13.1)	(11.5)	(7.5)	(11.0)	(15.6)	(18.4)	(. . .)
Ratio of capital to outstanding loans[5]	. . .	. . .	12.1	13.6	14.4	12.9	16.7	16.1	17.7	. . .
Number of bank deposit accounts (in millions)	. . .	5.3	21.0	22.6	24.9	25.6	23.7	20.2	19.5	18.6
Of which:										
Commercial banks	(. . .)	(. . .)	(10.1)	(13.3)	(15.1)	(15.2)	(14.0)	(12.6)	(12.4)	(11.8)
Thrift	(. . .)	(3.3)	(7.2)	(5.1)	(5.5)	(5.8)	(5.0)	(3.1)	(2.7)	(2.5)

Broad money/Total liquidity	...	...	100.0	94.2	95.6	95.3	86.3	74.3	68.7	...
Bank deposits (in billions of pesos, end of period)	...	27.6	90.4	100.1	116.7	140.0	152.2	167.5	166.3	159.8[4]
Of which:										
Commercial banks	(. . .)	(20.7)	(72.6)	(79.3)	(93.2)	(116.2)	(134.5)	(143.0)	(138.0)	(132.1)
Thrift	(. . .)	(1.6)	(7.9)	(7.2)	(9.3)	(11.2)	(7.1)	(10.5)	(13.0)	(13.2)[4]

Source: Central Bank of the Philippines.

[1] Unless otherwise specified.

[2] For 1970 and 1975, data refer to cumulative amounts between 1970 and 1974 and 1975 and 1979, respectively. Data for the rate of bank failure exclude the five commercial banks in distress which have been acquired by GFIs; they are: Republic Planters' Bank (1978); International Corporate Bank (1982); Union Bank of the Philippines (1982); Associated Bank (1983); and Philipinas Bank (1979). The numbers in parentheses refer to the year of acquisition by government financial institutions.

[3] September.

[4] June.

[5] Capital defined as "net worth" or unimpaired capital plus free reserves.

Monetary Management During the Crisis

Actions on Supply of Banks' Reserves

Between 1981 and 1986, CBP had increasing difficulty in achieving its often conflicting objectives of monetary stability, confidence in the banking system, and credit allocation to priority sectors, as both the financial crisis and the recession deepened.

Between 1981 and 1983, CBP gave priority to containing the spread of financial distress and stepping up selective credit policies. As a lender of last resort, CBP intervened appropriately by providing emergency credit during 1981 and by absorbing excess liquidity as the crisis abated in 1982 (see Table 12). Meanwhile, CBP increased concessional rediscount credit to financial institutions. In the aftermath of the banking panics of 1983 CBP also replenished the banks' loss of deposits and began to realize exchange losses on swap operations; as a result of these developments, reserve money jumped 48 percent between the end of 1982 and the end of 1983.

Between 1984 and 1986, to offset the expansionary effects on reserve money of the earlier policies and to restore monetary stability, the CBP absorbed huge amounts of liquidity from financial institutions through massive sales of its own securities and tighter access to rediscount facilities.[59] However, the effect of these actions was mitigated by the huge financing of the public sector deficit in 1984, following the drastic cutback in foreign financing of these deficits.[60] This policy stance caused inflation to jump from 12 percent in 1983 to 50 percent in 1984, and led to a crowding out of the private sector. Between 1985 and 1986, CBP finally brought inflation under control by maintaining a tight policy.

CBP continued to provide extensive emergency assistance between 1984 and 1985, reacting essentially to financial distress rather than to panics as in earlier years. To prevent failures of financially distressed firms, CBP, through the decisions of the MB, adopted a remedial rather than punitive approach. This approach, however, led to a trade-off between short-run stability and long-run cost effectiveness of rescue operations.

The long negotiations over corrective actions to rehabilitate troubled institutions may have prolonged the public's perception of uncertainty and raised the ultimate cost of rescue operations. Also, CBP's attempt to seek additional capital and merger partners for troubled banks proved difficult

---

[59] After 1983, CBP closed a number of special rediscount facilities and set the discount rate on the remaining ones at market-related levels.

[60] Despite the reduction in the public sector deficit (in percent of GNP) after 1983, CBP stepped up its financing to this sector in order to offset the sharp decline in foreign financing of the public sector budgetary deficit.

Table 12. Descriptive Statistics for Reserve Money and CBP Credit During the Crisis, 1981(I)–1986(IV)

	1981(I)–1986(IV)		1981(I)–1983(III)		1983(IV)–1986(IV)	
	Mean	Coefficient[1] of variation	Mean	Coefficient of variation	Mean	Coefficient of variation
Money and credit aggregates		*(In billions of pesos, unless otherwise specified)*				
Reserve money	25.8	40.6	16.1	9.6	34.1	20.4
Net domestic credit	15.8	70.3	23.3	11.4	9.5	123.0
To: Public sector	12.5	42.7	8.0	13.0	16.3	27.4
Of which:						
Government	(11.7)	(32.8)	(8.8)	(16.1)	(14.2)	24.4
Financial institutions	3.3	460.3	15.2	17.3	−6.8	−203.2
Of which:						
Assistance	7.6	72.5	2.7	30.0	11.7	35.9
Rediscounting	10.3	30.5	12.1	30.0	8.8	18.4
Open market operations	−14.6	−127.1	0.3	1,690.4	−27.3	58.2
Selected ratios		*(In percent of reserve money)*				
Net domestic credit	84.6	78.2	145.9	15.2	32.9	40.6
To: Public sector	49.2	18.1	50.0	11.1	48.5	23.0
Financial institutions	35.4	184.4	95.8	21.6	−15.7	−260.3

Source: IMF staff calculations.

[1]Defined as the ratio (in percent) between the standard deviation (σ) and the mean ($\bar{x}$).

between 1983 and 1986, when all domestic banks faced financial difficulties. As the MB was deliberating the appropriate disposition of problem institutions, CBP continued to extend emergency loans, overdrafts, and equity lending to prevent a collapse of the banking system. This policy, combined with the Government's massive issuance of treasury bills to finance its budget deficit, had expansionary effects on total liquidity after 1983 despite the decline in the money multiplier (see Charts 4 and 5).

Complications from Portfolio Shifts

Empirical results showed that the estimated demand for real M3 shifted downward in 1983(III) because investors shifted from deposit substitutes into treasury and central bank bills; as a result, M3 became an unreliable indicator of monetary policy.[61] CBP's overestimation of actual M3 contributed to the loose monetary policy and skyrocketing inflation observed until late 1984.

CBP then reversed its stance to bring inflation under control and began targeting reserve money. CBP tightened the supply of bank reserves through massive sales of central bank bills, but the surge in the demand for reserve money (partly reflecting the currency flight) probably led to excessive tightening and thereby caused the steep increases in nominal interest rates from late 1985 to the middle of 1986. Large increases in domestic government borrowing added upward pressure on nominal interest rates, and contributed to crowding out the private sector. Such increases, which occurred despite the tightening of fiscal policy, stemmed from the drying up of foreign financing after the announcement of the moratorium.

Credit Crunch

After 1981, declining economic growth compounded the negative effect of rising interest rates on the demand for real credit, particularly in the private sector. The increase in overdue loans, many of which were renegotiated between 1984 and 1986, mitigated the sharp decline in this demand. Indeed, with private investment (in percent of GNP) plummeting in 1981 and debts being liquidated, demand for new investment loans by the private sector nearly came to a halt.

Nonetheless, banks apparently curtailed the supply of real credit to the private sector by more than the drop in demand, thereby resorting to

---

[61] When the economic and financial environment became very uncertain in late 1983, investors moved interest-bearing securities issued by banks to their customers into safer assets (see Section I of this chapter). A recent study (Goldsborough and Zaidi (1989)) also provides evidence of instability in the demand for M1, an instability consistent with the currency flight taking place during the 1983(IV)–1986(IV) period of the crisis.

Chart 4. Movements of Seasonally Adjusted Aggregates, 1981(I)–1986(III)

——— L: Liquidity (i.e., M3 plus nonbank holdings of central bank and treasury bill securities)

⋯⋯ R: Reserve money

— — M3: Broad money stock

— ⋅ Cᴾ: Currency in circulation

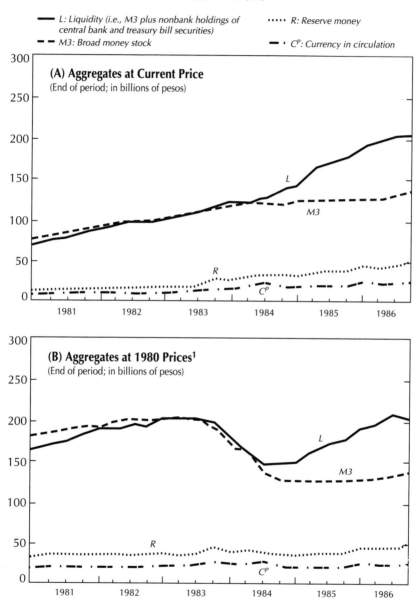

Sources: International Monetary Fund, *International Financial Statistics*.
[1] Deflated by consumer price index in Manila (end of period).

Chart 5. Evolution of Selected Monetary Ratios, 1981(I)–1986(III)
(In percent; end of period)

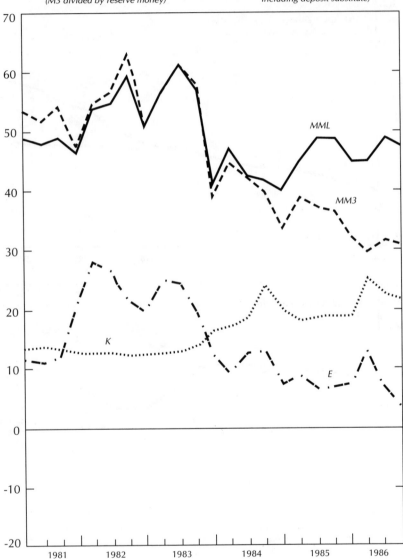

Source: International Monetary Fund, *International Financial Statistics Year Book*, 1989.

credit rationing as the crisis deepened. Between 1983 and the end of September 1986, real credit to the private sector fell a staggering 53 percent, and cumulative output fell by 9 percent. Consistent with their prudent lending policy, the uncertain economic outlook, and the chronic shortage of reserves, banks may have preferred to stop lending rather than to charge higher interest rates. Furthermore, banks found investing their liquidity in public securities (of treasury bills and central bank bills) more attractive than lending, for safety reasons. Banks' holdings of public securities rose sharply during the crisis, particularly between 1984 and 1986.[62] Banks' shift of funds to the public sector crowded out the private sector. Therefore, the banks' actions seem to have exacerbated the shortage of funds in the credit market and worsened the recession.

III. Measures to Deal with the Crisis

Measures to deal with the crisis included, in addition to emergency assistance and some liquidations, recapitalization through government funds, financial assistance to nonfinancial corporations, takeover of weak financial and nonfinancial firms by government financial institutions, and eventually a massive restructuring of some of the government financial institutions themselves.

Financial Assistance to Troubled Entities

During the 1981–86 crisis period, CBP and the Government provided massive financial assistance to troubled entities under various schemes.

Schemes

When the 1981 crisis broke out, the CBP lender-of-last-resort facility did not cover quasi-banks. To enable these quasi-banks to meet the demand for withdrawal of funds, CBP provided emergency loans through a special rediscount facility.[63] However, the primary issuers of commercial papers, mostly corporate businesses, continued to face liquidity problems and failed to honor their obligations as they came due. At that point, quasi-banks were the major holders of this paper.

CBP then set up the Industrial Fund with resources from CBP and the

---

[62] Between 1984 and 1985, banks (commercial, thrift, and savings) were the heaviest subscribers of government securities. These banks' holdings of government securities nearly doubled. See Paulino (1986), p. 29.

[63] Before 1981, the CBP law required the Central Bank to provide unlimited financial assistance during a crisis, but only to banks. This situation was corrected in 1982, when nonbanks became eligible for emergency assistance.

national government budget. Through the GFIs and unibanks, the Industrial Fund, in turn, lent these funds to troubled corporations, which then settled their obligations to the quasi-banks.[64] The latter, in turn, repaid the CBP emergency loans. This scheme amounted to a conversion of short-term emergency loans extended through the special rediscount window into long-term CBP lending through the Industrial Fund.

In early 1982, the Industrial Fund was replaced by a CBP special rediscount window, through which CBP extended medium- and long-term loans to universal banks, including PNB and DBP, to allow them to finance their acquisition of and merger with troubled entities (see Lamberte (1985)). That same year, CBP began to provide emergency loans and overdrafts to financial institutions facing unexpected liquidity shortages.

Similarly, the Government provided emergency lending and equity contributions to nonfinancial public corporations (mostly from 1981 to the middle of 1983) and to the government financial institutions (mostly from 1983 to 1985). The Government channeled its financial assistance directly through the capital budget, which recorded large deficits. Direct financial assistance to distressed public sector firms in 1981 and 1982 was aimed both at financing their operating deficits and at stepping up public investment to offset the decline in private investment after 1981. Assistance to government financial institutions, beginning in 1983, was aimed mostly at financing their acquisition and merger of distressed entities, and facilitated the conversion of debt owed to government financial institutions into equity. The Government provided both loans and equity funds to government financial institutions, thus allowing these institutions to absorb the loan losses and to assist distressed corporations by converting the bad loans provided to these corporations into equity. Because no dividends were expected from these corporations for a long time, this operation amounted to forgoing interest payments. In fact, the PNB lost an estimated ₽ 400 million in annual interest payments from the Construction Development Corporation of the Philippines as a result of such debt/equity conversion.

Government financial institutions took over large businesses that were virtually bankrupt, including the largest conglomerates that had been hit severely by the 1981 crisis. To illustrate, the National Industrial Development Corporation—a government financial institution and subsidiary of PNB—took over 9 corporations of the Construction and Development Corporation of the Philippines (CDCP) and 15 corporations of the Herdis Group; DBP and PNB took over 87 other CDCP corporations and 14

---

[64] Most of the universal banks involved in the scheme were major creditors of the troubled corporations (see Laya (1982)).

Herdis corporations.[65] The Social Security System (SSS), which had put 24 percent of its investment portfolio into the hotel sector during the 1970s, took over 9 hotels.

Volume

Between 1981 and 1985, the volume of financial assistance that the authorities granted to troubled entities mirrored the intensity of the crisis over its three phases. This volume more than doubled during the 1981 episode, continued to rise in 1982, and doubled again between 1983 and 1984 (Table 13). In addition, the role played by CBP and the Government, as well as the destination of their financial assistance, differed over these phases. During 1981 and in the period from late 1983 to 1985, both the CBP and the Government provided massive financial assistance to financial corporations. In 1982 and 1983, however, the Government provided the bulk of financial assistance, mostly to public corporations (financial and nonfinancial).

As the crisis progressed, the main recipients of government financial assistance shifted gradually from nonfinancial to financial public corporations. Until 1982, the Government provided assistance to troubled nonfinancial firms in part to maintain overall domestic investment, and in part to finance takeovers and acquisition of distressed and bankrupt corporations by government financial institutions. Beginning in 1983, the Government curtailed public investment to reduce budget deficits. As a result, financial assistance to nonfinancial corporations declined somewhat; but assistance to financial corporations accelerated.

Over the whole crisis period, the Government's financial assistance to troubled entities, which rose from 13.6 percent of all government expenditure in 1980 to 20.1 percent in 1985, aggravated the Government's own position.

Terms of CBP Financial Assistance

The terms of the CBP financial assistance rapidly shifted from penalty rates to subsidized rates. In 1981, for emergency loans and overdrafts of 60 days, CBP applied a rate of interest of 24 percent, plus 2 percent for each rollover of outstanding amount. Compared with the market rate of 16 percent charged by banks on short-term borrowing, this amounted to a heavy penalty rate. Moreover, CBP extended emergency loans against any collateral that troubled institutions could submit, even collateral previously unacceptable to CBP. With the establishment of the Industrial

---

[65] These figures are quoted from *Business Day* (1982), the publication of the Securities and Exchange Commission. This issue also reported (p. 294) that of the 20 biggest corporations 8 had substantial government investments in 1981.

Table 13. Authorities' Financial Assistance Flows to Distressed Corporations, 1980–85

	1980	1981	1982	1983	1984	1985
			(In millions of pesos)			
To financial corporations	277	3,054	1,574	2,077	14,289	13,549
From Central Bank						
Emergency loans/overdraft facilities[1]	120	2,424	163	1,900	5,900	2,800
From Government						
Emergency lending and equity contribution[2]	157	630	1,408	177	8,389	10,749
To nonfinancial corporations	5,040	8,380	10,178	7,955	5,641	5,328
From Government						
Equity contribution and net lending	5,040	8,380	10,178	7,955	5,641	5,328
Total (1) + (2)	5,317	11,434	11,752	10,032	20,230	18,877
Memorandum items			(In percent)			
Central Bank assistance/reserve money at end of previous period	0.8	13.6	0.8	9.6	20.3	8.0
Government assistance/total government expenditures	13.6	18.7	22.0	15.3	21.0	20.1
Flow of government assistance/budget deficit	—	31.5	17.9	−46.7	60.2	18.3
Government equity contribution (in percent of GNP)	2.0	2.7	2.8	1.5	1.8	2.4

Sources: International Monetary Fund, *International Financial Statistics*, 1988; data provided by the authorities; and IMF staff estimates.

[1]These figures represent changes from end of period stock. They exclude ₱ 700 million of promissory notes of Union Bank's borrowers such as the Rancom Corporation, and ₱ 2.8 billion of National Investment and Development Corporation promissory notes accepted as payments to clear emergency loans of Intercom (financed from the rediscount window). The figure for 1980 refers to commercial banks only.

[2]To government financial institutions only, financed from the budget.

Fund in the middle of 1981, however, CBP provided an implicit interest subsidy. On the medium- and long-term resources provided by that fund, CBP charged an interest rate of 16 percent, compared with the long-term market rate of 21.6 percent.

Between 1983 and 1985, CBP continued to accept less than first-rate collateral for its emergency loans. Furthermore, between 1984 and 1985, CBP provided interest rate subsidies on emergency loans and overdrafts as well as on medium- and long-term equity loans provided through the special rediscount window. For instance, on short-term loans of 180-day maturity CBP charged an interest rate of 27 percent (MRR plus 2 percent, see Table 14), which was lower than the comparable treasury bill rates.[66] Similarly, on medium- and long-term equity loans to finance mergers and acquisitions, CBP charged 11 percent, which was well below market rates.

Disposition of Private Banks in Distress

During the crisis, the authorities arranged for government financial institutions to take over four private commercial banks with ₱ 13.5 billion in assets in order to work out appropriate rehabilitation and decide on eventual disposition. If the two banks acquired in the late 1970s prior to the crisis are included, the Government owned, by the end of 1986, six formerly private banks with ₱ 20.3 billion in assets (12.7 percent of the total assets of the private banking sector).[67] The rehabilitation scheme for these banks consisted of an initial capital infusion from the government financial institution that took over each bank, placement of a central bank comptroller (if warranted) to work out restructuring, continued central bank financial assistance where needed, and arrangement of new private sector partners for mergers or acquisitions (sometimes on a "clean balance sheet basis").[68]

The eventual disposition of these banks has varied with the depth of their problems and the complexity of the litigation that followed. As of 1988, two banks had been successfully rehabilitated and were about to be reprivatized. Two others have been declared insolvent; one of these has been closed, but lawsuits by the owners have delayed liquidation of the other.[69] The fate of the other two banks remained undecided. The author-

[66] Beginning in December 1984, CBP applied the treasury bill rate plus 2 percent to emergency loans with 90-day maturity.

[67] Republic Planters Bank and Philipinas Bank were acquired in the late 1970s. The private banks acquired since 1982 were International Corporate Bank, Union Bank of the Philippines, Associated Bank, and the Commercial Bank of Manila.

[68] Only one proposal for merger of an insolvent bank was on this clean balance sheet basis. Bad loans would be taken out of the balance sheet and the new partner would bring in funds to recapitalize the bank.

[69] These two banks and the government-owned Philippine Veterans Bank are the three commercial banks that were actually liquidated during the 1980s.

Table 14. Terms of Financial Assistance to Distressed Corporations, 1982–85

Facility	Date	Circular No.	Rediscount Credit (in percent of bank loan)	Rediscount Rate (in percent)	Maturity
Special rediscounting					
Medium- and long-term[1]					
For acquisition of fixed assets	Feb. 1982	846	75	11	10 years or less (nonrenewable)
For investment in affiliates			70	14	7 years or less (nonrenewable)
Lender of last resort	Mar. 1982	864.907	80[2]		
Commercial bank				MRR[3] + 2 percent min.	90 days
Thrift bank				MRR + 2 percent min.	90 days
NGBGs				24 percent for loans of ₱ 150–300 million + 2 percent for each rollover	60 days
Emergency rediscounting	Dec. 1982	Section 90 RA 265/907		16 percent or MRR + 3 percent (whichever is higher)	90 days
	Dec. 1983			MRR + 2 percent	180 days
	Dec. 1985			TB[4] + 2 percent	90 days

Source: International Monetary Fund.

[1]Medium- and long-term; also covers lending for working capital in connection with a proposed or ongoing expansion development program, and investment in high-grade securities.

[2]Or as may be provided for under a Monetary Board resolution.

[3]MRR = Manila Reference Rate.

[4]TB = treasury bill.

ities intended to divest themselves and reprivatize all government-acquired banks. Change in ownership and management of these troubled banks was not always required. In one case, old stockholders were even allowed to maintain their equity position.

Rehabilitation/Restructuring of DBP and PNB

By the end of 1985, DBP and PNB, which together accounted for nearly one half of banking assets in the country, were recognized as insolvent. Their asset portfolios had deteriorated beyond repair; about 80 percent of the combined portfolio was regarded as nonperforming. This deterioration reflected the politically motivated loans these institutions had granted during the 1970s and early 1980s, plus their poor internal controls, auditing, and lending standards; their takeover of troubled corporations; the economic recession; and the massive devaluation of the peso.[70] The rehabilitation and restructuring of the two institutions began in November 1986.

The Rehabilitation Program[71]

The program of rehabilitating DBP and PNB included a restructuring of the finances, the establishment of new charters, the reorganization of staff and management, the setting up of new credit appraisal procedures, the introduction of improved budgeting and planning processes, and a rationalization of branch networks.

Following an external audit to re-evaluate the assets and liabilities of the two banks, most of their nonperforming assets[72] were transferred to the Assets Privatization Trust (APT) and others were written off. (APT, which was set up to facilitate the administration and disposition of nonperforming assets of government banks, mainly DBP and PNB, is discussed in the next subsection.) The Government recapitalized the banks and assumed the deposit liabilities equal in amount to the book value of nonperforming assets transferred minus the capital infusion. Government deposits constituted a large part of these deposit liabilities. The liabilities taken over by the Government, net of the Government's own deposits, became part of public debt.

The bailout operation involved the transfer of ₱ 107.5 billion of assets to APT, equivalent to 27.2 percent of the total assets of the banking system

---

[70] The special position of DBP and PNB allowed them unlimited use of government deposits, exemptions from taxes, and access to government-guaranteed borrowing.

[71] This program was supported by World Bank resources under its Economic Recovery Loan.

[72] Nonperforming assets also included real assets and some contingent liabilities.

Table 15. Financial Restructuring of GFIs, June 1986
(In billions of pesos)

	DBP¹				PNB²				Total			
	June 1986	Adjust-ment	Transfer	Remaining	June 1986	Adjust-ment	Transfer	Remaining	June 1986	Adjust-ment	Transfer	Remaining
Total assets	73.9	2.8	60.4	10.7	78.5	6.0	47.0	25.5	152.4	8.8	107.4	36.2
Of which:												
Loans	39.3	0.0	33.3	6.0	38.1	1.5	23.4	13.2	77.4	1.5	56.7	19.2
Equity investment and other bonds	6.7	0.0	5.9	0.8	7.0	0.0	2.3	4.7	13.7	0.0	8.2	5.5
Total liabilities and net worth	73.9	2.8	60.4	10.7	78.5	6.0	47.0	25.5	152.4	8.8	107.4	36.2
Of which:												
Peso deposits	7.9	1.4	5.0³	1.5	19.6	0.0	6.2	13.4	27.5	1.4	11.2	14.9
Borrowing	52.6	0.0	49.6	3.0	39.4	0.0	38.3	1.1	92.0	0.0	87.9	4.1
Of which:												
Foreign exchange	(35.2)	(0.0)	(35.2)	(0.0)	(22.3)	(0.0)	(21.9)	(0.4)	(57.5)	(0.0)	(57.1)	(0.4)
Capital	1.6	0.2	0.6	2.5	0.03	6.29	8.45	2.5	1.63	6.49	9.05	5.0
Contingent⁴	21.5	0.0	21.3	0.2	25.4	0.0	16.7	8.7	46.9	0.0	38.0	8.9

Source: Data provided by the Central Bank of the Philippines.
[1]Adjustments and transfers are subtracted from outstanding stock as of June 1986; adjustments for the DBP are *before* transfers.
[2]Includes the operations of the subsidiary, NIDC; adjustments are made after transfers.
[3]All government deposits.
[4]Includes outstanding and unavailed guarantees.

at the end of 1985 (see Table 15).[73] PNB accounted for ₱ 47 billion, of which ₱ 6 billion worth of nonperforming assets came from its subsidiary, the National Investment Development Corporation, which was also heavily involved in the rescue of failing businesses. DBP accounted for the remaining ₱ 60.5 billion. As a result, the balance sheets of these two government financial institutions were scaled down sharply. Total assets of PNB declined from ₱ 79 billion in 1985 to ₱ 26 billion in 1986, while total assets of DBP went from ₱ 74 billion to ₱ 11 billion.

Second, new management was introduced into both banks, and staffs were reorganized. The size of each staff was reduced over time. DBP staff was reduced from 4,147 employees in July 1985 to 1,981 employees by the end of October 1987; PNB staff was reduced from 6,500 to 4,700. The number of branches and the size of each head office also were reduced.

The rehabilitation plan established new charters for the two banks. DBP was given the status of a thrift bank and hence will be subject to normal central bank regulations governing thrift banks.[74] At first it will concentrate on lending for agriculture, small- and medium-scale industry, and housing. Expanded lending in other areas—including wholesale rather than retail lending—was to be permitted only after a three-year rehabilitation period (1987–89). PNB will continue to operate as a universal bank, but without access to special privileges or funds, and it will continue to serve as the principal banker for the Government and public enterprises, but within the rules prescribed for public deposits. After a two-year period of successful operations, PNB will be privatized through public offering of stock.

The Handling of Nonperforming Assets Through APT

As already mentioned, APT is a government entity set up to administer and dispose of the nonperforming assets and government corporations transferred to it.[75] It has a paid-up capital of ₱ 100 million, a five-man Board of Trustees appointed by the President of the Philippines, and an expected life span of five years.[76] The Government contributed the entire capital of APT.

---

[73] Bank credit to the private sector, in nominal terms, went from ₱ 153 billion at the end of 1983 to ₱ 96 billion (after transfer) at the end of 1986, compared with ₱ 114 billion before transfer at the end of 1986.

[74] These regulations include limits on equity investments, limits on exposure to any one borrower, and the use of guarantees. However, the gearing ratio for the DBP will not exceed 5:1 during the rehabilitation period although a 10:1 ratio is permitted for thrifts.

[75] In theory, APT could also receive public corporations that the Government wished to privatize.

[76] APT is supervised by the Committee on Privatization (COP), which is the first tier of the asset disposition mechanism. COP is a five-man interministerial body chaired by the

Banks were allowed to transfer any nonperforming account with a value in excess of ₱ 10 million as well as smaller loans they had made with a government guarantee. Transfers were effected at book value. In accordance with these criteria, legal titles on some 400 nonperforming accounts were transferred to APT in 1986 and 1987; about 75 percent of these are financial claims requiring foreclosure procedures that are expected to be long and costly. The remaining assets over which APT has physical control were being disposed of expeditiously.

APT was to dispose of transferred assets according to a given set of principles and disposition mechanisms, including the following:

- Sales were to be open to qualified buyers through competitive bidding or auction arrangements.
- Rehabilitation prior to disposal was to be undertaken only in exceptional cases, when it would lead to a justifiable increase in the assets' salability and price.
- As a general rule, nonperforming accounts were not to be returned to their original owners.
- In the case of deferred payment, terms were to be consistent among the various individual transactions.

APT could sell the transferred assets either directly or indirectly through the use of agents or brokers. The price and terms of settlement of the sale were to be decided on a case-by-case basis, upon approval by the Board of Trustees. Revenues from APT sales of nonperforming assets were to be transferred to the government budget as capital revenues.

Both DBP and PNB selected members of their staff to participate on loan-workout task forces and charged them with managing the nonperforming assets transferred to APT: preparing the assets for sale/recovery, preparing legal documentation preliminary to the sale or seizure of collateral, and so on.[77] A management contract was signed under which APT reimburses all expenses related to handling of these nonperforming assets by the task forces, including salaries of task force staff. This effective transfer of staff was done to ensure that the bank was protected from political influence during the recovery process. For nonperforming accounts retained in DBP and PNB (i.e., less than ₱ 10 million in value per account), additional task forces went to work to manage loan recovery, and loan recovery rates are reported to be satisfactory.

Minister of Finance. It is empowered to issue guidelines governing the disposition process, approve or disapprove individual disposition proposals on terms and purchasers, approve organizational and financial requirements of APT, and monitor the overall disinvestment program.

[77] The names of borrowers have become public and a number of them have now acted to settle their obligations.

IV. Main Findings

The paper has analyzed the causes of the Philippine financial crisis and the authorities' reactions to the crisis. The Philippine crisis followed a boom-bust phenomenon typical of those analyzed in crisis literature. After experiencing tremendous growth in the 1970s, both the real sector of the economy and the financial sector experienced a major contraction in the 1980s. The main conclusion of this paper is that factors within the financial system were instrumental in provoking and exacerbating the crisis, and thus, a key transmission mechanism of the crisis ran from the financial sector to the real sector of the economy. This feedback from the financial to the real sector constituted the main focus of the paper.

Although the deteriorating economy, the political climate, and the balance of payments crisis increased the financial fragility of corporate and noncorporate institutions, three phenomena originating inside the financial system provoked the crisis and exacerbated its impact on the real sector. First, improper sequencing of financial sector reforms in a period of macroeconomic and political shocks led to widespread loose lending practices, fraud, and mismanagement by numerous banks. In particular, the financial reforms neglected to tighten bank supervision as regulatory restrictions were dismantled in some areas (activity regulations, interest rate setting) and even kept in other areas (e.g., selective credit).

Second, the limited competition in loan markets (reflecting in part the domination by bank holding companies) played a key role, although competition in deposit markets (reflecting low concentration in the banking industry as a whole) was strong. Before the crisis, the bank holding company structure allowed banks that belonged to these holding companies to engage in excessive risk taking with newly created and inexperienced subsidiaries. Many of these subsidiaries would be hit by the limited crisis of 1981, causing the entire holding group to collapse. During the crisis, this structure contributed to the upward pressure on nominal lending rates. Statistical evidence suggests that, faced with mounting overdue loans, banks passed along to customers the cost of carrying overdue loans. Thus poor quality of the banks' own portfolios contributed to higher interest rates and exacerbated the effects of tight monetary policies.

Third, sharp portfolio shifts in the banking and nonbanking sectors appear to have complicated monetary and fiscal management, and contributed to crowding out the private sector. After 1983, monetary management based on indirect instruments not only became vulnerable to prediction errors and M3 was no longer a reliable intermediate target, but also faced conflicting objectives during a crisis—namely, maintaining monetary stability while preventing the collapse of the banking system. Also, despite a tighter stance and a reduction of the budgetary deficit (in percent of GNP) after 1983, the fiscal authorities had to step up domestic borrowing because foreign financing had dried up. These demand management policies, in turn, caused interest rates to skyrocket and reduced sharply domestic funds available to the private sector, thereby worsening the recession.

Banks' behavior also contributed to the recession as widespread uncertainty in the economic outlook and attractive rates on central bank and government securities led banks to ration private sector credit during the crisis and to allocate investible funds into safe outlets. However, this issue requires further empirical scrutiny.

In reaction, CBP and the Government took financial assistance measures to contain the crisis and long-term restructuring measures to restore the soundness of the financial system. The various support measures to deal with problem banks helped to contain the crisis during the difficult macroeconomic environment which existed between 1983 and 1986, and the Government eventually had to assume the large accumulated losses. The institutional solutions in this regard—the specific recapitalization and restructuring of the banking system and the method of disposition of problem assets—seem comprehensive and well conceived; their effectiveness in terms of minimizing future problems remains to be assessed.

Bibliography

Buhat, V., "Trends in Peso Deposits and Secured Loans of Commercial Banks (1981–1985)," *CB Review*, Vol. 38, No. 6 (June 1986).

—————, "Movements in the Manila Reference Rates and Lending Rates of Commercial Banks (1982–1986)," *CB Review*, Vol. 39, No. 2 (February 1987).

Business Day, "1,000 Top Corporations in the Philippines" (in cooperation with the Securities and Exchange Commission), Vol. 15 (1982); and Vol. 17 (1984).

Capie, F., and E.G. Woods, eds., *Financial Crisis and the World Banking System* (New York: St. Martin's Press, 1986).

Central Bank of the Philippines, *Statistical Bulletin*, 1982.

—————, *Banking Laws* (Manila: Central Bank of the Philippines, 1983).

—————, "Governor's Report," *CB Review*, Vol. 40 (February 1988).

—————, "The Philippines External Debt Monitoring System," *CB Review*, Vol. 41 (January 1989).

—————, *Philippines Financial Statistics*, 1982–85.

—————, "Rationale and Expanded Dimensions of Universal Banking in the Philippines," *Bondline* (April–June 1980) (Manila: Central Bank of the Philippines).

De Dios, Emmanuel S., *An Analysis of the Philippine Economic Crisis* (Manila: University of the Philippines Press, 1984).

Doherty, John F., "Who Controls the Philippine Economy: Some Need Not Try as Hard as Others," in *Cronies and Enemies: The Current Philippine Scene*, ed. by Belinda A. Aquino, Philippine Studies Occasional Paper No. 5 (Honolulu: Center for Asian and Pacific Studies, University of Hawaii, August 1983), pp. 7–35.

Edwards, S., and M. Khan, "Interest Rate Determination in Developing Countries," *Staff Papers*, International Monetary Fund, Vol. 32 (September 1985).

Fry, M., *Money, Interest and Banking in Economic Development* (Baltimore: Johns Hopkins University Press, 1988).

Goldsborough, D., and I. Zaidi, "Monetary Policy in the Philippines During the Period of the Financial Crisis and Changes in the Exchange Rate Regime," IMF Working Paper, WP/89/98 (December 1989).

International Monetary Fund, *International Financial Statistics Yearbook*, 1988.

Lamberte, Mario B., "Financial Liberalization: What Have We Learned?" *Journal of Philippine Development*, Vol. 12, No. 2 (1985).

Laya, Jaime C., *A Crisis of Confidence* (Manila: Central Bank of the Philippines, 1982).

————, *Gearing Toward Recovery* (Manila: Central Bank of the Philippines, 1983).

Licaros, G.S., "Regulations in the Financial System," *Bondline*, Vol. 23, No. 3 (Manila: Central Bank of the Philippines, 1979).

Lirio, Ricardo P., "The Philippine Banking Industry: A Historical Perspective," *Bondline*, Vol. 24 (April–June 1985) (Manila: Central Bank of the Philippines), pp. 4–13.

Lontoc, Francisco L., "A Time of Crisis and Reform," *Bondline*, Vol. 20 (November 1981) (Manila: Central Bank of the Philippines), pp. 7–13.

McKinnon, R.I., *Money and Capital in Economic Development* (Washington: The Brookings Institution, 1973).

Paulino, H., "Government Securities: A Review of 1985 Performance," *CB Review*, Vol. 38 (January 1986).

Robledo, Catalina T., "Deficit Financing of Government Corporations, 1973–83," *Central Bank Review* (May 1984) (Manila: Central Bank of the Philippines), pp. 12–15.

Saldana, Cesar G., "The Philippine Commercial Banking System: Structure, Performance, and the Impact of the Capital Buildup Program of 1972," *Philippine Review of Economics and Business*, Vols. 3 and 4 (1984), pp. 145–64.

Shaw, E., *Financial Deepening in Economic Development* (London: Oxford University Press, 1973).

Sicat, Gerardo P., "A Historical and Current Perspective of the Philippine Economic Problems," *Philippine Economic Journal*, Vol. 24, No. 1 (1985).

Sycip, Gorres, Velayo, and Co., "A Study of Commercial Banks in the Philippines" (Manila: Sycip and Others Publication Unit, various issues: December 1972, 1978, 1983, and 1986).

Teodoro, Procesa L., "Non-Bank Financial Intermediaries—A Decade of Performance," *Central Bank Review* (September 1985) (Manila: Central Bank of the Philippines), pp. 16–20.

APPENDIX

Appendix Table 1.   Estimation of the Determinants of Banks' Interest Margins, 1981(IV)–1986(IV)

(Annual percentages)

Dependent Variable (i_L-i_D)	Independent Variables				Summary Statistics	
	Constant	Inflation	Herfindahl-Hirschman index[1]	Overdue[1] loans	Adjusted R^2	Durbin-Watson statistic
Equation I	5.95 (0.38)	0.07 (1.77)	−0.40 (−0.29)	0.19 (1.13)	0.20	1.14
Equation II	0.14 (0.82)	0.06 (2.54)		0.22 (1.89)	0.23	1.17

Note: ($i_L - i_D$) = gross interest margin on short-term bank rates.
[1]Annual data were divided by four and repeated for each quarter.

**Appendix Table 2. Indicators of Activity
and Financial Performance of 1,000 Top
Industrial Corporations, 1980–84**

	1980	1981	1982	1983	1984
Total assets (TA)	*116.5*	*130.0*	*184.8*	*251.5*	*284.2*
Current assets (CA)	58.9	62.7	69.5	82.1	96.8
Fixed assets (FA)	47.3	53.8	96.3	136.1	160.4
Other assets (OA)	10.3	13.5	19.0	33.3	27.0
Total liabilities (TL)	*77.6*	*89.3*	*126.1*	*178.9*	*209.4*
Current liabilities (CL)	50.7	57.4	67.8	83.8	96.7
Long-term liabilities (LL)	26.9	31.9	58.3	95.1	112.7
Equity (E)	38.7	59.2	40.7	72.6	75.0
Net income (IN)	. . .	0.2	−1.7	−2.0	2.6
Gross revenue (R)	. . .	119.2	140.9	167.9	230.0
Sales	. . .	114.6	137.2	163.5	223.5
			(*In percent*)		
Selected financial ratios					
Leverage					
TL/E	2.1	1.5	3.1	2.5	2.8
Activity					
S/CA	. . .	182.8	197.4	199.1	230.9
S/TA	. . .	88.1	74.2	65.0	78.6
Profitability					
IN/E	. . .	0.2	−4.2	−2.7	3.5
IN/TA	. . .	0.1	−0.9	−0.8	0.9
Liquidity					
CA/CL	116.2	109.2	102.5	98.0	100.1

Source: *Business Day* (1981–84).
Note: The 1,000 top industrial corporations consist of the largest corporations in construction; electricity, gas, and water; manufacturing; and mining and quarrying sectors.

Appendix Table 3. Evolution of Nongovernment Sector Debt in Nominal Terms by Borrowers and Origin; Selected Years, 1972–85

(In billions of pesos at current prices; end of period)

	1972	1978	1980	1981	1982	1983	1984	1985
Nongovernment[1]								
Total	30.1	179.7	246.7	293.2	356.7	471.6	603.5	540.5
Domestic	27.1	104.4	150.3	153.6	196.5	214.4	233.3	200.1
Foreign	3.0	75.3	96.4	121.8	160.2	257.2	370.2	322.8
Enterprises[2]								
Total	8.7	90.8	117.4	141.8	170.2	248.7	328.3	277.1
Domestic	8.7	33.2	49.8	53.5	58.0	61.9	51.9	33.7
Foreign	...	57.7	67.6	88.3	112.2	186.8	276.4	243.4
Commercial banks								
Total	18.0	76.5	113.7	133.6	166.7	200.1	249.3	245.8
Domestic	15.0	58.9	84.9	100.1	118.7	129.7	155.5	166.4
Foreign	3.3	17.6	28.8	33.5	48.0	70.4	93.8	79.4
Individuals								
Total	3.4	12.4	15.6	17.8	19.8	22.8	25.9	17.6

Memorandum items:

(In billions of U.S. dollars)

Enterprises' foreign debt[3]								
Total	—	7.8	8.9	10.8	12.4	13.4	14.0	12.8
Of which:								
Short-term	(—)	(1.4)	(2.5)	(3.7)	(4.0)	(4.0)	(4.2)	(3.0)

(In billions of pesos)

Net national income[4]	45.8	157.5	211.0	243.2	270.4	302.4	426.2	468.8

Sources: Central Bank of the Philippines, *Annual Report*, 1983; *Philippines Financial Statistics*, 1984–86; and International Monetary Fund.

[1]Sum of debt contracted by enterprises, commercial banks, and individuals.

[2]Composed of business corporations (private and public), single proprietorships, partnerships and associations, and cooperatives. More than 80 percent of the debt was attributed to corporations.

[3]Contracted in local currency from domestic commercial banks. The debt contracted in local currency but re-lent by the Central Bank of the Philippines or commercial banks (including the DBP) is netted out. Such debt is included in the foreign currency debt because, as ultimate borrowers, these firms assumed the exchange risk.

[4]Includes foreign debt re-lent to enterprises.

5

Distressed Financial Institutions in Thailand: Structural Weaknesses, Support Operations, and Economic Consequences

R. Barry Johnston[1]

This chapter is one in a series of examinations of experiences with financial crises in different countries. Although each of these experiences reflects country-specific factors, each also provides general background on the potential causes and consequences of financial crises. A recurring theme in this book is the interrelationship between the stability and soundness of the financial system, the role of regulation and supervision of the financial institutions, and macroeconomic conditions. This chapter reviews the background for the deterioration in the conditions of financial institutions in Thailand, the remedial actions and support arrangements that were subsequently taken, and the consequences for macroeconomic conditions.

The financial system in Thailand faced a crisis in the first half of the 1980s. Poor managerial practices, accompanied by inadequate regulations and supervision, led to a gradual deterioration in the quality of the balance sheets of Thailand's financial institutions. The difficulties were exacerbated by a slowdown in economic activity in the early 1980s. Beginning in 1983, the Thai authorities had to intervene in the affairs of about 50 finance and security companies and 5 commercial banks, which together

---

[1] An earlier version of this paper was discussed at the IMF Seminar on Central Banking, November 28–December 9, 1988. I am grateful to V. Sundararajan and Tarisa Watanagase for their comments on an earlier draft of the paper, and to Anne Johannessen for her help in compiling the information in Section III.

234

accounted for about one fourth of the total assets of Thailand's institutions. Twenty-four finance and security companies were closed and 9 others merged into 2 new companies; 13 finance companies and 5 commercial banks continued to receive support, including financial subsidies in the form of "soft" loans. Remedial actions also continued; these included reductions in capital values, management restructuring, and the buildup of capital and reserves under financial programs set by the authorities. As a result of the crisis, the power of the authorities to supervise and restructure financial institutions was substantially strengthened. The macroeconomic impact of the crisis was probably procyclical, resulting in a more restrictive policy in 1984 and 1985 and a more expansionary policy in 1986 and 1987.

Section I reviews the structure of the financial system and the evolution of banks and finance companies; Section II discusses some indicators of the condition of financial institutions; Section III examines the reasons for the weakening position of financial institutions in Thailand, emphasizing structural and regulatory inadequacies; Section IV describes the arrangements to support the ailing financial institutions; Section V assesses the success of these support arrangements; Section VI examines the macroeconomic consequences of the financial crisis; and Section VII presents the conclusion and a summary of the main findings.

I. Structure of the Financial System and Evolution of Banks and Finance Companies

The financial system in Thailand appears relatively diversified. As of the end of 1987 it consisted of the Bank of Thailand (BOT), the central bank; 16 local commercial banks and 14 branches of foreign banks; a number of representative offices of foreign banks; nonmonetary financial institutions comprised 94 finance companies, 11 security companies, and 25 credit foncier companies; a number of government-owned or government-sponsored specialized financial institutions (the Government Savings Bank—GSB; the Bank for Agriculture and Agricultural Cooperatives —BAAC; the Government Housing Bank—GHB; the Industrial Finance Corporation of Thailand—IFCT; and the Small Industries Finance Office —SIFO); a large number of savings and agricultural cooperatives; 12 life insurance corporations; the Securities Exchange of Thailand (SET); short-term money markets; and a sizable unorganized financial system. Table 1 provides a summary of the main characteristics of the financial institutions. In practice, assets of the financial system are concentrated mainly among the commercial banks and the finance companies, which are predominantly private sector institutions, and the GSB. Because of the

Table 1. Summary of Structure of Financial Intermediaries, End-December 1987

	Commercial Banks	Finance Companies	Credit Foncier Companies	Government Savings Bank	Life Insurance Corporations	Savings Cooperatives[1]	Agricultural Cooperatives[1]	Bank of Agriculture and Agricultural Cooperatives	Industrial Finance Corporation of Thailand	Small-Scale Industries Financial Office	Government Housing Bank	Pawnshops
Total assets (*in billions of baht*)	943.3	163.2	3.8	111.5	24.9	19.6	8.5	33.6	22.6	0.1	15.4	5.4
Total number of institutions	30	94	21	1	12	732	1,157	1	1	1	1	336
Foreign owned	14	...	...	—	1	...	...	—	—	—	—	—
In which the Government holds												
50 percent or more of equity	2	12	—	1	—	—	—	1	1	1	1	—
With public quotations on the SET	12	22	—	—	—	—	—	—	—	—	—	—
Total number of branches[2]	2,004	22	—	452	724	...	...	70	3	—	—	—
Of which: In Bangkok	557	9	—	64	68[3]	...	...	...	...	...	...	...
Proportion of liabilities that are												
Demand deposits	4.7	—	—	0.1	—	...	...	—	—	—	0.1	—
Savings deposits	24.0	—	—	16.9	—	...	...	10.7	—	—	31.8	—
Time deposits	47.3	—	—	45.4	—	...	...	10.7	—	—	18.8	—
Capital funds	6.1	6.7	15.7	5.0	11.2	...	...	6.3	13.3	93.8	14.3	25.9
Other borrowing												
Bank of Thailand	4.5	5.8	...	—	...	...	...	8.9	0.2	—	6.5	—
Commercial banks	2.5	19.1	52.6	—	0.2	...	...	36.6	—	—	—	61.1
Government	2.5	—	...	2.0	...	...	...	0.9	1.8	—	16.9	—
Overseas	3.9	1.4	...	—	...	...	...	22.3	39.8	—	—	—
Other private sector	4.5	67.0	31.7	30.6	84.7	...	...	3.6	44.9	—	—	—

Proportion of assets held as claims on

Bank of Thailand	2.7	0.2	...	0.5	...	...	—	—	—	0.6	...
Commercial banks	2.4	2.8	5.2	13.1	12.0	...	11.6	3.6	50.4	1.9	3.7
Other financial institutions	5.5	5.5	—	1.9	...	...	—	5.8	5.0	5.2	—
Central Government	12.3	12.4	—	76.9	16.5	...	—	—	2.3	0.1	—
Public enterprises	1.6	0.6	—	1.9	...	...	—	0.1	—	—	—
Business and household sectors	65.2	65.9	55.3	1.4	34.9	...	74.7	49.6	—	82.5	88.8
Overseas	4.1	—	—	—	...	...	—	—	—	—	—
Regulatory framework											
Governing legislation	4,5,6	7	7	8	9	10	11	12	—	13	14
Licensing body	15	15	16	17	16	18	17	17	—	17	19
Supervisory agencies											
Primary	16	16	16	15	20	18	15	15	21	15	19
Secondary	16	—	—	—	...	...	—	—	—	—	—

Source: Bank of Thailand.

[1] Estimates based on 1985 data.
[2] Excluding head office.
[3] End of June 1987.
[4] Commercial Bank Act, 1962 and 1979 (revised).
[5] Bank of Thailand Act.
[6] Currency Act.
[7] The Finance Securities and Credit Foncier Act of 1979, amended by emergency decree, 1983.
[8] Government Savings Bank Act, 1946.
[9] Life Insurance Act, 1967.
[10] Cooperatives Act, 1968.
[11] Bank for Agriculture and Agricultural Cooperatives Act, 1966.
[12] Industrial Finance Corporation of Thailand Act, 1959.
[13] Government Housing Bank Act, 1953.
[14] Pawnshop Act, 1962.
[15] Ministry of Finance.
[16] Bank of Thailand.
[17] Act of Parliament.
[18] Ministry of Agriculture and Agricultural Cooperatives.
[19] Ministry of Interior.
[20] Ministry of Commerce.
[21] Ministry of Industries.

concentration of assets, a crisis among the banks and finance companies is tantamount to a financial sector crisis.

The establishment of local and foreign banks had proceeded at a rapid pace up to 1955, when the Thai Cabinet passed a resolution to restrict the approval of new banks; a virtual moratorium on new banking licenses was imposed from the mid-1970s (see Table 2). At the end of 1987 there were 16 local and 14 foreign-owned banks, virtually the same number as in 1966.[2] In addition to imposing a virtual moratorium on new banks, the Government restricted each foreign bank's branching activities to a total of 20 local branches. The local commercial banks, by contrast, developed an extensive branch network and at the end of 1987 the 16 local commercial banks had 1,964 local branches, excluding head offices, compared with 352 in 1960.

Most local banks were established by Thai-Chinese business families and trading houses to help finance their operations. The Bangkok Bank, the Thai Farmers Bank, the Bank of Ayudhya, the Bangkok Metropolitan Bank, and the Bank of Asia have remained effectively family-controlled institutions. The Government has also become an important participant in bank ownership: the Krung Thai Bank, and more recently the Sayam Bank, are government owned and the Government has minority share-holdings in several other banks.[3]

The banking system in Thailand is highly concentrated. Local banks account for 95–97.5 percent of total commercial bank assets, advances, and deposits (see Table 2). Within the commercial banking sector, business is concentrated among a few banks. At the end of 1986 the largest bank, the Bank of Bangkok, accounted for about 30 percent of total commercial bank assets and deposit liabilities, and the three largest banks (the Bangkok Bank, the Thai Farmers Bank, and the Krung Thai Bank) together accounted for about 57 percent of commercial bank assets. The smallest five local banks accounted for only 5–6 percent of commercial bank deposits and assets. The two government-owned banks, the Krung Thai Bank and the Sayam Bank, which have been operationally merged, are the second-largest banking organization; together they account for about 15 percent of bank assets. The banks have operated an effective interest rate cartel

[2] The only new bank opening after 1966 was the German-based European Asian Bank, which reflected both the lack of a previous German representation and the desire by the Thai Farmers Bank to open a branch in the western part of Germany. Of the 16 local banks, the Sayam Bank stopped accepting deposits and extending credits in April 1987, when its performing assets and deposit liabilities were transferred to the Krung Thai Bank (discussed later in this section and in Sections II and V).

[3] The Siam Commercial Bank, the Bangkok Bank, the First Bangkok City Bank, the Bank of Ayudhya, the Thai Military Bank, and the Union Bank of Bangkok all have some government ownership.

Table 2. Date of Opening and Distribution of Private Sector Deposits for Commercial Banks

Bank	Year of Opening	Deposits as a Percentage of Total (December 31, 1986)
Local commercial banks		
Siam Commercial Bank	1906	8.7
Nakornthon Bank[1]	1933	0.9
Bank of Asia	1939	2.4
Siam City Bank	1941	4.1
Bangkok Bank of Commerce	1944	4.7
Bangkok Bank	1944	26.6
Bank of Ayudhya	1945	5.9
Thai Farmers Bank	1945	14.1
Laem Thong Bank	1948	0.5
Union Bank	1949	1.9
Thai Danu Bank	1949	1.2
Bangkok Metropolitan Bank	1950	4.1
Thai Military Bank	1957	5.1
First Bangkok City Bank	1960	2.9
Sayam Bank[2]	1965	2.0
Krung Thai Bank	1966	12.7
Subtotal		97.8
Foreign commercial banks		
Hongkong and Shanghai Banking Corporation	1888	0.3
Standard Chartered Bank	1894	0.2
Banque Indosuez	1897	0.1
Four Seas Communication	1909	—
Bank of Canton	1919	—
Citibank[3]	1923	0.1
International Commercial Bank of China[4]	1947	0.1
Bharat Overseas Bank[5]	1947	0.1
Bank of America	1949	0.2
Mitsui Bank	1952	0.3
Bank of Tokyo	1962	0.4
Chase Manhattan Bank	1964	0.2
United Malayan	1964	0.1
Deutsche Bank (Asia)[6]	1978	0.1
Subtotal		2.2
Total		100.0

Source: Bank of Thailand.

[1] Previously Wang Lee Bank Ltd.
[2] Previously Asian Trust Bank Ltd.
[3] Previously Mercantile Bank Ltd.
[4] Previously Bank of China Ltd.
[5] Previously Indian Overseas Bank Ltd.
[6] Previously European Asian Bank Ltd.

organized around the Thai Bankers' Association (TBA); in recent years the cartel arrangements have been breaking down under pressure from foreign competition for bank loans to domestic customers and official encouragement of a more competitive interest rate structure; by the end of 1988, the competitive setting of local deposit rates had begun to emerge. About 60 percent of the value of commercial bank deposits is accounted for by deposits larger than B 500,000 (US$20,000), and some 70 percent of credits outstanding are for loans exceeding B 1.0 million (US$40,000). Because of various family and corporate connections among bank customers, the effective degree of deposit and loan concentration is even higher.

Finance and security companies make up the second major group of financial intermediaries. Finance companies—which, in contrast to commercial banks, are highly competitive institutions—first emerged in the early 1960s as the finance arm of retailers. Subsequently, finance companies expanded their activities into certain types of corporate finance; the first full-fledged finance company was established in 1969. The entry of new finance and security companies was first regulated by National Executive Council Announcement No. 58 issued in July 1972, but this order left the finance and security companies relatively free in their operations compared with commercial banks. Thus the effect of the Executive Council Order was largely to give official recognition to the companies, thereby significantly increasing their attractiveness to investors. Further controls were placed on the operations of finance companies by the Finance, Securities, and Credit Foncier Business Act, BE 2502, in 1979, when problems emerged with one finance company (Raja Finance). As described (in Section III), however, these controls were generally inadequate to regulate these companies.

The number of finance companies grew rapidly during the 1970s, when foreign and local banks set up such companies partly to avoid the moratorium on new banking licenses and on foreign bank branching, and partly to avoid the maximum interest rate and credit controls imposed on commercial banks. Initially, financial companies were not subject to interest rate ceilings, and when those ceilings were introduced, they were higher than the ceilings on commercial banks. The number of finance companies grew from 17 in 1971 to 78 in 1973 and 113 in 1979.

Chart 1 illustrates how finance company assets grew much faster than commercial bank assets up to 1979; Charts 2 and 3 show the positive relationship between the relative growth of finance company promissory notes and bank time deposits, and the differential in the interest rates paid by finance companies and banks up to 1979. The fluctuation in 1979 coincided with the emergence of problems with a finance company (already noted) which temporarily undermined general confidence in finance

Chart 1. Growth of Finance Company and Commercial Bank Assets, 1972–86
(In percent)

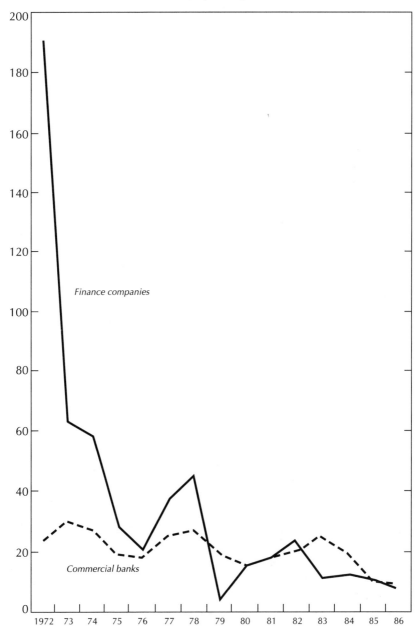

Chart 2. Growth of Time and Saving Deposits with Finance Companies and Commercial Banks, 1972–86
(In percent)

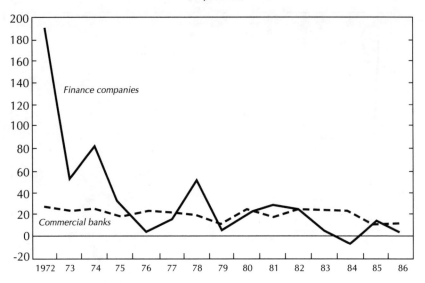

Chart 3. Interest Differential Between Finance Company and Commercial Bank Deposit Rates, 1972–86
(In percent)

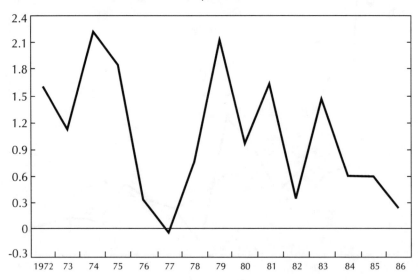

companies.

Thai finance companies engage in diverse activities. In December 1987, 22 were licensed only for finance company business (consumer installment lending, corporate advances, etc.); 11 only for securities business (essentially stockbroking); and 72 for both activities, performing functions not unlike those of merchant/investment banks. The largest finance company, with assets of B 8.4 billion, was about the same size as the third-smallest commercial bank, and 6 finance and security companies had larger assets than the smallest commercial bank. The 10 largest companies accounted for about 30 percent of the total assets of finance companies. Finance companies can borrow through the issuance of fixed-term promissory notes but cannot accept deposits. Because promissory notes can be at call and withdrawn on demand, however, the practical effect of this restriction has been limited. Business and household holdings of promissory notes accounted for 52 percent of the liabilities of finance and security companies.

II. Financial Position of Banks and Finance Companies

The financial position of Thai commercial banks and finance companies weakened during the first half of the 1980s.

Commercial Banks

Between 1980 and 1986, average bank net profits fell from 25 percent to 7 percent of capital funds, and capital/assets ratios declined from 6.4 percent to 5.7 percent (Table 3). An examination of the components of "other assets" of banks (Table 4) indicates the substantial buildup in interest and income earned but not received in recent years, equivalent to about 2 percent of total assets. About 15 percent of the total assets of Thai banks were estimated to be delinquent in 1987.

It is difficult to assess the financial position of institutions simply by focusing on a few ratios. For example, historical net profit figures are misleading because they include accrual of income and interest earned but not received. Moreover, because banks did not make adequate provision for loan losses, the banks' reported net profit was inflated. More recent net profit figures, which improved to about 11 percent of capital funds in the 12 months to June 1987, also are exaggerated because they have been boosted by the soft loan subsidy provided by the BOT (see Section IV). Similarly, the historical capital/assets ratios failed to give a true picture of bank solvency because little debt was provisioned or written off. More recently, capital values of banks have been written down against loan losses, and in 1986 and 1987 banks raised about B 15–20 billion in new

Table 3. Indicators of Financial Position of Commercial Banks, End of Period, 1980–87

	1980	1981	1982	1983	1984	1985	1986	1987
All banks								
Total assets (*in billions of baht*)	305.4	358.3	431.4	540.1	649.4	713.6	777.8	943.3
Annual percentage change	15.6	17.3	20.4	25.2	20.2	9.9	9.0	21.3
Annual growth of nonbank private sector								
Deposits	25.2	19.0	26.4	26.4	22.4	11.5	13.2	20.2
Loans	13.0	15.0	18.5	33.1	17.6	9.8	4.8	22.6
As percent of assets								
Capital accounts	6.4	6.0	5.7	5.2	5.6	6.0	5.7	6.1
Reserves with Bank of Thailand	3.4	3.3	3.0	2.8	2.3	3.0	2.8	2.7
Government securities[1]	12.9	14.0	15.4	12.5	14.6	13.8	16.2	12.3
Loans to nonbank private sector	73.8	72.3	71.2	75.7	74.0	73.9	71.0	72.2
Foreign assets	5.1	7.0	6.1	4.6	4.7	4.7	5.4	4.1
Nonbank private sector deposits	67.3	68.3	71.6	72.4	73.4	74.7	77.6	76.4
Borrowing from Bank of Thailand	5.5	5.6	4.9	4.3	3.7	3.7	4.3	2.5
Claims on nonmonetary financial institutions	6.4	5.0	4.9	4.7	5.2	4.6	4.7	5.5
As percent of nonbank private sector deposits								
Loans to nonbank private sector	109.6	106.0	99.4	104.6	100.5	99.0	91.6	94.5
Reserves with Bank of Thailand	5.1	4.8	4.1	3.8	3.1	4.0	3.7	3.6
Reserves plus government securities[1]	19.2	20.5	21.5	17.3	19.8	18.4	20.9	19.6
Demand deposits	12.2	10.5	7.8	6.0	6.1	4.8	5.6	6.2
Savings deposits	13.2	15.0	19.4	23.8	21.3	20.8	26.1	31.4
Time deposits	74.1	74.0	72.4	70.0	72.4	74.2	67.9	61.9
Local banks[2]								
Total assets (*in billions of baht*)	...	...	...	...	...	688.0	753.0	812.3[3]
Capital and reserves (*in billions of baht*)	...	...	...	...	...	39.1	40.6	44.8[3]
As percent of assets	...	...	...	...	...	5.7	5.4	5.5[3]
Reserves for loan losses (*in billions of baht*)	...	...	...	...	...	4.2	5.4	6.3[3]
As percent of assets	...	...	...	...	...	0.6	0.7	0.8[3]

Source: Bank of Thailand. Some figures are partly estimated.
[1] Includes Bank of Thailand bonds. [2] Excludes operations of foreign branches. [3] June 1987.

Table 4. Components of "Other Assets" of Commercial Banks, End of Period, 1983–86

	1983	1984	1985	1986
	(In billions of baht)			
Premises, furniture, and equipment	11.2	12.4	14.5	16.4
Properties foreclosed	1.5	1.7	1.8	2.6
Accrued interest receivable	3.7	5.5	8.2	11.0
Prepaid expenses	0.9	2.1	4.9	5.1
Income earned but not collected	1.9	2.3	2.9	4.5
Interoffice expenses	1.1	0.9	1.3	1.4
Sundry debtors	1.0	1.4	2.1	0.6
Other	4.3	4.9	4.9	5.7
Total	25.7	31.2	40.6	47.3
	(Percentage change)			
Premises, furniture, and equipment	. . .	10.7	16.9	13.1
Properties foreclosed	. . .	13.3	5.9	44.4
Accrued interest receivable	. . .	48.7	49.1	34.2
Prepaid expenses	. . .	133.3	133.3	4.1
Income earned but not collected	. . .	21.1	26.1	55.2
Interoffice expenses	. . .	− 18.2	44.4	7.7
Sundry debtors	. . .	40.0	50.0	− 71.4
Other	. . .	14.0	—	16.3
Total	. . .	21.4	30.1	16.5

Source: Bank of Thailand.

capital funds. As a result, the more recent capital/assets ratios imply a sounder financial position than the same ratios one to two years previously.

Indicators of the performance of individual local commercial banks in 1985 and 1986 are shown in Table 5. The capital/assets ratios of most banks were relatively low by international standards,[4] and the ratios for 8 banks declined in 1986. Seven banks, including the first-, third-, and fourth-largest banks, had capital/assets ratios below 5 percent. Eleven of the 16 local banks for which data are available recorded net profits in 1986; however, the net profitability of 10 of these banks declined relative to 1985. Two other banks slightly reduced their losses. Returns on equity fell by between 3 and 5 percentage points in 1986 to an average of about 7

---

[4] The Basle Committee of Banking Supervisors has recently recommended a minimum capital-to-risk assets ratio of 8 percent. See Bank for International Settlements, Committee on Banking Regulations and Supervisory Practices, *International Convergence of Capital Measurement and Standards* (Basle, July 1988).

Table 5. Performance of Local Commercial Banks, 1985–86
(Amounts in billions of baht unless otherwise stated)

Bank	Assets 1985	Assets 1986	Assets Percentage change	Loans 1985	Loans 1986	Loans Percentage change	Deposits 1985	Deposits 1986	Deposits Percentage change	Capital/Assets Ratio (percent) 1985	Capital/Assets Ratio (percent) 1986	Loan/Deposit Ratio (percent) 1985	Loan/Deposit Ratio (percent) 1986	Net Profit 1985	Net Profit 1986	Return on Assets (percent) 1985	Return on Assets (percent) 1986	Return on Equity (percent) 1985	Return on Equity (percent) 1986	Provision for Loan Losses 1985	Provision for Loan Losses 1986
Bangkok Bank	262.3	268.0	2.2	200.0	203.8	1.5	194.5	199.7	2.7	4.6	4.6	103.2	102.1	1.43	0.93	0.55	0.35	11.4	7.6	...	1.20
Thai Farmers' Bank	104.5	116.2	11.2	76.9	79.3	3.2	85.9	96.7	12.6	5.9	5.4	89.5	82.0	0.60	0.47	0.58	0.41	9.8	7.6	...	0.20
Krung Thai Bank Ltd.	93.5	105.6	12.9	64.9	69.7	7.4	77.9	85.1	9.2	3.9	4.2	83.3	81.9	0.06	0.15	0.06	0.14	1.6	3.4	0.01	0.08
Siam Commercial	65.3	73.1	11.9	48.8	51.6	5.7	52.6	60.8	15.4	5.3	4.8	92.8	84.9	0.54	0.35	0.83	0.48	15.6	10.1	1.60	1.29
Thai Military Bank	37.7	44.8	18.8	27.0	31.5	16.7	27.8	34.3	23.4	6.8	5.7	97.1	91.8	0.25	0.23	0.67	0.51	9.8	8.9	...	0.11
Bank of Ayudhya	38.8	41.6	7.2	27.0	28.9	7.1	30.6	35.3	15.4	5.8	5.5	89.1	81.9	0.19	0.16	0.49	0.37	8.3	6.9	...	0.66
Bangkok Metropolitan Bank	33.3	35.8	7.5	23.5	24.6	4.7	22.4	25.2	12.5	4.5	4.7	105.8	97.6	0.12	0.08	0.38	0.23	8.4	5.0	...	0.26
Bangkok Bank of Commerce	29.2	31.3	7.1	20.8	22.0	6.0	26.0	28.6	9.6	4.0	4.1	80.0	76.9	...	...	...	...	...	...	...	...
Siam City Bank	27.8	28.6	2.5	19.2	20.4	6.4	22.7	24.8	9.2	5.7	5.6	84.6	82.3	0.02	...	0.06	...	1.02	...	0.01	0.01
First Bangkok City Bank	27.5	27.5	—	19.7	16.6	-15.6	16.1	16.4	1.8	5.4	5.8	122.4	101.2	...	-0.10	...	-3.6	...	-6.3	...	-0.13
Sayam Bank	17.2	20.3	18.0	10.2	10.7	4.9	8.3	11.7	42.0	3.0	2.6	122.9	91.4	-0.70	-0.45	-4.07	-2.22	-136.66	-82.6	...	...
Bank of Asia Ltd.	15.5	17.2	11.4	10.9	11.8	9.9	13.0	14.9	14.8	5.2	6.3	83.9	79.2	0.03	0.03	-0.17	0.03	3.2	0.4	—	0.01
Union Bank of Bangkok	15.2	14.1	-7.2	9.2	9.7	5.4	10.3	11.3	10.4	4.6	5.2	89.3	85.8	0.05	0.04	0.29	0.30	6.4	5.9	0.01	0.01
Thai Danu Bank	7.9	8.9	12.7	6.2	6.6	6.7	6.2	7.5	20.3	8.1	7.3	100.0	88.0	0.06	0.05	0.81	0.55	10.10	7.5	0.02	0.04
Nakornthon Bank	5.7	6.4	13.4	3.6	4.5	22.7	4.3	5.2	20.7	4.5	4.4	84.8	85.9	0.03	0.02	0.45	0.27	9.6	5.9	...	0.03
Laem Thong Bank	4.5	4.7	3.8	2.9	2.9	—	2.3	2.4	5.2	16.6	20.1	126.1	120.8	-0.04	-0.01	-0.88	-0.07	-5.2	-0.04	0.01	—

Source: Annual reports of commercial banks.

[1]Accounts do not reflect B 4.9 billion in doubtful debts for which income is not available to make provision.

percent. Most banks added to their provisions for loan losses in 1986, but the typical provision amounted to much less than 1 percent of assets.

During 1987, 5 banks with assets amounting to about 25 percent of total commercial bank assets received official support, and 2 other banks were reported to be having financial difficulties (see Table 6).

Finance and Security Companies

The financial crisis among finance and security companies began in the autumn of 1983, when a finance company and two affiliates were closed as a result of large losses; between 1983 and 1986 a total of 20 finance companies and 4 security companies were closed. These closures were accompanied by a loss of confidence which resulted in a withdrawal of deposits. In the year to September 1984, finance and security company liabilities to businesses and households fell by 11 percent, but the growth in their liabilities to the banking system began to accelerate, as banks and the BOT moved to support ailing finance companies (Table 7). In 1985 business and household deposits recovered somewhat, but not enough to prevent a further increase in liabilities to the banking system, which rose to 25 percent of assets by the end of 1987. The capital/assets ratios of finance and security companies fell from 12 percent in 1980 to 6.7 percent in 1985. Reserves for loan losses rose to about 2 percent of assets, and delinquent debts were estimated at between 10 and 15 percent of assets.

Operating losses of finance and security companies were B 200 million in 1986, reduced from B 600 million in 1985 and B 400 million in 1984. However, as was true of the profit figures for the commercial banks, the underlying profit trends are difficult to discern because of the soft loan subsidy that has been provided by the BOT and the various provisions for loan losses. BOT loans to finance and security companies increased from B 3.7 billion at the end of 1984 to B 7.4 billion at the end of 1985 and B 9.1 billion by the end of 1987. Assuming that the interest subsidy on these loans averaged 7 percent, the BOT support arrangements might have increased finance and security company profits by B 300 million in 1984, B 600 million in 1985, and B 700 million in 1986. But companies increased their loan loss provisions by B 900 million in 1986. Similarly, the interpretation of the trends in the capital/assets ratios has been affected by the writing down of capital values against loan losses and the subsequent raising of new capital.

III. Reasons for Weakening Position of Banks and Finance Companies

A combination of factors contributed to the weakening financial position of banks and finance companies.

Table 6. Commercial Banks That Were Receiving Financial Support or Had Reported Financial Difficulties
(Position at end-December 1986)

	Total Assets		Capital/ Assets Ratio	Loan/ Deposit Ratio	Reported Difficulties	Recommendations by Bank of Thailand	Support Arrangements
	In billions of baht	As percent of total					
Bank of Asia	17.2	2.1	6.3	79.2	—	—	B 1.7 billion was provided as a soft loan by BOT in 1987.
Sayam Bank	20.8	2.5	2.6	86.3	—	—	Taken over by Government in August 1984 and operationally merged with Krung Thai Bank in February 1987. Monetary authorities provided B 3.5 billion in support in 1986: B 500 million to boost capital, B 1 billion to absorb bad debts, and remainder as a soft loan.
First Bangkok City Bank	27.5	3.3	5.8	101.2	At end-1985, bad debts were reported at B 2.8 billion; inclusion of doubtful debts would push figure to B 5 billion.	Value of capital was ordered reduced from B 1.365 billion to B 68 million, and then raised to B 2 billion.	Received a soft loan of B 3.8 billion with a 10-year maturity in May 1986 from BOT. RF stood ready to take up B 500 million of shares issued. BOT officials took over management of the bank.

Bank							
Siam City Bank	28.6	3.4	5.7	82.3	—	Ordered to reduce capital from B 800 million to B 40 million, and to increase it subsequently to B 1.5 billion. BOT to approve management.	Soft loans provided by BOT; raised B 1 billion of new shares in February 1987. RF was ready to take up B 500 million of shares issued.
Krung Thai Bank	105.6	12.6	4.2	73.6	Weak capital and reserve position. Also had experienced losses because of the overexposure of a financial subsidiary (IFCC).	—	Recapitalization of bank with a capital subscription of B 2 billion in 1987.
Other Banks with Reported Financial Difficulties							
Bangkok Metropolitan Bank	33.8	4.0	5.1	94.9	Loan exposure to the liquor sector and low capital funds.	Management structure to be revised to reduce family influence; exposure to liquor sector to be reduced; registered capital to be raised from B 500 million to B 1 billion.	The Government has supported the Sura Thrip Group (liquor group) to protect banking system.
Laem Thong Bank	4.6	0.6	19.9	110.3	Experienced loan losses and loss of confidence among depositors, leading to deposit withdrawals.		

Table 7. Indicators of Financial Position of Finance and Security Companies, End of Period, 1980–87

	1980	1981	1982	1983	1984	1985	1986	1987
Total assets (in billions of baht)	65.4	77.6	95.7	106.3	119.5	132.8	142.8	163.2
Annual percentage increase	14.9	18.7	23.3	11.1	12.4	11.1	7.5	14.3
Annual growth of business and household								
Deposits	22.3	28.8	25.4	5.2	−5.4	16.0	4.0	7.6
Loans	11.8	17.6	21.0	16.4	5.7	8.2	9.3	12.6
Net liabilities (in billions of baht) to								
Banking system	4.3	0.4	0.4	6.6	15.4	18.2	23.8	35.7
Bank of Thailand	1.0	0.2	−0.2	0.2	3.7	7.4	10.1	9.1
Commercial banks	3.3	0.3	0.6	6.4	11.8	10.7	13.7	26.6
Businesses and households	−9.0	−6.0	−4.9	−13.1	−21.7	−13.2	−15.5	−22.5
As percent of assets								
Capital accounts	12.0	10.4	9.2	9.7	7.6	6.7	6.8	6.7
Reserves for loan losses	...	...	...	...	...	1.1	1.7	1.7
Borrowing from banking system	9.6	5.6	6.5	10.1	15.9	17.3	19.3	24.9
Borrowing from households and businesses	63.2	68.5	69.6	66.0	55.5	57.9	56.0	52.1
Advances to households and businesses	57.3	58.8	56.6	60.0	60.7	58.2	58.8	56.9
Claims on Government	4.6	4.5	5.7	5.0	7.9	11.1	11.7	12.4

Source: Bank of Thailand. Some figures are partly estimated.

Institutional Weaknesses

The oligopolistic structure of the banking system, which allowed banks to make profits for many years, also led the banking industry to be inefficient and encourage bank management and shareholders to pay little attention to safety and soundness. The structure of bank ownership and the high concentration of banking activity also led to weaknesses in the banking system. In 1981, the Governor of the BOT summarized several of the management problems of commercial banks as follows:[5]

- Several managers were not professional bankers but were extensively involved in commercial enterprises and gave too little attention to running their banks;
- Inadequate internal controls and operating procedures provided scope for malpractice, irregularities, and fraud;
- Contrary to sound banking practices, the institutions extended credit and guarantees to businesses in which directors and shareholders of the banks were heavily involved;
- Banks constructed lavish and unnecessarily large headquarters and bank offices, which raised banks' operating costs excessively;
- Banks failed to diversify their share ownership and to include more small shareholders—practices that might have imposed greater discipline on the activities of directors and managers;
- Concentration of lending to a few large interrelated enterprises and industries magnified the risk exposure of the banks and reduced the supply of credit to smaller borrowers, thereby possibly impeding economic development;
- Lack of competition between banks may have raised lending margins and reduced deposit rates thereby discouraging savings and reducing the attractiveness of the organized vis-à-vis the unorganized financial markets.

Management weaknesses were especially notable in many finance and security companies. In contrast to commercial banks, finance companies were highly competitive in bidding for deposits, but their main objective often was simply to mobilize funds for use by their own or related companies. The management weaknesses were compounded by the generally lax regulatory framework and controls that were imposed on these companies' operations, and their faster rate of balance sheet expansion during the 1970s.

---

[5] Speech by Nukul Prachuabmoh, Governor, Bank of Thailand, to Thai Bankers Association, February 18, 1981.

Inadequate Legislative Framework

The internal weaknesses among the banks and finance companies might not have threatened the stability of the financial system if the authorities had had adequate powers to regulate, supervise, and intervene to direct the financial institutions. But the legal, regulatory, and supervisory framework had to be developed after problems emerged among financial institutions, and it has taken time to implement the new regulations fully.

The central bank is normally placed at the apex of the financial system, and the bank's powers over the financial system are clearly defined in its statutes. The Bank of Thailand Act, BE 2485 (1942), which established the BOT, however, restricted the BOT's powers and meant that detailed regulations had to be developed through separate laws and directives. As a result, the regulatory system was less flexible and more political, and may have been slow to react. Moreover, it took several years before the BOT was vested with sufficient power to supervise and regulate financial institutions adequately.

The original laws and regulations for banks and finance companies also were inadequately drafted and had to be amended. The original version of the current Commercial Banking Act BE 2505 (1962) (denoted here as CBA1)[6] was first amended in 1979 and was known as the Commercial Banking Act (No. 2), BE 2522 (denoted CBA2). This act was again amended in 1985 by the Emergency Decree Amending the Commercial Banking Act, BE 2505, BE 2528 (denoted EDCBA). The main statutory controls over finance and security companies were set out in the Act on the Undertaking of Finance Business, Securities Business, and Credit Foncier Business, BE 2522 (1979) (denoted FCA). The act was amended by Emergency Decrees in BE 2526 (1983) and BE 2528 (1985) (denoted EDFCA1 and EDFCA2, respectively). Table 8 shows the regulatory arrangements at the end of 1987.

Specific Regulatory Shortcomings and Amendments to Commercial Banking Act and Financial and Security Company Legislation

Concentration of Ownership and Portfolio

The original Commercial Banking Act (CBA1) provided insufficient safeguards against a high concentration of ownership. CBA2 set the maximum individual shareholding at 5 percent and the minimum number of shareholders per commercial bank to 250. Under CBA2 the registry of

---

[6] This act replaced the Commercial Banking Act, BE 2488 (1945).

shareholders was to be made available to the Bank of Thailand before any payment of dividends.

CBA1 placed no limits on banks' holdings of shares and debentures in companies as a percentage of the banks' own capital, thus permitting an excessive concentration of assets. CBA2 limited banks' holdings of shares and debentures to 20 percent of the banks' capital and reduced the limit on banks' holdings of another company's issued shares from 20 percent to 10 percent of the total shares sold. CBA2 also prohibited a commercial bank from purchasing the shares of another commercial bank, except when explicitly authorized to do so by the BOT.

Conflicts of Interest

CBA1 did not regulate the selection of directors, managers, and advisors; CBA2 listed the qualifications and exclusions for bank employees. CBA1 prohibited loans to a director or to the spouse of a director, or to partnerships in which they were involved, but it did not restrict directors' access to a number of channels through which directors could obtain finance. CBA2 imposed tighter restrictions on commercial banks' business transactions with their own directors; the definition of loans to directors was widened to include companies in which they held 30 percent or more of the shares issued, and the banks' boards were required to obtain approval for, and to notify the BOT about, certain transactions. EDCBA further tightened these restrictions by requiring that the BOT approve any transactions over a certain amount between a commercial bank and its directors. EDFCA2 introduced identical restrictions for finance companies. EDCBA also expanded the definition of loans to a director to include loans to subsidiaries of a company in which the director or the director's family members or associates were holding shares. EDFCA2 prohibited finance companies from lending money and guaranteeing any debt to its directors. CBA2 increased the penalties on interlocking directorships in commercial banks.

Changes in Supervisory Responsibility

To improve the supervisory arrangements, CBA2 transferred a number of regulatory responsibilities from the Ministry of Finance (MOF) to the BOT. The MOF retained responsibility for licensing head offices of domestic banks, but the BOT gained the power to regulate changes in the location of bank offices and to authorize domestic representative offices of foreign banks and foreign representative offices of domestic banks. EDFCA2 made the BOT responsible for authorizing domestic representative offices of foreign finance companies, for approving bank auditors, for setting banking hours and bank holidays, and for prescribing the form and frequency of commercial banks' summary statements.

Table 8. Summary of Main Statutory Requirements of Commercial Banks, Finance and Security Companies, and Credit Foncier Companies, End-1987

	Commercial Banks	Finance and Security Companies	Credit Foncier Companies
Minimum paid-up capital (in millions of baht)	—	60	30
Restrictions on share ownership			
Number of shareholders	150 holding 50 percent of shares	100 holding 50 percent of shares	100 holding 50 percent of shares
Foreign ownership	25 percent of shares	25 percent of shares	25 percent of shares
Maximum held by a single person	0.5 percent of total	0.6 percent of total	0.6 percent of total
Minimum ratio of holdings of capital (in percent) to			
Risk assets	8	6	6
Contingent liabilities	20[1]	25[2]	—
Exemptions of assets from the risk/asset ratios			...
Maximum lending in relation to capital (in percent)			
Loans to a single borrower	25	30	30
Other loan categories	20 percent of aggregate share holdings	5 percent for car hire purchase	20 percent for unsecured call loans to an individual institution and 100 percent in aggregate
Other lending restrictions			
Loans to directors	Prohibited	Prohibited	Prohibited
Overdraft lending to single borrower	Maximum B 50 million	—	—
Loan to deposit ratio	...	—	—
Minimum collateral requirements		Cash or notes equal to 70 percent of value of loans for security purchases[3]	...

Open foreign exchange position *(percent of capital funds)*	20	—	—
Reserve and liquidity requirements			
Cash reserve ratio *(in percent of deposits)*	7	—	—
Balances of Bank of Thailand	(>2)	(...)	(...)
Cash in hand	(<2.5)	(...)	(...)
Government securities	(2.5)	(...)	(...)
Liquid asset ratio *(percent of borrowing)*	—	7	5
Balances of Bank of Thailand	(—)	(>0.5)	(>0.5)
Unobliged government securities	(—)	(>5.5)	(>3.5)[4]
Deposits at call and loans to banks	(—)	(<1.0)	(<1.0)
Other restrictions on liabilities	Maximum interest rates	Maximum interest rates, minimum size of promissory notes;[5] demand and savings deposits prohibited	Maximum interest rates, minimum one-year maturity and size of promissory notes;[6] demand and savings deposits prohibited
Supervisory framework			
Regular reports to BOT	Monthly	Monthly	Monthly
BOT approval needed for Payment of dividends			
Appointment of auditors	Yes	Yes	Yes
On-site inspections by BOT staff	Yes	Yes	Yes
Formal loan classifications	Yes	Yes	Yes
Formal provisioning requirements	Yes	Yes	Yes

Source: Bank of Thailand; Commercial Bank Acts; Finance and Security Company, and Credit Foncier Acts.

[1] Some 28 items are excluded, including certain loans to priority sectors.
[2] Exempt 14 items.
[3] This figure is subject to the regulation of the SET but not less than 25 percent.
[4] Including unobliged government-guaranteed securities.
[5] B 10,000 in Bangkok metropolitan area, B 5,000 elsewhere.
[6] B 1,000.

Tighter Regulations and Penalties

Under CBA1, banks had been largely unrestricted in the types of activities they could undertake. Under CBA2, the banking business was defined in more detail, and any activity by banks that was unrelated to banking became either unlawful or subject to approval by the BOT. CBA2 also gave the BOT authority to set a capital requirement against contingent liabilities, to impose a liquid assets requirement, and to differentiate the cash requirement by type of deposit.

CBA2 specified more power for the MOF to revoke bank licenses and authorized the MOF to recommend that a commercial bank dismiss its directors or officers to avoid having its license revoked. EDFCA1 required finance companies to close their books at least every six months and specified that balance sheets and profit and loss accounts had to be approved by a general meeting of shareholders before being published and had to be submitted to the BOT within 21 days. EDCBA introduced the same regulations for commercial banks. EDFCA1 required that the BOT approve auditors for finance companies annually; EDCBA extended this requirement to commercial banks.

Stricter penalties were introduced for noncompliance with the law by CBA2 and EDFCA1. The most important changes in the penalties imposed on banks are given in Tables 9 and 10.

Expanded Supervisory Powers and Cease and Desist Arrangements

CBA1 provided for the appointment of bank inspectors but did not give inspectors the power necessary to conduct on-site examinations of commercial banks; moreover, the lack of BOT control over bank returns under CBA1 may have restricted off-site inspection. CBA2 gave inspectors more power, including the right to enter a bank's premises when they had reason to suspect that an offense had been committed. Inspectors could demand cooperation not only from directors, officers, and employees of commercial banks, but also from the banks' auditors. EDCBA and EDFCA2 gave inspectors (competent officers, in the case of finance companies) the right to enter the premises where data were analyzed or stored and to obtain information from, and to order cooperation by, persons responsible for collecting or analyzing data. With the approval of the Governor of the BOT or the MOF, bank inspectors also could enter the premises of and examine the operations of a commercial bank's borrower, or otherwise require the borrower or other persons to provide information necessary for the inspection of the commercial bank.

Under CBA1 the Minister of Finance could order, in the public interest, a license to be revoked or a bank to be placed under control following the inspector's report, but these broad powers were not used. CBA2 gave the

Table 9. Main Changes in Penalties for Noncompliance with the Commercial Banking Law Enacted by CBA2

New Offenses Subject to Penalties Under CBA2	Penalties for Bank	Penalties for Responsible Persons
Operating representative office domestically or abroad without obtaining authorization of BOT		Imprisonment of up to one year, maximum fine of B 100,000, or both
Failing to comply with regulations on concentration of ownership of shares	Maximum fine of B 100,000	
Failing to comply with special cash reserve requirements when in effect	Maximum fine of B 200,000	Imprisonment
Increased penalties for existing offenses		
Undertaking commercial banking without proper authorization		Imprisonment of up to five years, maximum fine of B 500,000, or both
Serving as director or holding any other position in two or more commercial banks simultaneously		Imprisonment of up to one year, maximum fine of B 100,000, or both
Establishing branch without proper authorization	Maximum fine of B 300,000	
Reducing bank's equity capital	Maximum fine of B 300,000 and/or B 3,000 a day	Imprisonment of up to one year, fine of B 300,000, or both

Source: Commercial Banking Act (No. 2), BE 2522.

BOT the power to demand that a commercial bank write off as worthless, assets that were found to be unrecoverable during the analysis of the summary statements—thereby allowing the BOT to impose some effective remedial measures. EDFCA1 established similar regulations for finance

**Table 10. Main Changes in Penalties for Noncompliance
with the Commercial Banking Law Enacted by EDCBA**

New Offenses Subject to Penalties Under EDCBA	Penalties for Bank	Penalties for Responsible Persons
Dismissed bank employees still working for bank or not cooperating with new employees by providing information		Imprisonment of up to one year and/or maximum fine of B 100,000
Prescriptions and conditions for noncompliance with following regulations:	Maximum fine of B 100,000 per offense	
Concentration of ownership of shares		
Minimum 250 shareholders per bank		
Bank purchase/ holding of shares in another bank		
Cessation of bank operations		
Transferral/dismissal of bank employees		
Maximum credit per borrower		
Liquid asset requirements		
Increase/reduction of equity capital		
Removal of directors		

Source: Emerging Decree Amending the Commercial Banking Act, BE 2505, BE 2528.

companies and gave the BOT the additional flexibility to require finance companies to provide special reserves to cover doubtful assets. EDCBA extended this additional power for the BOT to commercial banks.

EDCBA and EDFCA2 allowed the MOF, with the advice of the BOT, to stop all or parts of a commercial bank's or a finance company's operations temporarily in order to rectify the financial position of the bank or to protect the stability of the financial system. The BOT obtained power to enforce compliance with regulations through direct intervention, to order a commercial bank or a finance company to increase or reduce its capital in order to prevent any damage to the public interest, to remove any director or person responsible for operating a commercial bank or a finance company that threatened damage to the public interest, and to approve new officials.

Lax Regulatory Standards

Even when the regulatory framework was adequate in Thailand, implementation was weak.

Capital/Assets Ratios

The deterioration in the overall capital/assets ratio of banks partly reflected an easing of regulatory standards for commercial banks. In May 1983, the overall capital/risk assets ratio fell from 8.5 percent to 8 percent largely because of a lack of capital rather than because of any reassessment of the riskiness of banks' assets. This reduction in the overall capital/assets ratio was accompanied by a very rapid growth of bank loans to the private sector (34 percent in 1983, see Chart 4). Rapid balance sheet growth by itself can strain management resources and credit appraisal systems, and, combined with weak procedures for assessing the quality of loans, that growth in loans contributed to the banks' subsequent loan losses.

The definition of banks' risk assets also was weakened. First, a number of relatively high risk assets, such as lending to finance and security companies, were excluded from the definition; because these assets tended to grow rapidly, the quality of banks' balance sheets deteriorated. Second, in August 1986, the BOT reduced from 100 percent to 80 percent the proportion of loans extended to certain priority sectors that were counted as risk assets; this action also tended to weaken banks' balance sheets. Third, between October 1986 and April 1987, as a measure to reduce domestic currency liquidity in the financial system, the BOT temporarily increased the limits on banks' open foreign exchange positions from 20 percent to 40 percent of capital funds. It subsequently redefined banks' open foreign exchange positions to exclude positions in a bank's branches abroad, thus providing scope for avoidance of the restriction on banks taking an overall open foreign exchange position. Fourth, until 1985 the assets of Thai banks' foreign branches were excluded from their capital/assets ratios; and capital requirements remained to be completely consoli-

Chart 4. Economic and Financial Indicators
(In percent)

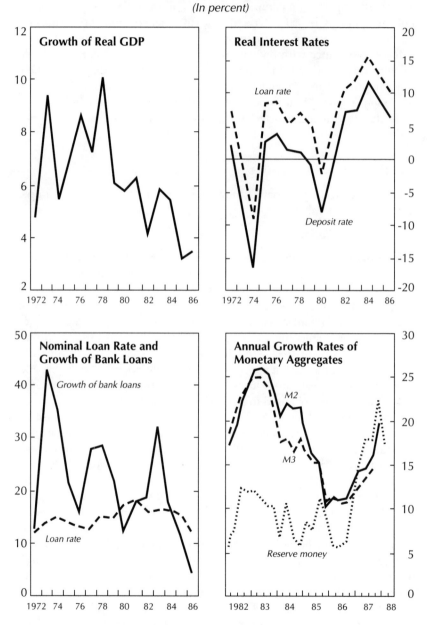

Sources: Data provided by the Thai authorities and International Monetary Fund, *International Financial Statistics.*

dated. As a result of the exclusions just mentioned, Thai banks' on-balance-sheet risk assets amounted to only 51 percent of their total assets at the end of 1986, compared with 64 percent in 1984 (Table 11). In addition, off-balance-sheet risks were substantial.

Off-Balance-Sheet Risks

A 20 percent capital requirement was imposed against contingent liabilities, but because the definition of contingent liabilities used in calculating this capital requirement covered only 12 percent of banks' off-balance-

Table 11. Assets, Off-Balance-Sheet Items, and Capital of Commercial Banks, 1982–86[1]

(In billions of baht)

	1982	1983	1984	1985	1986
Total assets	*496.2*	*614.7*	*741.4*	*806.8*	*870.1*
Risk assets[2]	247.0	326.7	396.1	450.5	439.6
As percentage of total assets	49.8	53.2	64.4	55.8	50.5
Off-balance-sheet transactions	*310.6*	*348.4*	*429.7*	*411.2*	*484.5*
As percentage of total assets	62.6	56.7	60.0	51.0	55.7
Contingencies[3]	...	43.4	54.7	61.0	57.5
As percentage of off-balance-sheet transactions	...	12.4	12.7	14.8	11.9
Contingencies and risk assets	...	370.0	450.7	511.4	497.2
Total assets plus off-balance-sheet transactions	806.8	963.1	1,171.1	1,218.0	1,354.6
Capital funds	24.5	28.0	36.1	42.3	43.9
As percentage of					
Total assets	4.9	4.6	4.9	5.2	5.1
Risk assets	9.9	8.6	9.1	9.4	10.0
Off-balance-sheet transactions	7.9	8.0	8.4	10.3	9.1
Contingencies	...	64.5	66.1	69.3	76.4
Contingencies and risk assets	...	7.6	8.0	8.3	8.8
Total assets plus off-balance-sheet transactions	3.0	3.6	3.1	3.5	3.2

Source: Bank of Thailand.

[1]Including overseas branches.

[2]Those assets subject to 8 percent capital requirements.

[3]Off-balance-sheet items defined under Section 10(3) of the Commercial Bank Act that are subject to a 20 percent capital requirement.

sheet transactions (see Table 11),[7] the capital requirement against total off-balance-sheet transactions averaged only 2–3 percent. Furthermore, this capital requirement has been imposed along with the 8 percent capital/risk assets ratio for on-balance-sheet risks using the same capital base. In other words, the balance sheet risk assets and contingencies have not been added together to arrive at a measure of total risk exposure in the portfolio for the purposes of determining capital adequacy.[8] Hence, to the extent that the capital has been fully employed as a safeguard against on-balance-sheet risks, it has not been available as a safeguard against off-balance-sheet transactions. Such transactions exceeded 50 percent of banks' total assets. The ratio of capital to gross total assets and off-balance-sheet transactions was approximately 3 percent (Table 11).

Dividend Payments and Interest Accruals

Although the BOT had power under Section 21 of the CBA2 to prevent the distribution of dividends and banks were slow to increase provisions for bad and doubtful debts, the BOT never exercised its power. Similarly, the BOT imposed no restrictions on the accrual of interest and income earned but not received in the balance sheets of commercial banks. Restrictions on dividend payments and interest accruals have been imposed on finance companies. Interest accruals boost recorded earnings and book profits, and unwarranted dividend payments could give a misleading impression to new shareholders when banks are raising new capital.

Loan Provisioning

The BOT defined worthless and irrecoverable assets in a circular, BE 2529, on March 18, 1986. The criteria were defined mainly in terms of the nonrecoverability of the debt, evidenced, for example, by death, bankruptcy, lack of collateral, or legal proceedings rather than by delinquency in meeting scheduled payments. Because there were no clear criteria for defining doubtful debts, which required provisioning in advance of loss, the result was to delay provisioning until the debt was actually a loss.

[7] Excluded from the definition were undrawn facilities, interest rate and currency swaps, options, and forward exchange rate and interest rate agreements. Such transactions were relatively new for Thai banks but have been growing rapidly, particularly because banks have been seeking to improve their profit positions by increasing their fee incomes and to avoid the capital/risk asset restrictions on their balance sheet activities. The BOT has been conducting a review of its treatment of off-balance-sheet transactions. Tejasmit and others, "Central Bank Policy on Off-Balance-Sheet Operations," Thailand Country Paper, presented to SEACEN Seminar, July 22–24, 1987, Bangkok, Thailand.

[8] This type of procedure is suggested by Bank for International Settlements, Committee on Banking Regulations and Supervisory Practices, *International Convergence of Capital Measurement and Standards* (Basle, July 1988).

Concentration of Ownership

Despite the regulations on share ownership, ownership appears to be highly concentrated, and this concentration has interfered with the professional management of some commercial banks. This problem was especially severe in banks where the regulations on lending to shareholders, directors, and management (or other affiliates) were being circumvented.

Economic Conditions

Although distinct structural and regulatory inadequacies were evident in the 1970s, the inherent institutional weaknesses were exacerbated by the downturn in economic activity in the first half of the 1980s (see Chart 4). In 1982 the Thai authorities substantially increased nominal and real interest rates. Real bank loan rates, which had averaged 4.2 percent between 1971 and 1981, averaged 12.4 percent between 1982 and 1986. Nominal bank loan rates rose above the growth of bank credit to the private sector in 1980 and 1981 and again in 1985 and 1986, resulting in a net transfer of resources from borrowers to commercial banks which acted to squeeze borrowers and caused loan delinquencies. As already noted, the rapid growth of bank lending in 1983 reflected the easing of the capital/assets ratio requirement. By 1983 the growth of the monetary aggregates slowed significantly (see Chart 4). The difference in the growth rates of M2 and M3 (M2 plus the consolidated liabilities of finance companies) in 1984 is indicative of the serious loss of confidence in finance companies in that year, which resulted in a shift of deposits out of finance companies into commercial banks (see Section VI). The average rate of real GDP growth fell from 6.9 percent between 1971 and 1981 to 4.4 percent between 1982 and 1986.

Also during the 1980s, competition in the supply of bank credits increased for several reasons. First, after 1985 the authorities encouraged a more competitive determination of bank interest rates and placed less reliance on interest rate ceilings. Second, between 1983 and 1986 the emergence of positive differentials between Thai and Eurodollar interest rates encouraged increased borrowing abroad by prime corporations. Third, in 1986 and 1987, the financial sector showed a high level of liquidity—a reflection of the improved balance of payments and foreign exchange reserve accumulation by the BOT. Fourth, between 1984 and 1986 loan demand was relatively sluggish and loan/deposit ratios fell (see Table 3). As a result, banks cut their lending rates to prime borrowers to 3 percentage points or more below posted "minimum lending rates"; the effective spread between the average cost of funds to banks and the average return on lending to banks then declined from 2.8 percent in 1982 and 1983 to 2.2 percent in 1984, 2.05 percent in 1985, and 1.95 percent in

1986. In some cases, the spread between borrowing and lending rates failed to cover the risks acquired in the portfolio, and, as already noted, the overall profitability of the banking system was reduced. An increase in competition inevitably put pressure on weaker institutions and made their recovery even more difficult.

The combination of weak institutions and economic downturn caused a crisis in 1983 when one finance company failed and others experienced runs on deposits. Because finance companies accounted for a relatively small proportion of total financial institution liabilities, they might have been allowed to fail without threatening financial sector stability, but in view of the sharp economic downturn, there was concern that any loss of confidence could have had serious economic implications. Hence the BOT decided to intervene in these companies either to pay off depositors or to support and restructure them. A loss of confidence in commercial banks was potentially much more serious, but except for deposit runs on the Sayam Bank, there was no evidence of a general loss of public confidence in the banking system.

IV. Support Arrangements and Remedial Actions

The restructuring and the support of ailing financial institutions in Thailand reflect the extent to which the arrangements were put into effect as part of crisis management or made in advance of the crisis. EDFCA1 (1983) expanded the supervisory power of the Minister/BOT over financially troubled companies. Any finance company that suspended repayment of its due obligations had to notify the MOF and the BOT immediately, and was prohibited from transacting any business without special authorization from the Minister. Upon receiving such a notification, the Minister had the power to appoint a competent officer to investigate the company. The BOT gained the power to order a banker or finance company to reduce or increase its capital, to remove directors and managers, and to appoint new officers in the public interest only in 1985 under EDCBA and EDFCA2. Hence the BOT could not really intervene when the crisis emerged in 1983. After 1985, the restructuring of institutions through mergers continued to be inhibited by the merger law, which required 100 percent agreement of creditors before mergers could take place. As a result, the remedial measures have been pursued mainly through direct government takeovers and attempts to rehabilitate existing institutions, rather than through mergers. In addition, there have been legal difficulties in recovering delinquent debts.

Support for Finance and Security Companies

The main elements of support for finance and security companies have been injections of liquidity through a number of schemes ("liquidity fund," "lifeboat" support, and credit from other financial institutions) and through capital and management restructuring.

Initial Liquidity Support

In late 1983, to provide general liquidity support to the ailing finance and security companies, the Government and members of the Thai Bankers Association (TBA) established a "liquidity fund" of B 5 billion, of which B 1 billion was provided by the Krung Thai Bank, acting on behalf of the Government, and the remainder by other commercial banks. The fund, which was used to support 18 companies, was managed jointly by representatives of the Krung Thai Bank (representing the TBA), the MOF, and the BOT. The TBA charged market-related interest rates on its loan to the fund (initially, 13 percent, equal to the BOT discount rate); rates on the loans provided by the fund to support institutions were also market related (set initially at 16–16.5 percent but subsequently reduced in line with the decline in market rates). Loans were initially granted for periods of up to three years but have subsequently been rolled over.

"Lifeboat" Support and Restructuring

In April 1984, after it became clear that a serious loss of confidence was developing in the finance companies, the MOF initiated a "lifeboat" scheme for the troubled companies, which provided additional support to the liquidity fund and gave the authorities a means to intervene in the finance companies (which the liquidity fund and the existing legal framework did not provide).

Under the lifeboat scheme, any troubled finance or credit foncier company that was not a bank affiliate could apply to join the lifeboat, which offered three types of financial assistance: credit lines at market rates, without a maturity date, to offset deposit withdrawals (the total amount available to be drawn was B 3.2 billion); capital injections through equity participation by the Krung Thai Bank[9] (B 2.4 billion); and BOT soft loans to be invested in government bonds (up to B 6.4 million). The soft loans carried a five-year maturity and an interest rate of 0.1–2.5 percent, depending on the interest rate on government bonds purchased.

To join the scheme, the company had to reduce the value of its shares

---

[9] These were later taken over by the Fund for Rehabilitation and Development of Financial Institutions (see below).

and existing management and major shareholders had to surrender additional collateral and to transfer to the MOF 25 percent of the shares plus another 50 percent of the voting rights; the latter 50 percent was to be transferred back to the original owners within five years at a price to be set by the MOF. As the authorities injected additional capital into the companies, their effective voting rights rose to about 90 percent of shares issued. The BOT and MOF were responsible for screening applicants; installing new management; and determining the amount, type, and terms of financial assistance. The BOT also had to monitor closely the performance of companies in the scheme.

Twenty-five companies joined the lifeboat scheme; 11 of these were viewed to be in a position that could be supported with soft loans, while the remaining 14 were judged to be in critical condition. Seven other companies refused to join the lifeboat scheme and were subjected to a detailed evaluation and restricted from accepting new deposits or granting new loans. Of these seven, 4 lost their licenses and were closed in October 1985; a fifth was closed in November 1986. The BOT has been paying off depositors in those 5 companies over a ten-year period without interest on the deposits. The controls on accepting new deposits and granting loans on the two others were lifted. In July 1986 4 security firms (which had not been in the lifeboat scheme) lost their licenses, reducing the number of security firms to 11.

In January 1987 a scheme was announced to resolve the problems of the finance companies in the lifeboat: (1) The Krung Thai Bank was to take over the management of the finance companies still in the lifeboat; staff from the Krung Thai Bank were appointed to join the management teams and to oversee the operation of these financial institutions; in addition, a task force consisting of analysts and examiners was set up at the BOT to follow activities of the firms and to provide management information and recommendations to policymakers; (2) The business of the companies was to be restructured to make them active in investment banking; (3) The cost of borrowing from the liquidity fund was to be cut to 8.85 percent (with a similar reduction in the return on placements with the fund); (4) The stronger companies in the scheme were to be reprivatized and the weaker companies were to be merged into new companies; (5) Foreign financial institutions were to be invited to join in the ownership and management of firms in the lifeboat and given incentives similar to those offered to encourage mergers (this proposal has faced difficulties); (6) Nonperforming assets of finance and security companies were to be rediscountable with the Fund for Rehabilitation and Development of Financial Institutions (RF), thus providing liquidity to these otherwise nonperforming assets. In addition to the funds it had provided to the liquidity fund, the Krung Thai Bank set aside a further credit line of B 4 billion to be extended to companies at market rates. This action brought the total credit lines provided under the support schemes to approximately B 19 billion. By the end of 1987 the net indebtedness of finance companies to the banking system had reached B 36 billion (see Table 7).

By the end of 1988, 5 of the 25 companies in the lifeboat had been resold to their previous shareholders and directors appointed by the authorities had been withdrawn, as originally envisaged when setting up the scheme, but the new management installed by the authorities was retained as part of the resale arrangement. The prices at which these companies were resold did not involve losses to the original shareholders, and additional soft loans were provided as incentives for the reprivatization of the companies. The authorities have encouraged other companies that have common shareholders or common debtors to merge and have provided incentive schemes such as the privileges to open branches and new lines of business (leasing). After two years of legal and administrative preparations, the first merger of 6 companies took place in late 1987; since then 3 other companies have merged too. The merged companies have remained in the lifeboat and continue to be supported by soft loans. At the end of 1988, 13 companies with assets of B 20 billion remained in the lifeboat.

Fund for the Rehabilitation and Development of Financial Institutions (RF)

The RF was set up within the BOT as a legally distinct entity with its own Board and management under the EDCBA to rehabilitate financial institutions. The RF's activities consist of lending (with proper collateral) to, placing deposits in, acquiring assets from, and holding equity in financial institutions; and offering assistance to depositors in, or lenders to, financial institutions during crises. Financial institutions are required to contribute to the RF at a rate set by its Board, up to 0.5 percent of outstanding deposits; the rate in 1988 was 0.1 percent. However, in November 1988 the BOT contributed the majority of the resources of the RF through a capital subscription and loans equivalent to 84 percent of the RF's total funds of B 12.2 billion. The RF has been active in underwriting and subscribing to capital issues by distressed financial institutions and has taken over the capital injections made earlier by the Krung Thai Bank under the lifeboat scheme. It has also provided liquidity support by rediscounting nonperforming assets of troubled financial institutions and providing soft loans. By November 1988, the RF had lent B 4.2 billion to commercial banks—the largest portion to the Krung Thai Bank—and invested B 4.3 billion and B 1.0 billion, respectively, in the equity of five banks and one finance company.

Support for Commercial Banks

The support and restructuring arrangements for commercial banks have also reflected the powers of the BOT to intervene and to order a restructuring of troubled financial institutions. The main arrangements used to support ailing commercial banks have been government takeover, soft loans from the BOT and the RF to be invested in government bonds by the institution (a de facto subsidy to banks' profits), and equity participations by the RF combined with a restructuring of the banks' managements under BOT guidance. Proposals to support ailing banks have been made by the Bank Supervision Department of the BOT. On the basis of these proposals the Board of the BOT can approve soft loans to the institution, and the Board of the RF can approve equity participations, rediscounts, and soft loans by the RF. As a condition of support, the BOT has set financial programs specifying paths for increases in capital and bad debt provisions of the banks. The purchase of shares by the BOT or the RF in supported institutions has meant that part of the gain in the net worth of the banks attributable to soft loan subsidies accrues to the BOT through an appreciation in share values.

Five banks have received financial assistance (see Table 6). The Sayam Bank, with about B 20 billion in assets (the eleventh-largest local bank), was judged insolvent in the early 1980s and, after suffering a run on deposits, it was taken over by the Government in August 1984. It has since received B 3.5 billion in support (equivalent to 20 percent of assets) from the monetary authorities and was operationally merged with the nationalized Krung Thai Bank in February 1987.

The Siam City Bank and the First Bangkok City Bank (the ninth- and tenth-largest banks, each with about B 28 billion in assets) were also judged to be insolvent but did not face deposit runs, and hence, emergency intervention and restructuring were not required. Because emergency measures were not called for, the BOT could more easily decide the timing and type of intervention and was able to utilize the new powers granted to it under EDCBA. After inspections of their books, the BOT ordered the value of the banks' capital to be reduced and new capital to be raised to a level that could support their activities, thus involving losses for existing shareholders. In each case, the banks were supported by soft loans from the BOT, and the RF stood ready to underwrite a large part of the new capital issue.

Once the BOT's powers of intervention had become established, it was easier for it to encourage further "voluntary" restructuring by certain commercial banks. In the case of the Bank of Asia (the twelfth-largest bank), the BOT provided soft loans when the bank agreed to a comprehensive restructuring package, and the shareholders and existing management were supported. However, the BOT retained the option of buying shares in the bank at below-market rates should the restructuring fail to advance as intended.

A package of support measures, including an equity participation of B 2 billion and loans by the RF, was announced in 1987 for the Krung Thai Bank, which had been active in supporting the ailing finance companies; consequently, the burden of financial institution support has come to rest even more heavily with the BOT.

V. Review of Support Arrangements

It seems important to distinguish between the support operations for the finance and security companies and the commercial banks. As already noted, the finance companies were financially less significant and substantially unregulated before the crisis and the insolvent companies had significant negative net worth, which has made their rehabilitation difficult. There would seem to be a prima facie case for closing these institutions rather than supporting them. On the other hand, the banks were quantitatively more important and were at least nominally subject to official regulation, and thus there would seem to be a better case for the support and restructuring operations. The restructuring operations for four of the five commercial banks were better planned, in that they were not undertaken in reaction to a crisis.

The success of the present support arrangements depends on the outlook for a recovery in profitability of the ailing financial institutions. The substantial recovery in the Thai economy in 1987 and 1988 to growth rates of 7–9 percent have improved loan performance, raised the value of collateral, and reversed the weak profit trends and declining bank lending margins noted during the 1980s, thus improving the prospects for success. On the other hand, competition between financial institutions has continued to intensify as the cartel arrangements between banks have continued to break down, keeping profit margins low. A competitive financial system may inevitably require that weaker firms disappear and new firms are permitted to enter, thus requiring a more fundamental restructuring of financial institutions and revisions to the present merger law.

The costs of keeping open the ailing institutions have turned out to be high. The direct annual cost of the support arrangements to the BOT, because of its soft loan subsidy, and indirectly to the central government budget, because of the lower BOT profits available for appropriation, is estimated to have amounted to about 1 percent of budgeted revenue in 1987/88[10] (equivalent to an annual cost of about 0.2 percent of GDP, and 2

---

[10] The contribution of BOT profits to budget revenues declined from B 2.3 billion (1.6 percent of total revenue) in 1984/85 to a budget estimate of B 1.2 billion (0.6 percent of total revenue) in 1987/88. Over this period there was a doubling of the BOT's net foreign assets,

percent of reserve money). The profitability of the Krung Thai Bank has also been adversely affected and has required support. Scarce resources—both human and financial—were also tied up in keeping open the ailing finance companies which might have been better employed in other activities.

The initial decision to support rather than close the insolvent finance and security companies was taken on the basis of the estimated comparative costs of paying back the depositors of the companies over a ten-year period (estimated in present value terms to be equivalent to 50 percent of the value of deposits assuming that no interest was paid on deposits) and of keeping open the ailing institutions. The estimates indicated that a salvage operation would be less costly. However, the costs of keeping open the ailing institutions turned out to be much higher than anticipated mainly because the magnitude of companies' bad debts was underestimated, the recovery of collateral was more difficult than anticipated, and also because the BOT staff, which took over the management of the companies, lacked commercial banking expertise. As a result the activities of the companies stagnated and their losses continued to increase. In these circumstances, new injections of capital were quickly wiped out and did not improve companies' solvency, but simply went toward paying interest to depositors.

An alternative would have been to develop at an early stage a program which would have involved a larger number of closures or the sale or merger of nonviable institutions with sound institutions. Nonviability might mean that there was a limited probability that the institution would achieve solvency and profitability in a reasonable period of time (say, three to five years). The closure of an institution would have required an injection of public funds to repay depositors. In a case where it would have been possible to sell the institutions (or merge them), which may be preferable to outright closure, it may have been necessary to have an initial injection of public funds equivalent to the institutions' negative net worth. The government budget has had to carry the cost of the support arrangements, albeit indirectly through reduced BOT (and Krung Thai Bank) profits, and the necessary one-time injection of public funds needed to restructure financial institutions might not have added to budgetary costs, taking a number of years together, while removing the burden of support from the authorities. Indeed, selling and merging the ailing companies could have placed them under more competent managements, and hence

---

which might have been expected to increase profits, although this may have been offset by a drop in interest rates which would have acted to reduce revenue. The cost to the BOT of its loans to commercial banks and finance and security companies, which amounted to B 28 billion at end-June 1987, might be estimated at B 2 billion annually, assuming an average soft loan rate of 1 percent and an average government bond yield of 8 percent.

their operations might not have stagnated, resulting in lower recovery and budgetary costs. Moreover, depositors could have been expected to bear some of the losses of finance companies, since they had benefited from the previous higher interest rates on finance company deposits. The interest differential paid by finance companies may have included a margin to cover the risks that deposits with finance companies would not be fully repaid, and so depositors may have anticipated some loss.

Such a program would have had to address the impediments to the restructuring of the financial system such as the commercial and bank-ruptcy laws which have made the closure and merger of financial institutions highly cumbersome, requiring direct intervention by the authorities. An easing of the restriction on foreign participation in local commercial banks, which has been limited to 25 percent of equity, could also have provided an injection of capital funds and management skills that would have facilitated the restructuring of financial institutions.

The BOT was able to restructure financial institutions as part of its support arrangements and in many cases imposed sanctions on bank managements and shareholders. Nevertheless, the approach to supporting existing financial institutions carried risks for financial sector efficiency when it prevented or slowed down a necessary restructuring of the finan-cial sector. In several cases shareholders were also insulated from the full losses incurred by their financial institutions, which could weaken share-holders' incentives to require the highest standards from the managements of the institutions concerned. The capital of banks was ordered reduced in some cases, but in others the shareholders were not penalized or at least did not bear the full losses of their institutions. Moreover, depositors in supported finance companies were fully bailed out by the authorities, even though the interest rates paid by these companies were at a premium to those offered by commercial banks. Intervention by the authorities may have raised problems for "moral hazard" and weakened self-regulatory systems.

VI. Macroeconomic Consequences

As regards the broader economic implications of the support arrange-ments, there are a number of possible channels by which the financial crisis could have influenced the macroeconomy. Since the BOT soft loans had to be invested in government securities sold from the BOT's portfolio, it is probable that a substantial part of the loans was automatically steril-ized and therefore did not have direct effects on economic activity. However, the requirement that soft loans be invested in government bonds might not prevent some leakage of these loans into other activities; for example, government bond purchases by these institutions might have taken place anyway. The higher budget deficit resulting from the lower

272 • R. BARRY JOHNSTON

profits of the BOT available for appropriation by the Government could contribute to monetary expansion if it were financed through the banking system.

A potentially more serious concern was that the stance of monetary policy was relaxed by the need to improve bank profitability rather than by macroeconomic considerations during 1986 and 1987. During these years the authorities permitted a high level of financial sector liquidity and the growth of reserve money increased sharply, reaching 20 percent in 1987. The increase in liquidity largely reflected balance of payments surpluses. The authorities had at their disposal the instruments—government bond repurchases and issues of central bank bonds—to restrict the liquidity expansion, and indeed the BOT became more active in its money market intervention in 1986 and 1987, but limited the amounts to certain nominal ceilings. As a result, interbank rates fell to very low levels and it has been suggested that this was partly to help weaker financial institutions by reducing borrowing costs; however, as noted above, the increase in liquidity also intensified competition for bank loans and therefore may have reduced bank lending spreads. During 1986 and the first half of 1987 the economy was in the early phases of recovery, inflation was low, and the balance of payments was in substantial surplus; therefore a looser financial policy may have been justified by macroeconomic conditions. Hence, there was no great conflict between supporting financial institutions and the macroeconomic policy stance during this period. Circumstances could have been otherwise, and there may be concern that the need for a future tightening of policy on macroeconomic grounds could be delayed by the need to support ailing financial institutions.

As is evident from Chart 4, there was a shift in the behavior of the M2 and M3 monetary aggregates in 1983 and 1984, associated with a movement of deposits out of finance companies into commercial banks following the financial crisis which distorted the monetary aggregates. Our estimated demand equation shows a significant increase in the demand for M2—currency and deposit liabilities of commercial banks—following the emergence of the crisis among finance companies in 1983.[11] The Thai

---

[11] The estimated demand equation for M2 is

$$\Delta lnM2 = \begin{array}{cc} -0.18 \\ (1.05) \end{array} \begin{array}{cc} + 0.27ln\,(GDP/M2(-1)) \\ (2.72) \end{array} \begin{array}{cc} - 0.08ln\,(GDPA/(GDP - GDPA)) \\ (1.21) \end{array}$$

$$\begin{array}{cc} + 0.03(r_{cb} - r_{fc}) \\ (3.28) \end{array} \begin{array}{cc} - 0.01(r_{cb} - \pi) \\ (0.48) \end{array} \begin{array}{cc} + 0.05D \\ (2.29) \end{array}$$

$\bar{R}^2 = 0.52$; DW = 2.09; estimated period 1971–86; t-ratios in parentheses;
where GDP = nominal GDP
$\quad GDPA$ = nominal GDP in agricultural sector

authorities have used multiple monetary targets as a guide to policy including the M2 monetary aggregate. The more rapid growth of this aggregate in 1983 and 1984 as a result of the portfolio shift out of finance company accounts into bank deposits could have contributed to the significantly tighter monetary policy during these years. But there would have been no necessary reason to tighten monetary policy simply because of a portfolio shift which would not have had expenditure implications.

Even if policy had not been tightened deliberately, an unanticipated tightening of policy could have occurred through two channels. First, since the cash ratio requirement was higher on bank deposits than on finance company promissory notes (see Table 8), the shift of deposits to banks from finance companies would have raised the demand for cash reserves. The authorities would have had to supply additional cash reserves to avoid an unanticipated tightening of policy, but there is no evidence of this. Second, in 1984 commercial banks were requested to restrict overall credit growth to the private sector and to restrict the opening of import letters of credit. The portfolio shift in deposits out of finance companies into banks meant that finance companies were less able to meet their credit demands and there was a sharp decline in the growth of their loans to the nonbank private sector (see Table 7); hence, there may also have been a portfolio shift which increased the demand for bank loans. Moreover, banks were increasing their lending to the finance companies which may have been caught under the restrictions on credit to the private sector, and which may have further crowded out other private sector borrowers. Thus the effect of the restrictions on commercial bank credit growth could have been tighter than anticipated because of the failure to allow for credit reintermediation and the increased demand for loans by finance companies as a result of the crisis. The precise impact of the financial crisis on real economic activity, inflation, and the balance of payments is very difficult to gauge. During 1983–85, economic policy had

---

r_{cb}	= savings deposit rate at commercial banks
r_{fc}	= deposit rate at finance companies
π	= rate of consumer price inflation
D	= dummy variable for the crisis among finance and security companies, taking value zero 1971–82 and one thereafter.

(-1) is the lag operator, ln the log operator, and
$\Delta X = X - X(-1)$ is the first difference.

This equation imposes the restriction that the long-run income elasticity of money demand is unity, which is an acceptable statistical restriction. Other equations estimated for M3 did not exhibit a significant shift dummy as would be expected when the shift was mainly between components within M3. The coefficient on the dummy implies that the crisis would cause the M2 aggregate to increase by 18 percent in the long run. Evaluated using end-1982 data, this implies an increase of B 67 billion, equal to the stock of business and household holdings of promissory notes with finance companies at end-1982, prior to the crisis.

been tightened to correct domestic and external imbalances and economic activity slowed sharply. It is precisely during this period that any disruption to credit availability and a misinterpretation of monetary aggregates because of emergence of the financial crisis could have resulted in a more restrictive policy and hence slower economic activity. Real GDP growth slowed to a very low level by Thai standards in 1984 and 1985 (see Chart 4). As noted, the subsequent recovery in activity was associated with the substantial growth of liquidity support by the BOT and economic activity recovered sharply in 1987 and 1988. Hence the crisis and the subsequent support may have influenced economic activity in a procyclical manner.

VII. Conclusion and Main Findings

The emergence of distressed financial institutions in Thailand had its origins mainly in weak managerial practices and an inadequate legal, regulatory, and supervisory framework for financial institutions. The indigenous private sector financial institutions were established by trading families and other powerful economic groupings and had a high concentration of ownership and, in several cases, of loan exposure to interrelated entities. Such institutions were not "self-regulatory" in the sense that there was a lack of normal checks and balances between shareholders, directors, and management, and this resulted in inherent management weakness. Moreover the regulation of interest rates and restrictions on branching and new bank offices encouraged the rapid growth of substantially unregulated finance companies.

Against this background, a high standard of external supervision and regulation was necessary if institutions were to develop sound and professional practices. However, the initial legislative framework establishing the BOT and covering the operations of financial institutions was very weak and did not give the authorities the powers to regulate or supervise the financial system. Finance companies were officially recognized—which acted to increase public confidence in these companies—but they were not regulated. Hence poor banking practices went on largely unchecked, leading to a problem of delinquent debts and erosion of the capital bases of the banks and finance companies. These problems were brought to the fore with the slowdown in economic activity in the early 1980s.

Initially, intervention occurred in a crisis environment and the authorities did not have flexible powers to intervene in and to restructure the ailing financial institutions. Only in 1985 were the legislative frameworks amended to give the BOT adequate powers to supervise and intervene in the financial institutions. The subsequent intervention in commercial banks using these powers was undertaken before a crisis was allowed to develop. This intervention could have been more systematic, involving financial programs that would return banks to solvency. However, cumbersome merger laws have continued to restrict the speed and scope for more fundamental restructuring of the financial system. It is difficult to avoid the conclusion that the crisis first could have been prevented, and second, could have been dealt with more expeditiously if the initial legislative system had been adequate and effectively implemented. That is, the central bank should have been given the appropriate powers to supervise and regulate the financial system and to intervene when the first signs of difficulties emerged.

The Thai authorities took a variety of remedial actions as the problems with financial institutions emerged, including a substantial strengthening of the legal, regulatory, and supervisory arrangements; the takeover of institutions by the Government; financial support through credit lines at market rates; soft loans and equity participation; direct intervention to order changes in management and capital restructuring; and mergers and closures with deposit payoffs by the BOT. The support arrangements maintained confidence in the financial system, but have been costly in terms of the use of public funds and scarce human and financial resources, and undermined efficiency in the financial system. In several cases, shareholders have been insulated from the full losses of their financial institutions, and depositors who invested with finance companies and earned higher interest rates have had their deposits underwritten by the authorities. Alternative arrangements might have been less costly and more effective, such as a more active policy of closures and mergers including legislative reform and the involvement of foreign financial institutions. The finance companies were relatively small and unregulated with significant negative net worth, and there would seem to be a good case for closing more of these institutions. More generally, the increased competitive structure of the Thai financial system may require a more fundamental restructuring of financial institutions.

The broader economic consequences of the financial crisis are difficult to gauge. A portfolio shift by depositors and borrowers out of finance companies into commercial banks could have led to an unanticipated tightening of policy because of an increased demand for reserve money and because the restraints on credit expansion by commercial banks may have been more restrictive than expected, since they did not allow for the reintermediation of credit to the banking system. The faster growth of the demand for M2 monetary aggregates could also have added to the monetary policy tightening, and to the already deflationary policies being followed by the authorities in 1983–85. The subsequent expansion in BOT liquidity support for financial institutions occurred during the recovery phase (1986–87). Hence, to the extent that the financial crisis had real economic effects, these were probably procyclical, leading to a deeper recession (1983–85) and stimulating the recovery (1986–87).

6

Liberalization and Financial Crisis in Uruguay, 1974–87

Juan Pérez-Campanero and Alfredo M. Leone

In 1982, a severe crisis emerged in the Uruguayan financial sector. This crisis undermined the country's financial stability and had far-reaching implications for the banking structure and the real economy in the subsequent five years.

This chapter provides an account of the main factors governing the crisis, tracing its causes, examining its major manifestations, and analyzing measures taken to deal with problem banks and borrowers. The consequences of some of the inconsistencies in the liberalization and stabilization policies during the 1970s are reviewed in order to highlight the linkages between stabilization, liberalization, and crisis.

Section I provides a general view of the characteristics of the economic environment and the progress of the stabilization and liberalization policies. The main traits of the recent economic history of Uruguay are recalled here, with special emphasis on the liberalization program implemented in 1974, and on the stabilization policies using the exchange rate as an anti-inflationary instrument. In Section II, the key features of the Uruguayan financial system are described. An account is given of the financial liberalization and the regulations governing the operation of financial intermediaries. Section III analyzes the effects of some of these policies on different economic variables and on the financial system, and, in the process, reviews some of the related empirical literature on Uruguay. The topics discussed include the growth of the financial sector, savings and investment, the behavior of interest rates, the repercussions on the financial structure of nonfinancial corporations, the market structure of the banking sector, and the process of currency substitution.

In Section IV the financial crisis and the policy responses to it are

276

described and analyzed. Two distinct approaches to the problem were tried. First, the Central Bank of Uruguay (CBU) came to the rescue of ailing institutions by providing emergency support funds, by arranging the sale of failed banks to healthy ones (while assuming the unrecoverable loan portfolio that caused the failure), and by purchasing the low-quality loan portfolio of any institution willing to make a seven-year loan in foreign currency. Later, the rights of debtors were favored over those of creditors when successive policy measures validated the generalized expectation of debt relief. These measures led financial intermediaries to an unsustainable position. One after another declared bankruptcy and was taken over by the Banco de la República (the state-owned commercial bank). Section V summarizes the findings and advances some conclusions.

I. Economic Environment and Financial Sector: Phases in Liberalization and Stabilization Policies

After nearly two decades of inward-looking economic policy and financial repression, the Uruguayan authorities began implementing bold liberalization reforms in the 1970s. These reforms, which included removal of trade restrictions and exchange controls and deregulation of financial markets, have received considerable attention in the literature.[1]

The next three subsections briefly review the pre-reform economic environment; the sequencing of major reforms that were put in place during the mid-1970s and their stylized outcomes; and some policy inconsistencies of the reform period. The objective of this review is to bring out the linkages among the macroenvironment, the financial sector, and financial crisis.

The Uruguayan Economy Before 1974

For more than twenty years after the early 1950s, policymakers resorted to import substitution and wide-ranging controls on domestic goods and financial markets; these controls were reflected in high tariffs and other trade barriers, negative interest rates in real terms, and extensive price distortions. Those years were characterized by very low and decelerating real GDP growth; high, volatile, and accelerating inflation rates; a low

---

[1] On liberalization and policies in Southern Cone countries, see *World Development* (1985); *Economic Development and Cultural Change* (April 1986); the contributions by Hanson (1986), Harberger (1986), and Edwards (1986); "Panel Discussion on the Southern Cone," *Staff Papers* (March 1983); Díaz-Alejandro (1981, 1985); Calvo (1986); Rodríguez (1982); McKinnon (1982); Ardito Barletta, Blejer, and Landau (1984). Hanson and de Melo (1983, 1985); de Melo (1985); Tybout (1985); Larraín (1986); and Corbo, de Melo, and Tybout (1986) focus on the Uruguayan case.

level of domestic savings; recurrent balance of payments crises; increasing fiscal deficits; and high unemployment.

The rate of growth of real GDP decelerated from 5.4 percent a year between 1944 and 1951 to 3.0 percent between 1951 and 1956, 0.1 percent between 1956 and 1967, and increased to 1.6 percent between 1967 and 1974.[2,3]

The inflation rate increased continuously, averaging 49.8 percent a year between 1965 and 1970 and 62.7 percent between 1971 and 1973, reaching 97 percent in 1973. The unemployment rate exceeded 8 percent between 1965 and 1973.

The balance of payments experienced recurrent difficulties owing to rising fiscal deficits, inadequate credit and exchange rate policies, and some external factors. The fiscal deficit, as a proportion of GDP, increased from an average of 1.9 percent during the 1965–70 period to 3.2 percent between 1971 and 1973.[4] The inadequate credit and exchange rate policies and the persistence of negative real interest rates provided incentives for capital flight, leading to a contraction in the size of the regulated financial market over time. During most of these years, multiple exchange rates and restrictive exchange controls prevailed. In March 1972 the authorities adopted a crawling peg while maintaining the exchange controls. Two main external factors compounded the balance of payments difficulties in 1974: the effects of the first oil shock and the closure of European Economic Community (EEC) markets to beef imports, the main Uruguayan export.

In July 1974, a new economic team responded to the country's weak economic performance and growing imbalances by implementing a package of deregulation policies.

A brief description of the reform process follows; more attention is paid to the reforms in the financial sector in Section II.[5]

The 1974 Economic Reform: Phase I, 1974–78[6]

The economic reform implemented in Uruguay in 1974 included measures to liberalize international trade and capital transactions, to remove distortions in domestic markets, and to eliminate fiscal imbalances. The liberalization of capital transactions with the rest of the world proceeded at

---

[2] Hanson and de Melo (1983), p. 479.

[3] Per capita output growth was also very low, averaging an annual rate of 0.7 percent from the end of World War II to 1973. See Larraín (1986), p. 4.

[4] Corbo, de Melo, and Tybout (1986), Table 1.

[5] A chronology of reforms is offered in Hanson and de Melo (1985), Appendix A.

[6] The delimitation of phases is based on Hanson and de Melo (1985); Corbo, de Melo, and Tybout (1986); and Larraín (1986).

the fastest pace and occurred before other major policy changes. While domestic financial markets were also liberalized relatively quickly, the rest of the liberalization program proceeded at a slower pace and suffered transitory reversals. By the middle of 1977, capital transactions were virtually free, while remaining exchange restrictions on current transactions were relatively minor. In contrast, trade restrictions remained severe and complex, with imports subject to a multiplicity of charges and exports subject to an array of taxes and subsidies that severely distorted production patterns.

In September 1974, capital flows were liberalized, with domestic residents permitted to hold dollar accounts with domestic banks for the first time; moreover, exchange rate controls were eliminated, and Uruguayans were also free to buy and sell assets denominated in external currencies without restrictions. Capital transfers were freely permitted through the financial market. A liberal foreign investment law was also approved in 1974, which required government authorization only for investment in specified activities. Foreign investors were guaranteed the transfer of capital and profits through the financial market.[7] During this phase of the reform, the exchange rate for financial transactions was freed, while the exchange rate for transactions in the goods market followed a passive crawling peg.

Although tariffs remained high and a number of restrictions on current payments or multiple currency practices prevailed, trade transactions were partially liberalized during this phase. From the middle of 1974 to early 1975, all quantitative restrictions on imports were removed. Imports of capital goods were further liberalized in early 1975, when they were exempted from special deposit requirements. On the export side, taxes on wool and beef exports were considerably reduced during 1974.

Further significant changes occurred in the trade and exchange system between 1975 and 1978. In 1975, import deposits and exchange taxes on beef exports were eliminated, and many trade taxes were reduced. In 1977, the system of import surcharges was further streamlined, leading to more uniform rates of effective protection. However, at the same time, a tax (*retención*) on beef exports was reintroduced, and export subsidies (*reintegros*) on nontraditional exports were reduced. In January 1978 a new tariff structure replaced the complex system of import duties and related charges with a basic rate of 20 percent and multiple rates ranging from zero percent to 150 percent. Export taxes continued to increase during 1978,

---

[7] Amortization or proceeds from liquidation of investment registered under this law could not be transferred abroad until three years after the date on which the investment was approved.

while subsidies on nontraditional exports continued to be reduced.

During this phase, the authorities began to remove the comprehensive price controls in the economy, but slowly. During 1974, controls were progressively eliminated or released on selected products and services, most of which were not included in the consumer price index (CPI). After a temporary reintroduction of price controls in 1975, all prices of goods considered to be competitively produced and not included in the CPI were freed in early 1976. Although price liberalization continued, by the end of 1978, 46 percent of products in the CPI basket were still subject to price control.

Tax reforms were also implemented to reduce tax evasion and simplify the tax system. Late in 1974, the tax on earned income and the inheritance tax were abolished, while the basic rate on the value-added tax was increased from 14 percent to 18 percent. During 1975, the coverage of the value-added tax was widened and its basic rate was increased to 20 percent, while the tax rate on income from industry and commerce was raised from 20 percent to 25 percent. During 1977 and 1978, the authorities strengthened tax administration and introduced severe penalties for tax evasion, together with indexation of late tax payments.

The stabilization strategy included an anti-inflationary policy based on reductions in fiscal deficits and in monetary growth. The fiscal position of the Central Government improved substantially owing to a strong rise in revenue collection and expenditure restraint. As a result, the overall deficit of the Central Government fell from the equivalent of 4.5 percent of GDP in 1975 to 1.3 percent of GDP in 1978 (see Statistical Appendix Table 1). However, monetary aggregates continued to grow rapidly (Chart 1). The stabilization plan also included an expenditure-switching policy, consisting mainly of a real devaluation followed by a passive crawling peg, and the promotion of nontraditional exports.

Economic performance clearly improved, despite an unfavorable evolution of the terms of trade. A period of rapid growth (Chart 2) replaced the pre-reform stagnation: real GDP grew at an average rate of 3.9 percent between 1974 and 1978. Inflation (Chart 3) declined from over 107 percent per annum in the last quarter of 1974 (CPI) to 41 percent by the end of the third quarter of 1978. The balance of payments strengthened substantially, with overall surpluses of US$167 million in 1976, US$102 million in 1977, and US$286 million in 1978 (Chart 4). This increase was due partly to large inflows of foreign private capital, attracted by the removal of exchange controls, the introduction of foreign currency deposits in local banks, the uncertain political situation in Argentina, and the high interest rates in Uruguay. The current account also improved, reflecting mainly the strong growth of nontraditional exports. Both unemployment and real wages fell.

Chart 1. Monetary Aggregates: Growth Rates
(In percent per annum)

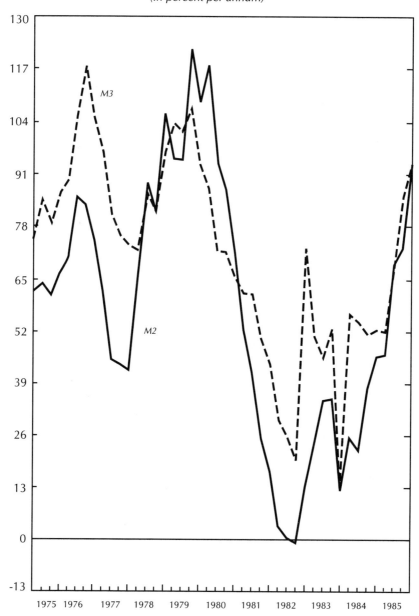

Source: Statistical Appendix Table 2.

Chart 2. Real GDP Growth Rates
(In percent per annum)

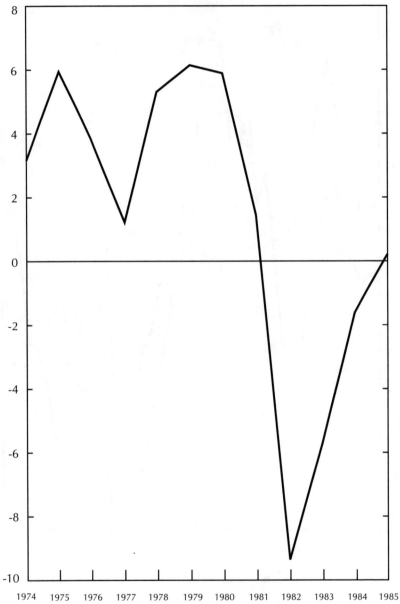

Source: International Monetary Fund, *International Financial Statistics.*

Chart 3. Price and Wage Inflation
(In percent per annum)

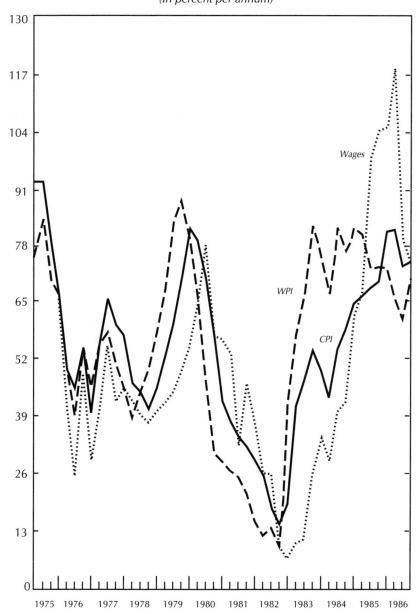

Source: Statistical Appendix Table 4.

Chart 4. Balance of Payments
(In millions of U.S. dollars)

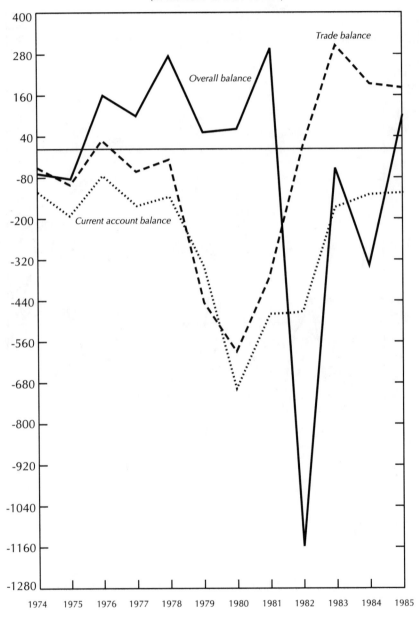

Source: Statistical Appendix Table 5.

Phase II: 1979–82

The second phase of the economic reform had three key elements: (1) the implementation of an active crawling peg, (2) the starting of a process of unification of import tariffs, and (3) an important tax reform. In addition, deregulation of foreign trade, commodity prices, and financial markets continued.

The strategy underlying this phase reflected disappointment with the stabilization measures taken in Phase I, which had failed to lower inflation to an acceptable level. To deal with this problem, the new strategy relied on using the exchange rate to influence inflationary expectations. On October 17, 1978, the dual exchange market was de facto unified when the Central Bank announced that it would buy and sell any amount of foreign exchange at rates that would be adjusted from time to time. On October 26, 1978, the Central Bank indicated for the first time the future rate of devaluation through the sale of three-month treasury bills redeemable in domestic currency or U.S. dollars; the redemption value (principal and interest) in U.S. dollars was indicated on the bills. On December 28, 1978, the Central Bank published a preannounced schedule of devaluations (informally known as the *tablita*).[8] This schedule indicated the daily exchange rates for the Uruguayan peso (in terms of U.S. dollars) through March 1979. On March 27, 1979, the schedule was extended through the end of 1979, and on July 10 through the first quarter of 1980. Thereafter, the schedules were announced six to nine months in advance.

Corbo, de Melo, and Tybout (1986) summarized the rationalization of this plan as provided by the Rodríguez (1982) model:

> Interest rate parity obtains continuously because of the absence of controls on capital flows and the assumption of perfect asset substitutability. The law of one price holds for tradeables, and the rate of change in the prices of nontradeable goods is a function of inflationary expectations-which are assumed to form adaptively—and of excess demand for nontradeable goods. The model predicts that the implementation of the *tablita* should immediately reduce nominal interest rates and, to a lesser extent, inflation. The decline in real interest rates should first stimulate demand, creating an excess demand for nontradeable goods and thereby inducing a temporary appreciation of the real exchange rate. As inflation falls, both the real interest rate and the real exchange rate should increase, approaching their long-run equilibrium from below. The economy should stabilize without undergoing the recession associated with traditional contractionary measures (p. 616).

Tariff reductions were accelerated during this phase. Import duties on a large number of imports were reduced or eliminated during the second

[8] Similar regimes were also adopted in Chile in February 1978 and in Argentina in December 1978.

half of 1978 and in 1979. Moreover, in December 1978, the Government announced a timetable to unify the numerous import taxes to a global tariff, and to reduce this global tariff gradually to an average level of 35 percent over the period January 1, 1980–January 1, 1985.[9]

Export subsidies were also reduced. On March 29, 1979, the system of export prefinancing (*preanticipos*) was eliminated. However, export subsidies for many products continued to be granted in the form of tax credit certificates.

In November 1979, a major tax reform went into effect. This reform included new taxes on agricultural income and sales, the merger of several excise taxes, the rationalization of a number of other taxes, and the substitution of higher value-added tax rates for several social security taxes. This tax reform's primary purpose was to increase the international competitiveness of Uruguayan products by lowering labor costs and eliminating taxes on exports of agricultural products.

Price deregulation continued during this phase, and the role of the price control agency gradually shifted from controlling prices to monitoring price movements and market behavior to protect consumer interests. Nevertheless, by March 1981, the prices of 24 percent of the goods and services constituting the consumer price index remained subject to control.

The foregoing measures succeeded for a time. The economic performance was impressive until the beginning of 1981. GDP growth exceeded 6 percent over the period 1979–80 (Chart 2). Moreover, after accelerating during 1979, the inflation rate receded from early 1980 until the third quarter of 1982 (Chart 3). The balance of payments was consistently in surplus (Chart 4), exports were greatly diversified, and official international reserves rose to a comfortable level. Balance of payments surpluses resulted mainly from capital inflows and tourism from Argentina. The peso appreciated in real terms with respect to the currencies of all major trading partners except Argentina (Statistical Appendix Table 6). Moreover, capital inflows fueled two booms, one in agricultural land, the other in real estate.[10] Confidence in the peso strengthened, and substantial amounts of private savings flowed into the domestic banking system.

Certain policy inconsistencies and several external factors resulted in the steady deterioration of Uruguay's economic and financial performance beginning in late 1980. Demand for Uruguayan exports weakened as a consequence of the recession in the world economy and the policy adjustments undertaken by Argentina and Brazil. Moreover, the deterioration of the terms of trade and the rising world interest rates adversely affected the

---

[9] However, to contain inflation, import duties on some products were lowered ahead of the planned timetable during the second half of 1979.

[10] Hanson and de Melo (1985), p. 10.

current account of the balance of payments. The public sector financial position also deteriorated as a result of a decline in the tax base, a large increase in social security payments,[11] and a surge in the burden of servicing the public foreign debt.[12] Finally, the Argentine devaluations of March 1981 fueled the growing expectations that the Uruguayan *tablita* was becoming unsustainable.

These factors led to a crisis in confidence in the *tablita*, resulting in major capital outflows and capital flight—which were evident in large changes in errors and omissions items of the balance of payments (Chart 5)—and a deep recession. Real GDP growth decelerated to about 2 percent in 1981, and in 1982 GDP declined almost 10 percent (Chart 2). Finally, in November 1982, the Government dropped its commitment to maintain the *tablita* and a major devaluation followed (Chart 6).

II. The Financial Sector and Evolution of the Regulatory Process

Financial markets in Uruguay evolved within an environment of excessive regulations during the 1960s and early 1970s, and a deregulation process was initiated in the middle of 1974. During the early 1960s the persistence of interest rate controls led to nonprice competition for a dwindling pool of savings, reflected in the increases in the number of bank branches, real estate speculation, and high spreads between loan and deposit rates.[13] Further regulation from the Government led to capital flight and loss of reserves, and the position of banks was weakened further.

In 1965, a generalized crisis of the banking system developed, and the number of bank failures multiplied. As a result, some very strict regulations were passed, including a ban on entry of new firms into the sector and a ceiling on the total number of branches (thus, if a bank wanted to increase the number of its branches, it could do so only if a competitor grew smaller); limitation of credit available to the private sector; direct subsidies; and interest rate controls.

In 1971, another wave of bank mergers and bankruptcies developed, spurred by the deterioration of bank assets caused by high real interest rates. Heavy regulation pervaded the financial activity, including preferential credit programs, high reserve requirements, compulsory purchase of government securities, and interest rate ceilings. An informal lending market developed (the *parabancario* market), operating through public notaries who certified the transactions between borrower and lender, thereby creating a tradable financial instrument (certified promissory notes).

[11] Hanson and de Melo (1985), p. 10.
[12] Larraín (1986), p. 19.
[13] See Daly (1967).

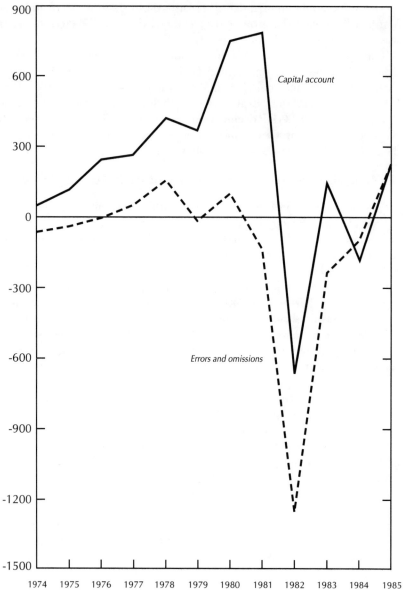

Chart 5. Balance of Payments: Capital Account and Errors and Omissions
(In millions of U.S. dollars)

Source: Statistical Appendix Table 5.

Chart 6. Nominal Exchange Rate
(Pesos per U.S. dollar, end of period)

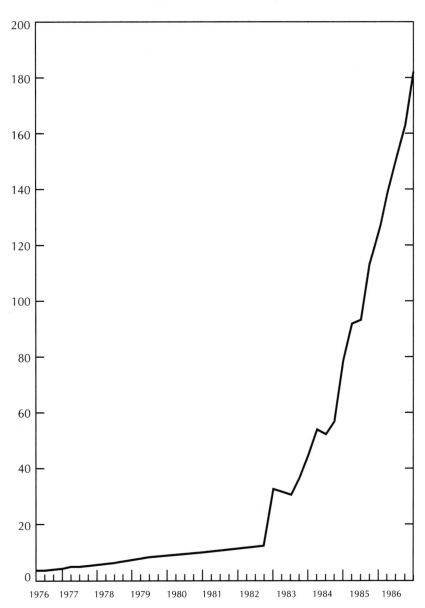

Source: International Monetary Fund, *International Financial Statistics.*

As Larraín (1986) notes,

At the time of the reforms, the role of the banking system as intermediator of funds was reduced to a critically low level, at approximately 35 percent of the real value of loans and deposits that it had in the early fifties (pp. 8–9).

The structure of the Uruguayan financial system prior to the middle of 1974 is described below.

- The Central Bank of Uruguay (CBU) was established in 1967 and was in charge of currency issuance, managing of international reserves, formulation and execution of monetary and credit policies, and control of the banking system.[14]
- The two state-owned banks Banco de la República Oriental del Uruguay (BROU) and the Banco Hipotecario (BH). The BROU, which was established in 1896, was the largest commercial bank in Uruguay. It handled all financial transactions of the central and departmental governments, controlled foreign exchange proceeds from exports, and collected some excise duties and tariffs.[15] The BH specialized in financing low- and middle-income housing.
- Private commercial banks: they could receive deposits in pesos and could extend loans in either pesos or foreign currency. Some of these banks were foreign owned.
- Banking houses (*casas bancarias*): they differed from commercial banks in that they were not allowed to accept deposits. They were allowed to intermediate in the bankers' acceptances market and in export-import operations. Their main activity was to borrow abroad and lend those funds in the domestic market.
- Financial intermediation cooperatives operated exclusively with their members.

There were significant differences in the evolution of these institutions between 1974 and 1985 (Statistical Appendix Table 7). The salient features were the small variation in the number of banks, the rapid increase in the number of banking houses after 1977, and the significant growth in the number of offices and employees.

Compared with banks in other countries, Uruguayan banks seemed to be relatively small: only 3 made the top 100 of Latin America as of 1986 (the BROU (No. 31), La Caja Obrera (No. 96), and Comercial (No. 99)).[16]

The share of "Banks, insurance, and other financial intermediaries" in nominal GDP at factor cost increased from 4.7 percent during 1975–77 to 6.5 percent during 1983–85 (Statistical Appendix Table 8).

---

[14] For a legal analysis of the role and functions of the CBU, see Delpiazzo (1983).

[15] This bank operated also as a monetary authority until the Central Bank was established.

[16] See *The Banker* (October 1986), p. 91.

Against this background, we will review now the process of deregulation of the financial markets, in the context of the liberalization-cum-stabilization experience of 1974–82.

Liberalization of International Financial Transactions

As noted in Section I above, in September 1974 domestic residents were allowed to trade in any kind of assets denominated in any currency, since exchange controls were eliminated altogether, and banks were authorized to receive deposits denominated in foreign currency. Moreover, the abolition of the personal income tax in July 1974 eliminated the need to report these transactions. Also, nonfinancial firms were allowed to borrow in foreign currency at home or abroad with no limitation, and nonresidents were allowed to repatriate both earnings and capital with no limit.

As Larraín (1986) notes,

> . . . this deregulation is all the more remarkable since before September of 1974 it was illegal for Uruguayans to hold dollars and stories are told about people sent to jail after being caught holding a hundred-dollar bill (pp. 21–22).

Interest Rates

The economic reform that began in 1974 included various adjustments to the ceilings on interest rates, culminating eventually in full liberalization of interest rates.

Effective September 25, 1974, the maximum interest rate (payable in advance) on bank *peso* loans was raised from 24 percent to 32 percent per annum. At the same time, the ceiling on bank commissions (also payable in advance) was reduced from 10 percent to 6 percent, while the tax on financial transactions (which could be passed on to borrowers) was kept at 6 percent. These measures increased the effective cost to borrowers (including the said tax) from a maximum of 66.6 percent to 78.6 percent per annum. The annual interest rate for loans in *foreign currency* had already been increased in July 1974 from 14 percent to 16.5 percent. The BROU kept preferential interest rates for public sector loans, and for a few priority sectors.

Interest rates on *peso* deposits continued to be fixed by the Central Bank until March 1976. Effective October 1, 1974, an annual interest rate of 10 percent was set on demand deposits, which previously had been non-remunerated. However, this measure was reversed a few months later. At the same time, the interest rate for savings deposits was increased by 10 percentage points to 18 percent a year. For time deposits the annual rates were increased by 15–23 percentage points ranging from 30 percent (for 3- to 5-month deposits) to 48 percent (for deposits of 12 months and over).

Rates payable on deposits in *dollars* were free throughout the period.

During 1976, the authorities attempted to reduce interest margins, improve the interest rate structure and encourage efficiency in banking operations. From January 1, commissions were eliminated and all interest rates were made payable at maturity, whereas before they were payable in advance. From April 1, all rates of interest on deposits were freed, but maximum lending rates continued to be set by the Central Bank. These changes enabled banks to pay positive real interest rates on deposits for the first time in many years. Nevertheless, the BROU continued to charge promotional rates on loans for nontraditional exports and for meat packing; these loans were rediscounted with the Central Bank. However, from April 1, 1976, the annual rate for all *new* central bank rediscount facilities, which had ranged from 8 percent (for rediscounts to the BROU) to 12 percent (for regular facilities to commercial banks), was raised to 17 percent. In September 1976, rediscount was restricted only to emergency lending to banks facing temporary liquidity problems and carried a penal interest rate.

The ceilings on lending rates were increased again in late 1977 and 1978. In addition, in May 1979, the tax on bank loans was substantially reduced. Finally, on September 12, 1979, all interest rate ceilings were eliminated.

Reserve Requirements

The level and structure of reserve requirements varied throughout the period, and the requirements were generally reduced, simplified, and unified between 1975 and 1979. This reflected a changing balance between the needs of raising revenue for the Government, inducing a certain portfolio composition, and promoting the liberalization program. Both peso and foreign currency deposits were subject to reserve requirements, whose level depended on the maturity of deposits, and which could be partially satisfied with government bonds during certain periods. (For a chronology of adjustments in the reserve requirements, see Appendix I.)

To assist banks that were placed in a difficult financial position because of the new interest rates announced in September 1974 (which implied a smaller spread for the commercial banks), effective October 1, 1974, the Central Bank reduced the reserve requirements. Early in 1975, the monetary authorities established a 40 percent marginal reserve requirement on the excess of *peso* deposits over their average level in December 1974.

A major reform in regulations on reserve requirements took place at the beginning of 1976. An important change was to disallow the use of any assets except cash in vault or deposits with the Central Bank for the fulfillment of reserve requirements. At the same time, however, it was decided that private commercial banks would have to keep in their portfolios government securities whose value was equivalent, at a minimum, to a certain proportion of their deposits. In June 1977 the requirement to hold government debt was eased, while reserve requirements were increased considerably.

Late in 1977 the authorities began to equalize the treatment of reserve requirements on local and foreign currency deposits. From January 1, 1979, all reserve requirements, both on *local and foreign currency* deposits, were unified at 20 percent of outstanding deposits at the end of 1978. All increments of deposits above that amount would have a zero reserve requirement. Finally, in May 1979, all basic reserve requirements were eliminated. After this measure, the only reserve requirement which remained in force was a marginal requirement of 100 percent, which applied to the amount of deposits in *local currency* exceeding 16 times a bank's capital and reserves. In June 1979, this limit was temporarily increased to 30 times capital and reserves, but was extended to *foreign currency* deposits, lines of credit, guarantees, and other obligations.

Entry Barriers

Under the 1965 law, no new banks were allowed, and a ceiling was set on the total number of branches. This law did not ban the establishment of new banking houses, but since they could not raise deposits, this was not a very important exception.

The first major change in entry regulations took place in 1976, when the Central Bank of Uruguay allowed banking houses to receive foreign currency deposits from nonresidents. This was a main factor in the rapid expansion of these houses after 1976, whose number increased from 2 in 1976 to 23 in 1981.

In November 1981 (Law 15207), the entry prohibition in the banking sector was lifted. New banks were allowed, in a number not to exceed each year 10 per cent of the number existing in the previous year; the ban on branch expansion was also lifted.[17]

Prudential Regulations

Uruguay's financial system was subject to a limited array of prudential regulations, most of which were in force for the whole reform period. No formal deposit insurance scheme existed at that time; banking supervision consisted primarily of control of capital and reserve requirements and on-site inspections; the accounting framework and off-site analysis were weak.

---

[17] See Olivera García (1982a and b) for a description of the legal details.

Maximum liability/capital ratios limited banks' expansion. Liabilities exceeding the maximum ratio were subject to a 100 percent reserve requirement. In February 1974 it was established that domestic deposits should not exceed an amount equal to 15 times each bank's capital. That ratio was raised to 16 some months later, but only for local currency deposits. The maximum limit for bankers' acceptances was set at 50 percent of the bank capital. In 1979, the liabilities/capital ratio was set at 30 times for banks and 20 times for banking houses, and was extended to cover both domestic and foreign currency deposits.

Minimum capital requirements were in force, varying according to the type of institution (higher for banks, lower for banking houses) and the location (higher for offices in Montevideo, departmental capitals, and the cities of Las Piedras, Pando, and Punta del Este) These requirements were updated periodically, and were in force throughout the period.

Maximum financing limits existed until 1979. When the reforms started in 1974, a bank's credit to a single client could not exceed 20 percent of the bank's capital and reserves (except for export prefinancing). In 1975, this limit was raised to 25 percent. A 1977 regulation forbade financing above 25 percent of the bank capital to corporations whose boards were linked to the banks' boards or managements.

In March 1979, all regulations on maximum financing and risk concentration were eliminated. They were reinstated in December 1980, when they were set at 25 percent for individuals or single firms, and at 35 percent for conglomerates or groups of firms. They applied to disbursed and nondisbursed loans, endorsements, etc. In August 1981, these limits were abolished and were replaced by a requirement that each borrower be subject to a detailed analysis, using a uniform methodology. In September 1982, lending to managerial personnel of firms was prohibited.

Foreign exchange exposure was not regulated. Thus, banks could borrow in dollars and lend in pesos without any limits.

Asset immobilization limits were set at 60 percent of capital and reserves in 1976, and raised during 1977 first to 70 percent and then to 100 percent.

Banking Supervision and Early Warning Indicators

Table 1 provides information on the number of on-site bank supervision visits.

These data suggest that the number of inspections the Central Bank carried out each year exceeded the number of banks and banking houses in operation. However, these numbers should be interpreted with caution. The numbers alone do not provide any information on the quality of the inspection or the criteria used for the audit, the amount of information made available to the auditors, or the penalties that could be applied.

Table 1.   On-Site Bank Supervision Visits, 1975–83

Year	Number of Visits
1975	36
1976	40
1977	97
1978	82
1979	66
1980	74
1981	. . .
1982	99
1983	96

Source: Central Bank of Uruguay, *Annual Report*, various issues.

According to Larraín (1986), supervision

has been mainly confined to the traditional control of capital and reserve requirements. Balance sheets and profit and loss statements are also reviewed to judge if they are appropriately drawn up so that they accurately reflect the financial situation of the bank (p. 29).

An interesting comment on this issue is made by J. Gil Díaz, President of the Central Bank of Uruguay from 1974 to 1982:

During my tenure . . . there was no legal norm that allowed the Central Bank to regulate the way in which the accounting information of financial institutions should be presented and evaluated.[18]

Similarly, there does not seem to have been any early warning indicators or other systematic or informal off-site analysis of banks in the Central Bank.[19] Nevertheless, the Central Bank management might have been aware of banking difficulties well in time, as Gil Díaz states:

. . . the Central Bank of Uruguay, within the limits of its capacity, discharged its responsibility of controlling the national banking system. Through its supervision, auditing, analysis of periodical information and special information requests, it soon detected that a group of institutions was weaker than the rest.[20]

[18] *Búsqueda*, No. 361, December 12, 1986, p. 14.
[19] See, for instance, the papers in Altman and Sametz (1977) for examples of alert indicators.
[20] *Búsqueda*, No. 361, December 12, 1986, p. 14.

III. Impact of Reforms on Macroeconomic Variables and the Financial Sector

Financial Intermediation and Growth of Financial Sector

Charts 7 and 8 illustrate the *financial deepening* process in Uruguay after 1974 by depicting the ratios of bank assets and liabilities relative to GDP.

The interest rate reforms and capital account liberalization generated important portfolio shifts and capital inflows with significant consequences for the Uruguayan financial sector after 1974. The ratio of M1 (currency in circulation plus sight deposits) to GDP declined from about 12 percent in 1974 to less than 8 percent in 1981, while the ratio of M3 (M1 plus savings and time deposits in foreign and domestic currency) to GDP increased from about 19 percent to about 43 percent over the same period.

The sequencing of the economic reform was also reflected in the evolution of the composition of M3. During the first years after the economic reform was initiated, liberalization of foreign currency deposits in Uruguay was quickly completed, while important regulations continued to prevail for domestic currency transactions. During this period, foreign currency deposits increased much faster than peso deposits. The ratio of foreign deposits to GDP increased about six times from 1974 to 1977 (with a large proportion held by nonresidents), while the ratio of domestic currency time and savings deposits to GDP increased only 33 percent over the same period.

After 1977, when interest rate ceilings were gradually removed and the authorities began to equalize the treatment of local and foreign currency deposits with regard to reserve requirements, domestic currency deposits became more attractive to investors. The ratio of savings and time peso deposits to GDP increased 2.5 times from 1977 to 1980, while the ratio of foreign currency deposits to GDP declined from 1978 to 1980. The factors that adversely affected the Uruguayan economy and contributed to the loss of confidence in the *tablita* reversed these trends after 1980.[21]

The question arises whether this growth of the financial sector translated into an increasing *availability of credit* to the private sector or whether funds were invested abroad or used to finance fiscal deficits.

Chart 8 shows a fast growth in credit to the private sector between 1974 and 1982. The remarkable reduction in fiscal deficits reduced government borrowing needs between 1974 and 1980. Most of the increase in private sector credit corresponds to credit in foreign currency, which, as a share of GDP, increased about five times over the period.

The problems faced in the early 1980s by the Uruguayan economy, and

---

[21] See also de Melo and Tybout (1986).

Chart 7. Financial Intermediation

(Liabilities of banking system as percentage of GDP)

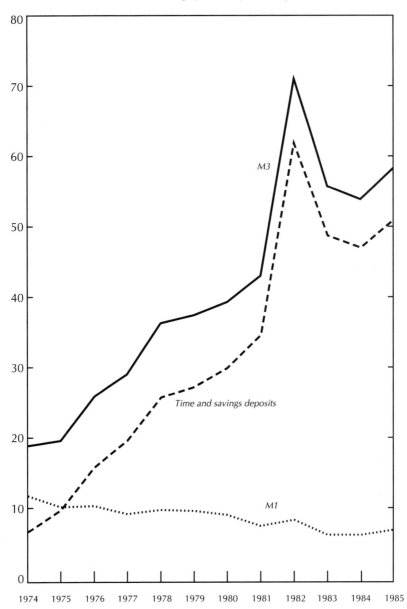

Source: Statistical Appendix Table 9.

Chart 8. Credit of Banking System
(As percent of GDP)

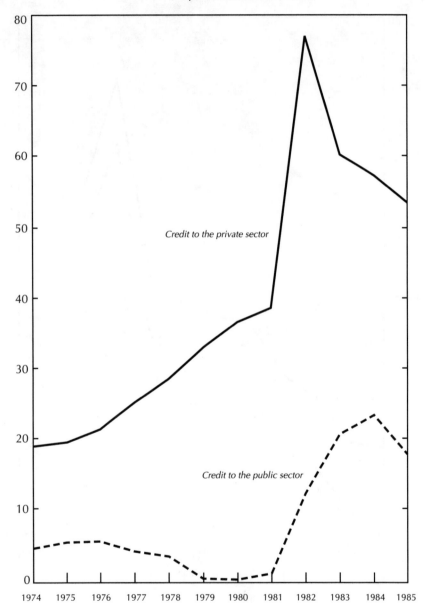

Source: *Statistical* Appendix Table 9.

particularly by its financial sector, tightened credit conditions. Moreover, fiscal deficits, which had been negligible before 1980, absorbed a larger share of domestic credit. Thus, credit to the private sector, and particularly credit in domestic currency, decreased after 1982 as a share of GDP.[22]

Hanson and de Melo (1985) stressed that a substantial share of private credit was in the form of consumer credit, whose share in total bank credit grew from 4 percent in 1979 to 12 percent in 1981. And that

> another part went to finance, and made possible, two asset price bubbles. The first was the agricultural land boom after the fourfold increase in domestic beef prices between August 1978 and August 1979 . . . . The second bubble—which followed immediately—was the real estate boom ignited by Argentine purchasers of real estate in Punta del Este (p. 12).

Effects on Savings, Investment, and Efficiency of Investment

The question arises as to whether the financial deepening described in the previous subsection resulted from an increase in savings or simply reflected portfolio shifts (financial operations which were carried out in informal markets being absorbed by the formal financial sector under the new policy regime), and capital inflows (attracted by the new conditions prevailing in the formal financial sector but also responding to conditions prevailing in neighboring countries). This subsection also discusses the effects of the liberalization on investment behavior.

Chart 9 presents data on aggregate savings and investment. Also, de Melo and Tybout (1986, p. 568) provide the following period average data:

	1955–63	1964–73	1974–78	1979–83
Domestic savings/GDP	11.9	12.5	11.0	11.7
Private savings/GDP	. . .	11.3	9.6	9.6
Foreign savings/GDP	2.9	− 1.7	2.5	2.9
Private investment/GDP	. . .	9.6	12.1	12.6

A straightforward reading of this evidence provides no support to the view that the domestic savings rate rose in response to interest rate deregulation. Although gross domestic savings seem to have been only slightly lower during the reform period, private savings fell during that period. Moreover, both gross domestic savings and gross national savings showed a declining trend after 1976, following two years of rapid increase (Chart 9).

---

[22] The 1982 peak in assets and liabilities of the financial sector reflects the devaluation impact when the *tablita* was abandoned.

Chart 9. Savings and Investment as Percentage of GDP

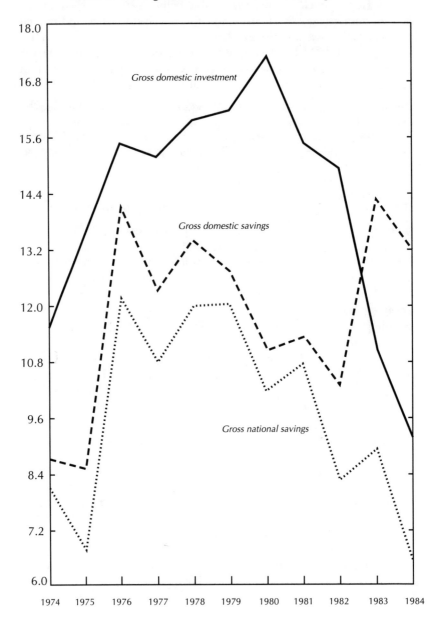

Source: Statistical Appendix Table 10.

De Melo and Tybout (1986) analyzed the influence of the financial liberalization on savings rates, and concluded that the effect of real interest rates on the savings rate was statistically not significant, although the savings rate shifted upward in the post-reform period. Foreign capital inflows and real exchange rates had the dominant impact on savings.

With respect to *investment*, the ratio of private investment to GDP rose in the reform period.[23] This could also be attributed, as de Melo and Tybout (1986) point out, to the exceedingly low return on capital in the pre-reform period, as documented in Harberger and Wisecarver (1977).

However, the shift in period averages masks two distinct trends apparent in the yearly data. Investment ratios (in relation to GDP) increase steadily until 1980 (from 7.7 percent for private fixed capital formation and 11.6 percent for gross domestic investment in 1974 to 11.8 percent and 17.4 percent, respectively, in 1980), with a marked decline thereafter (to 5.2 percent and 9.3 percent, respectively, in 1984).

De Melo and Tybout (1986) document structural shifts in the investment function (an upward shift of the intercept term and more responsiveness of investment to interest rates and real exchange rates) but this is not interpreted as evidence in support of the McKinnon hypothesis. Rather, they interpret the finding of significant accelerator-type effects to be a sign that Uruguayan savings were not constrained, despite the presence of "financial repression" in the pre-reform years. Larraín (1986) points out that the rationalization and decrease of profit taxes as well as the elimination of quotas on imports of capital goods were major determinants of the shift in post-reform investment function.

On the issue of the *efficiency of investment*, Hanson and de Melo (1983) find a 40 percent rise in the ex post incremental output/capital ratio from 1967–1974 (0.18) to 1975–1981 (0.25). They argue that the improvement in efficiency probably reflected not only the improved allocation of credit but also the improved utilization of capacity, the rapid growth in less capital-intensive industries (which benefited from the goods and financial market reforms) and the easing of restrictions on capital goods imports.[24]

Thus, even though the empirical evidence does not support a strong responsiveness of domestic savings to financial liberalization, the economic reforms implemented in Uruguay in the mid-1970s raised the level and efficiency of investment.

[23] This is in accordance with the McKinnon-Shaw thesis, which suggests that the dismantling of financial repression and the increase in real interest rates will contribute to increases in savings and investment, and in the average efficiency of investment, and will promote economic growth. See McKinnon (1973) and Shaw (1973).

[24] Further evidence on the allocative efficiency of investment is considered in the study by de Melo, Pascale, and Tybout (1985) using microeconomic data.

Behavior of Interest Rates

Nominal Interest Rates

Nominal interest rates fluctuated sharply as ceilings were lifted and economic conditions changed (Charts 10 and 11).

In general, nominal lending and deposit *peso* interest rates increased during the first years of the reform, but the ceilings continued to be binding until late 1977. Interest rates were relatively stable during the second phase (1979–82), particularly after late 1979. They jumped when the stabilization policy collapsed and inflation started to regain momentum. Nominal interest rates on *dollar* operations increased during the whole reform period, particularly during the second phase (under the active crawling peg regime). However, interest rate ceilings on dollar lending rates were also binding until late 1977. Nominal interest rates on dollar operations became highly volatile between the second half of 1979 and late 1982, when they started to fall steadily.

With regard to the second phase of the reform, Favaro (1985) also points out two stylized facts in relation to two nominal rates. First, the term structure of interest rates remained upward sloping (i.e., interest rates on short-term deposits were below the rates on longer-maturity deposits). Also, despite changes in economic circumstances and in the institutional scenario, domestic interest rates experienced little fluctuation.

The authorities attempted to reduce the spread between lending and deposit rates after 1976. However, only after 1979 did spreads decline markedly (Charts 12 and 13), when the tax on bank loans was substantially reduced and basic reserve requirements were eliminated. Increased competition in banking also contributed to the decline in spreads.[25] Spreads, particularly those on peso rates, widened considerably in late 1982 and early 1983. This measure of spread does not indicate intermediation costs or performance of the banking industry, as the net spread—net of the impact of taxes, reserve requirements, etc.—would do.[26]

However, there is not enough information available to analyze the evolution of costs of intermediation. Moreover, constantly evolving regulations on portfolio and reserve requirements for financial institutions make it difficult to construct a series on net spreads from the available information on gross spreads. Nevertheless, the available data show that the removal of different regulations greatly contributed to the reduction of financial spreads.

[25] Spiller and Favaro (1984) and Hanson and Neal (1986).
[26] For a study of different definitions of spread, see Hanson and Rocha (1986).

Chart 10. Annual Nominal Interest Rates (Peso)
(In percent)

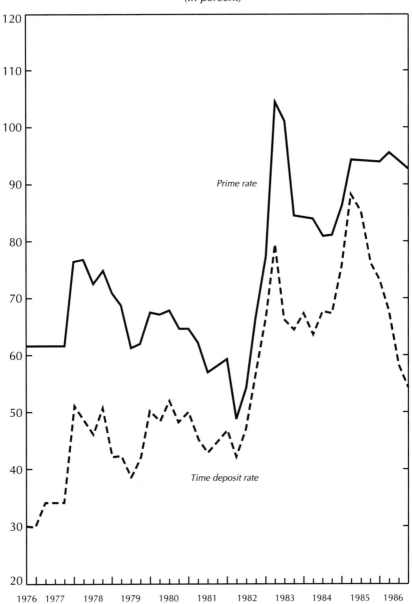

Source: Statistical Appendix Table 11.

Chart 11. Annual Nominal Interest Rates (Dollar)
(In percent)

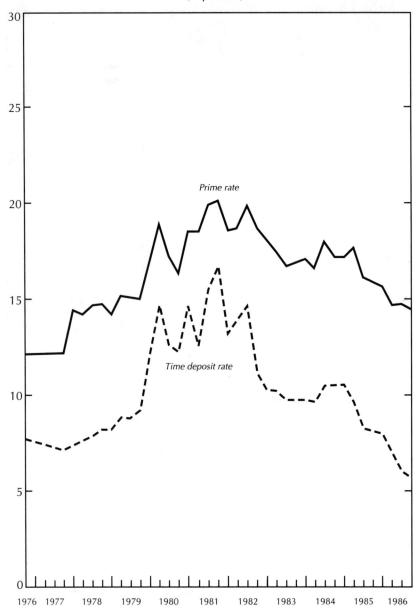

Source: Statistical Appendix Table 11.

Chart 12. Spread in Interest Rates (Peso)[1]
(In percent per annum)

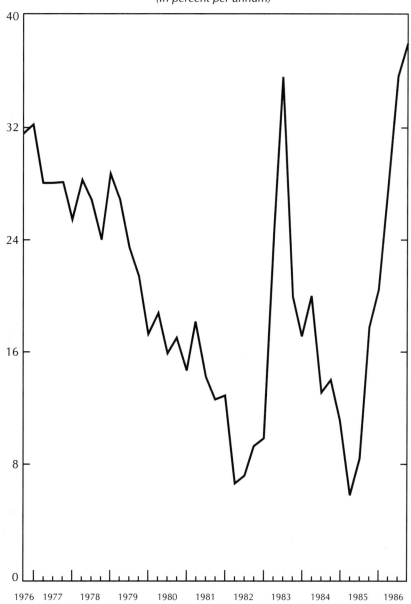

Source: Statistical Appendix Table 11.
[1] Prime loan rate less interest rate on time deposits of up to six months.

Chart 13. Spread in Interest Rates (Dollar)[1]

(In percent per annum)

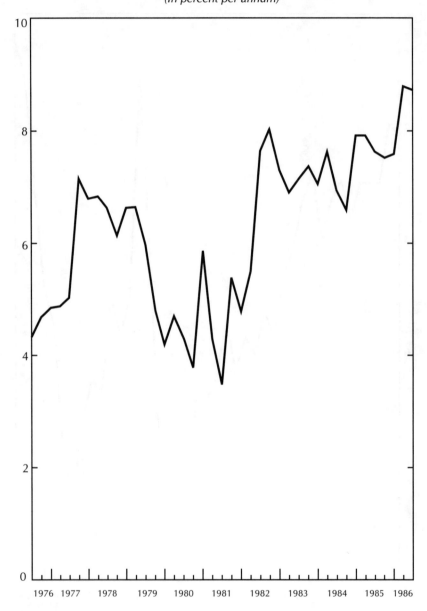

Source: Statistical Appendix Table 11.
[1] Prime loan rate less interest rate on time deposits under six months.

The Spread Between Peso and Dollar Rates

With free convertibility of the peso and no interest rate ceilings, it was expected that interest parity conditions would obtain, owing to asset market arbitrage. Therefore, the domestic interest rate would be determined by the world interest rate, adjusted for exchange rate risk.

The ex post spread between the rates on peso deposits and peso equivalent rates on dollar deposits was high and varied throughout the period (Chart 14). It widened after the adoption of the *tablita*, remained about constant in 1980, and dropped "sharply during the period of exchange guarantees extending over seven months starting in February 1981."[27]

The evolution of the spread between peso and dollar rates raises two issues: (1) why the rate of interest on assets in pesos exceeded the rate of interest on assets in foreign currency, even when the assets were traded in the same domestic market (so that we can abstract from country risk considerations), and (2) why this ex post realized premium kept changing over time.

The most common explanation for the existence of the premium is that of expectations of devaluation, i.e., the lack of credibility of the public in the exchange rate policy. If this is true, then the variation in the premium could be traced to the factors that affect those expectations. Moreover, a positive spread implies that expected devaluation was higher than realized devaluation.

Hanson and de Melo (1985) tested a model of interest rate determination along these lines, based on the uncovered interest rate parity using monthly data for November 1978 to December 1981. They concluded that the long-run elasticity of the peso deposit rate with respect to the rate on foreign currency deposits, 0.98, was not significantly different from the unitary elasticity predicted by the interest parity theorem, suggesting a constant ex ante spread. Moreover, the ex post rate of devaluation seems to have had an insignificant effect on the ex ante spread.

Favaro (1985) found the expectations of devaluation hypothesis unsatisfactory and proposed an alternative explanation, based on a model of financial cost minimization that introduces the existence of real costs of adjusting a given net foreign asset position. He emphasized that, under certain policy rules, limited arbitrage opportunities may result in a wide gap between the nominal interest rate and the rate of inflation and hence in movements of the real rate of interest. He also concluded that differences between domestic and foreign interest rates do not necessarily mirror expectations of devaluations, but reflect the existence of real adjustment costs of the debt structure owing to uncertainty in the policy regime and incomplete futures markets.

---

[27] Hanson and de Melo (1985), p. 13. Favaro (1985) also discusses the evolution of spreads.

Chart 14. Interest Rate Differentials[1]
(In percent per annum)

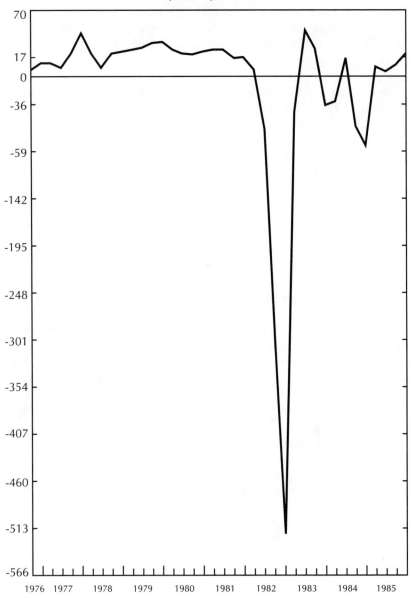

Source: Statistical Appendix Tables 11 and 12.
[1] Peso prime lending rate less peso equivalent of dollar prime lending rate.

Ex Post Real Interest Rates

Real interest rates (ex post) showed a high volatility between 1976 and 1985 (Charts 15 and 16). This volatility of real interest rates generated financing difficulties for the Uruguayan firms. Declining financial costs when real rates were negative (up to mid-1980) led to overindebtedness, which generated a large debt-service burden for Uruguayan firms when real rates went up to high levels in the next few years (up to mid-1982).

Blejer and Díaz (1986) conclude that external factors—foreign interest rates and tradable goods prices—were the major factors affecting the behavior of real interest rates in Uruguay, while monetary disequilibria and changes in the nominal exchange rate had insignificant effects on real rates. Also, they conclude that the exchange rate risk did not affect real interest rates.

Financing of Nonfinancial Sector Firms

A study by de Melo, Pascale, and Tybout (1985) discusses the interplay of real and financial shocks in the Uruguayan economy using financial statements of industrial firms. This study distinguishes three phases in the development of the financial crisis.

A first phase, of opportunities for nonoperating earnings,[28] is described as the time when "the seeds of disaster were sown."[29] In this phase (up to the late 1970s), with the opening of the capital account and the economic recovery under way, firms (especially in the exportable sector) took exposed positions in dollars to expand their capacity and to take advantage of currency arbitrage opportunities. Real borrowing costs were highly negative, owing first to the controlled interest rates and then to borrowing in foreign exchange. The authors explain that at the time, rapid dollar indebtedness may not have seemed inordinately risky because "operating earnings were clearly improving, prevailing interest rates posed no major debt-service problem, and government reserves seemed adequate to maintain the exchange rate regime indefinitely." These expectations would prove unwarranted in the end.

The second phase, of real side problems and rising financial costs, corresponds to the time when "the desire to survive . . . replaced the lure of easy money as the motive behind increasingly risky financial structures."[30] When expectations of the abandonment of the Argentine *tablita*

---

[28] Defined as "all income from nonoperating assets, net of real financial costs. Hence, unlike under the standard accounting definition, nonoperating income accrues to firms whenever real financial costs are negative" (Tybout, 1985, p. 6).

[29] *Ibid.*

[30] Tybout (1985), p. 15.

Chart 15. Ex-Post Real Interest Rates (Peso)
(In percent)

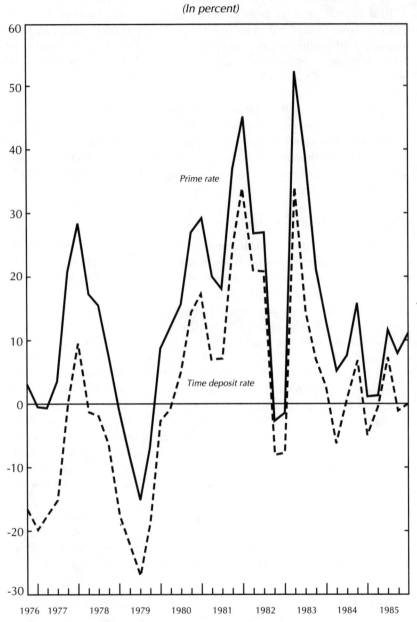

Source: Statistical Appendix Table 13.

Chart 16. Ex-Post Real Interest Rates (Dollar)
(In percent)

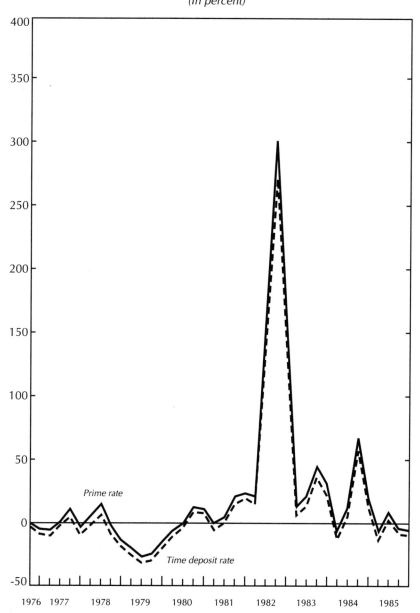

Source: Statistical Appendix Table 13.

policy and devaluation generalized, confidence in the sustainability of the Uruguayan exchange rate regime waned. Interest rates started to climb, which induced firms to borrow in dollars in the hope that the exchange rate regime could be maintained. The authors explain that although operating earnings were stable, reflecting Argentine demand, net earnings dropped, reflecting increasing financial costs. Corporations stepped up their borrowing, partly to offset the reduction in internal sources of funds, but also, surprisingly, to finance increased fixed investment and the continuance of large dividend payments. This situation affected especially the exportable sector (with export subsidies reduced or eliminated). Thus, the scenario of the financial crisis was set, with overindebted firms left in an illiquid position and highly exposed in dollars.

The final phase corresponds to the financial crisis itself. The confidence crisis triggered by Argentina's devaluation caused rapid deterioration in the situation in Uruguay, and led to the final collapse of the exchange rate regime in November 1982, with the abandonment of the *tablita* and a 100 percent devaluation. This shock devastated the firms heavily indebted in dollars and made an important part of bank loans nonperforming, with many banks becoming technically insolvent.

Mezzera and de Melo (1985) study the importance of different shocks based on interviews with managers in manufacturing, agricultural, and exporting firms. These subjective assessments also confirm the importance of financial shocks (impact of devaluation, rising costs of working capital, etc.).

Market Structure

Describing the situation before the banking crisis of 1965, Daly (1967) notes that the great expansion of bank branches represented nonprice competition in a context in which negative real deposit rates, liberal rediscounting policies, and real estate speculation allowed banks to sustain high profits, despite high operating costs and a small volume of deposits.

The 1965 law severely limited the installation of new banks and opening of new branches. Spiller (1984) notes that these restrictions to entry and the easy access to information on competitors' behavior (distributed by the Central Bank) promoted the development of cartel relationships.

Spiller and Favaro (1984) study the effects of the 1977 decree which allowed banks to raise deposits from nonresidents (see Section II above). The study focuses on interaction among oligopolistic firms. The authors' main conclusion is that the interaction among the four dominant banks was reduced after the legal change, and that firms in the fringe group (small firms with a market share of less than 2 percent) did not expect retaliation from dominant firms.

The effects of the 1981 law, which liberalized entry somewhat, have not been similarly studied. The effects of the banking crisis on the structure of the banking system have, however, overshadowed the effects of that law and other measures. Hanson and de Melo (1985) point out that 20 of 22 Uruguayan banks have changed hands since 1981. As the financial crisis worsened and the commercial banks were being intervened or capitalized directly or indirectly by the Banco de la República Oriental del Uruguay (BROU), the concentration in the sector has increased sharply, with the BROU and the banks owned by it holding more than 70 percent of the banking system deposits in 1986.

Currency Substitution

The share of foreign currency assets and liabilities in the Uruguayan banking system increased sharply between 1974 and 1985 (Charts 17 and 18).

The share of foreign currency deposits jumped from 11.8 percent of M3 and 31.7 percent of total time and saving deposits in 1974 to 65.6 percent and 75.4 percent, respectively, in 1985. On the credit side, whereas only about 18 percent of the credit of the banking system to the private sector was denominated in foreign currency in 1974, this share amounted to 77.4 percent in 1985. Moreover, although no statistics exist on foreign currency deposits held abroad by domestic residents, an idea of the trend of these deposits can be obtained from the U.S. Treasury Department data on deposits in U.S. banks held by nonbank Uruguayan depositors. These deposits grew steadily from 1974 to 1976, declined from 1977 to 1979, and regained strength beginning in 1980 (Chart 19).

A high and increasing proportion of foreign currency deposits in Uruguay have been held by nonresidents (mostly Argentines). The fraction of foreign currency deposits in the private banking system held by nonresidents increased from 16.8 percent in 1974 to 49.3 percent in 1982, declining thereafter to 45.0 percent in 1985 (Chart 20).[31]

These huge portfolio shifts and the sharp process of dollarization are most remarkable and have potentially far-reaching implications for the implementation of monetary policy. Banda and Santo (1983) analyze empirically the domestic money substitutes and their importance for the effectiveness of monetary policy, concluding that the closest substitutes for a narrow money definition are savings and time deposits, denominated

---

[31] However, Hanson and de Melo (1985) point out that official statistics may not be a good measure of the importance of nonresident deposits because they have been subject to different treatment during the period. For example, they initially were subject to higher reserve requirements than resident deposits, which encouraged banks to request that nonresidents declare a Uruguayan address.

Chart 17. Foreign Currency Deposits as Percentage of M3
(In percent)

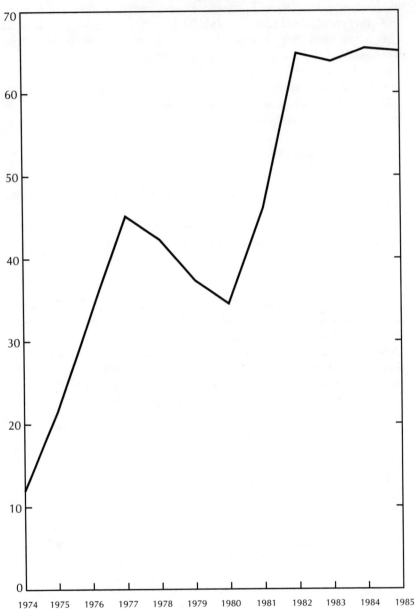

Source: Statistical Appendix Table 14.

Chart 18. Currency Substitution
(In percent)

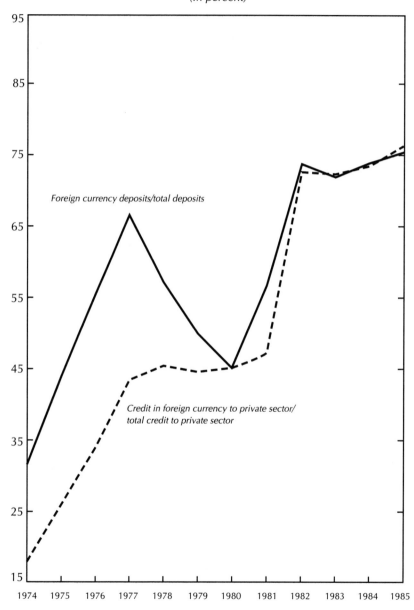

Foreign currency deposits/total deposits

Credit in foreign currency to private sector/
total credit to private sector

Source: Statistical Appendix Table 14.

Chart 19. Deposits in U.S. Banks by Uruguayan Nonbank Private Sector
(In millions of U.S. dollars)

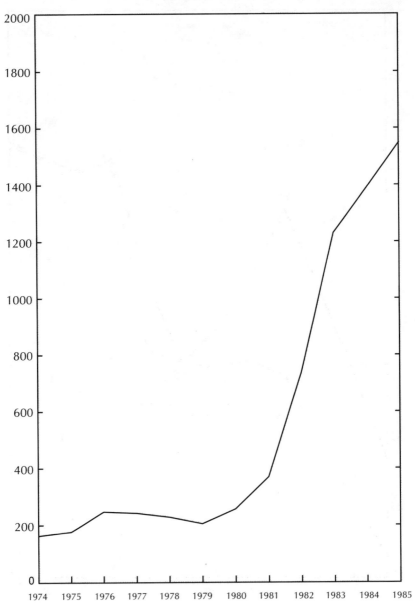

Source: *U.S. Treasury Bulletin,* various issues.

**Chart 20. Foreign Currency Deposits in Private Banks
Held by Nonresidents**
(Percent of foreign currency deposits)

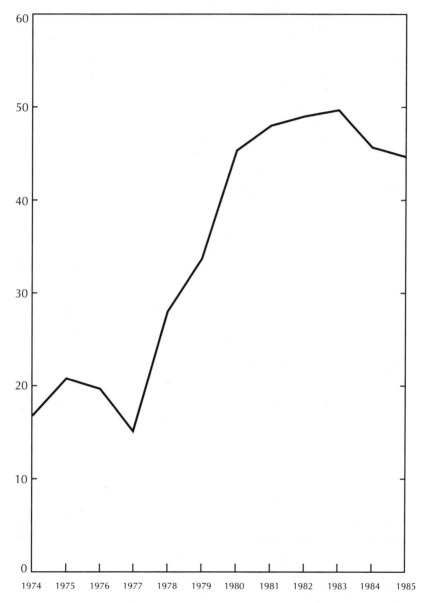

Source: Statistical Appendix Table 14.

in pesos, with a low elasticity of substitution between foreign currency and domestic deposits. They argued that after the capital account was opened, increases in foreign currency deposits reflected speculative capital flows from Argentina rather than a portfolio shift by domestic residents, and that this capital inflow was often monetized—resulting in an increase in M1. In contrast, Ramirez-Rojas (1985) concludes that currency substitution—defined as the demand for foreign fiat money by domestic residents—was empirically important in Uruguay, and should be taken into account in the implementation of economic policy.[32]

De Melo (1985) argues that a dollarization of the magnitude observed reflected more than an increase in the demand for fiat money. He suggests that it was caused by a portfolio adjustment between dollars abroad and dollars held in the Uruguayan financial system. He bases this contention on the evolution of the ratio of Uruguayan dollar deposits in the United States to dollar deposits in Uruguay. This ratio decreased sharply between 1974 (3.53 percent) and 1980 (0.24 percent) and then started rising again (0.85 in 1983) (Statistical Appendix Table 14). De Melo attributes these movements to changes in expectations about the evolution of the economy, and the maintenance of the exchange rate regime, and after 1982 to the impact of the domestic financial crises and insolvency of Uruguayan banks on people's confidence.

The turning point probably began during 1980 instead of 1982. At that time, deposits in U.S. banks by Uruguayans began to rise again (Chart 19) and at a faster pace than foreign currency deposits in Uruguay (see Statistical Appendix Table 14) while, at the same time, the share of foreign currency deposits in the domestic financial market also increased considerably (Charts 17 and 18). This evidence suggests that the external factors, which adversely affected the performance of the Uruguayan economy and more expansive fiscal policies, began to make the exchange rate policy less credible in 1980, promoting a new round of currency substitution.

IV. The Financial Crisis and Policy Responses

The Financial Crisis

As described above, the financial position of Uruguayan firms, especially in the tradables sector, deteriorated sharply between 1980 and 1982, owing to the increasing peso overvaluation, the rise in interest rates, and

---

[32] For theoretical models of currency substitution, see Calvo and Rodríguez (1977), Frenkel and Rodríguez (1982), and Calvo (1985); for empirical studies, see Ortiz (1983) and Márquez (1984). On the issue of "symmetrical" currency substitution (residents and nonresidents holding both currencies) see, for instance, Cuddington (1983).

the historical buildup of debt denominated in foreign currency. The collapse of the *tablita* and the accompanying devaluation were a major blow for enterprises—especially producers of nontradables who lacked foreign exchange cover—and triggered the financial crisis by inducing loan defaults which made many financial institutions technically insolvent.

The devaluation of the Argentine peso (78 percent in March 1981) provoked a massive outflow of capital in Uruguay, owing to the lack of confidence in the sustainability of the Uruguayan *tablita* once Argentina had abandoned its own. The capital outflow and the drop in Argentine demand together reduced the price of assets in Uruguay,[33] thus also reducing the value of collateral on bank loans.

As Chart 21 shows, banks' loan portfolios were clearly affected (see also Statistical Appendix Table 15). The stage for the crisis was set. By the beginning of 1982, many banks were in serious difficulties and there was a threat of a generalized banking crisis. When the peso was finally devalued, firms indebted in dollars were devastated, and to make things worse for banks, the value of collateral had dropped, making foreclosures more difficult.

Policy Responses

The authorities attempted a series of measures to overcome the financial crisis, but their response was complicated by the ongoing political transition. Expectations of a general debt relief were generated, and the attitude of "hold off payments, wait and see" was reinforced by the evolution of the legal developments and the workings of the judicial system, which tended to favor debtors.

The Bailout: Special Credit Facilities and the Portfolio Purchase Scheme

As nonperforming loans began to cause serious trouble for financial institutions, the Central Bank of Uruguay (CBU) devised a series of relief mechanisms.

In 1982, and particularly during the second half of the year, some emergency support funds were provided by the Central Bank of Uruguay to troubled financial institutions. The Banco Hipotecario received substantial financial assistance after early 1982. Net credit from the CBU to that institution increased over 1,500 percent from September 1981 to September 1982.[34]

---

[33] Fossati mentions that the price of urban real estate dropped from US$500 per square meter in 1982 to less than US$200 in 1984; and the price of pasture land, from more than US$600 to less than US$220, *Búsqueda*, No. 374, March 12, 1987, p. 3.

[34] It increased over 1800 percent during 1982. See Central Bank of Uruguay, *Boletín Estadístico*.

Chart 21. Ratio of Bad Loans/Net Worth in Consolidated Banking System

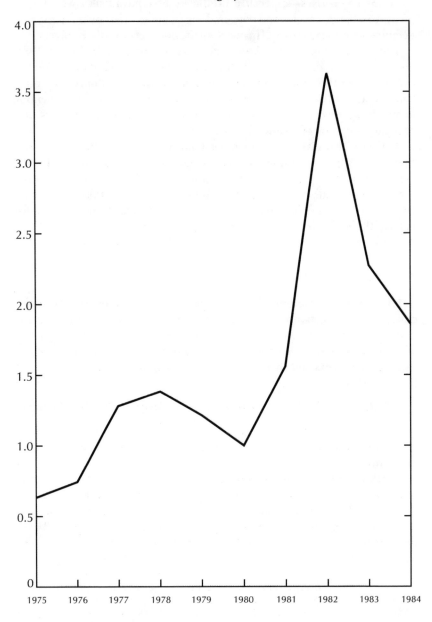

Source: Statistical Appendix Table 15.

Another source of monetary expansion during 1982 (but prior to the abandonment of the *tablita*) was net credit to the Central Government. It increased about 400 percent from September 1981 to September 1982.[35] Moreover, two special facilities were established to assist private sector borrowers: the export prefinancing scheme and a voluntary refinancing scheme. These schemes involved subsidized interest costs which were mostly borne by the Central Bank and subsequently caused a substantial expansion of the monetary base.

The export prefinancing scheme, abolished in 1979, was reinstated in September 1982 and eliminated when the *tablita* was abandoned two months later. This amounted to an exchange guarantee and was made available only to nontraditional exporters. Under the scheme, dollar loans from commercial banks against future export revenues were deposited at the CBU (for a six-month term) for their peso equivalent, and when the deposit matured, the CBU would refund the original amount (minus a 10 percent annual charge). After the devaluation, capital gains were reaped by exporters, with the losses absorbed by the CBU. The *voluntary refinancing scheme* allowed debtors in the agricultural, industrial, and commercial sectors to reschedule their debt (up to a maximum of 33 percent of the outstanding private commercial bank credit to those sectors) for a period of five years, with a two-year grace period. Maximum interest rates were to be 2 points above the London interbank offered rate (LIBOR) (for 180-day maturities) on foreign currency loans, and 90 percent of the average rate charged by banks on peso loans. During the grace period, the borrower would pay only three fifths of the interest cost of the rescheduled loan to his bank, with CBU covering the rest. Thus two fifths of interest cost would be capitalized and repaid as part of the amortization payments, once the grace period expired. However, the most decisive relief measure was the portfolio purchase scheme, which comprised two different operations: the portfolio purchase linked to loans to the CBU (*compra de cartera vinculada a préstamos al Banco Central*), and the portfolio purchase linked to bank intervention (*compra de cartera vinculada a negociación de bancos*). These two measures provided for the CBU to purchase commercial banks' nonperforming loan portfolios with dollar-denominated bonds and promissory notes issued by the CBU. In the first operation, the banks were to arrange for medium-term external finance to the CBU in a multiple of the amount of the loan portfolio transferred to the CBU while, in the second case, the CBU arranged for the sale of a bankrupt local bank to a foreign financial institution, and purchased the bad loan portfolio with the issue of bonds and the write-off of previous financial assistance.

Under both operations, which took place from late 1982 to 1984, the

[35] Central Bank of Uruguay, *Boletín Estadístico*.

CBU acquired assets for the equivalent of US$632 million[36] and received financing for the equivalent of US$328 million against the issuance of bonds and promissory notes for US$855 million and cancellation of financial assistance for US$105 million (see Statistical Appendix Table 16). Thus, Table 2 shows the effects of the operation on the balance sheet of the CBU, abstracting from interest payments within this two-year period.

Table 2. Changes in Central Bank Balance Sheet
(In millions of U.S. dollars)

Assets		Liabilities	
Credit to the private sector (portfolio purchased)	+ 632	Long-term debt (bonds and promissory notes issued)	+ 855
International reserves (resulting from external financing to CBU)	+ 328		
Claims on commercial banks (cancellation of financial assistance)	− 105		

A disaggregation by currency of portfolios acquired by the Central Bank of Uruguay is given in Charts 22 and 23. It is shown that 74.5 percent of portfolios purchased through the scheme that involved loans to the CBU and 65.1 percent of those acquired through the scheme that involved bank interventions were denominated in foreign currency.[37]

The loans purchased by the CBU were concentrated in the livestock sector (36.8 percent of peso portfolios and 25 percent of dollar portfolios), and the industrial sector (21.8 percent of peso portfolios and 37.8 percent of dollar portfolios) (Statistical Appendix Table 17).

The portfolios purchased by the CBU were highly concentrated in terms of the size of the debt. Less than 1.5 percent of borrowers (those

---

[36] This amount represented about 22 percent of total outstanding credit to the private sector granted by the consolidated banking system, and about 24 percent of total deposits in that system in 1983. It also represented about 60.5 percent of total 1983 Uruguayan exports.

[37] As shown in Statistical Appendix Table 14 for the years 1982–84 the fraction of credit to the private sector denominated in foreign currency averaged 73.8 percent; therefore, the currency composition of portfolios purchased corresponds roughly to that of total credit to the private sector.

Chart 22. Currency Composition of Loans Purchased
(As percentage of portfolio purchases linked to loans to CBU)

Source: Central Bank of Uruguay.

Chart 23. Currency Composition of Loans Purchased
(As percentage of portfolio purchases linked to bank intervention)

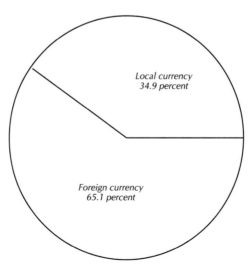

Source: Central Bank of Uruguay.

with outstanding loans of more than US$1 million) had debts totaling 48.3 percent of the debt purchased, and about 16.5 percent of borrowers (those with debt outstanding of US$50,000 or more) had debts equivalent to almost 92 percent of the total debt purchased (Statistical Appendix Table 18). Unfortunately, no similar figures for total credit are available for comparison.[38] In any case, the available information suggests that prevailing prudential regulations on risk concentration and maximum financing limits proved insufficient to preserve loan quality.

The administration and management of the portfolios purchased by the Central Bank of Uruguay kept switching throughout the period, from CBU delegating them to the BROU and the foreign banks involved in the purchase of local banks, to assumption by CBU, to administration by BROU, and, finally, to administration by one of the newly nationalized commercial banks. This is partly attributable to the lack of appropriate human and technical resources at CBU for the difficult task of managing such huge and diversified portfolios. Loan recovery undoubtedly has suffered from the indecisive management policy. It turned out that a good part of the loans was unrecoverable, with far greater costs to the CBU than had been anticipated.

Whether it was appropriate for CBU to use long-term dollar debt to pay for a portfolio partly denominated in pesos gave rise to some debate. It was justified by the Government on the basis of (a) the spreading out of the monetary effects over several years, and (b) banks' unwillingness to hold long-term peso assets. For instance, the then president of the CBU declared later in parliamentary testimony that monetary conditions prevented a cash payment; in his view, a cash payment would have been immediately used to purchase dollars. He also argued that payment with long-term notes in domestic currency was not feasible either: the nonexistence of this type of assets was proof that they would not have been acceptable.[39]

The portfolio purchase linked to loans to the Central Bank of Uruguay started in October 1982, when the Central Bank declared its readiness to purchase part of the loan portfolios of commercial banks, in return for foreign currency loans equivalent to 200–300 percent of the portfolio purchased. This proportion varied according to the quality of the loans purchased, of which at least 66 percent had to be of good quality—as judged by the CBU—or to be guaranteed by the selling bank. The operation was financed by the issue of promissory notes with seven years'

---

[38] Ideally, a time series of debt disaggregated by size would have provided information on the effects of regulatory changes on risk concentration, and its comparison with the bad loans data would have allowed to discuss whether or not banks' risk exposure was excessive.

[39] *Búsqueda*, No. 362, December 1986, p. 18–19.

maturity and three semesters' grace, which carried an interest rate of 1.5 points over the LIBOR, with repayment scheduled to be in 11 semestral installments, equal and consecutive.

The CBU did not select the portfolio, but did assess it. If according to this assessment, at least two thirds of the portfolio offered was not considered of good quality, offering banks could attempt a recomposition of the portfolio offered to CBU until that threshold was reached. For the election of transferable portfolios, banks would have to take into account borrowers' capabilities to meet the following conditions: (1) a minimum interest rate of two points over the LIBOR for dollar debts and 90 percent of the average market loan rate for peso debt, and (2) a maximum maturity of seven years, and a maximum grace period of three semesters.

As a result of the operation, the CBU purchased portfolios for the equivalent of US$216 million, receiving fresh loans in foreign exchange for US$328 million (i.e., the credit received from the commercial banks net of the purchased portfolio value) and financing the transaction with the issuance of notes for US$544 million (see Statistical Appendix Table 16).

This operation was decided on because the CBU was facing an acute shortage of reserves, triggered by the lack of confidence in the *tablita* and the massive intervention required to sustain the exchange rate. In 1982, international reserves fell by about US$1,000 billion (see Statistical Appendix Table 5).[40] Bertero (1985) argues that a feasible alternative would have been the sale of a part of the gold reserves, and her computations show that the CBU could have obtained the same amount of foreign exchange with the sale of about 21–25 percent (depending on market prices) of its gold reserves at international prices.

Charts 24 and 25 clearly show that the main sellers of the portfolios in this operation were the foreign commercial banks, with 60.2 percent of the loans denominated in pesos and 74.3 percent of the loans denominated in dollars. For comparison, only 24.8 percent of the peso-denominated assets and 24.6 percent of the assets denominated in dollars of the banking system were held by foreign banks in 1982.[41]

The more sizable portfolios acquired by the Central Bank of Uruguay under this operation were sold by the Citibank (the equivalent of US$74.8 million) and the Bank of America (the equivalent of US$49.9 million), totaling 58 percent of the portfolio purchased by CBU (against loans from the banks to CBU for US$297.3 million) (see Statistical Appendix Table 20). It is noteworthy that Citibank and Bank of America were among the

---

[40] J.M. Puppo, who assumed the presidency of the CBU in July 1982, stated that "the operation of portfolio purchase linked to loans to the Central Bank of Uruguay was decided given its financial need at that time" (*Búsqueda*, No. 362, December 1986, p. 18).

[41] Information provided by the Central Bank of Uruguay.

Chart 24. Portfolio Purchases Linked to Loans, Peso Denominated

(As percentage of portfolio purchases linked to loans to CBU)

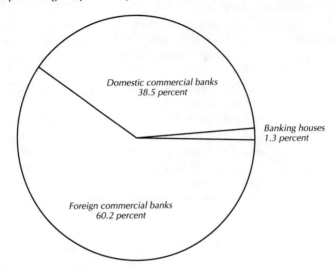

Source: Statistical Appendix Table 19.

Chart 25. Portfolio Purchases Linked to Loans, Dollar Denominated

(As percentage of portfolio purchases linked to loans to CBU)

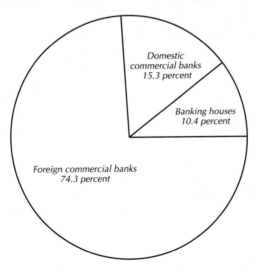

Source: Statistical Appendix Table 19.

creditor banks negotiating the external debt of Uruguay at the time.[42] The portfolio purchase transaction with Citibank was closed a month before the demise of the *tablita*, allowing this institution to make a sizable capital gain.[43]

The portfolio purchase linked to bank intervention was of a different nature. As the position of local banks worsened, the Central Bank of Uruguay stepped in to forestall bankruptcies by arranging the sale of insolvent local banks to foreign banks. As a condition for buying those insolvent institutions, the foreign banks got the CBU to acquire the portfolio of poor quality loans (for the equivalent of US$416 million) paying for it through the issue of bonds and promissory notes, denominated in U.S. dollars—with seven years' maturity, two years' grace, and at an interest one and a half points over LIBOR[44] (for a total of US$311 million), and through writing-off the equivalent of US$105 million in emergency financial assistance credits that had been granted to these institutions (no longer needed once they were taken over by the solvent foreign banks).

A total of five takeover operations took place. The ultimate rationale for these operations was the avoidance of a banking panic and the maintenance of the stability of the financial system. There have been claims of irregularities in some of these takeover deals, with the subsequent opening of parliamentary and judicial investigations.[45]

The authorities had in mind a monetary approach to the theory of financial crisis and sought to implement the unavoidable bailout (after emergency financial assistance failed to save the banks in difficulties) in what seemed the most efficient way.[46] The main arguments advanced in favor of this means of implementing the bailout instead of some alternative like direct intervention of the affected banks were as follows:[47]

- It allowed a case-by-case treatment, permitting more flexibility. Interventions cannot do this, owing to their adverse effect on expectations, which could trigger a generalized banking panic unless all interventions took place at the same time.
- Direct intervention amounts to a monetization of the deposits of insolvent banks with negative consequences for the conduct of mone-

---

[42] For a heated debate at the Uruguayan parliament on the issue, see *Búsqueda*, No. 275, pp. 12 and 32, April 1985.

[43] US$34.8 million out of the US$74.8 million of the portfolio sold to the Central Bank of Uruguay in October 1982 was peso-denominated (see Statistical Appendix Table 20).

[44] See *Búsqueda*, No. 224, February 1984.

[45] See *Búsqueda*, No. 275, April 1985, especially pp. 12 and 32.

[46] See *Búsqueda*, No. 361, December 1986, containing a justification along these lines from Mr. J. Gil Díaz, President of the CBU from December 1974 until July 1982.

[47] *Ibid.*

tary policy. In addition, the operating costs of the intervened banks must be borne by the central bank. On the other hand, the adopted scheme allowed the spreading of the bailout losses over several years, and minimized the losses for the state, since previous financial assistance could be recovered and did not entail bearing the operating costs of the distressed banks. Unfortunately, hardly any data exist on the recovery of the loan portfolio purchased under both schemes.

According to press reports[48] the terms initially offered to the debtors under both operations, i.e., portfolio purchases linked to loans to the CBU, and portfolio purchases linked to bank intervention were one-year's grace, two-years' amortization, and rates going from 71 percent to 79 percent, for peso debt; and two-years' grace, three-years' amortization, and 13 percent interest for dollar debt.

Some measures were taken in April 1984 to attempt the recovery of part of these nonperforming assets.[49] A National Office of Asset Recovery was created to administer the portfolios. Also, borrowers were classified into two groups: *high-standard* and *low-standard borrowers*. High-standard borrowers were those who had paid in 1983 at least 60 percent of the interest accrued during six months of that year and would have to pay, before May 15, 1984, 60 percent of the interest accrued during 1983 as a whole. This classification applied to both peso- and dollar-denominated debts.

High-standard borrowers benefited from the following measures:

- The equivalent of 20 percent (for borrowers in local currency) and 40 percent (for borrowers in foreign currency) of the interest accrued during 1983 was written off.
- Maturity periods were extended to five years with one year of grace for portfolios denominated in local currency purchased before 1984; to four years for portfolios denominated in local currency purchased during 1984; to eight years with one year of grace for portfolios denominated in foreign currency purchased before 1984; and to seven years with one year of grace for portfolios denominated in foreign currency purchased during 1984.
- Borrowers in local currency could opt to convert their debt outstanding on December 31, 1983, into indexed debt, to be repaid in 14 six-month installments at an annual interest rate of 4 percent over the adjusted principal. For each period, the adjustment factor to be applied would be the lower of (a) the change during the period in the exchange rate or (b) the change in the corresponding sectoral price index.

---

[48] *La Semana Uruguaya*, May 8, 1984, p. 16.
[49] *La Semana Uruguaya*, May 8, 1984, p. 16; and Central Bank of Uruguay (1984).

- Borrowers in foreign currency could opt to convert their foreign-currency-denominated debt as of December 31, 1983 into local-currency-indexed debt, with the same interest rate and conditions given to debtors in local currency who opted for converting their debt into indexed debt.

In addition, all borrowers who, before September 30, 1984, made prepayments 180 days before the due date would benefit from a write-off equivalent to the prepaid amount, up to a maximum equivalent to 25 percent of the debt outstanding at the time of prepayment. Those debtors making prepayments (180 days before the due date) after September 30, 1984 would also benefit from a write-off equivalent to the prepaid amount, up to 15 percent of the debt outstanding at the time of prepayment.

These measures improved somewhat the debt collection: data on recovery of outstanding debt as of August 31, 1984[50] show that 30 percent of the recovery on dollar debt and 34 percent of the recovery on peso debt took place between May 1 and August 31, 1984. Nevertheless, the recovery pace remained dismal. By December 31, 1983 the Central Bank of Uruguay had recovered only US$8.7 million (or 1.8 percent) of the dollar debt, and NUr$409.9 million (or 6.4 percent) of peso debt (see Statistical Appendix Table 21). By August 31, 1984, these figures had risen to US$13.7 million for dollar debt and NUr$724.5 million for peso debt. The recovery pace seems to have slowed down afterwards, against the background described in the next subsection.

This poor performance can be attributed to a number of different factors: (1) Actual insolvency of debtors, aggravated by debt concentration; (2) unwillingness to pay on the part of debtors, on the expectation of a general debt amnesty; (3) inadequacies of the judicial system, which have tended to favor borrowers and made it difficult to attach their property; and (4) the belief that the future improvement of economic conditions would increase the real value of collateral, allowing a better recovery performance.

The long-term impact of this purchased portfolio on the accounts of the Central Bank of Uruguay is hard to assess, and there is no public information on issues such as how the loans are being accounted for, which part is in arrears, and whether interests are being capitalized. It seems, though, that an important part of this portfolio may have been written off. Moreover, the data on total credit of the Central Bank to the private sector show sharp falls in the months of December, suggesting that a portion of these loans are written off as operational losses at the end of every year.[51]

---

[50] See *El País*, November 11, 1984. This is the last time that data on recovery were made public.

[51] See *Búsqueda*, August 28, 1986, p. 24.

The Backlash: The Domestic Debt Refinancing Law and BROU Takeovers

In the last few years of the period under study payment habits deteriorated. Growing expectations of a general forgiveness of debt pervaded society, with demands for a "political" solution to the debt problem becoming increasingly aggressive.

Regulations on compulsory selective credit to exporters were reinstated in 1984, and a forward exchange market linked to compulsory credit in pesos to exporters was also created.

Banks were confronted with an increase in arrears as debtors delayed payments in expectation of some sort of debt relief after the change in administration in March 1985 and, rather than lending to the private sector, preferred the safer returns from holding treasury bills. These expectations also affected the recovery of the portfolio purchased by the Central Bank of Uruguay under the schemes described above.

> According to a local observer, the demise of the *tablita* influenced notably the deterioration of respect for any kind of jurisdiction. This was aggravated by the belief that the private banks had accumulated huge profits during the period of the *tablita*. As a result, the issue of the inability of corporations to pay began to be considered as having a political origin and later, with the return of democratic political activity, these problems were added to the revisionist and demanding-of-damage compensation claims attitude developed since then.[52]

This climate is reflected in the figures on the fraction of loans in arrears and unpaid over the total liabilities of domestic debtors with private banks shown in Table 3.

Table 3. Loans Unpaid and in Arrears

Date	Total Loans (in percent)
September 1980	1.5
September 1981	3.0
September 1982	11.0
September 1983	18.0
September 1984	25.0
September 1985	34.0
March 1986	42.0
June 1986	56.0
September 1986	59.0

Source: *Búsqueda*, No. 374, March 12, 1987.

[52] Fossati, *Búsqueda*, No. 374, March 12, 1987.

The demanded "political solution" was offered by the Domestic Debt Refinancing Law (Law No. 15786), passed in November 1985, and the decrees complementary to the law (Decree 83/986 on the refinancing regime for the agricultural sector and Decree 84/986 on the refinancing regime for industry and services), issued in February 1986.[53] The purpose of the law was to alleviate the debt burden of financially viable firms and provide the legal environment for an orderly rescheduling of that debt, in order to allow those firms new access to borrowing. The law in itself favored debtors, and provisions in the law allowed solvent firms to postpone payments. Moreover, the law included a transitory moratorium for all debtors that applied for classification under the law. Evaluation and classification of debtors according to the provisions of the law was left to a specially appointed Financial Analysis Commission, whose work was delayed with the result that loans were not serviced in the meantime.[54] Financial intermediaries were squeezed by the nonperformance of assets, and one after another domestically owned banks became technically insolvent, and were taken over by the BROU.

The law's refinancing schemes were optional for private debtors. For debtors to the banking system, a two-stage process was established. First, the Financial Analysis Commission had to determine which debtors were eligible for refinancing. Then, commercial banks had to proceed with the refinancing agreement, which entered into effect if the debtor accepted it. However, if the debtor disagreed or was delinquent in servicing the refinanced debt for more than six months, he was subject to judicial procedures to liquidate his/her assets. The law aimed at providing debt relief to economically viable firms in financial difficulties, excluding from its provisions firms considered "solvent," firms considered "nonviable" (except for some special cases), and foreign-owned firms. The provisions of the law were complicated, containing different criteria, circumstances, and terms of refinancing for different debtors.[55]

The eligibility criteria to obtain refinancing differed across sectors. Solvent firms were excluded, as noted. For the agricultural sector, solvency was defined in terms of maximum indebtedness per hectare, which varied across subsectors. Firms exceeding that maximum limit (NUr$4,000) had access to refinancing. For industry, firms were considered solvent if the sales/liabilities (with the financial system) ratio was greater than 2.5, except for small firms, which were considered solvent if

---

[53] For a comprehensive legal analysis of this legislation, see Ferrere and Olivera García (1986) and Rodríguez Olivera and Varela Artagaveytía (1987).

[54] The CBU appointed the three members of this commission, which was also in charge of settling disputes between borrowers and lenders.

[55] See Rodríguez Olivera and Varela Artagaveytía (1987).

indebtedness per employee was less than NUr$20,000. For the commerce and services sector, firms were considered solvent if their liabilities were less than 60 percent of assets, except for small firms (indebtedness less than NUr$25,000 per employee in this case). Nonviable firms in the agricultural sector were those whose indebtedness per hectare exceeded a certain maximum (which varied according to the subsector); in the industrial sector, nonviable firms were those with a sales/liabilities ratio of less than 0.9 (priority activities) or 1 (other activities). In the commerce and service sectors, nonviable firms were those with a negative operative margin (special activities) or that operated with a negative margin and had debt exceeding NUr$2 million (general activities). All firms that were not solvent or nonviable were viable. Small agricultural and industrial nonviable firms were also eligible, as were debtors that refinanced their liabilities according to previous norms issued by the Central Bank of Uruguay.

In general, the conditions and terms of refinancing were contingent on the categorization of debtors. Debtors in the agricultural sector were classified in categories A, B, C, D, E, F, G, depending on the subsector, the size of the unit, and the amount of outstanding debt per hectare. For the industrial sector, categories included small firms, priority activities, nonpriority activities, and debtors that had rescheduled their liabilities under previous debt-relief programs and that had met the corresponding installments. The categories for the commerce and services sectors were small firms, special activities, general activities, and debtors that had refinanced their liabilities under previous debt-relief programs.[56]

The amount subject to refinancing was computed in two steps. First, the total amount outstanding as of June 30, 1983 was computed. For this, interest was capitalized up to January 1983 at the terms originally contracted, and after that date, penalty rates were not to exceed the market loan rate for domestic debt, or the preferential rate for dollar debt. Second, the outstanding debt as of October 15, 1985 was computed taking account of the outstanding debt as of June 30, 1983 previously calculated and using pre-established interest rates: for the favored debtors (those that originally contracted loans at preferential interest rates), it was the basic rate charged by the BROU for domestic debt, and 12 percent for dollar debt; for all others, the normal rate for peso debt and the preferential rate for dollar debt. *The grace period* was between one and three years, depending on the sector of activity, while *the payment period* was between five and ten years, also depending on the sector and categorization of the debtor. The interest rates were generally lower than the market rate (from 33 percent to 90 percent of the average market rate) for peso debt, depending on the sector and category, and equal to the market rate for obligations in dollars.

[56] See Ferrere and Olivera García (1986), Chap. 5 for details.

Interest payments were in some cases only a fraction of the required amounts, with the unpaid portion subject to capitalization. A fraction of the interest unpaid between June 1983 and October 1985 (depending on sector and category) could be deferred to the latter years of the repayment period. A premium of up to 20 percent for prompt payment was established for some sectors and categories. The amortization was quarterly, with amounts increasing over time as a fraction of the outstanding debt, with the precise schedule depending on sector and category.

Also, firms were not allowed to pay dividends until debt was reduced to one third of the original amount, and dividend distribution required approval of the Financial Analysis Commission and a majority of creditors (dividends were not to exceed 20 percent of profits in any case).

The debt-relief scheme involved cumbersome procedures, which allowed borrowers legally to delay servicing their debts. One of the first measures of the new parliament had been approval of a law suspending court attachment of debtors' property for all debt contracted after July 1978 for a period of 35 days (Law 15741, of April 10, 1985).[57] This period was subsequently extended through November 20, 1985. The law of domestic debt refinancing extended this period for another 60 days. More important, it established that after this extension lapsed, the moratorium would continue for all debtors applying for refinancing for as long as their application was under study.

The commission had to determine whether a debtor was subject to automatic refinancing under the provision of the law (i.e., was a viable firm or otherwise eligible firm) or not (nonviable firm). The procedure was likely to lead to delays. A debtor could submit his application to anyone (but only to one) of his/her creditors. Then, all these applications had to be centrally processed, and all the creditors notified of all applications presented by all the firms against which they held any financial asset, after a comprehensive list had been produced. Taking into account the number of debtors (tens of thousands) and the applications presented (estimated to be about 9,000, according to press releases),[58] a formidable amount of paperwork was involved.[59] It is not surprising then that the work of the commission was delayed for more than a year, until mid-1987.

As a result, bank losses continued to increase, and a new phase of the crisis arrived, marked by the takeover of banks by the BROU resulting in progressive de facto nationalization of the banking sector.

The first episode of government participation in the banking sector took

[57] See Ferrere and Olivera García (1986), Chap. 11.
[58] See *Búsqueda*, Nos. 331, May 1986, and 341, July 1986.
[59] Often debtors had to be summoned to provide required additional information. See *Búsqueda*, No. 344, August 1986.

place much earlier, at the beginning of 1984, when the Banco del Plata was liquidated, with deposits being reimbursed.

At the beginning of 1985, before further takeovers by the BROU, the three largest private banks in Uruguay were the Banco Comercial (10.2 percent of deposits), the Banco Pan de Azúcar (9.9 percent), and the Banco de Italia (4.7 percent).[60]

In May 1985, the Banco de Italia was taken over. It was the local branch of an Argentine bank that had been intervened by the Central Bank of Argentina. The local branch was solvent, though, according to press reports.[61] The CBU ordered the intervention and the BROU assumed the majority of the equity.

In July 1985, the Banco Pan de Azúcar was taken over. It had become insolvent, and its head office in Chile was also in the process of liquidation. The BROU assumed the equity capital without indemnization.

In April 1986, Banco Pan de Azúcar and Banco de Italia merged, under the name of Banco Pan de Azúcar. About 83 percent of the equity of the new institution was held by the BROU.[62]

In March 1987, the Banco Comercial, by then technically insolvent, was recapitalized by BROU in an operation ordered by the CBU. Its capital was raised from NUr$750 million to NUr$10,000 million (with a priority right for the acquisition given to former shareholders), and roughly 90 percent of the capital was held by the BROU at the end of the operation.[63]

In June 1987, the Banco Pan de Azúcar—in which BROU had assumed the majority of shares—acquired Banco La Caja Obrera (which was the last domestically owned private commercial bank in Uruguay), following a run on the latter's deposits. As a result, 75 percent of deposits ended in government-owned banks, amounting to a sort of "de facto" nationalization of the banking sector.

This nationalization was a highly debated topic in Uruguay, with some arguing in favor of a de jure nationalization, integrating the purchased banks in the official bank system, and others in favor of a reprivatization.

Developments in the Late 1980s: New Measures to Deal with the Consequences of Portfolio Purchases by the CBU

In recent years both the BROU and the CBU have adopted measures to address the domestic debt problem. Most important among these measures are (a) the rescheduling of certain nonperforming loans by the BROU; (b) the introduction of a debt-to-debt conversion scheme by the CBU; and (c)

---

[60] See *Búsqueda*, No. 376, March 1987.
[61] See *Búsqueda*, No. 334, June 1986, p. 21.
[62] *Búsqueda*, March 20, 1986, p. 24.
[63] See *Búsqueda*, No. 376, March 1987, p. 13.

the strengthening of regulatory and supervisory procedures in the CBU.

In 1987, BROU began to reschedule loan order terms more favorable than those established in the 1985 refinancing law. This decision was triggered by the increasing share of nonperforming assets in the portfolio of the BROU following the takeover of Banco Comercial and Banco La Caja Obrera in early 1987. In selected cases, the BROU allowed debt-to-debt conversions, involving the repayment of domestic debt with external claims on BROU purchased abroad at a substantial discount. Moreover, the BROU resumed lending to those delinquent debtors who had rescheduled their debt.

The CBU has also addressed the problem of limited collection on its private loan portfolio which has become the major source of its quasi-fiscal losses in recent years. In late 1987, the CBU introduced its own debt-to-debt conversion scheme. Through this mechanism, private debtors are able to cancel their liabilities to the Central Bank with public external debt purchased in the secondary market. Moreover, in early 1988, the CBU transferred to the BROU the administration of its impaired private sector loan portfolio.

In 1989, the Government launched an extensive reform of the financial sector with assistance from the World Bank. The main objectives of this reform are the strengthening of the banking system and the restoring of necessary safeguards to normal credit operations to avoid a repetition of previous lending practices. The reform includes the rehabilitation of three of the failed banks absorbed by the BROU with a view to their subsequent privatization and the liquidation of a fourth insolvent bank. This reform is supported by a strengthening of the CBU's regulatory and supervisory procedures for evaluating credit applications, determining reserves for potential operational losses, and rating of uncollectible loans. New accounting procedures for commercial banks were introduced, including standardized balance sheets, guidelines for classifying credits in arrears, and special solvency and liquidity checks. At the same time, banking inspection was stepped up. In this context, the BROU is required to conform to the new banking and accounting standards applicable to private banks and to report separately to the CBU on its banking and nonbanking operations and their financing.

V. Summary and Conclusions

A major financial crisis developed in Uruguay in 1982 with far-reaching effects in subsequent years. A wide range of factors—both macroeconomic and regulatory—contributed to the crisis, which seriously disrupted the functioning of the Uruguayan economy.

In 1974 a profound economic reform was initiated. The reform implied a significant change in past policies and practices, and immediately improved the performance of the economy in terms of growth and efficiency. However, the sequencing of the reform—whereby the liberalization of capital transactions with the rest of the world was completed quickly, the liberalization of domestic financial markets was at a slower pace, and the removal of distortions in domestic commodity and labor markets and trade barriers proceeded at the slowest pace and suffered transitory reversals—together with prevailing conditions in neighboring countries (Argentina and Brazil) promoted important capital inflows that led to a surge in borrowing, particularly in foreign currency.

The reforms did not affect the CBU's supervisory techniques and procedures, which remained basically unchanged with respect to those prevailing during the pre-reform period. Supervision was confined to the traditional control of capital and reserve requirements. No legal norms regulated the way in which the accounting information of financial institutions had to be presented and evaluated. Most important, there were no early warning indicators or other systematic or informal schemes for off-site analysis of banks by the CBU.

Delays in removing trade barriers and other restrictions in domestic commodity and labor markets, together with the important capital inflows, complicated the management of monetary policy and contributed to high inflation during the first years of the reform process. In attempting to solve these problems, in late 1978 the authorities introduced an active crawling peg, announced a timetable to remove trade barriers, implemented an important tax reform, and continued to improve the fiscal position of the (nonfinancial) public sector and to liberalize domestic markets. Even though they succeeded in decelerating the inflation rate (particularly after late 1979), some adverse shocks affected the Uruguayan economy beginning in 1980.

The early 1980s was a time of recession in the world economy. It was also a time of important policy adjustments in Argentina and Brazil. As a result, demand for Uruguayan exports weakened and terms of trade deteriorated. At the same time, international interest rates increased. These developments caused a deterioration in the current account of the balance of payments. The public sector financial position also deteriorated owing to a shrinking tax base and large social security payments. Monetary management became more difficult because of the increasing financial needs of the Government and the deteriorating financial position of some financial institutions (mainly official banks). As a consequence, continuation of the active crawling peg regime (known as the *tablita*) became less credible and a renewed process of currency substitution began to develop. Domestic interest rates became highly positive in real terms (particularly those on assets and liabilities denominated in local currency), reflecting the increasing risk of devaluation and adversely affecting the financial position of borrowers. This process was considerable fueled by the Argentine devaluation of early 1981, which created major capital outflows and capital flight.

When confidence in the *tablita* receded, and the expectation of a devaluation generalized, the position of nonfinancial firms, overindebted and exposed in dollars, was threatened. Already squeezed by rising real interest rates and by the fall of collateral prices after the reverse of the speculative upsurge caused by Argentine demand, the beginning of the peso float by a substantial devaluation represented a major blow. The financial sector saw the quality of its portfolio worsen rapidly, and the injection of emergency funds from the Central Bank was insufficient to revitalize the banks.

After the first indications of banking panics were detected and a generalized banking crisis was feared, the CBU bailed out depositors by arranging the sale of troubled banks to foreign banks, which only accepted the deal insofar as the CBU assisted the troubled banks by purchasing their bad loans. The CBU spread out the monetary effects of such purchases over a period of seven years.

In addition, the depletion of foreign exchange reserves at the Central Bank and the contemporaneous renegotiation of the external debt led the CBU to agree to purchase the poor-quality loan portfolio of some foreign banks in return for a loan in dollars. The deal was repeated later with a number of local banks, but the situation had deteriorated and the portfolios bought from local banks were of poorer quality. Owing to a number of factors, most of the debt that the CBU acquired through these schemes has proved so far impossible to recover.

The issue turned highly political, as debtors presented organized resistance to foreclosure procedures and resisted repayment in general, demanding a "political" solution. A law was passed in late 1985 that compromised between these demands and the need to resume normal lending operations by providing a legal framework for orderly rescheduling.

In the meantime, the position of banks became increasingly fragile, with some of them being affected also by the weak position of their head offices in other Latin American countries. One after the other, banks became insolvent, suffered bank runs, and the BROU stepped in, taking over failing banks by means of a recapitalizing operation sponsored by CBU. As a result, in 1987, the BROU held 75 percent of deposits while foreign banks held the rest.

The limited collection on the loan portfolio acquired by the CBU through the different portfolio purchase schemes during 1982–84 became a major source of losses in recent years. Also, the assistance provided by the

BROU to the troubled banks that it absorbed and its relief to delinquent debtors decreased its profitability. These factors have increased the financial needs of these official financial institutions, jeopardizing their autonomy, and complicating monetary management.

To address these problems, several measures were adopted in recent years. In late 1987, the CBU introduced a debt-to-debt conversion scheme under which over US$50 million of its foreign liabilities were canceled. The BROU rescheduled certain nonperforming loans under terms more favorable than those provided for under the 1985 rescheduling law. It also implemented a selective debt-to-debt conversion scheme by allowing loan cancellations against its foreign liabilities purchased abroad at a discount.

Later, in June 1989, the Government launched an extensive financial sector reform. The main objectives have been the rehabilitation of three of the failed banks absorbed by the BROU and their subsequent privatization, and the liquidation of an insolvent bank. In addition, the CBU has started a review of the accounting rules for financial institutions and has strengthened its regulatory and supervisory role.

References

Abalo, C., "Uruguay, un largo viaje hacia la sombra," *Comercio Exterior*, Vol.32, Nos. 5 and 6 (1982).

Academia Nacional de Economía, *Contribución a la Historia Económica del Uruguay* (Montevideo: 1984).

Ache, E., A. Banda, and R. Lopez Murphy, "La base monetaria: Hacia una definición operativa," *Monetaria*, Mexico (July–September 1986), pp. 263–82.

Altman, E., and A. Sametz, eds., *Financial Crisis: Institutions and Markets in a Fragile Environment* (New York: J. Wiley, 1977).

Banda, A., and M. Santo, "Una aproximación empírica al estudio de los sustitutos del dinero en Uruguay," *Monetaria*, Mexico (July–September 1983), pp. 301–314.

The Banker (October 1986).

Barletta, Ardito Nicolas, Mario Blejer, and Luis Landau, eds., *Economic Liberalization and Stabilization Policies in Argentina, Chile, and Uruguay: Applications of the Monetary Approach to the Balance of Payments* (Washington: World Bank, 1984).

Bernanke, B., "Bankruptcy, Liquidity, and Recession," *American Economic Review* (May 1981), pp. 155–59.

—————, "Nonmonetary Effects of the Financial Crisis in the Propagation of the Great Depression," NBER Working Paper No. 1054, National Bureau of Economic Research (January 1983).

Bertero, E., "The Banking Crisis in Uruguay (1980–82): Macroeconomic Causes and Policy Response" (unpublished; International Monetary Fund, 1985).

Blanco H., and P. Garber, "Recurrent Devaluation and Speculative Attacks on the Mexican Peso," *Journal of Political Economy* (1986), pp. 148–66.

Blejer, M., and J. Gil Díaz, "Domestic and External Factors in the Determination of the Real Interest Rate: The Case of Uruguay," *Economic Development and Cultural Change* (1986), pp. 589–606.

Bordo, M., "Some Historical Evidence 1870–1933 on the Impact and International Transmission of Financial Crisis," NBER Working Paper No. 1606, National Bureau of Economic Research (April 1985).

Bryant, M., "A Model of Reserves, Bank Runs and Deposit Insurance," *Journal of Banking and Finance* (1980), pp. 335–44.

Búsqueda (Montevideo), various issues.

Cagan, P., *Determinants and Effects of Changes in the Stock of Money* (New York: Columbia University, 1965).

Calvo, G., "Trying to Stabilize Some Theoretical Reflections Based on the Case of Argentina," in *Financial Policies and the World Capital Market: The Problem of Latin American Countries*, ed. by P. Aspe-Armella, R. Dornbusch, and M. Obstfeld (Chicago: University of Chicago Press, 1983).

————, "Currency Substitution and the Real Exchange Rate: The Utility Maximization Approach," *Journal of International Money and Finance*, Vol. 4 (June 1985), pp. 175–88.

————, "Fractured Liberalism: Argentina under Martinez de Hoz," *Economic Development and Cultural Change*, Vol. 34 (1986), pp. 511–36.

————, and C.A. Rodríguez, "A Model of Exchange Rate Determination Under Currency Substitution and Rational Expectation," *Journal of Political Economy* (June 1977), pp. 617–25.

Central Bank of Uruguay, "Administración de las carteras del Banco Central del Uruguay," mimeograph (April 1984).

————, *Boletín Estadístico*, various issues.

————, *Reseña de la Actividad Económica Financiera*, various issues.

————, *Memoria*, various issues.

Choksi, A., and D. Papageorgiou, eds., *Economic Liberalization in Developing Countries* (New York: Basil Blackwell, 1986).

Cline, W., and S. Weintraub, eds., *Economic Stabilization in Developing Countries* (Washington: The Brookings Institution, 1981).

Corbo V., and J. de Melo, eds., "Scrambling for Survival: How Firms Adjusted to the Recent Reforms in Argentina, Chile, and Uruguay," World Bank, Staff Working Paper No. 764 (1985).

————, and J. Tybout, "What Went Wrong with the Recent Reforms in the Southern Cone?" *Economic Development and Cultural Change*, Vol. 34 (1986), pp. 607–40.

Cuddington, J.T., "Currency Substitution, Capital Mobility and Money Demand," *Journal of International Money and Finance*, Vol. 2 (August 1983), pp. 111–33.

Cumby, R., and S. van Wijnbergen, "Fiscal Policy and Speculative Runs with a Crawling Peg: Argentina 1979–1981" (unpublished, IMF Seminar Series No. 1987–3, 1987).

Dale, R., *Bank Supervision Around the World* (New York, 1982).

Daly, H., "A Note on the Pathological Growth of the Uruguayan Banking Sector," *Economic Development and Cultural Change*, Vol. 16 (1967), pp. 91–96.

de Juan, A., "From Good Bankers to Bad Bankers: Ineffective Supervision and Management Deterioration as Major Elements in Banking Crisis," mimeograph (1987).

Delpiazzo, C., *El Banco Central del Uruguay* (Montevideo: Ediciones Jurídicas A.M. Fernández, 1983).

de Melo, J., "Financial Reforms, Stabilization and Growth Under High Capital Mobility: Uruguay 1974–83," World Bank, DRD Discussion Paper No. 138 (1985).

————, and J. Tybout, "The Effects of Financial Liberalization on Savings and Investment in Uruguay," *Land Economics* (1986), pp. 561–87.

————, R. Pascale, and J. Tybout, "How the Financial Statements of Uruguayan Firms in 1973–81 Reflected Stabilization and Reform Attempts," World Bank, Staff Working Paper No. 696 (1985).

Diamond, D., and P. Dybvig, "Bank Runs, Deposit Insurance, and Liquidity," *Journal of Political Economy* (June 1983), pp. 401–419.

Díaz, R., "Uruguay's Erratic Growth," in *World Economic Growth*, ed. by A.C. Harberger (San Francisco: ICS Press, 1984).

Diaz-Alejandro, C., "Southern Cone Stabilization Plans," *Economic Stabilization in Developing Countries*, ed. by W. Cline and S. Weintraub (Washington: The Brookings Institution, 1981).

————, "Good-Bye Financial Repression, Hello Financial Crash," *Journal of Development Economics*, Vol. 19 (1985), pp. 1–24.

Dooley, M., and D. Mathieson, "Financial Liberalization and Stability in Developing Countries," IMF Working Paper, WP/87/19 (1987).

The Economist Intelligence Unit, *Country Profile: Uruguay, Paraguay, 1987–88* (London, 1987).

Edwards, S. (1984a), *The Order of Liberalization of the External Sector in Developing Economies*, Princeton Essays in International Finance, No. 156 (1984).

———— (1984b), "The Order of Liberalization of the Balance of Payments: Should the Current Account Be Opened Up First?" World Bank, Staff Working Paper No. 710.

————, "The Order of Liberalization of the Current and Capital Accounts of the Balance of Payments," in *Economic Liberalization in Developing Countries*, ed. by A. Choksi and D. Papageorgiou (New York: Basil Blackwell, 1986).

————, and S. van Wijnbergen, "The Welfare Effects of Trade and Capital Market Liberalization," *International Economic Review* (February 1986), pp. 141–48.

Favaro, E., "Interest Rate Differences: Expectations of Devaluation Versus Costs of Adjustments of Net Asset Position" (Montevideo: Banco Pan de Azúcar, 1985).

Ferrere, M., and R. Olivera García, *La Refinanciación del Endeudamiento Interno* (Montevideo, 1986).

Finch, M.H.J., *A Political Economy of Uruguay Since 1970* (New York, 1981).

Fisher, I., *Booms and Depressions* (New York: Adelphi, 1932).

————, "The Debt-Deflation Theory of Great Depressions," *Econometrica* (October 1933).

Flood, R., and P. Garber, "A Systematic Banking Collapse in a Perfect Foresight World," NBER Working Paper No. 691 (National Bureau of Economic Research, 1981).

Frenkel, J., "Comments" on McKinnon, *Carnegie Rochester Conference Series on Public Policy*, No. 17 (1982).

————, "Panel Discussion on the Southern Cone," *Staff Papers*, International Monetary Fund (March 1983).

————, and C.A. Rodriguez, "Exchange Rate Dynamics and the Overshooting Hypothesis," *Staff Papers*, International Monetary Fund (March 1982).

Friedman M., and A. Schwartz, *A Monetary History of the United States, 1867–1960* (Princeton, New Jersey: Princeton University Press, 1963).

Fry M., "Money and Capital or Financial Deepening in Economic Development?" *Journal of Money, Credit and Banking* (1978), pp. 464–75.

————, "Savings, Investment, Growth, and the Cost of Financial Repression," *World Development* (1980), pp. 317–27.

————, "Models of Financially Repressed Developing Economies," *World Development* (1982), pp. 731–50.

Galbis, V., "Financial Intermediation and Economic Growth in LDCs: A Theoretical Approach," *Journal of Development Studies* (1977), pp. 58–72.

Gilbert, R.A., "Bank Market Structure and Competition: A Survey," *Journal of Money, Credit and Banking*, Part II (November 1986).

Giovannini, A., "Savings and the Real Interest Rate in LDCs," *Journal of Development Economics* (1985), pp. 197–217.

Gordon, G., "Bank Suspension of Convertibility," *Journal of Monetary Economics*, Vol. 15 (1985), pp. 177–93.

Hanson, J., "What Went Wrong in Chile?" in *Economic Liberalization in Developing Countries*, ed. by A. Choksi and D. Papageorgiou (New York: Basil Blackwell, 1986).

Hanson, J., and J. de Melo, "The Uruguayan Experience with Liberalization and Stabilization, 1974–81," *Journal of Interamerican Studies and World Affairs* (1983), pp. 477–508.

————, "External Shocks, Financial Reforms and Stabilization Attempts in Uruguay: 1974–83," (unpublished; World Bank, February 1985).

Hanson, J., and C. Neal, *Interest Rate Policies in Selected Developing Countries, 1970–1982*, Industry and Finance Series (Washington: World Bank, 1986).

Hanson, J., and R. Rocha, *High Interest Rates, Spreads, and the Cost of Intermediation*, Industry and Finance Series (Washington: World Bank, 1986).

Harberger, A., "El rol de los factores fiscales en la inflación uruguaya," *Cuadernos de Economía* (1975), pp. 33–46.

————, "Welfare Consequences of Capital Inflows," in *Economic Liberalization in Developing Countries*, ed. by A. Choksi and D. Papageorgiou (New York: Basil Blackwell, 1986).

————, and D. Wisecarver, "Private and Social Rates of Return to Capital in Uruguay," *Economic Development and Cultural Change* (1977), pp. 411–45.

Ho, T.S.Y., and A. Saunders, "The Determinants of Bank Interest Margins: Theory and Empirical Evidence," *Journal of Financial and Quantitative Analysis* (November 1981).

International Monetary Fund, *International Financial Statistics*, various issues.

──────── , "Panel Discussion on the Southern Cone," *Staff Papers* (March 1983).

Kahkonen, J., "Liberalization Policies and Welfare in a Financially Repressed Economy," *Staff Papers*, International Monetary Fund (1987), pp. 531–47.

Kapur, B., "Alternative Stabilization Policies for Less-Developed Economies," *Journal of Political Economy* (1976), pp. 777–95.

Khan, M., and M. Knight, "Stabilization Programs in Developing Countries: A Formal Framework," *Staff Papers*, International Monetary Fund (1981), pp. 1–53.

Khan, M., and R. Zahler, "The Macroeconomic Effects of Changes in Barriers to Trade and Capital Flows: A Simulation Analysis," *Staff Papers*, International Monetary Fund (1983), pp. 223–82.

Kindleberger, C.P., *Manias, Panics, and Crashes: A History of Financial Crises* (New York: Basic Books, 1978).

Kruger, A., "Problems of Liberalization," in *Economic Liberalization in Developing Countries*, ed. by A. Choksi and D. Papageorgiou (New York: Basil Blackwell, 1986).

Lanyi, A., and Saracoglu, R., *Interest Rate Policies in Developing Countries*, IMF Occasional Paper No. 22 (1983).

Larraín, F.B., "Financial Liberalization in Uruguay: Success or Failure" (unpublished; Pontificia Universidad Católica de Chile, September 1986).

Londono, F., and M. Glen de Tobon, "La intervención del Estado en la Banca Latinoamericana," *Integración Latinoamericana* (1981), pp. 43–55.

McKinnon, R., *Money and Capital in Economic Development* (Washington: The Brookings Institution, 1973).

──────── , "The Order of Economic Liberalization: Lessons from Chile and Argentina," *Carnegie Rochester Conference Series on Public Policy*, No. 17 (1982), pp. 159–86.

Márquez, J., "Sustitución de monedas, dualidad e indeterminación del tipo de cambia: Análisis empírico de la experiencia venezolana," *Cuadernos de Economía*, Santiago de Chile (December 1984).

Mathieson, D., "Financial Reforms and Capital Flows in a Developing Economy," *Staff Papers*, International Monetary Fund (September 1979), pp. 450–89.

──────── , "Financial Reform and Stabilization Policy in a Developing Economy," *Journal of Development Economics* (1980), pp. 359–95.

──────── , "Inflation, Interest Rates, and the Balance of Payments during a Financial Reform: The Case of Argentina," *World Development* (1982), pp. 813–27.

──────── , "Estimating Models of Financial Market Behavior During Periods of Extensive Structural Reform: The Experience of Chile," *Staff Papers*, International Monetary Fund (1983), pp. 350–93.

──────── , and R. McKinnon, *How to Manage a Repressed Economy* (Princeton, New Jersey: International Finance Section, Princeton University, 1981).

Mezzera, J., and J. de Melo, "Adjustments by Industrial Firms in Uruguay During 1974–82," in Scrambling for Survival, ed. by V. Corbo and J. de Melo (World Bank, 1985).

Minsky, H., "A Theory of Systemic Fragility," in *Financial Crisis: Institutions and Markets in a Fragile Environment*, ed. by E. Altman and A. Sametz (New York: J. Wiley, 1977).

———— , "Can 'It' Happen Again?" *Essays on Instability and Finance* (New York: M.E. Sharpe, Inc., 1982).

Mitchell, W.C., *Business Cycles* (Berkeley: University of California Press, 1913).

Molho, L., "Interest Rates, Savings and Investment in Developing Countries," *Staff Papers*, International Monetary Fund (1986), pp. 90–116.

Mussa, M., "The Adjustment Process and the Timing of Trade Liberalization," in *Economic Liberalization in Developing Countries*, ed. by A. Choksi and D. Papageorgiou (New York: Basil Blackwell, 1986).

Olivera García, R. (1982a), *Instalación de Bancos en el Uruguay* (Montevideo, 1982).

———— , (1982b), *Sistema de Intermediación Financiera en Uruguay* (Montevideo, 1982).

Ortiz, G., "Currency Substitution in Mexico: The Dollarization Problem," *Journal of Money, Credit and Banking*, Vol. 15 (May 1983), pp. 174–85.

El País (Montevideo), November 11, 1984.

Ramirez-Rojas, C., "Currency Substitution in Argentina, Mexico and Uruguay," *Staff Papers*, International Monetary Fund (December 1985), pp. 629–67.

Rodríguez, C.A., "The Plan of the 20th of December," *World Development*, Vol. 10 (1982), pp. 801–811.

Rodríguez Olivera, N., and P. Varela Artagaveytía, "Comentarios a la Ley de Refinanciación del Endeudamiento Interno" (Montevideo, 1987).

Santomero, A., "Modeling the Bank Firm: A Survey," *Journal of Money, Credit and Banking* (1984), pp. 576–616.

La Semana Uruguaya (Montevideo), May 8, 1984.

Shaw, E.W., *Financial Deepening in Economic Development* (New York: Oxford University Press, 1973).

Spiller, P., "Comments on Uruguay," in *Economic Liberalization and Stabilization Policies in Argentina, Chile, and Uruguay: Applications of the Monetary Approach to the Balance of Payments*, ed. by Nicolas Ardito Barletta, Mario Blejer, and Luis Landau (Washington: World Bank, 1984).

———— , and E. Favaro, "The Effects of Entry Regulation on Oligopolistic Interaction: The Uruguayan Banking Sector," *Rand Journal of Economics* (1984), pp. 244–54.

Stockman, A., "Comments" on McKinnon, *Carnegie Rochester Conference Series on Public Policy*, No. 17 (1982).

Tybout, J., "Interest Controls and Credit Allocation in Developing Countries," *Journal of Money, Credit and Banking* (1984), pp. 474–87.

———— , "A Firm Level Chronicle of Financial Crises in the Southern Cone," World Bank, DRD Discussion Paper No. 139 (1985).

United States, Treasury Department, *Treasury Bulletin*, various issues.

van Wijnbergen, S. (1983a), "Credit Policy, Inflation and Growth in a Financially Repressed Economy," *Journal of Development Economics*, Vol. 13 (1983), pp. 45–65.

—————— (1983b), "Interest Rate Management in LDCs," *Journal of Monetary Economics* (1983), pp. 533–52.

Veblen, T., *The Theory of Business Enterprise* (New York: Charles Scribner and Sons, 1904).

Wolfson, M., *Financial Crisis* (New York: M.E. Sharpe, Inc., 1986).

World Development (August 1985) .

APPENDIX I
Major Regulatory Changes in the Uruguayan
Financial Sector, 1974–86

Interest Rates

Uruguayan financial regulations have traditionally included interest rate ceilings. This continued to be the case during the first few years of the reform process. Later, interest rates were freed for a few years, after which followed a period of more intervention ("moral suasion" or administrative ceilings on interest rates).

CBU Circular No. 524 (6/28/74) set the ceiling for foreign currency loan rates at 15.5 percent per annum paid at maturity; the ceiling was raised to 16.5 percent effective July 22, 1974.

CBU Circular No. 549 (9/24/74) set local currency maximum loan rates at 32 percent per annum, paid in advance (about 61.3 percent at maturity); the same circular set a 6 percent limit on commissions and fees paid in advance.

CBU Circular No. 550 (9/24/74) limited annual interest rates on domestic currency deposits as follows: 10 percent for checking accounts, with interest paid only if daily average balance exceeds NUr$100,000; 18 percent for savings accounts; for time deposits above NUr$50,000: 30 percent for 3- to 5-month deposits, 36 percent for 6- to 11-month deposits, and 48 percent for deposits with maturities of 12 months and over.

CBU Circular No. 614 (4/3/75) modified the ceiling for foreign currency loan rates, setting it at 14.5 percent per annum. Effective April 1, 1976, this rate was set at 12 percent per annum.

Beginning in March 1975, no interest was paid on checking account deposits.

CBU Circular No. 728 (3/5/76) set the maximum interest rate for lending operations in local currency with banks' own resources at 62 percent paid at maturity. At the same time, all interest rates on time and savings deposits could be fixed freely by banks. CBU Circular No. 730 (3/5/76) established that private financial intermediaries should communicate monthly to the CBU the most frequent interest rates charged or offered on their operations.

CBU Circular No. 869 (10/14/77) set maximum legal interest rates on loans at 90 percent for those in domestic currency and 15 percent for those in foreign currencies.

Effective June 1, 1978, the maximum interest rate on foreign currency loans was increased from 15 to 20 percent per annum.

CBU Circulars Nos. 941 and 950 (9/7/78 and 11/20/78) defined a "Basic Interest Rate," equal to an average of the more frequent deposit interest rates paid by the five most important banks.[64] These circulars also indicated that the basic rate would apply to export prefinancing schemes and to the lines of credit granted by the CBU to assist private banks.

In 1979, CBU Circular No. 990 (9/11/79) (based on Law 14887 and Decree 450/979) abolished all interest rate ceilings. A period of free interest rate determination followed.

Beginning in July 1983, CBU began using "moral suasion" with private banks to bring interest rates down from the prevailing levels at the time. Another brief period of formal administrative regulation followed soon thereafter.

In November 1984, an interest rate ceiling of 85 percent per annum was set for domestic currency loans. The ceiling was raised to 87 percent in December of the same year, to 90 percent in January 1985, and to 95 percent in February 1985.

Finally, interest rate ceilings were abolished again in December 1985. In the most recent period, and against the background of a stagnant financial system, the state commercial bank BROU played a major role in setting the market pace for interest rates.

Reserve Requirements

Reserve requirements were traditionally high, and continued to be so during the first few years of the liberalization period. In 1979, reserve requirements were eliminated, although they were reinstated later, and— together with compulsory investment coefficients—have been raised in recent years. All through this period the reserve requirement policy has been changing in terms of the percentages required, the type of assets that can satisfy the requirements, and the type of deposits subject to them. The main developments may be summarized as follows:

CBU Circular No. 548 (9/24/74) set the following requirements, effective October 1, 1974:

(i) For domestic currency deposits: 30 percent on sight deposits; and

---

[64] Importance was defined in terms of relative share in total deposits in domestic currency.

10 percent on time deposits with maturities exceeding 30 days. The requirement could be satisfied with cash in vault (up to 85 percent of the requirement); deposits with monetary authorities (with CBU or BROU); holdings of government bonds (up to 40 percent of the requirement, with a minimum of 10 percent in treasury notes and a minimum of 5 percent in adjustable mortgage bonds); and gold.

(ii) For foreign currency deposits, 20 percent, which could be satisfied with sight deposits in foreign currency at CBU or BROU (minimum 25 percent of the requirement); and government bonds denominated in foreign currency (up to 75 percent of the requirement).

CBU Circular No. 502 (2/12/74) established a 100 percent reserve requirement for all deposits exceeding 15 times the capital and reserves of the bank (see section on liabilities/capital ratios). This limit was later raised to 16 times (CBU Circular No. 548, 9/24/74), effective January 1, 1976.

CBU Circulars Nos. 593 and 595 (1/30/75 and 2/6/75) created an additional reserve requirement: 40 percent of the increase in deposits in local currency over the level of December 1984. The requirement could be satisfied with sight deposits with CBU, yielding 20 percent per annum interest rate; and special local currency treasury notes. These additional reserves were then reduced to 20 percent for domestic currency time deposits with maturities exceeding a year.

CBU Circular No. 703 (12/30/75) unified the basic and additional legal reserve requirements. Effective January 1, 1976, these requirements were 40 percent for sight deposits and deposits of less than 30 days; 20 percent for 30-day to 360-day time deposits; 5 percent for deposits of over 360 days; and 10 percent of capital for financial houses. This circular established that these reserve requirements could be fulfilled only with deposits with the CBU or cash.

Beginning in March 1976, private banks were forced to hold government bonds for 19 percent of local currency deposits, of which at least 11 percent were required to be in treasury bills, and at least 4 percent were required to be in mortgage bonds.

CBU Circular No. 679 (10/8/75) determined that government bonds held in fulfillment of foreign currency reserve requirements must be deposited exclusively with the CBU.

CBU Circulars Nos. 753 and 769 (6/3/76 and 6/30/76) eliminated the remunerated deposits in local currency as a form of holding reserves.

CBU Circular No. 799 (12/29/76) established a gradual increase in required reserves on foreign currency deposits, to 23 percent as of February 1977 and to 28 percent as of July 1977. At the same time, it established a remuneration on foreign currency of 2 percent over LIBOR, provided that the deposits were made for at least three months and for at least US$100,000.

CBU Circular No. 808 (2/10/77) ordered a 100 percent reserve requirement for transitory deposits in banking institutions, to be met with cash and domestic currency deposits at the CBU.

CBU Circular No. 832 (5/9/77), which became effective as of June 1, 1977, established the following reserve requirements: 50 percent for sight deposits and time deposits with a maturity of less than 30 days; 35 percent for 30-day to 360-day time deposits; and 12 percent for deposits of more than 360 days.

CBU Circular No. 877 (10/14/77) ordered that, starting November 1, 1977, legal reserve requirements would be 50 percent for sight deposits and time deposits with a maturity of less than 12 months; 30 percent for 30-day to 360-day time deposits; 6 percent for deposits of more than a year; and 32 percent for foreign currency deposits.

Bankers' acceptances (including financial houses) were to be subject to the following reserve requirement ratios: 30 percent for acceptances of up to 12 months; and 6 percent for acceptances of more than a year.

CBU Circulars Nos. 840, 855, 865, and 876 (5/20/77, 7/28/77, 9/15/77, and 10/14/77) regulated the remuneration of reserves.

CBU Circular No. 875 (10/14/77), which came into effect as of November 1, 1977, set the required reserves for banks and financial houses at 32 percent on foreign currency deposits. Government bonds were eliminated from the required reserves.

Effective June 1, 1978, it was established that prevailing legal reserve requirements on all kinds of deposits would be applied to the monthly average deposits of each bank for the month of April 1978. All increments of deposits above this amount would have a unified reserve requirement of 20 percent.

At the same time, the legal reserve requirement for foreign currency deposits outstanding as of April 1978 was set at 28 percent. All increments of foreign currency deposits above this amount would also have a reserve requirement of 20 percent.

CBU Circular No. 945 (10/27/78) reduced the reserve requirement ratio for foreign currency deposits outstanding as of April 1978 from 28 percent to 24 percent.

CBU Circular No. 951 (12/7/78) unified (effective January 1, 1979) the reserve requirement ratio for both domestic and foreign currency deposits at 20 percent. These requirements applied to the stock of deposits of each bank outstanding at the end of 1978. All increments of deposits above this amount carried a zero reserve requirement.

CBU Circular No. 905 (3/8/78) established a remuneration for required reserves on domestic currency deposits of up to 15 percent a year for 30-day to 360-day liabilities subject to reserve requirements. The excess would also be remunerated up to an amount equal to 6 percent of domestic currency deposits with maturities exceeding 360 days.

CBU Circular No. 936 (8/7/78) limited to 10 percent of liabilities subject to reserve requirements the fraction of reserves to be remunerated. CBU Circular No. 951 (12/7/78) set this limit at 2.5 percent, beginning in December 1978.

CBU Circular No. 976 (5/8/79) eliminated all reserve requirements, except those related to maximum liabilities/capital ratios: deposits over 16 times the capital and reserves became subject to 100 percent required reserves. CBU Circular No. 979 (6/27/79) raised this ratio from 16 to 30 times the capital and reserves.

Reserve requirement ratios were reintroduced after the failure of the preannounced devaluation regime. CBU Circular No. 1127 (12/29/82) established that, starting in 1983, reserve requirement ratios would be set at 5 percent for local currency deposits outstanding as of December 1982; and 20 percent on the increment in local currency deposits over those outstanding in December 1982. These reserves would be remunerated at a variable rate.

CBU Circular No. 1128 (1/5/83) increased reserve requirements to 10 percent of liabilities in domestic currency existing by the end of December 1982 (from 5 percent previously); and to 40 percent for increases over that level (from 20 percent). CBU Circular No. 1137 (3/10/83) increased from 10 percent to 13 percent the reserve requirement on liabilities in domestic currency, and CBU Circular No. 1149 (9/21/83) lowered the marginal requirement from 40 percent to 25 percent. CBU Circular No. 1153 (12/1/83) ended this transitory period by setting a 14 percent reserve requirement ratio and eliminating the marginal requirement.

CBU Circulars Nos. 1124 and 1149 (2/8/83 and 9/21/83) spelled out the penalties for not satisfying legal reserve requirements.

Entry and Branching Regulations

Law 13,330 of 1965, passed after the banking crisis of 1965, forbade both the installation of new banks and the opening of additional branches or offices of existing banks (a new branch could be opened only if another office was closed by the same or another institution).

Banking houses were not included in the prohibition, because at the time only one banking house existed, and its weight in the financial system was negligible.

CBU Circular No. 799 (12/29/76) allowed banking houses for the first time to receive foreign currency deposits from nonresidents.

Law 15,207 of 1981 lifted the entry prohibition in the banking sector. New banks were allowed to enter the sector, in a number not to exceed 10 percent of the number that had existed the previous year, and the ban on branch and office expansion was lifted.

Risk Concentration and Maximum Financing Limits

Before the reform, maximum financing limits to a single client were in force, and risk concentration regulations applied for most of the period except for a brief interval of less than two years.

CBU Circular No. 547 (9/24/74) maintained the prohibition against lending to a single client more than 20 percent of the bank capital and reserves, with the exception of export prefinancing.

CBU Circulars Nos. 640, 642, and 706 (6/15/75, 6/27/75, and 12/2/75) removed some pre-existing norms on banned lines of financing and on promoted lines of credit, and raised the maximum credit to a single person or firm to 25 percent of the bank capital (with some exceptions).

CBU Circular No. 860 (7/24/77) addressed the issue of interlocking boards of directors by forbidding financing above 25 percent of the bank capital to corporations whose board of directors included members of the bank board or management.

CBU Circular No. 964 (2/22/79) modified the regime of exceptions to the financing limit to a single customer.

CBU Circular No. 971 (3/29/79) eliminated all regulations on risk concentration and maximum financing. A deregulated period followed.

CBU Circular No. 1048 (12/10/80) reintroduced legal maximum risk concentration limits, which were set at 25 percent of the bank capital (as of the next-to-last month) for individuals or single firms and 35 percent for conglomerates or groups of firms (with no single firm within the group exceeding the 25 percent limit). The limits included disbursed and nondisbursed loans, banking acceptances, and endorsements.

Some exceptions were considered for guaranteed loans and loans with more than three years to maturity, if covered by the Credit Insurance Fund.

For a transition period of three months (January–March 1981), banks that did not satisfy the limits when the regulation was issued had to observe limits of 40 percent for single firms and 60 percent for conglomerates, to be gradually adjusted to the 25 percent and 35 percent limits.

The limits were abolished in August 1981, when restrictions were replaced by requirements for detailed information on borrowers, to be provided to the Central Bank of Uruguay according to a uniform methodology.

Liability to Capital Ratios

Throughout the period, the capacity of banks to take deposits or to incur liabilities was linked to the bank capital.

CBU Circular No. 501 (2/12/74) established a maximum bank deposits/capital ratio of 15 times. CBU Circular No. 548 (9/24/74) of the same year raised that ratio to 16, with a 100 percent reserve requirement for all deposits exceeding the limit.

CBU Circular No. 735 (4/1/76) regulated bankers' acceptances, setting a limit of 50 percent of the bank capital. It also set a maximum limit for discounting commercial paper.

CBU Circular No. 782 (5/25/76) set the limits on bankers' acceptances at either 50 percent of the bank capital or up to 20 percent of the deposits in local currency subject to reserve requirements.

CBU Circulars Nos. 971, 980, 982, and 999 (6/27/79, 7/6/79, 7/22/79, and 11/15/79) defined maximum legal limits to the liabilities in local currency or foreign currency that the financial intermediaries could have. This was set at 30 times the capital for banks. Also, for banks that, as of June 30, 1977, had liabilities in excess of 30 times their capital, and for banking houses with liabilities in excess of 20 times their capital, the following transitory regime was established, effective December 1, 1979: the 100 percent reserve requirement for liabilities above the limit was waived until March 1980; increases in liabilities above the level of June 10, 1979, were subject to a 100 percent reserve requirement.

CBU Circular No. 1150 (9/23/83) set a maximum level for bank liabilities equal to 20 times the sum of their capital plus reserves at the CBU plus holdings of government bonds not affected to meet reserve requirements.

Minimum Capital Requirements

Throughout the period, regulations on legal minimum net worth (capital and reserves) for banking firms were in force, and were updated periodically to take account of inflation.

Decrees 439 and 614 (of 1976) updated previous minimum capital requirements for financial intermediaries, setting basic requirements at NUr$3.5 million for banks; NUr$1.5 million for banking houses; NUr$350,000 for *cajas populares*; and an additional minimum capital requirement of NUr$300,000 for every office in Montevideo department, in the capitals of all other departments, and in the cities of Las Piedras, Pando, and Punta del Este; and NUr$150,000 for each office in any other location.

Decree 540 and CBU resolution of October 14, 1977, redefined minimum capital requirements. The basic requirements were set at NUr$6 million for banks; NUr$3 million for banking houses; NUr$6 million for *cajas populares*; and the additional minimum capital was set at NUr$500,000 for offices in Montevideo department, in the capitals of other departments, and in the cities of Las Piedras, Pando, and Punta del Este; and

NUr$250,000 for offices elsewhere.

CBU Circular No. 960 (1/23/79) again updated these minimum requirements. The basic requirements were set at NUr$7.8 million for banks; NUr$3.9 million for banking houses; and the additional ones at NUr$650,000 for offices in Montevideo department, in the capitals of all other departments, and in the cities of Las Piedras, Pando, and Punta del Este; and NUr$325,000 for offices at all other locations. Also, a requirement of NUr$325,000 for exchange house offices was set.

CBU Circular No. 1007 (12/12/79) set the requirements at NUr$46.5 million for banks; and NUr$27.9 for banking houses.

CBU Circular No. 1032 (9/14/80) stated that holdings of domestic financial corporations equity would not count for the fulfillment of minimum capital requirements, and that general equity or bonds could be counted only up to 5 percent of capital.

CBU Circulars Nos. 1082, 1083, 1098, and 1110 (issued in 1982) raised the minimum capital requirements.

CBU Circulars Nos. 1140 and 1150 (5/6/83 and 9/27/83) again updated minimum requirements to NUr$145 million for banks; NUr$87 million for banking houses; NUr$7.25 million for credit cooperatives.

The minimum capital requirement regulations continued in force afterward, and were periodically updated.

Asset Immobilization

CBU resolutions of January 7, 1977 (Circular No. 801), and February 16, 1977, established limits on immobilized assets in the balance sheets of banking firms at no more than 60 percent of the capital and reserves, to be raised to 70 percent after September 1977.

A CBU decision dated October 14, 1977, set this limit at 100 percent of capital and reserves.

APPENDIX II
Statistical Appendix

Statistical Appendix Table 1. Government Finance (Central Government), 1973–84

	1973	1974	1975	1976	1977	1978	1979	1980	1981	1982	1983	1984
	(In millions of new Uruguayan pesos)											
Total revenue	370.2	587.9	985.5	1,722	2,938	4,350	8,424	14,955	21,260	19,552	29,486	39,797
Total expenditure	406.5	789.5	1,348.8	2,048	3,179	4,751	8,301	14,880	21,377	30,761	36,897	55,473
Current	372.2	709.4	1,203.8	1,808	2,796	4,021	7,260	13,081	18,817	27,503	33,159	50,560
Capital	34.3	80.1	145.0	240	383	730	1,040	1,799	2,559	3,258	3,738	4,913
Deficit or surplus	−36.3	−201.6	−363.3	−326	−241	−401	123	75	−117	−11,210	−7,411	−15,676
	(Deficit or surplus as percent of GDP)											
	1.4	−4.4	−4.5	−2.5	−1.2	−1.3	0.02	0.01	−0.01	−8.7	−3.9	−5.3

Source: Larraín (1986).

Statistical Appendix Table 2. Money Supply, 1974–85

(In millions of new Uruguayan pesos)

Year	Quarter	Currency with Public	Demand Deposits	M1	Peso Savings, Time, and Other Deposits	M2	Ratio M2/M1	Foreign Currency Deposits	M3	Ratio M3/M1
1974	I	214.7	166.6	381.3	169.6	550.9	1.4	48.3	599.2	1.57
	II	217.3	159.4	376.7	197.2	573.9	1.5	52.7	626.6	1.66
	III	235.7	180.7	416.4	217.3	633.7	1.5	71.0	704.7	1.69
	IV	315.7	223.8	539.5	218.6	758.1	1.4	101.2	859.3	1.59
1975	I	328.7	286.6	615.3	278.4	893.7	1.5	155.2	1,048.9	1.70
	II	349.7	271.7	621.4	320.6	942.0	1.5	215.1	1,157.1	1.86
	III	348.1	292.8	640.9	378.5	1,019.4	1.6	240.8	1,260.2	1.97
	IV	469.8	351.5	821.3	434.3	1,255.6	1.5	345.0	1,600.6	1.95
1976	I	520.1	410.2	930.3	587.9	1,518.2	1.6	465.3	1,983.5	2.13
	II	598.6	435.6	1,034.2	713.0	1,747.2	1.7	643.5	2,390.7	2.31
	III	626.2	464.4	1,090.6	784.4	1,875.0	1.7	867.1	2,742.1	2.51
	IV	784.2	542.8	1,327.0	876.0	2,203.0	1.7	1,091.4	3,294.4	2.48
1977	I	829.7	624.4	1,454.1	1,003.1	2,457.2	1.7	1,458.3	3,915.5	2.69
	II	811.7	644.4	1,456.1	1,085.1	2,541.2	1.7	1,788.1	4,329.3	2.97
	III	831.6	674.2	1,505.8	1,197.8	2,703.6	1.8	2,135.3	4,838.9	3.21
	IV	1,112.4	745.4	1,857.8	1,273.9	3,131.7	1.7	2,597.6	5,729.3	3.08
1978	I	1,120.7	865.2	1,985.9	1,975.7	3,961.6	2.0	2,769.5	6,731.1	3.39
	II	1,347.8	940.2	2,288.0	2,514.2	4,802.2	2.1	3,244.4	8,046.6	3.52
	III	1,271.8	903.4	2,175.2	2,742.6	4,917.8	2.3	3,949.3	8,867.1	4.08
	IV	1,809.3	1,257.5	3,066.8	3,387.8	6,454.6	2.1	4,712.6	11,167.2	3.64
1979	I	1,777.8	1,537.5	3,315.3	4,385.9	7,701.2	2.3	6,016.2	13,717.4	4.14
	II	2,119.7	1,857.9	3,977.6	5,388.0	9,365.6	2.4	6,865.1	16,230.7	4.08
	III	2,226.1	1,916.9	4,143.0	6,762.5	10,905.5	2.6	7,571.5	18,477.0	4.46
	IV	3,105.2	2,597.8	5,703.0	7,811.9	13,514.9	2.4	8,060.2	21,575.1	3.78

Statistical Appendix Table 2 (concluded). Money Supply, 1974–85

(In millions of new Uruguayan pesos)

Year	Quarter	Currency with Public	Demand Deposits	M1	Peso Savings, Time, and Other Deposits	M2	Ratio M2/M1	Foreign Currency Deposits	M3	Ratio M3/M1
1980	I	3,671.5	2,521.5	6,193.0	10,614.0	16,807.0	2.7	8,797.4	25,604.4	4.13
	II	3,344.9	2,730.8	6,075.7	12,104.8	18,180.5	3.0	9,739.7	27,920.2	4.60
	III	3,439.6	2,927.4	6,367.0	14,196.5	20,563.5	3.2	11,166.6	31,730.1	4.98
	IV	5,089.7	3,571.2	8,660.9	14,939.7	23,600.6	2.7	12,489.5	36,090.1	4.17
1981	I	4,747.8	3,600.4	8,348.2	17,771.7	26,119.9	3.1	15,599.5	41,719.4	5.00
	II	5,312.1	3,371.7	8,683.8	17,706.9	26,390.7	3.0	19,236.4	45,627.1	5.25
	III	5,019.4	3,252.2	8,271.6	17,675.9	25,947.5	3.1	22,004.3	47,951.8	5.80
	IV	6,146.2	3,523.6	9,669.8	18,495.1	28,164.9	2.9	24,350.5	52,515.4	5.43
1982	I	5,523.0	3,142.2	8,665.2	18,619.2	27,284.4	3.1	27,520.4	54,804.8	6.32
	II	5,442.5	2,951.7	8,394.2	18,290.4	26,684.6	3.2	32,261.7	58,946.3	7.02
	III	5,305.6	2,560.8	7,866.4	17,890.6	25,757.0	3.3	32,858.0	58,615.0	7.45
	IV	7,879.3	3,589.9	11,469.2	20,362.0	31,831.2	2.8	59,423.6	91,254.8	7.96
1983	I	7,543.9	2,848.4	10,392.3	22,915.3	33,307.6	3.2	50,767.5	84,075.1	8.09
	II	6,139.5	3,200.1	9,339.6	26,992.1	36,331.7	3.9	50,236.5	86,568.2	9.27
	III	5,854.7	3,476.6	9,331.3	25,809.1	35,140.4	3.8	54,974.2	90,114.6	9.66
	IV	8,405.1	4,378.3	12,783.4	24,383.8	37,167.2	2.9	66,559.4	103,726.6	8.11
1984	I	8,363.4	4,387.2	12,750.6	29,421.4	42,172.0	3.3	89,839.3	132,011.3	10.35
	II	8,861.4	4,294.7	13,156.1	31,891.3	45,047.4	3.4	89,801.2	134,848.6	10.25
	III	9,359.4	4,202.1	13,561.5	34,361.2	47,922.7	3.5	89,763.6	137,686.3	10.15
	IV	12,105.2	7,499.6	19,604.8	35,091.2	54,696.0	2.8	104,806.7	159,502.7	8.14
1985	I	14,984.0	6,234.0	21,218.0	40,805.7	62,023.7	2.9	139,521.0	201,544.7	9.50
	II	16,725.0	8,974.3	25,700.1	49,969.9	75,670.0	2.9	146,086.4	221,756.4	8.63
	III	15,413.9	10,220.0	25,633.9	57,673.8	83,307.7	3.2	172,373.2	255,680.9	9.97
	IV	23,274.8	16,886.8	40,161.6	66,122.4	106,284.0	2.6	203,086.3	309,370.3	7.70

Source: Central Bank of Uruguay, *Boletín Estadístico*, various issues.

Statistical Appendix Table 3.   Exchange Rates, 1976–84

(In new Uruguayan pesos)

		1 U.S. Dollar		1 Argentine Peso		1 Brazilian Cruzeiro	
		Buyer	Seller	Buyer	Seller	Buyer	Seller
1976	Average	3.30	3.34	0.0153	0.0155	0.2701	0.2727
	December	3.94	3.98	0.0150	0.0150	0.2700	0.2700
1977	Average	4.65	4.68	0.0117	0.0118	0.2774	0.2779
	December	5.38	5.39	0.0093	0.0093	0.2740	0.2746
1978	Average	6.05	6.06	0.0077	0.0077	0.2820	0.2826
	December	6.97	6.98	0.0070	0.0070	0.2688	0.2693
1979	Average	7.84	7.86	0.0060	0.0061	0.2526	0.2534
	December	8.41	8.43	0.0052	0.0052	0.1921	0.1930
1980	Average	9.08	9.10	0.0049	0.0049	0.1613	0.1623
	December	9.92	9.95	0.0050	0.0050	0.1497	0.1507
1981	Average	10.79	10.82	0.0025	0.0026	0.1079	0.1089
	December	11.50	11.53	0.0010	0.0011	0.0729	0.0739
1982	Average	13.85	13.91	0.0006	0.0006	0.0545	0.0553
	December	28.21	28.51	0.0004	0.0005	0.0704	0.0718
1983	Average	34.38	34.54	2.7860	2.8680	0.0426	0.0433
	December	42.50	42.73	1.7410	1.7490	0.0343	0.0346
1984	Average	55.89	56.12	0.7822	0.7892	0.0286	0.0289
	December	71.98	72.23	0.3970	0.4020	0.0200	0.0201

Source: Central Bank of Uruguay, *Boletín Estadístico*, various issues.

Statistical Appendix Table 4. Price and Wage Inflation, Fourth Quarter, 1974–Third Quarter, 1986
(Annual percentage change in end-of-period indices)

Year	Quarter	Consumer Prices					Wholesale Prices				Wages
		CPI[1]	Food	Clothing	Housing	Other	WPI[2]	Manufacturing	Agriculture	Construction	
1974	IV	107.4	105.5	72.7	111.4	129.5	87.5	88.7	45.1	75.1	96.9
1975	I	92.9					75.6	93.7	60.9	69.1	
	II	93.0					84.4	82.2	40.6	62.1	
	III	79.7					70.6	75.9	35.8	46.2	
	IV	66.8	53.1	68.0	88.6	77.3	65.0	54.4	33.5	39.8	61.6
1976	I	49.9					49.2	44.4	23.8	29.5	41.2
	II	44.8					39.3	57.1	49.0	41.6	24.6
	III	53.9					55.2	45.1	45.3	44.3	49.9
	IV	39.9	38.5	36.4	43.5	41.1	45.1	56.8	52.5	46.1	29.2
1977	I	56.0					55.8	60.8	52.6	53.2	41.4
	II	65.7					59.0	50.6	46.9	46.8	55.9
	III	59.4					49.8	41.7	55.8	44.9	43.0
	IV	57.3	59.5	46.6	66.5	50.1	44.8	34.4	56.7	39.0	45.6
1978	I	54.9					39.2	38.4	71.4	40.4	42.5
	II	44.7					45.3	39.0	96.5	38.3	39.3
	III	40.8					51.4	49.3	92.0	40.8	38.1
	IV	46.0	48.4	39.5	45.6	44.9	59.6				41.0
1979	I	55.2					70.4	57.0	112.1	49.8	42.8
	II	62.9					84.7	72.6	121.1	65.1	45.3
	III	73.4					88.5	80.5	109.0	76.7	50.6
	IV	83.1	86.0	95.2	78.8	76.9	77.1	82.7	63.4	93.6	56.8
1980	I	78.1					62.8	74.3	36.7	88.9	68.8
	II	67.8					40.5	51.9	13.5	74.3	78.8
	III	56.6					30.7	41.3	7.1	51.5	57.4
	IV	42.8	33.5	27.7	63.7	47.9	28.6	32.9	16.7	35.7	57.0

1981 I	38.7					26.5	33.8	5.1	38.0	52.7
II	34.8					25.0	29.8	9.9	28.3	32.2
III	32.7					25.2	29.7	11.9	33.5	48.2
IV	29.4	25.2	18.8	42.9	26.3	14.9	18.1	5.2	21.1	30.3
1982 I	22.3					11.9	12.4	10.1	12.7	26.5
II	18.9					14.0	13.4	16.2	12.8	25.5
III	14.7					9.3	10.2	6.1	8.6	10.3
IV	20.5	13.3	8.0	28.8	27.9	33.5	37.9	17.9	30.7	7.0
1983 I	42.9					60.0	59.3	62.6	45.0	10.8
II	47.2					67.0	67.0	67.1	44.1	11.3
III	55.1					84.1	81.0	95.3	50.7	29.8
IV	51.5	59.7	64.76	30.9	59.8	73.8	62.9	118.6	38.8	35.2
1984 I	43.9					67.7	63.1	84.7	39.9	29.9
II	56.2					84.0	77.4	108.0	52.7	41.9
III	60.4					78.3	73.9	92.5	61.6	41.8
IV	66.1	77.5	89.6	38.9	68.0	84.0	82.0	90.3	65.8	66.1
1985 I	67.9					81.8	80.6	85.7	78.7	69.2
II	70.5					73.7	80.4	52.8	88.2	99.2
III	72.0					73.7	85.1	40.2	95.8	106.8
IV	83.0	72.2	92.0	77.1	102.9	74.2	85.5	41.1	93.3	107.7
1986 I	83.2					68.0	73.4	50.7	81.5	120.9
II	74.8					63.1	62.1	67.1	69.2	82.0
III	76.5					72.3	59.3	122.8	57.9	75.6

Source: Central Bank of Uruguay, *Reseña de la Actividad Económica Financiera*, various issues.
[1]Consumer price index (CPI)
[2]Wholesale price index (WPI)

Statistical Appendix Table 5. Balance of Payments, 1974–85

(In millions of U.S. dollars)

	1974	1975	1976	1977	1978	1979	1980	1981	1982	1983	1984	1985
Current account balance	-118.0	-189.5	-73.6	-159.8	-127.0	-316.8	-692.0	-478.2	-468.2	-171.1	-129.2	-120.2
Trade balance	-52.3	-109.1	28.4	-68.1	-23.7	-437.8	-592.3	-384.0	-15.5	305.4	192.3	178.2
Exports (f.o.b.)	381.2	385.0	565.0	611.6	686.1	788.1	1,058.5	1,215.4	1,022.9	1,045.1	924.6	853.6
Imports (c.i.f.)	-433.5	-494.1	-536.6	-679.7	-709.8	-1,125.9	-1,650.8	-1,599.4	-1,038.4	-739.7	-732.3	-675.4
Net service payments	-40.5	-16.1	-37.3	-30.4	-33.6	71.7	-8.0	-30.1	-266.2	-199.7	30.1	41.7
Net investment income	-42.6	-71.2	-72.4	-67.9	-76.8	-57.8	-100.4	-73.8	-187.6	-196.9	-361.6	-350.9
Net transfers	17.4	6.9	7.7	6.6	7.1	7.1	8.7	9.7	10.4	11.0	10.0	10.8
Capital account balance	49.3	104.1	240.7	261.7	413.4	360.3	745.6	779.7	-681.1	136.7	-198.1	232.4
Public sector	53.0	119.4	101.0	35.2	54.2	114.2	174.3	289.4	857.7	506.8	73.9	157.9
Private sector (Excluding errors and omissions)	64.3	27.7	149.7	183.3	199.9	269.4	476.8	631.9	-277.3	-121.4	-158.6	-164.7
Errors and omissions	-68.0	-43.0	-10.0	43.2	159.3	-23.3	94.5	-141.6	-1,261.5	-248.7	-113.4	239.2
Allocation of SDRs	—	—	—	—	—	11.4	11.5	10.9	—	—	—	—
Overall balance	-68.7	-85.4	167.1	101.9	286.4	54.9	65.1	312.4	-1,149.3	-34.4	-327.3	112.2
Gold valuation adjustment	0.0	0.0	0.0	0.0	0.0	0.0	0.0	9.7	150.7	71.6	3.1	0.4
Change in reserves	-68.7	-85.4	167.1	101.9	286.4	54.9	65.1	322.1	-998.6	37.2	-324.2	112.6

Source: Central Bank of Uruguay, *Reseña de la Actividad Económica Financiera*, various issues.

Statistical Appendix Table 6.   Real Effective Exchange Rates, 1978–84
(Index 1978 = 100)

	1978	1979	1980	1981	1982	1983	1984	1985[1]
Argentina	100.0	141.0	185.2	170.8	94.9	80.5	95.0	90.1
Brazil	100.0	90.4	80.7	99.1	104.5	84.8	85.1	86.4
Mexico	100.0	105.9	118.2	133.5	95.6	84.3	98.0	109.7
United States	100.0	97.5	98.0	111.2	124.7	129.1	139.6	153.4
Uruguay	100.0	108.6	135.7	152.7	164.3	103.8	98.9	95.8

Source: World Bank, "Country Economic Memorandum on Uruguay, 1986," Table 9.7.
[1]January – June.

Statistical Appendix Table 7.   Banking System Structure, 1974–85

Year	Government-Owned Banks	Commercial Banks		Casas Bancarias	Number of Offices	Number of Employees
		Domestic	Foreign			
1974	2	12	8	2	248	5,718
1975	2	13	8	2	263	5,336
1976	2	13	8	2	248	5,718
1977	2	13	8	4	261	5,777
1978	2	13	8	11	274	6,280
1979	2	13	8	17	299	6,655
1980	2	13	8	20	316	7,500
1981	2	13	8	23	318	7,980
1982	2	12	10	20	325	7,839
1983	2	13	9	19	332	7,856
1984	2	13	9	17	. . .	. . .
1985	2	13	9	16	. . .	. . .

Source: Central Bank of Uruguay.

**Statistical Appendix Table 8. Value-Added of the
Financial Sector Relative to GNP, 1975–85**
(In percent)

1975	4.61
1976	5.08
1977	4.35
1978	5.18
1979	4.97
1980	5.06
1981	5.28
1982	6.08
1983	6.47
1984	6.44
1985	6.72

Source: Central Bank of Uruguay.

Statistical Appendix Table 9. Financial Intermediation, 1974–85
(Assets and liabilities of the banking system as a percent of GDP)

Year	M1	Peso Savings, Time, and Other Deposits	M2	Foreign Currency Deposits	Total Savings and Time Deposits	M3	Net Public Sector Credit	Private Sector Credit			Domestic Credit	M3/ Domestic Credit	M3/Credit Private and Public Sector
								Peso	Dollar	Total			
1974	11.87	4.81	16.68	2.23	7.04	18.91	4.59	15.35	3.38	18.73	19.92	0.95	0.81
1975	10.06	5.32	15.38	4.22	9.54	19.60	5.54	14.39	5.09	19.48	17.51	1.12	0.78
1976	10.50	6.93	17.43	8.64	15.57	26.07	5.50	14.16	7.30	21.46	18.97	1.37	0.97
1977	9.33	6.40	15.73	13.04	19.44	28.77	4.33	14.14	11.03	25.17	16.77	1.72	0.98
1978	9.92	10.95	20.87	15.24	26.19	36.11	3.45	15.33	13.09	28.41	16.11	2.24	1.13
1979	9.90	13.56	23.46	13.99	27.55	37.45	0.70	18.15	14.91	33.06	23.73	1.58	1.11
1980	9.39	16.20	25.59	13.55	29.75	39.14	0.48	20.16	16.88	37.04	28.39	1.38	1.04
1981	7.90	15.10	23.00	19.89	34.99	42.89	1.66	20.19	18.68	38.87	30.74	1.40	1.06
1982	8.91	15.82	24.73	46.17	61.99	70.90	12.70	20.37	57.18	77.55	63.41	1.12	0.79
1983	6.91	13.18	20.09	35.98	49.16	56.07	21.50	16.45	44.59	61.04	45.27	1.24	0.68
1984	6.66	11.92	18.58	35.61	47.53	54.19	24.26	14.71	43.17	57.88	47.14	1.15	0.66
1985	7.60	12.52	20.12	38.45	50.97	58.57	18.35	12.23	41.82	54.05	48.17	1.22	0.81

Sources: Central Bank of Uruguay, *Boletín Estadístico*, various issues, and International Monetary Fund, *International Financial Statistics*, various issues.

imf;66258tab6b   d1   kat   14;29   11-08-91   p0001   0024

Statistical Appendix Table 10.   Savings and Investment as a Percent of GDP, 1974–84

	1974	1975	1976	1977	1978	1979	1980	1981	1982	1983	1984
Gross domestic savings	8.7	8.5	14.1	12.3	13.4	12.8	11.0	11.4	10.3	14.4	13.3
Gross national savings	8.0	6.7	12.2	10.8	12.0	12.1	10.2	10.8	8.3	9.0	6.7
Net domestic savings	5.6	4.5	9.2	7.5	8.4	5.9	4.1	4.1	2.0	5.2	
Net national savings	4.8	2.7	7.4	6.0	7.0	5.2	3.2	3.6	0.0	-0.3	3.2
External financing	3.6	6.7	2.7	4.4	4.0	5.3	7.8	4.3	6.2	1.0	9.3
Gross domestic investment	11.6	13.4	15.5	15.2	16.0	16.2	17.4	15.6	15.1	11.0	9.3
Fixed capital formation	10.3	13.3	15.5	15.2	16.0	16.2	17.4	15.6	15.1	11.0	9.3
Public sector	2.6	4.6	6.5	7.0	8.0	6.5	5.6	5.7	7.2	4.1	4.1
Private sector	7.7	8.7	9.0	8.2	8.0	9.7	11.8	9.9	7.9	6.9	5.2
Changes in stocks	1.3	0.1	-0.6	-0.0	0.0	1.2	0.6	-0.5	-0.6	-1.0	0.6
Depreciation	3.2	4.0	4.9	4.8	5.0	6.9	7.0	7.2	8.3	9.3	
Net domestic investment	8.4	9.4	10.0	10.4	11.0	10.5	11.0	7.9	6.2	0.7	

Source: World Bank (1986).

Statistical Appendix Table 11. Nominal Interest Rates, 1974–86

(In percent per annum)

Year	Quarter	Loan Rates				Deposit Rates			
		Local currency		Foreign currency		Local currency		Foreign currency	
		Preferential	Prime	Preferential	Prime	1–6 months	Above 6 months	Time	Sight
1974	IV	...	...	...	...	30.0	41.4	8.0	5.5
1975	IV	...	...	...	...	30.0	41.4	8.0	5.5
1976	III	45.0	61.5	...	12.0	30.0	41.4	7.6	5.6
	IV	47.6	62.0	...	12.0	30.2	45.2	7.4	5.6
1977	I	45.9	62.0	...	12.0	34.0	45.2	7.2	5.5
	II	50.0	62.0	...	12.0	33.8	45.6	7.1	5.2
	III	50.3	62.0	...	12.0	34.1	46.4	7.0	5.2
	IV	65.2	76.6	13.6	14.3	51.4	63.0	7.2	5.4
1978	I	65.8	76.9	...	14.2	48.9	56.8	7.4	4.9
	II	61.6	72.8	12.7	14.6	46.4	51.2	7.7	4.6
	III	62.6	74.6	13.3	14.6	50.8	52.6	8.0	5.0
	IV	59.7	71.2	13.3	14.2	42.6	45.4	8.0	5.5
1979	I	50.1	69.2	13.5	15.2	42.6	43.0	8.6	6.0
	II	46.8	62.0	12.6	15.2	38.9	40.4	8.6	5.5
	III	47.1	62.6	12.7	15.0	41.4	43.0	9.0	6.0
	IV	49.9	68.1	15.8	16.8	50.6	49.2	11.9	5.5
1980	I	49.3	67.4	15.9	18.8	48.8	49.4	14.6	5.9
	II	52.0	68.3	15.0	17.1	52.2	52.6	12.5	5.6
	III	48.9	65.6	14.4	16.4	48.8	51.8	12.1	6.0
	IV	49.8	65.1	18.1	18.5	50.3	52.7	14.6	5.7

Statistical Appendix Table 11 (concluded). **Nominal Interest Rates, 1974–86**

Year	Quarter	Loan Rates				Deposit Rates			
		Local currency		Foreign currency		Local currency		Foreign currency	
		Preferential	Prime	Preferential	Prime	1–6 months	Above 6 months	Time	Sight
1981	I	49.4	63.7	17.3	18.4	46.0	46.3	12.5	6.0
	II	44.1	57.4	16.5	19.9	43.3	43.0	15.5	5.3
	III	45.5	58.6	19.0	20.1	45.8	46.4	16.6	5.6
	IV	46.5	59.8	16.8	18.4	47.4	49.8	13.1	5.5
1982	I	44.0	49.0	17.3	18.7	42.5	42.6	13.9	5.0
	II	47.7	54.8	18.5	20.0	47.6	47.4	14.5	5.7
	III	53.2	65.9	18.5	18.8	56.8	57.2	11.1	4.3
	IV	56.7	76.3	17.2	18.2	66.2	67.3	10.2	5.8
1983	I	75.7	105.5	16.6	17.6	80.8	75.0	10.3	6.7
	II	67.9	102.0	15.3	16.8	66.6	61.6	9.8	6.0
	III	70.2	85.0	15.3	17.0	65.2	59.6	9.8	6.3
	IV	65.5	85.0	15.5	17.2	67.8	66.0	9.8	6.2
1984	I	64.3	84.4	15.1	16.8	64.4	64.2	9.7	6.2
	II	65.0	82.0	17.0	18.2	68.4	72.6	10.5	6.2
	III	68.2	82.0	15.8	17.5	68.0	73.8	10.5	6.5
	IV	69.3	86.6	14.2	17.3	75.2	79.0	10.6	6.5
1985	I	80.1	95.0	14.5	17.8	89.2	93.2	9.8	6.2
	II	74.4	95.0	13.6	16.3	86.2	86.4	8.3	6.0
	III	78.6	95.0	12.4	16.0	77.0	79.6	8.1	5.1
	IV	80.0	95.0	12.5	15.8	74.4	76.2	8.1	5.4
1986	I	76.0	97.0	12.9	15.0	69.0	68.8	7.3	5.2
	II	82.0	95.0	12.5	15.0	59.2	57.4	6.1	5.0
	III	75.8	93.6	12.7	14.7	55.8	54.6	5.8	3.9

Sources: Central Bank of Uruguay, *Boletín Estadística*, and *Reseña de la Actividad Económica Financiera*, several issues.

Note: Domestic currency loan rates are for loans of up to six months; foreign currency loan rates are for commercial operations; foreign deposit rates are for deposits of up to six months.

Statistical Appendix Table 12. Ex Post Peso Equivalents of Dollar Interest Rates, 1974–85

(In percent per annum)

Year	Quarter	Ex Post Annual Devaluation Rate for Subsequent Six Months	Loan Rates		Deposit Rates	
			Preferential	Prime	Time	Sight
1974	IV	139.0	...	...	158.1	152.1
1975	IV	51.0	...	...	63.1	59.3
1976	III	40.7	...	57.5	51.4	48.6
	IV	35.0	...	51.2	45.0	42.6
1977	I	35.0	...	51.2	44.7	42.4
	II	39.5	...	56.2	49.4	46.8
	III	27.7	...	43.0	36.6	34.3
	IV	15.6	31.3	32.1	23.9	21.8
1978	I	35.0	...	54.2	45.0	41.6
	II	43.5	61.7	64.5	54.5	50.1
	III	32.9	50.6	52.3	43.5	39.5
	IV	28.6	45.7	46.9	38.9	35.7
1979	I	23.4	40.1	42.2	34.0	30.8
	II	17.1	31.9	34.9	27.2	23.5
	III	12.1	26.3	28.9	22.2	18.8
	IV	11.7	29.3	30.5	25.0	17.8
1980	I	16.0	34.4	37.8	32.9	22.8
	II	22.5	40.9	43.4	37.8	29.4
	III	23.4	41.2	43.6	38.3	30.8
	IV	18.2	39.6	40.1	35.5	24.9

Statistical Appendix Table 12 (concluded). Ex Post Peso Equivalents of Dollar Interest Rates, 1974–85

(In percent per annum)

Year	Quarter	Ex Post Annual Devaluation Rate for Subsequent Six Months	Loan Rates		Deposit Rates	
			Preferential	Prime	Time	Sight
1981	I	15.1	35.0	36.3	29.5	22.0
	II	14.9	33.9	37.8	32.7	21.0
	III	15.1	37.0	38.2	34.2	21.5
	IV	15.6	35.0	36.9	30.7	22.0
1982	I	18.8	39.3	41.0	35.3	24.7
	II	132.2	176.3	179.8	167.0	146.5
	III	472.6	578.5	580.2	536.2	497.2
	IV	210.8	264.3	267.4	242.5	228.8
1983	I	29.0	50.4	51.7	42.3	37.6
	II	42.6	64.4	66.6	56.6	51.2
	III	86.9	15.5	118.7	105.2	98.7
	IV	82.8	111.1	114.2	100.7	94.1
1984	I	40.4	61.6	64.0	54.0	49.1
	II	57.0	83.7	85.6	73.5	66.7
	III	123.2	158.5	162.3	146.6	137.7
	IV	99.1	127.4	133.5	120.2	112.0
1985	I	57.7	80.6	85.8	73.2	67.5
	II	63.8	86.1	90.5	77.4	73.6
	III	53.3	72.3	77.8	65.7	61.1
	IV	44.7	62.8	67.6	56.4	52.5

Sources: Nominal rates from Statistical Appendix Table 11; devaluation rate from International Monetary Fund, *International Financial Statistics*.
Note: Ex post peso equivalents of dollar rates are computed using the annualized six-month devaluation rate (change in the average market exchange rate) for the subsequent six months.

Statistical Appendix Table 13. Real Interest Rates, 1974–85

(In percent per annum)

Year	Quarter	Ex Post Annual Inflation Rate	Loan Rates				Deposit Rates			
			Local currency		Foreign currency		Local currency		Foreign currency	
			Preferential	Prime	Preferential	Prime	1–6 months	Above 6 months	Time	Sight
1974	IV	77.4	...	...	...	...	−26.7	−20.3	45.5	42.1
1975	IV	34.8	...	...	...	...	−3.6	4.9	21.0	18.2
1976	III	56.0	−7.1	3.5	...	1.0	−16.7	−9.4	−2.9	−4.7
	IV	61.5	−8.6	0.3	...	−6.4	−19.4	−10.1	−10.2	−11.7
1977	I	63.3	−10.7	−0.8	...	−7.4	−17.9	−11.1	−11.4	−12.8
	II	56.5	−4.2	3.5	...	−0.2	−14.5	−7.0	−4.5	−6.2
	III	34.1	12.1	20.8	...	6.6	0.0	9.2	1.9	0.1
	IV	37.4	20.2	28.5	−4.4	−3.9	10.2	18.6	−9.8	−11.4
1978	I	50.1	10.5	17.9	...	2.7	−0.8	4.5	−3.4	−5.7
	II	48.6	8.7	16.3	8.8	10.7	−1.5	1.7	4.0	1.0
	III	58.8	2.4	9.9	−5.2	−4.1	−5.0	−3.9	−9.6	−12.2
	IV	71.1	−6.7	0.1	−14.8	−14.1	−16.7	−15.0	−18.8	−20.7
1979	I	81.4	−17.3	−6.7	−22.8	−21.6	−21.4	−21.2	−26.1	−27.9
	II	88.5	−22.1	−14.1	−30.0	−28.4	−26.3	−25.5	−32.5	−34.5
	III	76.6	−16.7	−7.9	−28.5	−27.0	−19.9	−19.0	−30.8	−32.7
	IV	53.8	−2.5	9.3	−15.9	−15.1	−2.1	−3.0	−18.7	−23.4
1980	I	49.3	0.0	12.1	−10.0	−7.7	−0.3	0.1	−11.0	−17.7
	II	45.4	4.5	15.7	−3.1	−1.4	4.7	5.0	−5.2	−11.0
	III	29.7	14.8	27.7	8.9	10.7	14.7	17.0	6.6	0.8
	IV	27.5	17.5	29.5	9.5	9.9	17.9	19.8	6.3	−2.0

Statistical Appendix Table 13 *(concluded).* **Real Interest Rates, 1974–85**

(In percent per annum)

Year	Quarter	Ex Post Annual Inflation Rate	Loan Rates				Deposit Rates			
			Local currency		Foreign currency		Local currency		Foreign currency	
			Preferential	Prime	Preferential	Prime	1–6 months	Above 6 months	Time	Sight
1981	I	35.0	10.7	21.3	0.0	1.0	8.1	8.4	-4.1	-9.6
	II	32.5	8.8	18.8	1.1	4.0	8.2	7.9	0.2	-8.7
	III	16.2	25.2	36.5	17.9	18.9	25.5	26.0	15.5	4.6
	IV	9.6	33.7	45.8	23.2	24.9	34.5	36.7	19.3	11.3
1982	I	16.9	23.2	27.5	19.2	20.6	21.9	22.0	15.7	6.7
	II	20.8	22.3	28.1	128.7	131.6	22.2	22.0	121.0	104.1
	III	68.7	-9.2	-1.7	302.2	303.2	-7.1	-6.8	277.1	254.0
	IV	77.4	-11.7	-0.6	105.4	107.1	-6.3	-5.7	93.1	85.3
1983	I	33.9	31.2	53.5	12.3	13.3	35.0	30.7	6.3	2.8
	II	41.4	18.7	42.9	16.3	17.8	17.8	14.3	10.7	6.9
	III	51.5	12.3	22.1	42.2	44.4	9.0	5.3	35.4	31.2
	IV	59.8	3.6	15.8	32.1	34.0	5.0	3.9	25.6	21.5
1984	I	72.9	-5.0	6.7	-6.5	-5.1	-4.9	-5.0	-10.9	-13.4
	II	67.4	-1.4	8.7	9.7	10.9	0.6	3.1	3.6	-0.4
	III	55.5	8.2	17.0	66.2	68.7	8.0	11.8	58.6	52.9
	IV	81.4	-6.7	2.9	25.4	28.7	-3.4	-1.3	21.4	16.9
1985	I	89.6	-5.0	2.8	-4.7	-2.0	-0.2	1.9	-8.6	-11.7
	II	72.4	1.2	13.1	7.9	10.5	8.0	8.1	2.9	0.7
	III	79.0	-0.2	8.9	-3.7	-0.7	-1.1	0.3	-7.4	-10.0
	IV	75.0	2.9	11.4	-7.0	-4.2	-0.3	0.7	-10.6	-12.9

Sources: Nominal rates from Statistical Appendix Tables 11 and 12; inflation rate from International Monetary Fund, *International Financial Statistics.*

Note: Ex post real interest rates are computed using the annualized six-month inflation rate (change in CPI) for the subsequent six months.

Statistical Appendix Table 14.   Currency Substitution, 1974–85

(In percent)

	1974	1975	1976	1977	1978	1979	1980	1981	1982	1983	1984	1985
Foreign currency deposits/ total deposits[1]	31.68	44.23	55.49	67.08	58.19	50.78	45.55	56.84	74.48	73.19	74.92	75.44
Foreign currency deposits/M3[1]	11.79	21.53	33.14	45.32	42.20	37.36	34.62	46.37	65.12	64.17	65.71	65.65
Percent of foreign currency deposits in private banks held by nonresidents[2]	16.78	20.92	19.70	15.13	28.34	33.74	45.52	48.32	49.34	50.00	45.97	44.98
Residents' deposits in U.S. banks/foreign currency deposits in Uruguay[3]	3.53	1.81	1.60	0.81	0.58	0.27	0.24	0.26	0.43	0.85	...	...
Credit in foreign currency to private sector/ total credit to private sector[1]	18.05	26.13	34.02	43.82	46.08	45.10	45.57	48.06	73.73	73.05	74.59	77.37

[1]Statistical Appendix Table 9.
[2]Central Bank of Uruguay, *Boletín Estadístico*, several issues.
[3]de Melo and Tybout (1986).

Statistical Appendix Table 15.   Banking System Performance Ratios, 1975–84
(In percent)

	1975	1976	1977	1978	1979	1980	1981	1982	1983	1984
Bad loans/net worth	0.65	0.75	1.30	1.41	1.23	1.03	1.55	3.64	2.29	1.90
Operational profits/ net worth	...	0.72	0.47	0.41	0.7	0.51	0.47	0.96	0.45	0.33
Administrative costs/ gross profits	...	5.54	4.01	4.59	2.33	1.94	0.05	1.21	−3.18	6.35
Nonperforming assets/ net worth	...	...	...	1.69	1.21	0.75	0.55	0.28	0.41	0.29
Net profits/net worth	...	0.57	0.34	0.31	0.57	0.43	0.29	0.53	−0.08	0.10
Administrative costs/ loans and deposits	...	0.049	0.037	0.035	0.028	0.025	0.024	0.015	0.018	0.017

Source: Central Bank of Uruguay, Research Department.

Statistical Appendix Table 16.   Portfolio Purchase Scheme
(In millions of U.S. dollars)

	Portfolio Purchased	Cash Received	Cancellation of Financial Assistance	Bonds Issued
Linked to loans to the Central Bank	216	328	. . .	544
Linked to bank intervention	416	. . .	105	311

Source: *Búsqueda*, No. 224, February 1984.

Statistical Appendix Table 17.   Structure of Portfolios Purchased by Central Bank by Sector of Activity of Borrowers
(In millions of new Uruguayan pesos and percent)

	Debt Denominated in Local Currency		Debt Denominated in Foreign Currency	
	NUr$	Percent	NUr$	Percent
Agriculture	127	3.4	3.6	0.9
Livestock	1,379	36.8	96.7	25.0
Industry	817	21.8	145.7	37.8
Commerce (nonretail)	543	14.5	68.4	17.7
Commerce (retail)	318	8.5	21.6	5.6
Services	377	10.1	44.4	11.5
Consumption	182	4.9	5.9	1.5
Total	3,743	100.0	386.3	100.0
Pemar and Banco de Londres	44		36.1	
Total	3,787		422.4	

Source: Central Bank of Uruguay.

Statistical Appendix Table 18.   Structure of Portfolios Purchased by Central Bank by Size of Debt

Thousands of U.S. dollars	Number of Debtors	Percent of Total	Amount of Debt (*In millions of U.S. dollars*)	Percent of Total
>1,000	88	1.4	234.1	48.3
500–999	133	2.2	78.9	16.3
400–499	46	0.8	20.1	4.1
300–399	70	1.2	24.5	5.1
200–299	107	1.8	26.8	5.5
100–199	256	4.2	38.4	7.9
50–99	306	5.0	22.9	4.7
0–49	5,072	83.4	39.2	8.1
Total	6,078	100.0	484.9	100.0

Source: Central Bank of Uruguay.

Statistical Appendix Table 19.   Portfolio Purchases Linked to Loans to Central Bank by Type of Bank

	Peso-Denominated Debt (*In millions of new pesos*)	Dollar-Denominated Debt (*In millions of U.S. dollars*)
Domestic commercial banks	429.6	24.5
Foreign commercial banks	672.7	119.1
Banking houses	14.4	16.6

Source: Central Bank of Uruguay.

Statistical Appendix Table 20. Portfolio Purchases Linked to Loans to Central Bank

Institution	Contract Date	In Domestic Currency			Debt Denominated in Foreign Currency		Loans Received by Central Bank (In millions of U.S. dollars)		
		Millions of new pesos	Exchange rate (new pesos per US$1)	U.S. dollar equivalent	Millions of U.S. dollars	Total	External resources	Domestic resources	Total
Citibank	10/27/82	470.7	13.52	34.8	40.0	74.8	175.0	—	175.0
Bank of America	12/8/82	16.6	29.0	0.6	39.4	40.0	95.0	—	95.0
Bank of America	5/24/83	14.5	31.75	0.5	9.4	9.9	27.3	—	27.3
Surinvest	1/10/83	1.4	30.0	—	1.6	1.6	2.7	—	4.6
Surinvest	4/14/83	—	34.0	—	0.5	0.5	—	3.0	1.1
Montevideo	1/27/83	19.7	26.25	0.8	3.4	4.2	—	9.3	9.3
Nación Argentina	1/28/83	12.6	26.75	0.5	3.8	4.3	12.9	—	12.9
River Trade	2/2/83	0.7	26.0	—	10.0	10.0	29.5	—	29.5
UBUP	2/8/83	19.6	30.5	0.6	1.5	2.1	—	6.3	6.3

Statistical Appendix Table 20 *(concluded).* **Portfolio Purchases Linked to Loans to Central Bank**

Institution	Contract Date	In Domestic Currency			Debt Denominated in Foreign Currency		Loans Received by Central Bank (In millions of U.S. dollars)		
		Millions of new pesos	Exchange rate (new pesos per US$1)	U.S. dollar equivalent	Millions of U.S. dollars	Total	External resources	Domestic resources	Total
Exprinter	2/10/83	4.6	28.75	0.2	2.8	3.0	3.4	4.0	7.4
Hollandes Unido	2/25/83	45.2	31.0	1.5	2.4	3.9	—	9.4	9.4
Boston	2/28/90	49.8	31.0	1.6	4.0	5.6	15.0	—	15.0
Comercial	3/9/83	28.9	32.0	0.9	5.8	6.7	—	19.3	19.3
Credito	3/25/83	361.4	32.5	11.1	13.6	24.7	12.0	51.7	63.7
La Caja Obrera	4/14/83	—	34.0	—	0.1	0.1	—	0.2	0.2
Trade Development	5/12/83	11.2	33.0	0.3	9.2	9.5	24.7	—	24.7
Extep Banca	5/13/83	7.7	32.7	0.2	1.4	1.6	3.6	0.5	4.1
Sudameris	4/14/83	0.5	34.0	—	0.1	0.1	—	0.2	0.2
Sudameris	10/14/83	35.8	37.05	1.0	1.8	2.8	—	7.2	7.2
Londres	4/14/83	—	34.0	—	0.4	0.4	0.8	—	26.2
Londres	2/23/84	15.6	46.95	0.3	8.4	8.7	26.2	—	26.2
EISA	12/14/83	—	42.75	—	0.3	0.3	—	0.7	0.7
Total		1,116.5		54.9	160.1	215.0	428.8	111.6	540.4

Source: Central Bank of Uruguay.

Statistical Appendix Table 21.   Debt Recovery of Central Bank
(In millions)

	As of 12/31/83		As of 04/30/84		As of 08/31/84	
	New pesos	U.S. dollars	New pesos	U.S. dollars	New pesos	U.S. dollars
Amount	409.9	8.7	479.9	9.6	724.5	13.7
Percent of total	6.4	1.8	. . .	. . .	. . .	. . .

Sources: Central Bank of Uruguay (1984), and *El País*, November 11, 1984.